THE DECLASSIFIED EISENHOWER

PUBLISHED BOOKS BY BLANCHE WIESEN COOK

Crystal Eastman on Women and Revolution
(Oxford University Press, 1978)

Past-Imperfect: Alternative Essays in American History,
2 vols. (Alfred A. Knopf, 1973), coeditor

Garland Library on War and Peace,
a 360-volume reprint series
(Garland Publishing, 1970–78), senior editor

Bibliography on Peace Research in History
(American Bibliographic Center, Clio Press, 1969)

THE DECLASSIFIED EISENHOWER

A Divided Legacy

Blanche Wiesen Cook

B
E36
C1

DOUBLEDAY & COMPANY, INC.
GARDEN CITY, NEW YORK
1981

This book is dedicated to my godchildren:

To Daniel Wayne Lessem and Douglas Jed Lessem,
who are still too young to read it

To Elizabeth Lorde-Rollins and Jonathan Lorde-
Rollins, who said over dinner one night
during the summer of 1980: We grew up with
this book; and now we are about to be drafted.

May they inherit a legacy of peace.

81077   c. 1

Library of Congress Cataloging in Publication Data

Cook, Blanche Wiesen.
The Declassified Eisenhower

Includes index.
1. United States—Foreign relations—1953–61.
2. United States—Foreign relations—1945–53.
3. Eisenhower, Dwight David, President, United States, 1890–1969.
4. Presidents—United States—Biography. I. Title.
E835.C57   327.73′0092′4
ISBN: 0-385-05456-4
Library of Congress Catalog Card Number 80–699
Copyright © 1981 by Blanche Wiesen Cook

Preface

"I believe that the people in the long run are going to do more to promote peace than any governments. Indeed, I think that people want peace so much that one of these days governments had better get out of their way and let them have it." Eisenhower said that to Prime Minister Harold Macmillan during a BBC television interview on 31 August 1959. I first read those words in London during the summer of 1970 while researching British antimilitarist organizations founded during World War I. With the war in Vietnam still raging, and no end in sight, Eisenhower's words, which were reprinted in a pamphlet that celebrated the activities of Britain's World War I pacifists, seemed particularly appropriate. It also seemed that Eisenhower's reputation as a golfer devoted to double-talking press conferences, a President who did little and understood less, merited further scrutiny.

After browsing through the public record, it became apparent that Eisenhower was the most undervalued and misunderstood statesman of the twentieth century. Maligned by liberals and conservatives alike, he was accused of being soft on communism, destroying our military security, and creating first a "bomber gap" and then a "missile crisis." Alternatively, he was criticized for escalating tensions on three continents and threatening the world with imminent nuclear holocaust. William Shannon called the Eisenhower years "the time of the great postponement," when nothing was done at all. "It has been," he wrote at the close of the fifties, "the age of the slob." Senator J. William Fulbright said Eisenhower's first administration was a period when Americans "could bask in the artificial sunlight" of "luxurious torpor," because the government "did not bother with serious things." Most historians shared that evaluation. Eric Goldman wrote an essay entitled "Good-By to the 'Fifties—and Good Riddance." Goldman considered the Eisenhower years possibly "the dullest and dreariest in all our history." In 1963, a poll of seventy-five historians ranked Eisenhower twenty-second in "presidential performance," behind Chester Alan Arthur.

By 1972, I believed that Eisenhower was a presidential pacifist. Based on the public record, I wrote a column, originally syndicated on 1 November by the Los Angeles *Times* and later expanded and published by Forum Press, "Dwight David Eisenhower: Antimilitarist in the White House." In that article, I noted that Eisenhower's military experiences caused him to conclude that war was an outmoded strategy. He hoped that World War II might be "the last civil war" to tear civilization apart. In 1956 he announced that war had become "preposterous." Not only did he believe that there was "no alternative to peace"; for eight years he actually found alternatives to war.

Subsequently, research in Eisenhower's private papers, long closed and classified, revealed a far more complex reality. Eisenhower's commitment to peace was real, but it was limited to nuclear détente and the prevention of large-scale international warfare. There was partial confirmation for my earlier judgment in, for example, his assertion to his press secretary, James Hagerty, on 8 February 1955: "You know, if you're in the military and you know about these terrible destructive weapons, it tends to make you more pacifistic than you normally have been." Eisenhower assured Hagerty that was true for the military in the Soviet Union as well. He did not believe the Soviets wanted war, brinkmanship notwithstanding. But Eisenhower's alternatives to war involved a range of political-warfare activities that included covert operations and counterinsurgency in Iran, Guatemala, the Middle East, Africa, and Asia that were kept entirely secret: undercover, and classified for decades.

After years of research and thousands of documents declassified with the aid of the Freedom of Information Act, Eisenhower's shabby place in history was explained. He worked largely undercover. America's most popular hero was America's most covert President. Eisenhower participated in his own cover-up. His presidency involved a thorough and ambitious anti-Communist crusade marked by covert operations that depended on secrecy for their success. While he cannot be credited with inventing the political-warfare wheel, he presided over its development. Harry S Truman introduced NSC-68 in April 1950.* Basic national security policy, that directive—to employ "any means, covert or overt, violent or nonviolent" to destabilize and then to transform Communist nations, and Communist parties—was expanded, intensified and made fully operative during Eisenhower's presidency. Similarly, the postwar economic institutions that emerged during the Bretton Woods Conference, of 1944, to restore economic stability were refined, extended, and generally transformed during Eisenhower's presidency. The International Monetary Fund and the International Bank for Reconstruction and Development (the World Bank) were technically to have been United Nations agencies. But Eisenhower's foreign economic policy emphasized the expansion of private capital investment abroad, protected by United States diplomacy as well as

---

* "The Report by the Secretaries of State and Defense on 'United States Objectives and Programs for National Security,' April 7, 1950" (NSC-68) was declassified on 27 February 1975 and reprinted in full in the *Naval War College Review* (May–June 1975), pp. 51–108.

fiscal and military support. Economic warfare became a respectable weapon in the United States' arsenal. Together with political warfare, it would over time lead the offensive. Although Eisenhower sincerely deplored the military-industrial complex, it was empowered as never before during his presidency.

Shrouded in secrecy, long obscured and trivialized, the fundamental realities of the Eisenhower years have been consistently belittled and ignored. With our historical documents classified and hidden, it has been possible to dismiss Ike as a bumbling, inarticulate, and very tired general. The foxy bridge player, the power broker, the international statesman has been slow to emerge. Now, after almost a decade of appeals for sources under the Freedom of Information Act, it is possible, and necessary, to revise the popular view of Eisenhower as a nowhere man, doing nothing on the presidential road to retirement.

Much remains closed or classified, including many activities in the Middle East, Tibet, Europe, and Africa, including all matters relating to private business interests, political finances, and crucial national security policy papers. But the evidence now available provides a new understanding. The State Department's release of the Guatemala file offers for the first time an account of the daily discussions of and the government rationale for the kind of counterinsurgency that has become traditional. With minor modifications for local differences, the Guatemala model has been used again and again. In addition to the documents declassified by the government and now available for research in Washington, the Eisenhower Library at Abilene, Kansas, has recently opened the most significant papers of his presidency. These include the Whitman file, comprising his letters, telephone logs, and diary entries kept by his secretary, Ann Whitman; parts of the Gordon Gray and Robert Cutler NSC files; Hagerty's diaries; and files relating to foreign economic policy. Without these papers, it has been impossible to understand the complexities of Eisenhower's presidency and the nature of his leadership.

Writers have traditionally depended on archival manuscripts for a factual record of the past. Recent history, steeped in myth and secrecy, has altered that tradition. In April 1975, I participated in a conference, sponsored by the American Assembly, on "The Records of Public Officials," which recognized that the papers of Presidents are essentially public property and recommended that: "The government must acknowledge, by law and regulation, a legitimate, enforceable and paramount public interest in insuring that as many as possible of these records of permanent historical significance be preserved, that they be made available as soon as possible and to the fullest extent possible."

Regarding the records of Presidents, the American Assembly concluded: "The practice of recognizing ownership of presidential records by presidents or their heirs should be ended immediately."[1] Without such legislation, without access to the documents of our past, there will be only wretched history; and a dangerously uninformed public. In these times of crises, the citizens of this democracy have the right to know what decisions—life-and-death decisions—are being made in our name, allegedly on our behalf.

Eisenhower presided over an unprecedented moment of economic growth, military expansion, and political retrenchment. He intended to destabilize communism worldwide, eradicate New Deal "socialism" domestically, and globalize American business and America's values. In a world of upheaval and constant change, his success cannot be measured except in terms of repression and reaction. That is in part Eisenhower's legacy. But there is another part: Eisenhower understood that no country "can *permanently* and by itself support abundance in both guns *and* butter." He feared that the United States might become a garrison state, that in the process of fighting communism it could lose its own identity and be transformed into a dictatorship—militarily burdened, financially exhausted, politically destroyed. He warned against the military-industrial complex. He intended his farewell address to be as significant as George Washington's. Eisenhower always corrected and rewrote his own speeches. "Everyone agrees," Eisenhower wrote Henry Wallace in 1957, that Washington "substantially corrected, and possibly re-wrote, Hamilton's draft of his Farewell Address. I've often felt the deep wish that The Good Lord had endowed me with his clarity of vision in big things, his strength of purpose and genuine greatness in mind and spirit."[2] And so his own farewell address would be the most important statement of his career: "We have been compelled to create a permanent armaments industry of vast proportions. . . . We annually spend on military security more than the net income of all United States corporations. . . . We recognize the imperative need for this development. Yet we must not fail to comprehend its grave implications. . . . In the councils of government we must guard against the acquisition of unwarranted influence, whether sought or unsought, by the military-industrial complex. The potential for the disastrous rise of misplaced power exists and will persist."

Eisenhower's fear of a garrison state, and his farewell warning to the citizens of the United States, were genuine reflections of his deepest sentiments. Every recently declassified letter and diary entry reveals that Eisenhower was, in many ways, a man of decency and conviction, of moderation and caring. But he inconsistently extended his finest attributes to people of color, and countries, such as Guatemala, whose struggles he seemed barely to consider. Globally, he pursued balance, a policy of military sufficiency and negotiation. Nevertheless, since 1960 the world's military-industrial complex has come to dominate every aspect of life. Since 1960, military spending has quadrupled. In 1978, world military expenditures were an estimated $425 billion. Estimated in constant prices, the world military budget was 70 percent higher in 1980 than it was in 1960. This situation has done nothing to ensure national security, but it has contributed to the fact that the gap between richer and poorer nations doubled between 1960 and 1980. According to Ruth Leger Sivard, former chief of the Economics Division of the United States Arms Control and Disarmament Agency, ". . . in pounds per person, the world has more explosive power than food."[3] The seeds of this global condition were planted during Eisenhower's presidency.

With the documents now available, it is clear that Eisenhower's legacy is counterinsurgency and political warfare; without Eisenhower's restraint, it is a protracted arms race, and an independent, private multinational economic system that begins to challenge the future of the traditional nation-state. Eisenhower declassified reveals an awesome legacy, and a challenge for change.

SOUTHAMPTON, NEW YORK
3 SEPTEMBER 1980

ACKNOWLEDGMENTS

Many people have helped to make this book possible. In the beginning, Diane Lampert's enthusiasm led me to investigate Eisenhower's presidency more seriously. Preliminary research resulted in a column syndicated by the Los Angeles *Times* on 1 November 1972. From that time to this, I have been grateful for the ongoing support of my agent, Betty Anne Clarke, and to Doubleday. I want to thank in particular Samuel S. Vaughan, who suggested this book, asking only that I be "fair" to President Eisenhower; John Ware, who saw the idea through its early stages; and my splendid editor, Lisa Drew, who remained encouraging throughout this time. I also want to thank Lisa Drew's efficient and congenial staff, Janice Rusin, Shirley Alves, and Anne Hukill; and Frank Hoffman for his careful and precise copy editing.

My research was supported in part by a grant from the Professional Staff-Congress and the City University of New York's Research Foundation. I am grateful for the assistance of Brenda Newman, Miriam Korman, and Elizabeth Walldov, of the Research Foundation of the City University of New York; and to the administration of John Jay College for the time made available to me through a sabbatical-year leave and a year's leave of absence. I am also indebted to my friend William Preston, chair of the History Department, who consistently supported my work.

Many archivists have assisted me through several stages of this project. At the Library of Congress, I am particularly grateful to Carolyn Hoover Sung, formerly head of Reference and Reader Services, Manuscript Division, and to David Wigdor, a keenly knowledgeable specialist on twentieth-century political history who facilitated my work on Guatemala; at Columbia University I appreciate the always helpful and cheerful staff, especially Henry Rowen and Mary Bowling; at the Dwight David Eisenhower Library at Abilene I want to thank Alan Kenyon, Rod Soubers, David Haight, James Leyerzapf, George Curtis, Don Wilson, and John Wickman.

Many inspiring hours were spent with Dr. Milton S. Eisenhower, the Honorable John S. D. Eisenhower, and Dr. George B. Kistiakowsky, formerly Eisenhower's special assistant for science and technology, in long and thorough interviews. I also want to thank Barton Bernstein and Stephen Pelz for sharing with me their new research on Korea; and Larry Wittner for his work on Greece.

My several visits to Abilene, spanning many weeks in each season, were made pleasant by the warm hospitality of several people. The Senner family provided not only a home but the use of a horse; Burton and Diane Kaufman and George and Margo Kren provided many hours of pleasant leisure—as well as a car and a motorcycle.

Gaudencio Thiago de Mello, Jaqueline Bernard, Renée Llanusa-Cestero, and Marge Barton helped me to translate rapidly fading Xeroxes copied from microfilm. I cannot thank them enough. I deeply appreciate the work of Doris De Vito, a superb and patient typist, and my friend Marge Barton, who carefully assisted during many stages of manuscript preparation.

I owe both intellectual and emotional debts to several friends and colleagues. My thanks go to Michael Meeropol, Alex Rosner, Michelle Cliff, and Adrienne Rich, who read sections of the manuscript. Clare M. Coss, Martin Fleischer, Alice Kessler-Harris, Gerald E. Markowitz, and Marilyn Young read the entire manuscript. I have benefited extensively from their challenges toward greater understanding. A special word of thanks goes to Gerry Markowitz, whose insightful criticism over time and during crises lifted my spirits when most needed. Because this is a book that deals with controversies that continue to involve us, it should be noted that all errors of fact and interpretation are strictly my own.

My father, David Theodore Wiesen, who died on Election Day 1972, might have enjoyed this book—if only for the good arguments we would have had. This work has been sustained by his memory and infused by the continued enthusiasm of my mother, Sadonia Ecker Wiesen.

Clare Coss, Joan Kelly, Martin Fleischer, Audre Lorde, and Frances Clayton traveled with me through many years and across many islands—accompanied as we were by an ongoing manuscript. This book would not have been written without their friendship. Above all, I am grateful to Clare Coss, who remained steady through an eight-year process of learning and change.

CONTENTS

INTRODUCTION
DWIGHT DAVID
EISENHOWER
AND THE
AMERICAN
CENTURY

The United States emerged from World War II with its global power mightily enhanced. While the war devastated Europe and witnessed the imperial decline of Britain and France, it ushered in America's greatest moment of military triumph and unequaled economic power. For a significant group of statesmen, publicists, businessmen, and generals, including Eisenhower, the end of World War II came to be regarded as the beginning of "the American Century." With the realities of the careful economic and political planning for postwar America abundantly classified, the public was treated to celebrations of unlimited United States power in the name of virtue and self-sacrifice. Henry Luce, America's most enterprising and influential publicist, had called for an American Century.

Almost immediately upon publication in *Life* magazine in February 1941, Henry Luce's essay became the beacon by which America was to be guided to alter its vision of itself, its national goals, its sense of power in the world. Throughout the country and across the political spectrum it was hailed and reviled, but nowhere ignored. Henry Luce was, after all, the owner and publisher of *Time, Life,* and *Fortune.* He did not write often, and his words were rarely treated lightly. He had called upon Americans to "consider the 20th century. It is ours not only in the sense that we happen to live in it but ours also because it is America's first century as a dominant power in the world. . . ." For Luce, the American Century would be a century of abundance and freedom, of trade and prosperity. It was rather vague and undetermined, but somehow entirely American.*

Since America "became in the 20th century the most powerful and the most vital nation in the world," it was necessary for Americans "to accommodate themselves spiritually and practically to that fact." And that meant "to exert upon the world the full impact of our influence, for such purposes as we see fit and by such means as we see fit." Specifically that meant "a system of free enterprise" guaranteed by America, with "America as the dynamic leader of world trade." It meant American direction in the arts, technology, and the entertainment industry. America's skills and values, America's educational leadership, Luce wrote, are "needed and will be eagerly welcomed." Finally, the American Century required that America become "the Good Samaritan of the entire world." Responsibility for the feeding and caring of the world would parallel America's defense of the world, to be achieved by "a very tough attitude toward all hostile governments." "For every dollar we spend on armaments, we should spend at least a dime in a gigantic effort to feed the world—and all the world should know that we have dedicated ourselves to this task. . . ."

The Good Samaritan of the American Century was above all to be a creature of high ideals. America the world power was to become not merely the "sanctuary" of civilization but "the powerhouse of the ideals of Freedom and Justice," the "dynamic center of ever-widening spheres of enterprise," "the training center of the skillful servants of mankind." Not only did Henry Luce envision the Americanization of the world, he believed that his vision was shared "by most men living." Shared or not, it became the public rhapsody of the postwar period, as spearheaded by Luce's publications and all his media allies. After the war, to call the idea of the American Century arrogant or imperialist was to be a Communist dupe or traitor.

As fatuous or extravagant as it might seem, to avoid a Nazi century or a Communist century, there would be a concerted effort to create an American Century.[1] Across party lines, political visionaries and practical engineers introduced the structures necessary for its implementation. No treaty, no negotiation was free of its shadow. Whether or not it embodied New Deal or "socialistic" tendencies seemed somehow irrelevant. It would be sufficiently broad-based so as to be bipartisan. It would be dynamic, vigorous, powerful. And it would involve the Americanization of the world. An alternative ideological mantle had

---

* Historically, the proprietary use of the word "American" denotes an expansionist view of the United States that embraces North, Central, and South America.

been draped over the war. All political decisions made during the course of World War II carried its decree. After the war, and particularly during Eisenhower's presidency, it was shaped and coordinated. Unevenly charted, pragmatic and experimental, the features of the American Century did not become clearly distinct until Eisenhower's administration. Until Richard Nixon's fall, it was impossible to name those features fully or accurately. It is now clear, the shortest century in history has been among the most violent.

For years—decades, really—a great historical myth has prevailed. That myth involved the notion that the United States benefited accidentally—and almost against its own best instincts—from the imperial rivalries of Europe. But the United States did not inherit by default the resource-rich world that had represented the brightest jewels in the imperial crowns of Britain and France. The American Century was not an accident of war or fate. With all its profits and burdens, the American Century was as carefully ordered and organized as a Five Year Plan. And that organization developed largely during the presidential administration of Dwight David Eisenhower.

In 1941, Eisenhower was a professional soldier in Roosevelt's Army. Not overtly political, few knew his political affiliations, or whether in fact he had any. He was obscure, unknown, and unremarkable. Born in Texas, a West Point graduate, class of 1915, Eisenhower grew up in Abilene, Kansas. Though he never saw troop command in Europe, he had some experiences between World War I and World War II that would serve him well in later years. In November 1929, Major Eisenhower became assistant executive in the office of the assistant secretary of war, to supervise "the procurement of all military supplies and other business of the War Department. . . ." Eisenhower's task was to assure America's mobilization capabilities, to oversee "matériel and industrial organizations essential to wartime needs."

That assignment enabled Eisenhower to meet and negotiate with industrialists whose productivity might in the event of war be converted to military needs. It involved precise investigations of America's resources, its raw materials, its stockpiles, its ability to manufacture synthetic substitutes for scarce supplies. It meant thinking about such questions as price controls, "manpower controls," and fair profit and tax issues in times of crisis. It meant serving on the U. S. War Policies Commission, which prepared the way for the Special Senate Committee to Investigate the Munitions Industry, chaired by Senator Gerald P. Nye from 1934 to 1936. Senator Nye's inquiry into the profits of munitions makers, many of whom had international business interests, especially in Germany, convinced many during the 1930s that the close association between industry and the military was treacherous. According to the Nye Committee report, World War I mobilization involved "shameless profiteering" and forged "an unhealthy alliance" that "brings into being a self-interested political power which operates in the name of patriotism and satisfies interests which are, in large part, purely selfish, and . . . such associations are an inevitable part of militarism, and are to be avoided in peacetime at all costs."[2] To the end of his career, Eisenhower's interwar assignment influenced his values, priorities, and goals for America. During that period, he achieved a profound understanding of what he would later call the military-industrial complex.

Eisenhower, always a reluctant politician, was above all a moral statesman. His was a morality that developed during World War II out of his hatred for fascism, for the garrison states of Europe. On the eve of World War II, Eisenhower listened with friends to a shortwave radio broadcast from London as Neville Chamberlain announced on 3 September 1939 that Britain was at war with Germany. Eisenhower wrote his brother Milton that it was "a sad day for Europe and for the whole civilized world." The "final result will be that Germany will have to be dismembered." Deprived of a European post during World War I, Eisenhower sought a fighting assignment in this war. Five days after Pearl Harbor, Walter Bedell Smith, then a colonel and secretary to the Joint Chiefs of Staff, called from Washington and ordered Eisenhower, recently promoted to brigadier general, "to hop a plane and get up here right away."[3]

At once dreaded and awaited, it was the phone call that changed his life. By the end of the war, Dwight David Eisenhower was among the world's most celebrated generals and statesmen. Popularly regarded as a man of peace, the architect of victory, "the greatest military strategist of our time," Eisenhower was as beloved as Roosevelt had been. And Roosevelt was dead. Astute observers lost no time recognizing Eisenhower's political charisma. His presidency received a popular mandate of enormous enthusiasm. Then, through no fault of his own, and quite abruptly, he was deemed very simply and utterly a dud.

For the past twenty years, historians have tended to leap over the Eisenhower years, flying from the optimism of Roosevelt's New Deal to the crystal years of Jack Kennedy and on to the sagging times of Nixon's Watergate. Despite all the recent evidence to illustrate Eisenhower's varied strengths, the popular estimation of his public career is unchanged. As recently as 23 July 1980, New York *Post* columnist Max Lerner announced that Ronald Reagan "likes uneventful presidents like Coolidge and Eisenhower." And as for Eisenhower, Lerner noted, he "was caught up in events he couldn't manage, from Little Rock to the U-2." Some recall with a misplaced nostalgia that the alternative to Eisenhower in 1952 was Adlai Stevenson, and think that Stevenson would have been either more dashing or more peaceable or, somehow, both. Yet in 1956 Stevenson accused Eisenhower of permitting half of Indochina to become a "new Communist satellite" and of letting America emerge "from that debacle looking like a paper tiger." Stevenson also attacked Eisenhower for NATO's decline and charged that he missed "great opportunities to exploit weaknesses in the Communist ranks. . . ."

In fact, the Eisenhower era was the height of the American Century. Developed slowly during the war, it was forged by the Truman Doctrine and the Marshall Plan. During Eisenhower's presidency, the United States expanded vigorously and thoroughly throughout the world. All the structures required to introduce and defend the American Century were redesigned and implemented. The United States' business and commerce, U.S. fashions in literature, entertainment, dress and architecture, all accompanied the penetration of the United States' military and political presence. The need to protect the United States' worldwide interests from both war and social upheaval resulted in new kinds of intelligence operations, new kinds of political activities, and a massive program of psychological warfare unprecedented in scope and intensity. From private talks to "brinkmanship," a massive multilevel strategy to combat communism and to extend the influence of capital development was introduced. Political warfare during Eisenhower's presidency involved everything from the manipulation of elections in Italy to the overthrow of the elected government in Guatemala, including the overthrow of Mossadegh in Iran and the assassination of Lumumba in the Congo. The very nature of political warfare was transformed under Eisenhower. Eisenhower introduced all the elements of détente with the Soviet Union while he pursued all the imperial activities demanded by the global ideology of the American Century.

As the American Century wound down, the United States was revealed over time as a power not unlike other powers: arrogant, shallow, self-interested, cruel. But, fresh from the anti-Fascist alliance and the great victories of World War II, the United States seemed uniquely suited for leadership, boasting leaders who appeared both benevolent and truthful. With his notable warmth, his dazzling smile, and his open candor, General Eisenhower seemed above all to embody what was virtuous and fine about America.

Eisenhower believed profoundly in America. He believed that all the

success, all the responsibilities and honors that had come to him had
something to do with the fact that he was lucky enough to have been
born in America's heartland. Then too, Eisenhower believed that he
owed to his country a great debt. In service to the United States he
had triumphed. He had moved far beyond his modest boyhood home.
All of North Africa and Europe had been under his command. His circle of friends, his vision, his world had expanded beyond his most dar-
ing imaginings, his most secret personal ambitions.

In January 1950, Eisenhower affirmed his determination "to try,
however feebly, to return to the country some portion of the debt I
owe." Only in America, Eisenhower believed, could a poor boy,
the third of six brothers, raised in Abilene, Kansas, long past its romantic and rugged frontier prime, succeed as he had succeeded. Very
simply, if he could succeed, then anybody with sufficient initiative and
vigor could succeed. As a result, Eisenhower was convinced that one
of the greatest virtues of the American Century would be the worldwide extension of opportunity for poor young people such as he had
been.

In the beginning, Eisenhower was not specifically political. Although
he opposed the "welfare liberalism" of the New Deal and would later
call Roosevelt, Truman, and all New Dealers "socialistic," he defined
politics in such a way that he could call himself a "militant liberal."
He was both nonpartisan and anti-ideological. But after the war he was
increasingly surrounded by friends—new friends such as Tom Watson,
of IBM; Phil Reed, of the General Electric Company and soon to become president of the International Chamber of Commerce; Cliff Roberts, an investment banker; W. Alton ("Pete") Jones, president of
Cities Service Company; George Whitney, president of J. P. Morgan &
Company; Henry Luce; and William Robinson, president of Coca-Cola
and vice-president of the New York *Herald Tribune*. They golfed and
played bridge together; and they talked decisively about the future of
America.

They were loyal and influential. They encouraged Eisenhower to
consider the presidency of Columbia University. And they persuaded a
reluctant general to think seriously about his role in America's future.
They were dedicated to the expansion of Eisenhower's vision and to
the development of his political awareness. On a new electric type-
writer that Tom Watson had given him, Eisenhower practiced his typ-
ing and carried on a lengthy dialogue with his mentors. On 1 January
1950, he wrote that since "there is no difference between the two great
parties . . . I belong to neither." Specifically, Eisenhower insisted: "I
do not want a political career." But he did want "to return to the
country some portion of the debt I owe . . ."

My family, my brothers and I, are examples of what this country with its system of rights and freedoms, its boundless resources and its opportunities for all who WANT to work, can do for its citizens, regardless of lack of wealth, political influence, or special educational advantage. Nowhere else on earth has this type of material, intellectual and spiritual opportunity been so persistently and so successfully extended to all. Regardless of all faults that can be searched out in the operation of the American system, I believe without reservation that in its fundamental purposes and in its basic structure it is so far superior to any government elsewhere established by men, that my greatest possible opportunity for service is to be found in supporting, in renewing public respect for, and in encouraging greater thinking about these fundamentals. . . .

From 1945 until his nomination in 1952, Eisenhower denied interest in, but prepared fully for, the presidency. His acceptance of what he considered his part of the responsibility to shape the American Century took him first to the presidency of Columbia University. In that environment, he was introduced to civilian society—to the society of the responsible: to business leaders and publicists. His acceptance of that responsibility also returned him to Europe, to military leadership and the task of building the European Defense Community. The World War II alliance, so quickly dissolved, needed not only to be rebuilt but rebuilt with different participants and for a different purpose. The Fascists were defeated. The Communists thrived. The United States had entered a new phase of the Cold War. Everything that Eisenhower had seen as Supreme Commander of the World War II alliance had now to be refocused through a different prism. By 1952, he had come to regard communism as humanity's primary enemy. But Eisenhower had seen too much during the war to forget a vow that he had made to himself while touring the concentration camps of Ohrdruf Nord and Buchenwald. In those places, on that day in April 1945, Eisenhower had decided to dedicate his life to avoiding World War III. Part of his postwar commitment was to work for a stable peace and to promote that combination of American ideals that he believed would best serve "the future of this worry-torn world."[4] Another part of his commitment involved building the American Century, containing communism: the policy of "rollback," nuclear deterrence, political warfare, counterrevolutionary activities, military-assistance programs. For Eisenhower, the American Century meant global involvement, the perpetual threat of war, the endless pursuit of peace.

NOTE ON SOURCES

This book is based largely on the newly opened collections at the Dwight David Eisenhower Library at Abilene. To the best of my knowledge, I was the first to see many of these papers as they were opened. Through a process of mandatory review and requests made with the assistance of the Freedom of Information Act, many documents were declassified after appeal.

The superbly catalogued Ann C. Whitman files represent the most significant collections at Abilene. They include the personal papers and diaries of the presidency and are collected in the Administration, Diary, Name, and International series. Both the D. D. Eisenhower Diary series and the Ann C. Whitman Diary series contain minutes of meetings and conferences and monitored telephone calls. I also used the personal papers of the pre-presidency period, notably the Diary and Name series. Mrs. C. D. Jackson permitted me to use the Papers and Records of C. D. Jackson—an important, ninety-five-box collection basic to an understanding of political warfare. In addition, I researched the White House Central Files; James Hagerty's Diaries; the Joseph Rand, Gabriel Hauge, and William Robinson papers; several collections filed in the recently opened Council on Foreign Economic Policy series, Office of the Chairman (Joseph Dodge and Clarence Randall); and the papers opened in the Gordon Gray and Robert Cutler collections, of the Office of the Special Assistant for National Security Affairs.

At Columbia University, I used the five-volume collection of Edward Bermingham's correspondence; and selected interviews made for the Eisenhower Administration Oral History Project, including those with Sherman Adams, Joseph Alsop, Richard Bissell, Herbert Brownell, Lucius D. Clay, Eleanor Lansing Dulles, Milton S. Eisenhower, Clarence Francis, Andrew J. Goodpaster, Gordon Gray, Robert Keith Gray, Alfred A. Gruenther, Gabriel Hauge, James M. Lambie, Robert Lovett, William F. Knowland, John J. McCloy, Robert D. Murphy, Maxwell Rabb, Raymond J. Saulnier, and Murray Snyder.

At the Library of Congress, I used the Guatemalan papers and the Joseph Alsop collection. Chapters VI and VII are based largely on the enormous collection of papers of the Arbenz regime deposited in the Library of Congress, and the Guatemalan record released by the Department of State as a result of Freedom of Information Case 840606.

These significant materials, now being made available for the first time, have engendered a new generation of Eisenhower-era scholarship. I am grateful to Richard Immerman, who sent me two examples of this recent work: Immerman's "Eisenhower and Dulles: Who Made the Decisions?" *Political Psychology*, Autumn 1979, pp. 3–20; and Fred I. Greenstein, "Eisenhower as an Activist President: a Look at new Evidence," *Political Science Quarterly*, Winter 1979–80, pp. 575–99.

All published sources that I used are cited in my footnotes. Two outstanding works deserve, however, special mention: Herbert S. Parmet, *Eisenhower and the American Crusades* (Macmillan, 1972); and Peter Lyon, *Eisenhower: Portrait of the Hero* (Little, Brown, 1974). Lyon's work, based on documents made available to him by the President before they went to Kansas, remains the best full-life biography available. For bibliographies of secondary works, see Parmet, Lyon, and Charles C. Alexander, *Holding the Line: The Eisenhower Era, 1952–1961* (Indiana University Press, 1975).

CHAPTER I
WORLD WAR II
AND THE
ORIGINS OF
EISENHOWER'S
INTERNATIONALISM

"In the final analysis, public opinion wins most of the wars and always wins the peace."

DWIGHT D. EISENHOWER,
20 DECEMBER 1944

Some scholars tend to date the origins of the Cold War very specifically. They cite 20 July 1945, the fourth day of the Potsdam Conference, as the moment Franklin D. Roosevelt's vision of a grand design for a future of peace and international cooperation between Great Britain, the United States, and the Soviet Union began to dissolve. The Potsdam Conference was the first major postwar meeting of the Grand Alliance; it was the first time Truman, Churchill, and Stalin talked privately together. They met in a suburb of Berlin at the ceremonial Cecilienhof Palace, the home of the vanquished Hohenzollerns, to seal the peace, negotiate the spoils of war, and reconfirm the wartime alliance.

Potsdam, however, settled nothing. The future of all major areas of contention remained unresolved. On 20 July, Truman's behavior altered so dramatically that many observers noticed an aggressive hardening in tone and spirit. On that day, an army courier had arrived with the full details of the new, atomic weapon that had exploded over the desert at Alamogordo, in New Mexico, on 16 July, the day the leaders of the alliance had assembled at Potsdam. Truman knew that it had exploded successfully. But not until the full details of its enormous power were related was it clear that the carefully created atmosphere of Allied amity might be ended.

The scientists said that the bomb was "brighter than a thousand suns," stunning and frightful. For Truman and Churchill, it was "exhilarating." Surpassing all hopes regarding its relentless power, the atomic bomb freed Truman and Churchill from any need to compromise or parley. Dreams of Soviet-American cooperation in peace, as it had triumphed in war, had been rendered obsolete.[1]

But not everybody agreed with Truman and Churchill. Theirs was not, for example, Eisenhower's view in 1945. But theirs was the view that prevailed. It prevailed because the Cold War did not in fact begin in July 1945; it began in October 1917. It began as soon as Lenin's socialist government announced that Russian workers and peasants had ended class rank and social privilege. The Bolsheviks withdrew one sixth of the earth's surface from capitalist investment. Forevermore, the Soviet Union's symbol of the hammer and sickle, signifying to socialists the unity of industrial workers and farm workers, would be regarded in antisocialist circles as the emblem of torture and persecution.

The new Russian state was theoretically dedicated to Karl Marx's doctrine of class warfare. Change was declared planetary and inevitable. It was in something called the dialectic. Change had a life of its own. It was tumultuous and violent; and it was unstoppable. And in 1917, revolution had a life of its own. It was everywhere, as were reaction, counterrevolution, and very high hysteria. Within a framework of starvation, runaway inflation, and pitiful despair, the fallout of revolution and counterrevolution spread throughout Europe—emerging, so it seemed, from the ashes of a war-torn civilization that had just toppled all of its historical empires. The Hohenzollern, the Hapsburg, the Romanov, and the Ottoman empires had all collapsed. National boundaries were changed boldly and with little regard to ethnic unity or economic coherence. All colonial interests were destabilized. Much of Asia, the Middle East, and Africa were once again up for grabs. And a variety of anticolonial nationalists journeyed to the peace conference at Versailles to seek independence for their countries. Ho Chi Minh, for example, was among those who accepted at face value Woodrow Wilson's promise of self-determination for all nations. Woodrow Wilson refused to meet with him. His appeals for the independence of Indochina were impolitely scorned. Ho Chi Minh returned home a revolutionary. Nothing would ever be the same after 1917.

At Versailles, an irregular line of nations, north to south from Finland to Albania, with Britain controlling Greece and Turkey, was designated a *cordon sanitaire* to divide Europe into two parts. Carved out of the toppled Hohenzollern, Hapsburg, and Ottoman empires, with sections from Germany, Poland, and Russia, redesigned political entities such as Estonia, Latvia, Lithuania, Czechoslovakia, and Yugoslavia—together with Hungary, Albania and Bulgaria—were to be the political and economic buffer zone to separate Russian communism from Western capitalism. Since the West seemed to begin at Vienna, and much of the West still consisted of kingdoms and tyrannies, talk of democracy and dictatorship, of Bolshevik "slavery" and the "free world," had not yet begun in 1917.

But the Cold War was underway. The era from Versailles to Potsdam to Vietnam to détente to our own moment of rapid and awesome global upheaval, revolution and counterrevolution, represents an unbroken time of historical tension and bloodshed and change. There is no way to make sense of appeasement, the twisted course of World War II, or the second phase of the Cold War, which began in 1945, without understanding that it all began in 1917. In 1917, all traditions were open to question, and everywhere the ordered world of noblemen and kings, of Enlightenment democrats and landless peasants was in turmoil. And in 1917, throughout the vast stretches of Russia—from Leningrad to Vladivostok—which dips into the Sea of Japan and borders Korea and for hundreds of miles is contiguous with China—in that place, revolutionary communism had actually taken root, removing one sixth of the world's land mass from private capital investment and threatening to become a worldwide system unrelated to the free-market economy. For such liberal internationalists as Woodrow Wilson and frank colonialists such as Winston Churchill, as well as for the remnants of Europe's toppled monarchies, such a state was untenable, unacceptable, unimaginable.

More than the pious tones of Woodrow Wilson's liberal internationalism and the outrage of Winston Churchill were necessary to meet the Soviet challenge. Armed, secret Allied intervention sparked by fire the reality of the Cold War. In 1919, Allied troops from Great Britain, North America, France, and Japan invaded Russia to overthrow the new regime. It was an ambitious scheme involving French troops in Odessa and Georgia, British activity in Transcaucasia (the crucial area between the Black Sea and Iran), and U.S., Czech, and Japanese troops in Siberia. Although mercenaries were hired by the hundred, and the counterrevolutionary forces under Romania's Admiral Kolchak were well supported, the success of the Allied intervention depended on a mass upheaval, a vigorous popular repulsion of the Soviet regime. But it never occurred. The Allied intervention, long a secret operation, little discussed either in history books or by the contemporary press, failed.[2] The new Russian state survived. And it threatened, most European and American statesmen believed, everything Western transatlantic civilization had stood for.

For such statesmen as Wilson and Winston Churchill, civilization meant very specific things. To begin with, it meant Anglo-American liberty. And liberty, as they understood it, meant not only democracy but a liberal economy, which they defined as a free-market economy, with government support but without government interference. It was no surprise, therefore, that men like Churchill abhorred the new Soviet state and that the entire United States diplomatic world acted simply as if Russia had ceased to exist.

Until 1933, when Roosevelt finally recognized the Soviet Government, United States diplomats observed the Soviet Union from Riga, a port city in the Baltic Sea. Largely German in culture and origin, Riga, then the capital of Latvia, became a center of anti-Soviet activities. At Riga, American specialists on Russia saw little and concluded much. They determined that the Soviet Union was civilization's enemy. Liberty would survive only if it was overthrown.

At the same time, in the face of the socialist threat, liberty itself was redefined. In the United States, it was restricted to mean elective government for nonsocialists, democracy for anticommunists. During the Red scare of the 1920s, all opponents of World War I, all anarchists, socialists, and political dissenters became the target of massive arrests, and a moment of political repression unparalleled in United States history occurred. Thousands of immigrants and dissenters were arrested during the raids ordered by Attorney General A. Mitchell Palmer without warrant or cause. Although hundreds of women and men were deported, most of those arrested were released for lack of evidence of wrongdoing. Censorship of the free press prevailed. Such liberal or antiwar magazines as *The Nation, The New Republic* and *The Masses* were confiscated and barred from the mails. *The Freeman's Journal* was suspended, for example, for quoting Thomas Jefferson's arguments on behalf of Irish independence; the *Irish World,* for editorializing that Palestine should not become a Jewish state; and *Four Lights,* the journal of the Woman's Peace Party of New York, for hailing the Russian Revolution "with mad, glad joy." Elected socialist officials were turned out of the United States Congress, and in many states and municipalities where socialists were elected, they were removed. In Britain, Clare Sheridan, Winston Churchill's cousin, scandalized polite British society when, in 1923, she went to Moscow to sculpture portraits of the Bolshevik leaders. She explained the vehement reaction of her horrified family in family terms:

> Winston Churchill (who is talked of as the likely leader of a Fascist party in England) says Fascism is the shadow of Bolshevism, and that if we must be ruled by one or the other he would rather be ruled by Fascist violence than by Bolshevik violence. . . .[3]

Just as there was a firm link that connected the Red scare of the 1920s with the McCarthy years, so there was a taut line maintained by the professional standard-bearers of international diplomacy that stretched from 1917 to 1945. For many career diplomats, World War II was an interlude. It was an unfortunate diversion from the primary problem. Appeasement was a part of that problem. For many statesmen in Britain, France, the United States, and China, the new Fascist regimes in Italy, Spain, and Germany were perfectly acceptable alternatives to communism.

The Fascist governments, after all, remained faithful members of the privately financed family of nations. And in so far as Fascist states were territorially ambitious, they looked east, toward the area of the newly erected *cordon sanitaire*. There was reason to hope, therefore, that these new and unattractive systems would battle each other, would cancel each other out. Russia, from the time of the czars, proclaimed itself the leader of the Slav nations. Now the Nazis of Germany proclaimed the same group of nations racially, geographically, rightfully their own. The battlefield was predetermined: The unstable territory so recently loosened from its ancient monarchical moorings and designated cynically at Versailles the *cordon sanitaire* was created to contain the Soviet menace.

If the Communists and the Fascists destroyed each other in Central Europe, then the "free world" could return to its traditional pursuits, at home and abroad. Some spokesmen for this position were crudely specific. Sir Alan Brooke, Chief of Britain's Imperial General Staff, whose position paralleled General George Marshall's during World War II, hoped, for example, that the Nazis and the "Red Hordes" would destroy each other so that "Britain might dominate an exhausted Europe."[4]

But the Fascists were greedy. Eventually Adolf Hitler went too far. He was, moreover, unwholesome. By 1939, frightened and horrified liberals of all persuasions, including the most vigorous anti-Communists, agreed that Hitler and fascism had to be stopped. In the United States, for example, Henry Luce was, in 1939, finally dismayed by Hitler. Luce's magazines, *Time, Life,* and *Fortune,* had until 1939 argued that Hitler was maligned and misunderstood. Apparently Luce had chosen Adolf Hitler to be *Time*'s Man of the Year for 1938. But, on 2 January 1939, he was portrayed on the cover of *Time* as a monster, a demon of murderous hate. And in the accompanying editorial, Hitler was designated "the greatest threatening force that the democratic, freedom-loving world faces today. . . . The Fascintern, with Hitler in the driver's seat, with Mussolini, Franco and the Japanese military cabal riding behind, emerged in 1938 as an international revolutionary movement. . . . The Fascist battle against freedom is often carried forward under the false slogan of 'Down with Communism!' . . . Civil rights and liberties have disappeared. . . . Germany's 700,000 Jews have been tortured physically, robbed of homes and properties. . . . Out of Germany has come a steady, ever-swelling stream of refugees, Jews and Gentiles, Catholics as well as Protestants. . . ."

According to his biographer, Luce approved the text personally, "after criticizing it for being too anti-Fascist and adding a paragraph listing Hitler's achievements within the Reich."[5] After Luce and his associates agreed that fascism was the primary danger, a dramatic shift occurred in policy-making circles. It became acceptable to deplore fascism without being labeled a Communist sympathizer.

During World War II, there were those who abhorred fascism even more than they feared Russia. There is now evidence that Eisenhower believed sincerely in the Grand Alliance. And he believed it could survive World War II. He was not alone. But, in professional diplomatic circles, such judgments were not highly regarded. While nobody doubted Russia's military importance to the Allied cause, the State Department's opposition to the alliance existed on two levels. Some State Department functionaries, such as A. A. Berle, feared that Russia might at any moment abandon its commitment to wartime unity and make a separate peace with Germany. After all, wrote Berle, the Soviets had already done so twice, by ending World War I at Brest-Litovsk in 1918 and again by signing the Soviet-German agreement of 23 August 1939. For Berle, those agreements rendered Russia untrustworthy.[6] Other State Department officials remained anti-Soviet in general and on principle. Subsequently known as the professional cold warriors, during World War II their influence was limited.

Although Roosevelt kept the cold warriors largely under wraps for the duration of World War II, they were present at every decision-making level. Moreover, the Grand Alliance was, even on the presidential level, unevenly pursued. The most spectacular example of Russia's secondary position in the alliance was Roosevelt and Churchill's 1942 decision to limit the Manhattan Project to Anglo-American participation. How can history explain that decision except in terms of the limitations of Roosevelt's own faith in the future of the alliance? Especially since he knew, as did all the scientists associated with the project, that all the earth's leading physicists shared the same fundamental knowledge. During the 1920s, they had worked together at, for example, the University of

Göttingen, in Germany. For over a decade, they had lectured, shared experiments, exchanged papers, and pursued the secrets of energy contained within the atom. All of them—British, Russian, Hungarian, Polish, North American, Italian, German—Sir Ernest Rutherford, George Gamow, Smoluchowski, Leo Szilard, Edward Teller, Eugene Wigner, J. Robert Oppenheimer, Enrico Fermi, Albert Einstein. When, in 1933, Hitler expelled the Jewish physicists, they and other scientists who left in protest went to Britain, to Denmark to work with Niels Bohr, to the United States, or to the Soviet Union. There was nothing that some of them could do that the others could not. Some scientists, such as Wernher von Braun and Werner Heisenberg, continued to work in Germany. That was, after all, what the urgency of the Manhattan Project was all about.

To exclude the Allied scientists of Russia was in fact a symbolic gesture. It was not, however, an isolated one. As early as 31 July 1941, A. A. Berle noted in his journal a State Department conference "on the Russian demand that we turn over our military secrets to her, and give her engineers access to the plants making our secret military weapons. The extreme Anglophile view is that we should turn over everything to the Russians at once." The British apparently believed that the Russians "will be in all respects a part of their train." But Berle was "in no way sanguine" and was delighted that "the Army, Navy and FBI" voted no, as he did. "We are much better off," Berle concluded, "if we treat the Russian situation for what it is, namely, a temporary confluence of interest."[7]

World War II was thus fought on two levels: The Grand Alliance against fascism was marked by a strained, limited, and uneven military détente. It was a period of suspended Cold War with Russia. Below the presidential level, the Grand Alliance was from the beginning a sham. Wherever the cold warriors possessed authority—and they shared authority in all key areas, such as North Africa, Italy, France, and finally occupied Germany—the alliance was grudgingly, ineffectively, and meanly administered.

Robert Murphy's important and revealing book *Diplomat Among Warriors* provides one of the best accounts of a cold warrior's frustrations during World War II. Robert Murphy considered the Grand Alliance a supreme folly, myopic and wasteful. A career diplomat first assigned to Munich in 1921, Robert Murphy has been called everything from a monarchist to a sentimentalist to a

Fascist. A dedicated specialist in political warfare who went earnestly about his business, Murphy was probably none of those things. Tough, hard-working and hard-boiled, if he was soft on anything it was the romantic and courtly past. He lamented the passing of Italy's "thousand-year" House of Savoy, and he adored good German efficiency. From his account, one does not discover that the kings of Italy and Belgium were unpopular because they collaborated with the Fascists. Rather, there is a sense of mourning for the passing of royal traditions. From his account, we get a sense of the limited political alternatives available during World War II.

Communism or Fascism. From the beginning, partisan politics influenced or determined every step taken during World War II. And partisan politics in Europe were a vastly different reality from U.S. exchanges between the Republican and Democratic parties. In 1938, Henry Luce reported to his staff during his European tour:

> Communism is a much bigger thing in Europe than it is in America. There were MILLIONS of actual official Communist votes in Germany before Hitler. In France there is a very large block of actual Communist votes seating 72 Communist Congressmen and there are whole suburbs around Paris which are Communistic—not merely in the alarmist American sense of the word, but as an actual party organization.[8]

Throughout World War II, the organized resistance to fascism was led largely by Communists and Communist sympathizers. Everywhere the Allied armies went, they were protected and supported and preceded by the organized Resistance. There were important instances of monarchist anti-Fascists, such as Yugoslavia's mountain hero General Draža Mihailović. Ironically, Churchill supported his opponent, Josip Broz Tito, a Communist whose activities were of greater importance to the Allied cause. And then there was de Gaulle.

The United States did not recognize General Charles de Gaulle as the leader of the Free French forces. The United States supported instead the Vichy leaders of North Africa, led by Admiral Jean Louis François Darlan. Darlan was a notorious Nazi collaborator who aided Rommel's Afrika Korps against the British in

Libya. America's alliance with the Vichy in North Africa and its passive acceptance of their many atrocities scandalized public opinion in Britain and the United States and influenced Franco-American relations for many decades to come.

The politics of North Africa rocked Eisenhower's prestige, aroused suspicion about his judgment, and dismayed anti-Fascist forces throughout the world. Eisenhower maintained that all political decisions in North Africa were militarily necessary. Vichy support was essential for America's military intervention in the area. But the politics of North Africa had more than temporary military significance.

In February 1941, President Roosevelt had sent Robert Murphy as his personal undercover emissary to North Africa to select alternatives to de Gaulle and his followers who would be more acceptable to the United States, and to negotiate an economic agreement in the area. Robert Murphy's trade agreement with Vichy's General Maxime Weygand, the "Murphy-Weygand Accord," of February 1941, ended the Allied blockade of Fascist North Africa. Condemned widely as "appeasement," the Murphy-Weygand Accord represented the United States' first successful step in Roosevelt's new policy of "economic penetration" in this traditionally Anglo-French preserve.

Roosevelt believed that France's colonies were "visibly withering on the vine." America's political decisions heralded its new level of interest in the future of France's colonial empire. The great oil-rich territories were no longer to be the exclusive properties of France and Britain. The "Darlan Deal" had served to announce America's presence in the area. From 1941, the United States would participate directly and fully in North Africa. Murphy had negotiated the simple exchange: Vichy support for the United States landing in North Africa in return for recognition of the legitimacy of the Vichy Fascists under Darlan.

America's refusal to support de Gaulle created a rift between England and the United States. De Gaulle was England's ally. Moreover, Britain subsidized de Gaulle and the Free French forces handsomely and at great cost to the war-torn nation. Britain and the Free French were in fact in a state of undeclared war against Vichy France. In July 1940, the British Navy had destroyed a Vichy naval squadron at Mers-el-Kebir, Algeria, killing over one thousand French sailors. Britain had attempted to capture Dakar, French West Africa, with de Gaulle personally leading the attack. In July 1941, British and Free French troops occupied Syria and Lebanon, and there were over sixty thousand casualties. Britain did not recognize the Vichy government of Marshal Pétain. Britain deplored publicly and relentlessly Vichy's Nazi decrees, the anti-Jewish laws, its concentration-camp roundups of all anti-Fascists, the atrocities that accompanied the establishment of the Vichy government.

At the same time, Britain supported de Gaulle's commitment to maintain the French Empire intact. Opposed to the nationalist independence movements in the area of their traditional dominance, Britain and de Gaulle recognized that America's support for the hated Vichy would only further destabilize colonial control over North Africa. In this area, their potential political differences were diminished by their shared colonial heritage. Churchill considered de Gaulle a "strong central authority" around whom the disunited Berbers, Moors, and Jews could unite in opposition to the Vichy regime. America's economic penetration of North Africa would occur only at great cost to traditional colonial influence and prestige in the area.

Eisenhower became the major target of Allied outrage over the Darlan Deal. Eisenhower considered it essential to his military operations. He believed that all respectable and responsible leaders in North Africa supported Darlan. But Eisenhower was badly misinformed.

As soon as the Allied "liberators" ratified the Fascists, all French officials who had assisted the Allies were jailed. Gaullists and newspaper editors who welcomed the Allies were arrested, and their newspapers were censored. Nazi laws against Jews and political dissenters were reinforced, and thousands of additional prisoners were sent to concentration camps. France's Compagnons, modeled on the Hitlerjugend, restrained during the period of negotiations, now paraded daily through the streets.[9]

Eisenhower's support of Darlan and the Fascists rapidly became untenable. In December 1942, Roosevelt dispatched Dr. Milton Eisenhower, the general's brother and associate director of the Office of War Information (OWI) to Algiers with four "specific assignments: (1) to study the work of OWI in psychological warfare and make changes if they were needed; (2) to find out why the Darlan agreement and our military actions were being misrepresented and make corrections . . . ; (3) to develop at least the preliminary phases of a plan for psychological warfare in subsequent military operations . . . ; and (4) to see what could be done with the French refugees who were fleeing from occupied France through Spain and Portugal to North Africa, where they threatened to impede our military operations."

The professional journalists and psychological warriors who represented the largest initial overseas group within the OWI had consistently opposed the continuance of the Vichy regime in North Africa. Independent and professional journalists, most of the women and men of the OWI considered Darlan and company a public-relations disaster. They insisted that the Allied war effort depended on Allied unity and the enthusiasm with which British and American troops might work with each other under the banner of a just and noble cause. To die for fascism in the world's crusade against fascism seemed to many of them an inordinately nasty thing. Edward R. Murrow, for example, blasted the Darlan Deal: "What the hell is all this about?" he demanded. "Are we fighting Nazis or sleeping with them?"[10] One OWI representative in London despaired:

> Oh, for one little act. . . . Just the name of one patriot released from jail, one honest man restored to his post, one fascist put out of the way. Or just one photograph of a Jewish schoolboy returning to his classroom, or of a refugee eating the bread of the liberators.[11]

But Milton Eisenhower was more concerned about "misleading information," anti-American "propaganda" and, according to Robert Murphy, "his brother's reputation." Not only had elements of the Anglo-American press labeled the general a "fascist," Dr. Eisenhower was appalled to discover that the world acquired its news from Radio Maroc, which was, he wrote, "amazingly" controlled by "Free French sympathizers." Milton Eisenhower, reported Murphy, wanted "drastic action taken immediately" before his brother's career was "irreparably damaged." "'Heads must roll, Murphy!' he exclaimed. 'Heads must roll.'" The Free French sympathizers were removed and replaced by OWI personnel who moved into North Africa with General Patton. Until suitable replacements went to work, North Africa was sealed off from all newspaper and radio reporters. Total media censorship prevailed throughout the winter of 1942–43.[12]

Like his brother, Dr. Eisenhower seemed undisturbed by Darlan. Milton Eisenhower acknowledged Darlan's "hatred of the British," but he did not see "in him any liking for the Nazis." He concluded that Darlan was "a conservative patriot, prepared to do whatever he had to do for the benefit of France. . . ." Milton Eisenhower was far more disturbed by his OWI subordinates. He complained that the women and men "recruited into the overseas division of OWI were former foreign correspondents, an independent group, usually more at ease criticizing public policy than in disseminating information concerning it." They were frequently "indifferent" to their new "responsibilities as representatives of the United States Government." And Milton Eisenhower judged their hostility to the politics of the North African campaign "insubordination, almost treason."[13]

It was not until C. D. Jackson was flown into North Africa to take "full charge of OWI operations" that Milton Eisenhower considered the situation finally "satisfactory." C. D. Jackson was one of Henry Luce's leading apostles, the editor of *Fortune* and a vice-president of Time-Life, Inc. Jackson, who was later to figure prominently in General Eisenhower's presidential administrations, was delighted with his new job. And a considerable job it was: As head of the Psychological Warfare Board (PWB), Jackson was to integrate psychological warfare into America's overall military strategy. In October 1943, Jackson wrote enthusiastically to Henry Luce about Eisenhower's acceptance of the Psychological Warfare Board as a regular part of Allied Force Headquarters. It was

> both interesting and exciting to be part of a propaganda organization which is used by a military high command, just as it would use any other arm of warfare. When a plan is being drawn up we are in on the drawing up, just as air and tanks and infantry; and the days of the rugged soldier looking down his nose at you and saying "We fight with bullets not with words, so please don't bother me" are pretty much over. Too much credit cannot be given to Eisenhower and his staff for having overcome the original hurdle of soldierly distrust, and for having accepted us as something more than a newfangled nuisance. . . .

The Psychological Warfare Board was one of the earliest units to achieve a truly allied organizational structure. Jackson described the structure to Luce:

We really have quite a show over here now. PWB has over 700 soldiers and civilians, British and American, all inextricably mixed up; and so completely integrated that none of us think in terms of nationality or organization. . . . No one thinks of himself . . . as either British or American, and the initials OWI, PWE, MOI are practically never mentioned. It is all PWB. And, miracle of miracles, we must have a dozen OSS officers working here now, all of whom have also been absorbed into PWB. . . . We own and operate two 50,000 watt radio stations and one 100,000 watt station. We are operating in Sicily and now in Italy, with combat propaganda teams with the Armies and occupation teams following them into the various centers as soon as they have been taken. We run radio photo from the front for distribution all over the world. We have mobile printing presses and mobile radio units. We set up our own communications channels. We start up the newspapers when the troops move into a town. We really print and distribute between seven and ten million leaflets a week. We have radio monitoring setups all over the place, which are used not only by us but by headquarters, advance headquarters and the fighting Armies. And, stepping out of my PWB role into OWI, I also have Cairo, Beirut, Istanbul to coordinate into the overall propaganda picture. . . . BBC and ourselves are in constant monitoring touch in order that we will all be telling the same story in the same way; and, of course, OWI short-wave is also integrated into the picture. . . .

I assure you I don't think of myself in these global terms during the daytime when the details crowd in. But when I do have time to add it all up . . . it is really pretty terrific. . . .[14]

Dwight David Eisenhower was one of the earliest champions and most consistent supporters of America's unique brand of psychological warfare. His acceptance of the PWB as an integral part of military strategy and planning was based on his understanding of the nature of American democracy, which depended so much on winning and maintaining the loyalty of favorable public opinion. Psychological warfare for the United States reflected, during World War II and later, during Eisenhower's presidency, his firm conviction that "in the final analysis, public opinion wins most of

the wars and always wins the peace."[15] Over time, Eisenhower
acted upon that conviction unevenly and inconsistently. But it
represented a basic belief that continued to inform, as general and
as statesman, each of his diplomatic acts.

In the spring of 1943, Milton Eisenhower attempted to define
the specific value of psychological warfare in the North African
campaign, and for the future. During an address before the Kansas
Bankers' Association, in Topeka, Dr. Eisenhower explained that
"the propaganda front" was "a vital part of total war." The psychological "battles we are waging . . . involve a struggle for men's
minds no less intense and no less urgent, in terms of ultimate victory, than the struggles for men's blood. Wars are not won by the
winning of men's minds, to be sure. . . . But the struggle on the
battle field is the physical expression of a conflict of convictions
and, in the end, the convictions of one side will prevail. If we
weaken the convictions of our enemies, we weaken their will to
fight; and if we strengthen the convictions of our allies and ourselves, we strengthen our capacity to win. . . ."

In the "struggle for men's minds," the United States, he said,
had "one great advantage, one 'secret weapon,'—the Truth." Regarding France and North Africa, America's policy "has been consistent. It is that the French and American people are Allies, and
that no German collaborationists or officials temporarily in charge
could change that fact. We stress the friendship and warm affection of the American people, our determination to liberate France
and then to permit the French people to choose their own leaders.
Our information to France is steadfastly factual, with a distinctive
American personality."[16]

Shortly after Milton Eisenhower had returned from his visit to
North Africa, on Christmas Eve 1942, Darlan was shot. To contemporary war-weary assassination observers, Darlan's death might
resemble political events to become more familiar in later decades.
A lone and allegedly crazed assassin was immediately caught and
immediately ordered executed. His death was ordered by General
Jean Marie Bergeret, the deputy high commissioner under Darlan,
"with no questions asked or encouraged." Bergeret then took out
after those few remaining Gaullists who had somehow eluded his
previous dragnets.[17]

Darlan's assassination did not remove the Fascists. The situation was still untenable. And Eisenhower remained puzzled by the unceasing protests against his policies. In January 1943, Eisenhower told Harold Macmillan, Britain's political adviser in North Africa (whose tasks paralleled Robert Murphy's): "I can't understand why these long-haired, starry-eyed guys keep gunning for me. I'm no reactionary. Christ on the Mountain! I'm as idealistic as hell." Moreover, Eisenhower reported to Macmillan, Darlan's death enabled the United States to make some changes: "We are going to get a new governor for Algeria." Marcel Peyrouton. "They tell me he's a fine guy."

Apparently nobody had told Eisenhower that Marcel Peyrouton had been Vichy's Minister of the Interior. The United States' new governor-general had been the man responsible for the arrest, torture, and execution of the French who had resisted Nazism and for administering the Nazis' anti-Jewish decrees. Darlan had nominated him, Murphy had recommended him, and the U. S. State Department, over the vigorous dissent of Undersecretary of State Sumner Wells, had approved him. Eisenhower's reaction to the "howls of anguish at home" regarding Peyrouton's appointment was confided to his diary: "Who DO they want? He is an experienced administrator and God knows it's hard to find many of them among the French in Africa." Eisenhower would not have had such a hard time finding good administrators if, as Peter Lyon has pointed out, he had "looked in the right places." All those places where anti-Fascists were imprisoned or in hiding; or if he had been permitted to accept the leadership of de Gaulle and his supporters.[18]

The United States designated instead General Henri Honoré Giraud as the leader of the French Government. Eisenhower minimized the differences between Giraud and de Gaulle as little more than petty partisan rivalry. The United States ignored the intensity of the conflict between the Vichy leadership and the anti-Fascist Resistance under de Gaulle. That France was in a state of civil war that reflected the full bitterness of World War II was continually denied by Eisenhower, and by Roosevelt, who personally shaped North African policy. This remained the case even after Eisenhower saw clearly that Giraud was "Reactionary, old-fashioned . . . , and without political acumen."[19] And it remained the case long after it was clear to many Allied observers that the trouble with de Gaulle was not his abrasive and haughty personality. The trouble with de Gaulle was his independence. He was a popular leader. The United States could not control de Gaulle. And above all, he was committed to the full restoration of France as a world power—and that included the reacquisition of the entire French Empire.

Months before de Gaulle arrived in Algeria and declared himself leader of the Free French forces and the Committee of National Liberation, and therefore President of France, Assistant Secretary of War John J. McCloy sent a secret memorandum dated 1 March 1943 to Eisenhower urging specific changes in policy.

I have had a great many talks and been around quite a bit and my general conclusions are as follows:

POLITICAL: Things are moving too slowly toward the liberalization of restrictions on personal freedom. I can find no good reason why the Nazi laws still obtain here. Their repeal . . . would produce a profound change for the better in American opinion toward the whole North African business and it would have a good effect in France and other non-Nazi areas. In fact, I can find no sound argument against it. . . .

Eventually the laws will be repealed, unless we are to write down the job as a failure, and if they are only repealed after the DeGaullists arrive, it will be DeGaulle and not Giraud who will get the credit. In fact, already Giraud is late, because even now if he repeals the laws it will be said he did it under the gun of DeGaullist arrival. . . .

Revealing the complex and conflicting nature of America's interests in North Africa, McCloy urged Eisenhower to pay keen attention to the problem of "personalities." For public-relations reasons, he counseled Eisenhower to shun or at least not publicly promote specific Vichy leaders, notably Jacques Lemaigre-Dubreuil. From the beginning one of Robert Murphy's "boldest French colleagues," Lemaigre-Dubreuil was a well-traveled, well-placed, "wealthy, aggressive industrial promoter." His numerous business interests throughout France as well as West and North Africa provided him with "immensely useful high-level contacts" and "ready access" to top German and Vichy authorities. Lemaigre-Dubreuil was accused of being a Nazi collaborator who amassed a wartime fortune as a "king of petroleum," but Murphy (who insisted that his fortune was in "the peanut oil industry") considered him an "irreplaceable" and "perfect intermediary" and believed in his anti-Nazi convictions.

Lemaigre-Dubreuil had advised Murphy that notable French "big businessmen believed that their interest would best be served by a German victory, because they thought that a British victory would result in the bolshevization of Europe." Lemaigre-Dubreuil told Murphy that "he opposed such ideas but that he had to pretend to agree with them."

Whatever his beliefs and no matter Murphy's enthusiasm for him, John J. McCloy wrote to Eisenhower that he did not think that Lemaigre-Dubreuil "is the sort that we can afford to have tied to our stars if we ever move into France. He is an ultra reactionary, smart monopolist. I do not doubt his loyalty to the cause, although he is said to have his dealings with the Germans which resulted in considerable preferment to him. . . .

"Some of his past history has been well advertised in the U.S. and any prominence given his name would not produce a good effect there. He should be prepared, and I gather from Murphy is, to work without public recognition. I like him and he is sensible, but I just think we are in for another headache like the Darlan-Pcyrouton affair if we advance him."[20]

Clearly, to maintain a policy that combined anti-fascism with the military needs of warfare, as well as an intense regard for America's economic future, was not a simple matter. On 29 June 1943, the general sent to his brother Milton his own analysis of the military victory in North Africa:

. . . The broader problems of war have a habit of presenting themselves without a pedigree of precedent. In this instance, a large Allied force invaded an officially neutral territory, but one in which there were known to exist definite Axis influence and glaring examples of deplorable racial and political discrimination that not only cried aloud for quick correction, but were of the type that our people were determined the war should eliminate. Every dictate of conscience and of upbringing in a free country urged us all to attempt immediately drastic and arbitrary reformation. But it was necessary to conduct an exceedingly risky campaign, far to the eastward of our original landings, and . . . we had to have the *active* cooperation of French forces. . . . I repeat, we then needed the *positive* cooperation of French forces, not merely passive non-resistance. The size of the eventual military victory certainly justified the policy of evolution rather than revolution in the political field. . . .

For Eisenhower, this military necessity "called for anxious thought, earnest effort and complete disregard for what might or might not be immediately popular to the public. Such success as we have acomplished over the whole front has come about, I firmly believe, because we did not attempt to put the cart before the horse."[21]

Insulting to the anti-Fascist French and abusive to de Gaulle, America's policy in North Africa was based in part on mistaken intelligence estimates. On 24 June 1943, Eisenhower had cabled General George Marshall that "within a matter of weeks De Gaulle will, in the opinion of all our people and of the conservative French . . . have declined to a position of practical impotency."[22]

"ALL OUR PEOPLE" and *"THE CONSERVATIVE FRENCH."* A pattern was initiated, and firmly set. Our intelligence operatives simply ignored the opposition, no matter how valid, how popular, or ultimately how significant it might be to the success of the United States' own expressed goals. Based on entrenched, traditional, and conservative sources, America's intelligence was for four decades to be locked into the service of the needs of a foreign economic policy that Roosevelt introduced in North Africa. Having concluded that the French Empire "tottered," Roosevelt considered it time for the United States to control the strategic areas of Indochina, Syria, and Lebanon; Dakar, in French West Africa; and Bizerte, in Tunisia. When Milton Eisenhower returned from his Algeria tour and reported to the President, Roosevelt's primary concern was very clear. He was, Dr. Eisenhower wrote, "in a pensive mood." He wanted to know all about the agricultural situation and the resources of North Africa, and he spoke enthusiastically of his plans for the region: "You know, Milton, when the war is over it would be wonderful to go to North Africa and trap the waters that now flow from the Atlas Mountains into the ocean. We could build dams and create one of the finest irrigation systems in the world. . . ."[23]

The victory in North Africa was not a victory over fascism. It was not even a victory for the Grand Alliance, which Eisenhower sought vigorously to create and firmly establish. Britain opposed

America's meddling in North Africa and colonial business, and continued to support de Gaulle. For his part, de Gaulle would never again trust "Anglo-Saxons," including his Anglo-American allies. Like other vigorous nationalists, he would forevermore be an unpredictable "swing man" in matters of international relations, pursuing an independent national course frequently unrelated to Anglo-American interests. But Eisenhower's victory in North Africa ended nineteenth-century colonial alignments. It closed the exclusive era of British-French imperial dominance. It was a dramatic and profound victory for the United States.

The politics of Eisenhower's North African campaign reflected the needs of America's military and economic interests. It occurred before Roosevelt established a political policy to guide the activities of the wartime alliance. Roosevelt's mandate for a Grand Alliance of Britain, the United States, and Russia was not defined until after a meeting of the Allied foreign ministers in Moscow in October 1943, which prepared the agenda and laid the political foundations for the first face-to-face meeting of the Big Three—Churchill, Roosevelt and Stalin—to meet in Iran at Teheran in November.

Secretary of State Cordell Hull returned from the Moscow conference of foreign ministers a changed man. His enthusiastic vision of permanent peace deeply influenced Roosevelt. Robert Murphy, on the other hand, was "astonished" at how "emotional" and "almost mystical" Hull was about the "epochal" conference. The public reaction to Hull's report of the conference, which was delivered before a joint session of Congress, was also epochal. Never again, Hull declared, would the world be divided by spheres of influence, military alliances, all those unfortunate arrangements that have failed in our "unhappy past" to safeguard the security of nations. Hull's address before Congress was an unprecedented event, and the response to it was overwhelming. It engendered a moment of high optimism that permanent peace was possible.[24]

Roosevelt went to Teheran not only committed to a strategy that involved coordinated military activities but looking forward to creating a sincere sense of Allied unity. A. A. Berle wrote of Teheran that "on its face, it was an agreement . . . to cooperate in winning the war and in keeping the peace." Also at Teheran, the Allies acknowledged Russia's military and security needs and agreed to open the long-requested "second front," a cross-Channel assault

upon Nazi power in the West. "Russia's paramount interest in
Eastern Europe was also recognized at this conference." Berle
noted that certain "unhappy souls" in the State Department were
already beginning to speak of an "'Eastern Munich.'" Indeed
Robert Murphy deplored the fact that after Teheran Roosevelt
seemed committed to Soviet-American cooperation "above any
other prospective Alliance."[25]

In terms of military efficiency and the coordination necessary for
as quick a military victory as possible, Roosevelt's new emphasis
suited Eisenhower's needs perfectly. After the politics of North
Africa, so damaging to his prestige as a military leader, Eisenhower was grateful to be able to postpone all political considerations and to defer all political concerns until the military requirements of the war were met. Then too, the United States
military was eager to begin its long-postponed plans for a second
European front against Germany.* At Teheran, Roosevelt agreed
with Stalin that the time had clearly arrived to begin an all-out invasion against the Nazis through northern France, an invasion that
had been postponed at the insistence of Churchill. While Britain
and the United States were preoccupied in North Africa and the
Pacific, Russia's armies faced 185 German divisions on the Eastern
Front. In Europe, Russia fought alone as the Nazis and the Ger-
man-satellite states Hungary, Romania and Bulgaria battled vigorously and mostly on Russian soil for over one thousand miles,
from Leningrad to Sevastopol.[26]

Roosevelt's Teheran decision rejected Churchill's strategy, so integral to Britain's primary economic and colonial interests in
North Africa and the Mediterranean, of going through the "soft
underbelly" of Europe in the interests of establishing an Anglo-
American presence in Italy, Greece, Yugoslavia, and Hungary.
Churchill's argument for a quick drive into the Balkans was based
on very specific considerations. It was madness, he insisted, to lose
the political advantages of an Allied presence in the area from
Italy to Budapest.

---

* A. A. Berle refers to negotiations for a second front throughout the spring
and summer of 1942. On 21 July 1942, for example, he wrote in his journal that
Russia continued to agitate for a second front. "I think they are right—and do
not know the military considerations which have prevented its being established
already (p. 417, *Navigating the Rapids* [Harcourt Brace Jovanovich, 1973]).

As a result of Churchill's insistence, Eisenhower's team had, in the spring of 1943, moved immediately from North Africa to Sicily. Eisenhower and the United States command were less than enthusiastic about "Operation Husky," the invasion of Italy. Eager to embark on plans for the cross-Channel invasion, Eisenhower cabled the Combined Chiefs on 7 April that if there were more than two German divisions in Sicily, the operation should be reconsidered. This cable infuriated Churchill, who recognized the disparity between Eisenhower's enthusiasm for the cross-Channel invasion and his attitude toward Churchill's favored area of activities. Churchill complained that "the operations must either be entrusted to someone who believes in them, or abandoned. . . . I regard this matter as serious in the last degree. . . . We have told the Russians that they cannot have their supplies by the northern convoy for the sake of HUSKY, and now HUSKY is to be abandoned if there are two German divisions (strength unspecified) in the neighborhood. What Stalin would think of this when he has one hundred and eighty-five German divisions on his front, I cannot imagine."[27]

Robert Murphy, who had been sent to Italy directly from North Africa, had worked carefully to establish a political base he believed reflected America's best interests and was chagrined by the changes demanded after the Moscow and Teheran conferences. From the Allied landing in Sicily at dawn on 10 July 1943, Murphy and his British compeer Harold Macmillan had assiduously avoided compromising Anglo-American dominance in the area. Originally neither France nor Russia had a place on the Allied Advisory Council on Italy and the Balkans, established to forge a military alliance against Germany and "for the future political revolution of Italy and the Balkans."

At the Moscow meeting, both France and Russia were granted an "advisory" role to the Advisory Council. A Russian and a French delegate were actually to sit in conference with Murphy and Macmillan regarding all major decisions. It was a compromise that displeased France and Russia, since both nations had fought invading Italian forces in their own territories, and their peacemaking role was in no way equal to that which Britain and the United States maintained for themselves. Murphy, however, judged the compromise terrible. He believed that Britain and the United States had thereby opened the door to communism in Italy and the Balkans.[28]

Immediately after Mussolini's fall, on 25 July, Murphy and Macmillan sought private and intensive negotiations with King Victor Emmanuel III and his new premier, Marshal Pietro Badoglio. Once again, the anti-Fascist press was dismayed. On Mussolini's resignation, King Victor Emmanuel immediately announced Badoglio's appointment and his "determination to continue the war alongside the Germans." Badoglio was best known for leading Mussolini's forces in his effort to colonize Abyssinia. Once again, the Anglo-Americans ignored the anti-Fascist forces as they courted Fascist leadership in an effort to maintain order and continuity in areas they liberated. Political reality, wrote Robert Murphy, demanded that the Allies negotiate with Fascists. After all, he protested to his critics, after twenty-one years of fascism, "every Italian of consequence who had remained in Italy" supported or was a part of the regime. Besides, Murphy was charmed by the gracious king, impressed by the longevity of the "1000 year old House of Savoy," and argued that, like Vichy's General Giraud, Badoglio had maintained a sublime disinterest in political questions.[29]

For Murphy there were limited choices. When members of the underground, the international resistance, and Italians long in exile appeared publicly to participate in the reconstruction of their country, Murphy attempted to block or diminish their efforts. They were Communists or Communist sympathizers, he declared. And they threatened everything he and Macmillan had worked so hard to create.

There were of course anti-Communist opponents to fascism. For many months, Count Carlo Sforza, the former Minister of Foreign Affairs, who had been in exile in the United States, had attempted to create "the equivalent of a 'DeGaulle government for Italy.'" New York's Mayor Fiorello LaGuardia and such State Department advisers as A. A. Berle favored Sforza. But Sforza was anticlerical and antimonarchist. He had called for the King's abdication and so was entirely unacceptable to Churchill.[30] Churchill's high-handed rejection was in turn unacceptable to Roosevelt. Monarchy was not, after all, part of the American tradition. Roosevelt insisted on Sforza's right to return to Italy to help organize a new political coalition.

The Allied and German bombings continued through the winter of 1943–44. It was for Italy a cruel and hideous time. When it was over, the Allies were still negotiating with the King. Count Sforza complained that this monarchical enthusiasm was politically disastrous. Throughout Italy, he explained, there were long queues to apply for membership in the Communist Party. Everybody, he told Murphy, business executives and professionals, women and men of all classes, were standing in line affirming the existence of a Communist revolution. It was time at least to dethrone the King. Reluctantly, Murphy and Macmillan agreed. The King said mournfully: "A republican form of government is not suited to the Italian people. They are not prepared for it either temperamentally or historically. . . . The only people who would profit would be the Communists."

There was no getting by it:—In Italy, most of the anti-Fascists were Communists. General Mark Clark's armies did not reach Rome until 4 June 1944, just thirty-six hours before D-day. And, Murphy wrote, Mark Clark's victory was mostly a Communist triumph.[31]

Anglo-American differences regarding postwar Italy contributed to that triumph. In May 1943, Churchill had journeyed to Washington for a two-week conference to schedule "a decisive invasion of the Axis citadel" and to discuss with Roosevelt America's occupation of Italy. A. A. Berle noted that ". . . our General Staff is adamant against it, feeling that there is nothing to be got by the occupation of Italy except the liability to feed a dependent population:—better leave that to the Germans. . . ." For the Allies, the main issue was the nature of Italy's postwar government. But here again Britain and the United States differed. Britain adamantly opposed Count Sforza and other moderate liberals. Moreover, the State Department believed that Britain sought dominance, even "control of Italy, as part of their complete control of the Mediterranean."[32]

Only in their mutual opposition to Communist influence in Italian politics were Britain and the United States in agreement. The political-warfare advisers of both nations agreed, therefore, on the temporary expediency of the King and Badoglio. As with the North African campaign, this decision evoked howls of protest from the Anglo-American press and from the United States' Office of War Information.[33]

On political questions, basic unity seemed to exist only between Murphy and Macmillan, who from the beginning attempted to minimize the role of the Communist Party in Italy through their work on the Allied Advisory Council on Italy and the Balkans. Without access to the secret military files at Allied headquarters that Macmillan and Murphy shared, the French and Russian advisers to the Council were severely handicapped. Indeed their very presence seems to have been repugnant to Murphy. On the other hand, France's Couve de Murville and Russia's Alexander Bogomolov were highly regarded career diplomats. Bogomolov had been ambassador to France and then England. Like Macmillan and Murphy, he was sent first to Algiers and then to Italy. But Russia supported de Gaulle, and in Algiers Bogomolov was designated personal ambassador to de Gaulle.

Despite his acknowledged charm and erudition, Bogomolov was treated socially as rather a curiosity by Murphy. Murphy appears to have been scandalized personally by the fact that, on Bogomolov's arrival in Italy, "Mark Clark even had a little ceremony to bestow a decoration on the Russian envoy." Murphy's attitude was not personally motivated. His resentment was political and far-ranging: Bogomolov's presence tacitly acknowledged, Murphy wrote, Russia's interest in Mediterranean affairs. Murphy insisted that Russia's thoroughly "approachable" and skilled diplomats Bogomolov and Andrei Vishinsky (Russia's Vice-Minister of Foreign Affairs, also sent first to Algiers and then to Italy) had "in five months" planted Communist movements throughout Europe east of Italy. Ultimately, Murphy blamed the situation largely on Secretary of State Hull's "extravagant confidence in a lasting Soviet-American partnership," which had resulted in such a tremendous "outburst of public optimism" as to cripple Murphy's ability fully to promote Anglo-American interests on the Allied Advisory Council.

Murphy and Macmillan were handicapped in their anti-Communist unity by the fact that, north of Rome, particularly in Milan and Turin, Communists were fighting earnestly. According to

Murphy, they were the "effective" opposition to the Nazis in Italy. The roots of partisan politics in Italy and eastward lay deeper than Russia's presence on the Council. Murphy—a clear-eyed political warrior—recognized that truth. After World War I, the Communist Party in Italy, he explained, had "come very close to power." He did not explain, however, that, as in Spain and Germany, only deadly Fascist opposition and political assassination had suspended Communist influence in partisan politics immediately prior to and during the war in all Fascist-controlled areas. Nothing had really changed. The situation Murphy and the political warriors inherited as the Second World War wound down was the same situation that prevailed after World War I.

Eisenhower apparently knew that, and upon entering Italy in August 1943 he decided to retain Mussolini's ban on the freedom of speech and press and on all political-party activity. Again, the Anglo-American press criticized him vigorously. The Russian advisers said nothing. Macmillan and Murphy believed the situation too unpopular to be tenable and advised Eisenhower to reconsider his policy and lift the ban. When it was finally lifted, the Communist victories in all districts were overwhelming. Italy was by then administratively in the hands of Britain. Eisenhower was in England preparing Overlord, the final invasion of Europe.

At that time, in January 1944, Palmiro Togliatti, the exiled leader of the Italian Communist Party, was permitted to return to Italy. Highly regarded, trained in guerrilla warfare, and entirely committed to the Grand Alliance (the war against the Fascists, he repeatedly said, "always comes first"), his return was supported by the U. S. Government. Murphy was instructed to treat him as he would any political leader. Better disposed to Togliatti than to Bogomolov, Murphy did not object to the assignment. Togliatti, after all, wrote Murphy, was suave and learned and an "agreeable dinner guest." Togliatti, indeed, was occasionally "invited to lend a piquant touch" to VIP gatherings.[34]

After the war in Italy, there were Fascists and Communists and the party supported by the Papacy, the Christian Democrats. This situation prevailed throughout Western Europe. After the war, the Anglo-American allies attempted to strengthen the parties that represented a counterforce to the two "extremes" of fascism and communism.[35] The triumph of "Christian Democracy" was to become one of the major goals of the American Century. With a lot of help—economic, political and military aid directly introduced—these parties began to flourish, particularly during Eisenhower's presidency.

But during the brief era of the Grand Alliance, the demands of military victory came first. And when, on 13 February, Budapest was liberated by the Russian armies, the people of the Western European resistance cheered—as did the entire Allied high command. The real tests of the Grand Alliance, and the future peace as envisioned by Roosevelt's grand design, focused on the political settlement of Germany and points east.

During the war, the attitude of the military had enhanced the Grand Alliance. And Generals George Marshall and Dwight David Eisenhower were of one mind regarding political warfare after 1943: It was somebody else's business. Eisenhower as general and as President fervently believed, as a primary article of faith, in civilian control over military affairs. The military unconfined, he believed, resulted inevitably in the formation of garrison states. And he had seen the results at close range. Overt fascism was not, and as far as Eisenhower was concerned must never become, the American way.

It is, moreover, now clear that Eisenhower shared Roosevelt's post-1943 enthusiasm for a united organized Allied peace that included the Soviet Union. Evidently, the only political suggestion that Eisenhower made to Roosevelt regarding the postwar period was that SHAEF (Supreme Headquarters Allied Expeditionary Force) be retained. Eisenhower hoped that Russia would join the Anglo-American organization and that there would be a permanent unified Allied command. He was disappointed when Russia rejected the idea and Roosevelt agreed to geographical zones instead.[36]

Eisenhower affirmed repeatedly that he based all his strategic decisions regarding the war's end game on military, not political, considerations. Since no military act was free of political significance, he frequently enraged the political warriors. His decision to stop at the Elbe River, for example, and not to take Berlin became a subject of long and bitter controversy. For Eisenhower the rationale was simple: To capture Berlin would have cost between ten thousand and one hundred thousand Anglo-American

lives. His projections were correct. During the battle to take
Berlin, Russia lost more than one hundred thousand troops. Berlin
was deep inside the Soviet zone, as agreed to at Yalta. Eisenhower
thought it absurd to sacrifice one hundred thousand Anglo-
American lives only to greet the Russians in their own city, and
leave as per agreement.[37]

As the war ended, the uneasy British-American-Russian alliance
began simultaneously to unravel. It did not happen suddenly. The
transition between World War II and the resumption of explicit
antagonism between the Anglo-American allies and their Russian
associate was neither smooth nor specifically predictable. There
was nothing inevitable or preordained about the origins of the second phase of the Cold War. Both Roosevelt and Eisenhower were
committed to a policy of postwar peace with Russia, and to a
United Nations organization that would ensure the permanence of
wartime amity.

The second phase of the Cold War followed from a specific series
of choices that were made between 1945 and 1947. These choices
involved a variety of interests—economic, ideological, and imperial. They involved actions that had occurred on behalf of those interests all during the war—beginning with the political events in
North Africa, Italy, and France. The distrust that loosened the
bonds of alliance emerged from such exercises of independent diplomacy as, for example, the "Berne incident."

In March 1945, Allen Dulles, representing the Office of Strategic Services (OSS) and apparently on his own initiative, met in
Berne, Switzerland, with Karl Wolff, an SS Obergruppenfuehrer, to
negotiate Germany's surrender in northern Italy. Wolff, the commander of SS police forces in Italy, and Allen Dulles had a mutual
fear: the powerful resistance activities and Communist demonstrations (generally suppressed by British force) in the major industrial centers of northern Italy, Turin, and Milan. The Dulles-
Wolff talks offended Russia. Roosevelt explained they were a
"misunderstanding." Molotov insisted that Russia believed they
were "something worse." Eisenhower was chagrined that Russia
doubted "our good faith." General Marshall cabled Stalin that
there were "no political implications" in the Dulles-Wolff talks and
that the Allies should continue to maintain vigilance against "persistent" German efforts "to create dissension."

After the Dulles-Wolff talks, Hitler removed at least two divisions from Italy. Germany was interested not only in blocking Russia's entry into German territory but in destabilizing the alliance. Predictably, Hitler's actions caused Stalin to become suspicious of America's plans for the future. Germany's persistent efforts to create dissension between the Allies was based on Hitler's assumption that an alliance between "ultra-capitalist states" and "ultra-Marxist states" was unnatural. In December 1944, he assured his generals that such a "heterogenous" alliance representing "such totally divergent objectives" had never before existed in all history. "One day," he assured his generals, "it can happen any moment, . . . this coalition may dissolve." Hitler's Thousand Year Reich depended on that.[38]

But the alliance did not dissolve on Hitler's behalf. Not one Anglo-American leader, political or military, underrated the value of the Russian military contribution. Politically, America's propaganda pamphlets addressed themselves directly to the significance of Russia's participation in the war against fascism, and to some of the postwar implications of Russia's courageous and costly victories.

In 1942, Freedom House, which was organized by C. D. Jackson and others to mobilize public opinion during the war, published a pamphlet, *World-Wide Civil War,* by Herbert Agar, Lewis Mumford, and Frank Kingdon. Herbert Agar, the president of Freedom House, wrote that the United States

is at war because a world revolution against civilization has been going on in increasing violence for 20 years. . . .

. . . The only nation in the Western World which has so far fought back successfully is Russia, which was organized on a system that made it possible for the entire nation to be put into the war when Russia was attacked. . . .

The United States of America is not organized on that system. The United States of America does not want to be organized on that system. . . .

Agar then denounced Russia's war effort as representing "the slave system, used by our enemies." In cold-warrior fashion, Agar left the reader to assume that Russia, representing "the slave system," was in 1942 one of America's "enemies." And "since we don't want," Agar concluded, "to be totalitarians and we don't want to be failures," we have got to create a new, democratically united "third system."

The president of the Union for Democratic Action, Frank Kingdon, was more specific; his remarks concluded the pamphlet:

. . . There is no use in trying to hide the fact, as so many people are doing in this country because they are afraid somehow to speak of Russia, that the enormous effort of Russia has been of priceless value to the United States.

I have no good word to speak for Communism. . . . But I do know that the people of Russia have put the people of the United States in such a debt that we should be forever ungrateful if we forgot to recognize them.

Let me add this word because I think it needs to be added. There are a great many people running around the United States saying, "Oh, isn't it dreadful? Russia is doing so well that when the peace comes she is going to sweep us all into the fold of Communism! Wouldn't it be better, really if Hitler licked the Russians so we wouldn't have Communism?"

For heaven's sake, haven't we any faith in democracy? Can't we realize that if we are going to be exposed to Communism, Russia is going to be exposed to democracy? And in that kind of conflict, democracy can always prove itself. . . .[39]

Freedom House's 1942 pamphlet represented the wartime contours of American political thinking. Russia was for some political warriors one of the enemies, to be classed and treated as such. Russia was for others an ally that might, appropriately managed, remain an ally—and possibly even be influenced to change in ways more to our liking as a result of the close and enforced contact of the Grand Alliance.

Militarily, Field Marshal Sir Alan Brooke in 1943 represented the first school. Consistent with his fantasy that the Nazi and Red hordes might obliterate each other somewhere over Central Europe in humanity's interest, he tried to diminish Marshall's and Eisenhower's enthusiasm to open a second front. The field marshal believed "that in ground conflict in a large theater," Anglo-American forces would "be at a great disadvantage and would suffer tremendous and useless losses." Sir Alan Brooke insisted that the Russian Army "was the only land force that could produce decisive results."[40]

Dwight David Eisenhower as Supreme Commander of Overlord represented the second view. His strategy involved a speedy, entirely coordinated and non-competitive victory. Russian troops triumphed against the Nazis across Poland, Hungary, and Austria. And, at Eisenhower's request, the Russians' offensive into Germany was launched ahead of schedule. Churchill had cabled Stalin:

THE BATTLE IN THE WEST IS VERY HEAVY. . . . IT IS EISENHOWER'S GREAT DESIRE AND NEED TO KNOW IN OUTLINE WHAT YOU PLAN TO DO. . . . I SHALL BE GRATEFUL IF YOU CAN TELL ME WHETHER WE CAN COUNT ON A MAJOR RUSSIAN OFFENSIVE . . . DURING JANUARY. . . .

Stalin responded that, "taking into account the position of our Allies," Russia would begin "large-scale offensive operations . . . not later than the second half of January . . . we shall do everything possible to render assistance to the glorious forces of our Allies."[41] The Russians attacked on 12 January 1945.

Anglo-American forces had defeated the Nazis west of the Rhine. And thanks to an intact bridge—a gift to the American GIs from the Belgian Resistance—the Rhine had been crossed at Remagen. The great German centers of industry, of coal and iron and steel, the mills and mines of the Ruhr, had been captured. And the Ruhr, the center of Nazi industrial power and wartime ability, had been captured intact. The fate of the Ruhr and the Saar Valley had been the subject of a long and bitter debate in Washington. There were those, like Secretary of the Treasury Henry Morgenthau, who believed that this enabling center of cruelty and military danger should be dismantled entirely. In 1945, Eisenhower agreed with the goal of returning Germany to an agricultural community. Indeed, although he later denied it, some, including Henry Morgenthau, were to say that a pastoral Germany was Eisenhower's idea in the first place. The view that prevailed, however, was represented by such political warriors and international economic planners as Robert Murphy, John J. McCloy, and Lewis Douglas, all later to serve prominently during the Eisenhower presidency. The Ruhr and over two thirds of German industrial might were under Anglo-American authority. The Russian zone was to be agricultural. The war in the Yalta-zoned West was over.[42] Only Berlin was left.

Berlin, one hundred miles inside the Soviet zone, had become for many Anglo-American strategists the symbol of military victory—and the prize. During a press conference on 27 March 1945 Eisenhower was asked: "Who do you think will be into Berlin first . . . ?" He answered, the Russians. "They have a shorter race to run, although they are faced by the bulk of the German forces." Russian forces were thirty-three miles outside Berlin; and American troops were two hundred fifty miles away.

They were, moreover, directed by Eisenhower toward Leipzig and Dresden—a route that enraged Churchill and all the British high command. It was important, insisted Churchill, to "shake hands with the Russians as far to the east as possible." Since the Russian armies seemed certain to enter Vienna and liberate Austria, Churchill feared that if "we deliberately leave Berlin to them, even if it should be in our grasp, the double event may strengthen their conviction, already apparent, that they have done everything."[43]

Churchill specifically rejected what apparently had been Eisenhower's contention that "junction with the Russians . . . would be a superior gain." "It was," wrote Churchill, an "idea" that "does not commend itself to me." In the United States, Churchill's point of view had many adherents. For Secretary of the Navy James Forrestal; the new Secretary of State, Edward R. Stettinius; and Averell Harriman, the ambassador to Moscow, the wartime alliance was over. An entirely new relationship, forged out of the fires of "a quid pro quo," was now, insisted Harriman, required. Only a strong, economically reconstructed Europe, refinanced largely by United States capital, would deter communism's march across the continent. In 1945, Averell Harriman, an international banker, believed that only aggressive international trade and "the working capital and raw materials" necessary to get that "trade going again" would limit Soviet ambitions. Harriman believed "that Stalin hoped to get to the Atlantic." The industrial regions of the Ruhr and Saar were not bombed, because the economic salvation and reconstruction of Europe required their service. German industry would be enlisted to serve the West's economic war against communism instead of the Thousand Year Reich.[44]

Thus even before World War II was over, one group of American statesmen based their future policies in large part on Germany's economic majesty. It was not a point of view likely to please the European victims of Germany's quest for power. Thirty million people had been massacred in the process of that quest, twenty million of them Russian. It was, moreover, a point of view that entirely contradicted Roosevelt's vision of postwar amity. In 1945, Eisenhower specifically and enthusiastically supported Roosevelt's vision. Averell Harriman explained that Eisenhower's belief that the United States and Russia "could get along" was based on the fact that Russia had been a dependable ally. Since "Stalin had carried out his military commitments," wrote Harriman, it was to be years before a very "reluctant" Eisenhower would "finally agree" with Harriman that the wartime alliance was over.[45]

Eisenhower's reluctance to accept Harriman's view was based on his abhorrence of fascism in general and of Nazi militarism in particular. Patton's Third Army had captured Ohrdruf and Buchenwald. And on 12 April 1945, Generals George Patton, Omar Bradley, and Eisenhower inspected the two concentration camps at Ohrdruf Nord and Buchenwald. All their senses were assailed as they stood before one of history's remarkable monuments to humanity's capacity for evil. When before had man created, with all the efficiency, technology, determination, and learning at his command, a more vile testament to the potential for human depravity? The sights and sounds and smells of unspeakable suffering that marked the Nazi movement have undoubtedly hardened us all. Forevermore, Nazi technology will stand as a measure of what we are all capable of, of what we can inflict on each other in pursuit of power and greatness, or in the name of ideology or country or God.

Born in the nineteenth century, the three American generals had been educated for war in a simpler time. On 12 April 1945, Bradley became ill. Patton walked away to vomit. Eisenhower, "his face frozen white," examined every detail of the camps, the conditions of victims from every country in Europe. The stench was overwhelming, the sights unimaginable. Eisenhower walked slowly through it all so that he could "testify at first hand about these things" in the event that anybody ever claimed that Nazi atrocities were only wartime propaganda. As Eisenhower passed through the lines of people, members of the Resistance—Jews and Catholics and Communists and Gypsies—scores of barely alive skeletons, their eyes burning with emotion and the intensity of their effort, pulled themselves up to salute their liberator. Eisenhower would never forget that sight. On that day, he vowed that he had borne witness to the suffering unleashed by the last civil war humanity would ever have to fight. The immediate implication of that vow was to do nothing that would antagonize Russia. "Eisenhower's hatred of Nazism," wrote Robert Murphy, "intensified his determination to have no conflict with Russia about Germany."[46]

That night, Eisenhower learned that Franklin D. Roosevelt was dead. Roosevelt was dead and nobody knew for sure what he had over time negotiated privately with Stalin. Roosevelt was dead and the future of world peace depended on the fulfillment of his grand design, the particulars of which had never been worked out. For the moment, the only certainty was that Eisenhower was in charge of all military operations to end the war in such a way as to ensure the peace. Politically, the era of private negotiations between the world's most powerful leaders—Stalin, Churchill, and Roosevelt— was over. Roosevelt had been the ameliorator. He had engendered the compromises while at the same time he had negotiated on behalf of America's new international economic interests; he had balanced Anglo-American differences while at the same time he had sought a formula for permanent Allied harmony. Now he was dead, and his successor knew nothing about international affairs. Harry S Truman had been confined to narrow political and domestic horizons. Churchill, long a friend to senators and congressmen involved with foreign relations, many of whom he courted earnestly, had never even met Truman.

It was up to Eisenhower. Supported by his most trusted colleagues, Generals Walter Bedell ("Beetle") Smith and Lucius Clay, and his boss, General George Marshall, the future of the world's peace depended on the strategy Eisenhower would choose. And he was steadfast. On 13 April, Russian forces entered Vienna. On 25 April, Russian forces encircled Berlin and established contact with American forces seventy miles south of the city, at Torgau, on the Elbe.

Eisenhower carefully coordinated the end game. Russia would occupy the Moldau Valley, including Prague. In this instance, Patton was only sixty miles outside the city and the Russians were farther away. When the Russian commander requested that Patton's armies be halted outside Prague, Eisenhower agreed. Moreover, he ordered Patton not to accept the surrender offered by thousands of Nazi troops who had fought on the Eastern Front. Ignoring intense and frequently contradictory political pressures, Eisenhower held steady, and the Yalta agreements were enforced militarily.

On 30 April, Hitler put a pistol into his mouth and shot his brains out. He was buried in a Russian shellhole in his flower garden. But the war did not end. To the very last, the German hierarchy hoped that a new military alliance of Anglo-Americans and Germans would be forged and the war would continue in the East against communism, against Russia. Churchill continued to urge eastward action. George Patton begged Eisenhower to allow him to move from his advance headquarters at Pilsen straight on to Moscow, claiming that he could reach Moscow in thirty days. But Eisenhower held steady.

The Supreme Commander of the Allied forces saw no reason to "endanger the life of a single American or Briton to capture areas we soon will be handing over to the Russians." Eisenhower negotiated the withdrawal of American troops from the Prague area and ordered Robert Murphy to investigate rumors that Hitler's designated successor, Grand Admiral, now Fuehrer, Karl Doenitz, was creating tension between SHAEF and Russia from his headquarters at Flensburg, in Schleswig-Holstein, on the Danish frontier. Fuehrer Doenitz was forthright in his talks with Murphy: Now was the time for all Westerners to work together "to prevent the Bolshevization of Europe." He was committed to protecting the "German race from Bolshevism." Proudly Doenitz reported to Murphy his radio campaign to induce a million Germans to flee westward and his arrangements to move Germany's ablest scientists from the East. Doenitz, concluded Robert Murphy, appeared "entirely unaware that the entire continent hated and feared Germany more than Russia." Doenitz seemed shocked that the Western Allies did not plan to permit the Nazi government to survive under his leadership.[47]

As soon as Murphy reported his findings to Eisenhower, he ordered Fuehrer Doenitz arrested. On 8 May, the war in Europe was over. Dwight David Eisenhower's strategy had salvaged the Grand Alliance. As the Allied troops converged, from the east and the west, they marched through Maidanek, Buchenwald, Auschwitz, Dachau, and Belsen. These courtyards of hell engendered considerable international support for Morgenthau's plan to strip Germany of the industrial capacity ever to rearm again. An agricultural Germany, a disarmed, demobilized, disabled German potato patch occupied by a watchful Allied army seemed to millions of Europeans—and a significant group of Americans as well—an appropriate thing. But that thought was for the future, and nothing about the future was settled. Geographic boundaries, reparations, the nature and function of occupation zones, all political and economic issues—all these were still to be negotiated, or, more accurately, renegotiated.

In the spring of 1945, all that was settled was that Eisenhower had salvaged the Grand Alliance. And he expected that he might serve in some future capacity in order to salvage at least part of the grand design. On 14 June, the day before he was to leave Europe for a victory tour across the United States, Eisenhower spoke openly and firmly about that during a farewell press conference in Paris:

Q: There has been a considerable campaign recently . . . to talk about a "Russo-American war." There is nothing in your experience with the Russians that leads you to feel we can't cooperate with them perfectly?

EISENHOWER: On my level, none. I have found the individual Russian one of the friendliest persons in the world. He likes to talk with us, laugh with us. . . . The peace lies, when you get down to it, with all the peoples of the world, not just for the moment with some political leader who is trying to direct the destiny of a country along a certain line. If all the peoples are friendly, we are going to have peace.

I think the Russians are friendly. I know all the officers I have met are.[48]

Consistent with his wartime policies, over the next fifteen years

Eisenhower promoted anti-Communist activities that served America's interests while he sought to avoid military confrontations with Russia. The decisions he had made during World War II regarding Western-designated territories—the Darlan Deal, what Peter Lyon has called the "neo-Fascist botch" in Italy, Eisenhower's acquiescence in and material support for British atrocities in Greece, his entire French policy—did not in any way contradict his conclusion that postwar amity with Russia was possible. Like Stalin, Eisenhower accepted the political arrangements of the World War II era, the arrangements of Teheran and Yalta. He took them seriously and, as Stalin did in Greece, interpreted them legalistically. In the West, Eisenhower was willing to bolster a variety of anti-Communist politicians, including royalists and frank reactionaries. In the East, where specific areas of Russian concern were involved, Eisenhower was far more cautious and conciliatory. That distinction prevailed throughout his public career. It was to become the banner of his presidency: the Cold War during Eisenhower's presidency would come to mean all anti-Communist activity, both possible and practical, short of war with the Soviet Union.

America's monopoly of the atomic bomb upset the delicately balanced structure of the grand design before the specifications for a postwar agreement had even been made. But the new weapon did not shatter Eisenhower's commitment to the wartime alliance. Nor did it dissolve the intensity of that silent vow he made to himself at Ohrdruf Nord: To do all in his power to prevent World War III. In July at Potsdam, Eisenhower expressed his opposition to the use of the bomb against Japan. He believed it militarily unnecessary and morally unsound. Even in retirement in 1963, when so many of his views had hardened, when so many disappointments had rendered his judgments even about his own achievements harsh, he maintained his initial reaction to Secretary of War Stimson's briefing at Potsdam. Listening to Stimson's enthusiastic description of the atomic tests, Eisenhower did not become jubilant, as expected. He became depressed. He believed that Japan was already defeated. News of Japan's readiness to surrender was well known at Potsdam. Eisenhower believed, in 1945, and he repeated his conviction, in 1963, that "Japan was already defeated and that dropping the bomb was completely unnecessary." In addition, Eisenhower "thought that our country should avoid shocking world opinion. . . ." On 11 April 1960, President Eisenhower met with

Professor Herbert Feis, the former State Department official then renowned for his series of books on World War II: *The Road to Pearl Harbor; Churchill, Roosevelt, Stalin;* and the final volume, on Potsdam, about which he sought Eisenhower's views. During that 1960 meeting, Eisenhower spoke at length of his initial reaction fifteen years before to Secretary Stimson's triumphant report at Potsdam that the "baby was born." He recalled that when he told Stimson that "he hoped his country would not be the first to use this weapon," "Mr. Stimson really hit the ceiling. . . ." Eisenhower said that "he knew from intelligence reports that the Japanese were at that moment trying to surrender. The Japanese in Tokyo were in communication with their Ambassador in Moscow about this." Feis agreed, and commented that "reading intelligence reports at that time gave a very clear impression that the Japanese were defeated. Even a careful reading of the *New York Times* would make it completely evident."

In August 1945, Harry S Truman hailed the nuclear destruction of Hiroshima as "the greatest thing in history." On 6 August, sixteen hours after Hiroshima was bombed, President Truman announced, "We have spent two billion dollars on the greatest scientific gamble in history—and won." Eisenhower was appalled. He could find nothing virtuous about incinerating untold numbers of people when it was no longer necessary for military reasons.[49]

Eisenhower was entirely excluded from the decision-making process in the Pacific theater of operations. On 9 July, he wrote to Captain Swede Hazlett, his lifelong friend from Abilene High School and the recipient of his most analytic correspondence: "I haven't the slightest idea of what is happening or is to happen in the Pacific. I do know that I am not to be officially connected with it in any way. . . ."[50] On 6 August, the first atomic bomb was dropped on Hiroshima. On 9 August, Nagasaki was leveled. World War II was over. For Eisenhower, the struggle to keep the peace had just begun.

CHAPTER II
THE DEMISE OF
THE GRAND
ALLIANCE AND THE
YEARS OF
EISENHOWER'S
PUBLIC ECLIPSE

Eisenhower was in Moscow on the night that Japan surrendered. Over the future hung a cloud of unknown vapors filled with elements not yet specifically identified. With no biologist on the team, and no particular foresight, the scientists who worked on the Manhattan Project could not imagine the cruel way by which their new weapon was soon to unite us all. They had anticipated neither radioactive fallout nor radiation poisoning. They could not know that never again would earth's children be born without such elements as strontium 90 in their bones, iodine 137 in their thyroids, and cesium 131 in their muscle tissue. Nobody in 1945 could have predicted the coming planetary epidemic of leukemia and cancer. In August 1945, the only discernible effect was that the United States had something big, something different in its arsenal.

With the secret of the atom and the might of the bomb, the United States embarked on the American Century. But General Eisenhower was in the Soviet Union to celebrate the peace, the Allied victory. Of all the high command, Admiral William D. Leahy

and Eisenhower had counseled against the use of the United States'
new weapon. Over the next few years, the transition years that led
to the arms race he opposed and the threat of resumed warfare he
dreaded above all, Eisenhower would frequently stand alone in political circles in his insistence on the possibilities of Soviet-American
amity. Nothing he saw, nothing he experienced during this five-day
journey weakened his conviction that permanent peace with Russia
was possible.

Eisenhower was accompanied by Generals Lucius Clay and
T. J. Davis, his son John S. D. Eisenhower, and Marshal Georgi
Zhukov, his official host. On the flight east from Berlin, the two
commanders sat together and shared their memories, and their
hopes. Zhukov and Eisenhower liked each other. They had mutual
interests—notably an enthusiasm for duck hunting; and they
agreed on major issues of military policy. Khrushchev, for example, later credited Zhukov, his Minister of Defense, with Russia's
post-Stalin policy of reducing military expenditures. According to
Khrushchev, Russia's military "cuts were made on Zhukov's initiative," because there were "many abuses and excesses." Zhukov also
persuaded the Soviet leadership to reduce Russia's standing army
by half and to negotiate reciprocal arms-control agreements with
the West.[1] While we do not have a record of the conversation between Zhukov and Eisenhower on 11 August en route from Berlin
to Moscow, it is not irrelevant that these changes in Russian military affairs paralleled Eisenhower's vision of America's national security needs and coincided with changes he would make during his
first year as President, shortly after Stalin's death, in the spring of
1953.

In Moscow, General Eisenhower was publicly honored in unprecedented ways. During the great Physical Culture Parade on
Sunday, 12 August, Stalin invited Eisenhower to watch the proceedings—the demonstration of one hundred thousand women and
men from all over European and Asian Russia—from atop Lenin's
tomb. This was a symbolic gesture of considerable significance.
Until Eisenhower and his party were invited only revolutionary citizens had ever stood in that place. Everywhere Eisenhower went,
he received a hero's welcome of unrestrained enthusiasm. One evening during a soccer game, the announcer told the audience of
sixty thousand that there were present two guests, Zhukov and Ei-

senhower. According to Ambassador Averell Harriman, the outburst of cheering in the stadium "surpassed anything I had ever heard." When Eisenhower, in response, put his arm around Zhukov, a roar of public approval arose that would not be forgotten over time.

Eisenhower's entire trip was marked by such sincere warmth and spontaneous happenings that, according to John Eisenhower's account of the trip, the "American Military Mission were astonished." During Eisenhower's last evening in Moscow, he received word to try to keep everybody at Spaso House, the American Embassy, as long as possible, because Harriman would return late with an important message. At one o'clock on the morning of 15 August, Averell Harriman announced that Japan had surrendered. The Soviet-American celebration that night in Moscow ended forever the reputation Russian officers had acquired among United States observers for cold aloofness, the much-mentioned Communist incapacity for joy. Never again would local embassy officials be "astonished to hear" Russians and Americans singing together, and to each other. The range of possibilities for the future seemed, during that celebration, unlimited. Kathleen Harriman, who worked for the OWI, and her father, at the embassy, wrote home about the evening: "We had a very hard time getting rid of some of our drunker Soviet guests. I took a great shine to Marshal Zhukov. He's very genial and fun and apparently easy to work with. Once during the evening he called Eisenhower 'Ike'—a great departure for a Soviet."[2]

Eisenhower never doubted that the people, the ordinary people of the world, wanted peace. And he never doubted the capacity for the deepest bonds of personal friendship between the peoples of Russia and the United States. It was to be years before his advisers, his political superiors, his associates in and out of public office would convince him that the alliance with Russia was over. Like Eisenhower, General Marshall also discounted the anti-Soviet attitudes fast becoming more and more prevalent. According to Harriman, the "fact that Stalin had honored his military commitments during the war was paramount in the thinking of both men." When General Walter Bedell Smith was appointed to replace Harriman in Russia, Marshall told Smith: "You must talk to Harriman, of course, in view of his long experience. But you ought to discount what he says. The Russians gave him a hard time and that made him too pessimistic."[3]

Thoroughly briefed by State Department officials, Walter Bedell Smith was impressed by the negative attitudes of the professional diplomats "long experienced in dealing with the Soviet Union and familiar with history of Czarist Russia. They felt," Smith explained, "that the Soviet Union, owing to its peculiar structure and the political philosophy which motivated it, was almost incapable of collaborating with other governments. . . ." But General Smith, like Eisenhower and Marshall, was "inclined to take a more optimistic view, encouraged by my conversations with senior Russian officers. . . . I felt that the first essential was an effort to restore confidence and mutual understanding. . . . It was in this mood that I was ready to leave Washington for Moscow."[4]

Neither Smith nor Marshall nor Eisenhower anticipated the full impact of the United States' atomic explosions. On the one hand, they freed certain policy makers in the United States from their commitment to the concept of the Grand Alliance. The architects of the American Century believed that their temporary technological superiority enabled them to reconsider all agreements mandated by military necessity at Teheran, Yalta, and Potsdam. Eisenhower was aware that the use of the bomb seriously destabilized his vision of permanent military accord between the wartime allies. Privately he expressed his deepest concerns:

> Before the atom bomb was used, I would have said yes, I was sure we could keep the peace with Russia. Now, I don't know. I had hoped the bomb wouldn't figure in this war. Until now I would have said that we three, Britain with her mighty fleet, America with the strongest air force, and Russia with the strongest land force on the continent, we three could have guaranteed the peace of the world for a long, long time to come. But now, I don't know. People are frightened and disturbed all over. Everyone feels insecure again.[5]

And Russia, historically the target of Western animus, invaded by counterrevolutionary Western armies, diplomatically never an equal among equals, devastated with 20 million dead, and economically exhausted, viewed the new military situation with considerable suspicion.

Russia was quick to observe the changes in attitude, quick to understand the implications of the fact that there were those among the Allies who had wanted to continue the war in Europe right through to Moscow, and now, as occupation officials, refused to follow Eisenhower's denazification orders. Moreover, Stalin had been specifically rebuffed in Japan. Although his troops were deep inside Manchuria, and an agreement had been reached to divide Korea, temporarily, at the thirty-eighth parallel, the Soviet Army had been denied permission to land on the Japanese islands. The war was over. The peace was yet to be finalized. And there were tensions in every occupied district, discord at every conference. Stalin had trusted Roosevelt, and he considered Eisenhower "a very great man, . . . not only because of his military accomplishments but because of his human, friendly, kind and frank nature."[6] But Roosevelt was dead. And Eisenhower was no longer clearly in command.

Eisenhower, in turn, found Stalin "benign and fatherly." He believed, moreover, that Zhukov would succeed Stalin—and he believed that an era of permanent peace would be ensured should that occur. At a press conference on 14 August, Eisenhower said: "I see nothing in the future that would prevent Russia from being the closest possible friends." And he warned against the effect of American publications so intent on inflaming tensions between the United States and Russia: "All I suggest is that we all keep our sense of values and not be upset by the lies or propaganda of a few crackpots."[7]

On the return from Moscow to Berlin, the enormity of that problem became crudely apparent to Eisenhower. Toward the end of the trip, Marshal Zhukov asked if he might have some American magazines for his daughter. Eager to please their "hospitable and effervescent" companion, Eisenhower and his son "frantically leafed through the racks, trying to look casual in selecting those that had nothing anti-Russian in them." According to John Eisenhower, the "abundance of *Time* magazines was no help at all." Luce publications had begun to attack allied unity vigorously in 1944. On 4 September 1944, *Life*'s editorial was William C. Bullitt's picture of "The World from Rome."

> It is an old picture . . . a picture of western Europe and Western civilization threatened by hordes of invaders from the East. . . . Great Britain alone will not be strong enough to stop the threat from the East. . . . The Italians . . . look beyond the end of the

fighting with little hope and much fear because they are afraid the withdrawal of American and British forces . . . will leave them at the mercy of the Soviet Union. . . .

A sad joke going the rounds in Rome gives the spirit of their hope: What is an optimist? A man who believes that the third world war will begin in about 15 years between Soviet Union and western Europe. . . . What is a pessimist? A man who believes that western Europe, Great Britain and the U.S. will not dare to fight. . . .

Shortly after this editorial, Luce appointed repentent former Communists Willi Schlamm, of Austria, to *Fortune* and Whittaker Chambers to the position of *Time*'s foreign-news editor. Earlier in the war, Chambers had been prevented from writing about Soviet issues because his views were considered so fanatical as to be dangerous to the war effort. Chambers was delighted with the change in policy and wrote that when the ban on his "editing or writing of Soviet or Communist news had at last been broken," his assignment sent "a shiver through most of *Time*'s staff, where my views were well known and detested with a ferocity that I did not believe possible. . . . With my first few Foreign News sections, the shiver turned into a shudder."[8] From that moment forward, *Time-Life-Fortune* emphasized the "flesh-creeping" threat of Russian dominance and called repeatedly for the alienation and isolation of the Soviet Union on behalf of the interests of the American Century.

That was the material the Eisenhowers tried to keep from Zhukov. As embarrassing as Luce rhetoric might have been to General Eisenhower, the fact was that the views Luce popularized had begun to influence decisions on all levels of government. Rules were not enforced; protocols were not enacted; agreements were suspended. There were shifts on all major and sensitive issues that had so recently seemed to involve considerable Allied consensus, such as the denazification of Germany. Even before Germany's surrender, in May, Eisenhower had issued a directive, Joint Chiefs of Staff 1067 (JCS 1067), forbidding all association with Nazis. The denazification of Germany required removing all Fascists from business, professional, and official positions. Eisenhower himself, according to Robert Murphy, "found it easy to obey" his directive. He hated fascism and refused either to consort or to confer with Nazis on any level. But Eisenhower's associates, including Robert Murphy, General Patton, and General Clay, considered

JCS 1067 not only impossible to enforce but absurd. Murphy and Clay resented the prohibition against hiring business executives and skilled workers, who, they argued, were needed "to get things running again—utilities, railroads, factories." Patton as military governor in Bavaria routinely refused to remove Nazis from office. During a news conference in September, Patton was asked about his failure to enforce the denazification order. He replied that there were no alternatives: "Do you want a lot of Communists?" Then he added, as if by way of explanation, that he knew nothing about politics or political parties: "The Nazi thing is just like a Democrat and Republican election fight."[9]

Patton's attitude created for Eisenhower a significant scandal. Not only did Patton insult his Russian associates whenever possible, he continued to boast that his troops could make a successful run to Moscow within six weeks. Moreover, his news conference occurred shortly after the publication of the report of Earl G. Harrison, the State Department's representative on the Intergovernmental Committee on Refugees. Harrison's report was based on his inspection tour of "displaced persons" camps, many of which were in Patton's area of command, and was submitted to Truman in August: "DPs"—mostly Jewish refugees—were still confined in camps behind barbed wire in prison uniform. Conditions were deplorable. German guards continued to staff the camps. Harrison reported that "we appear to be treating the Jews as the Nazis treated them except that we do not exterminate them."[10]

Eisenhower's response to this situation was to reassign Patton and to restate JCS 1067: German commerce and industry were to be denazified. Former Nazis must not remain in their former positions. They might be employed as common laborers. Ironically, Robert Murphy, a vigorous opponent of JCS 1067, was sent to investigate the law's effectiveness. Eisenhower insisted that the refugee camps be cleaned up and "ordered the DPs to be properly housed even if German civilians had to be ousted from their homes."[11] But Eisenhower was no longer capable of securing the changes he ordered. On 10 October 1945, John J. McCloy, Assistant Secretary of War, later president of the International Bank for Reconstruction and Development (the World Bank), sent a message to Eisenhower regarding conditions in the European Theater. This "Top Secret/Eyes Only" document, not declassified until

1973, goes a long way toward explaining the nonenforcement of the denazification policy:

> Have concluded a visit to BERLIN, FRANKFURT, VIENNA and BUDAPEST and it is about the same welter of problems wherever you go: Food, transportation, communication, displaced persons, the oppressions of occupation, particularly the weight of Russian forces and their requisitions scarcities with no continuing means of restoring the needs, no industry with all metropolitan areas on a virtual relief basis, everywhere the fear of hunger, disease and Russians. . . .

> Our emphasis has been on demobilization, denazification, decentralization. All of Middle EUROPE needs the restoration of some industry unless we are to establish permanent soup kitchen feeding. For all practical purposes there is no industry in GERMANY or AUSTRIA and unless there is it is a constantly losing game. . . .

> There should be greater consultation with the native leaders on matters relating to their social, economic and political restoration. Above all we should not hesitate to encourage the reestablishment of more industry and commerce. I repeat without it there will be collapse and progressive physical and social deterioration of the people in an area whose influence is such that it will set the level of European living so low that we also will be demoralized by it. Moreover unless we do there will be little hope for the reestablishment of anything like political wisdom in the area. . . .

Regarding DPs, including the political refugees from Austria and Czechoslovakia, McCloy referred to OSS reports of "horrible situations developing in Eastern *Germany* due to the expulsions from *Poland*. Behind *Churchill's* black curtain the reports are that we are having repeated some of the horrors that used to appall us in *Asia Minor* at the time of the Armenian expulsions. . . ." McCloy called, therefore, for long-range planning free of burdensome time limits: "If we do not proceed on a thoroughly planned basis," McCloy warned, "we will soon have on our hands scenes and episodes which will revolt us." Regarding Jewish DPs, McCloy assigned members of his staff to inspect the camps independently. They reported that the camps varied "from good to indifferent," with none particularly "scandalous or anywhere near so." Although improvements were needed, McCloy referred to the "heavy difficulty of disciplining the inmates to the constant necessities which go with clean and pleasant camp conditions. There is no problem with the educated Jew but the bulk of the population of the camps are of a peasant or low living standard type. . . ."

Referring specifically to the Harrison report and to Eisenhower's suggestions for housing, McCloy wrote:

It is fantastic for anyone to say that their condition is the same as it was under HITLER except for the extermination policy and the Jews who seem friendly resent this statement as much as anyone. We must fix a definite policy toward these people. We must determine how far the preference is to go, for the mere movement of them into a former German's or Austrian's house does not solve the problem. Are they to receive permanently higher rations than the non-Nazis about them or preferment in business? It may well provoke a more acute anti-semitism if an attempt is made to make permanent any preferment. . . .

In Russian areas of control established by the Teheran, Yalta, and Potsdam agreements, McCloy counseled a continued United States military presence, particularly in Austria and Hungary. He also suggested that all food and supply credits as well as UNRRA (the United Nations Relief and Rehabilitation Administration) benefits "be held up pending [Soviet] withdrawal." McCloy considered it "incongruous to send in American financed food when the country is being reduced to poverty by the requisitions of unnecessarily large [Soviet] forces." The presence of United States troops, McCloy wrote, was "not burdensome because we mainly feed ourselves and we give the population hope against the Russian fear. There is no doubt that the presence of troops during this period is a substantial aid to our policy in these areas of Middle *Europe.* . . ."

There is no doubt that local political opposition to Russian pressures gains encouragement in this control period by our mere presence. The presence of well disciplined, well behaved and well disposed troops affords a continuously favorable impression on both the people and indirectly on the Russians. The dislike of the Russian is creating a political condition unfavorable to him and the local Communist elements which can only have tangible results as long as we are on the ground. . . .[12]

Although JCS 1067 remained the paper law until General Clay became military governor, in 1947, the long-range goals and immediate political considerations of the United States, as related by

McCloy, rendered denazification unenforceable at all levels. From the beginning, Clay's economic adviser, General William H. Draper, a New York investment banker, and Clay's financial adviser, Lewis W. Douglas, a former Arizona congressman and president of a major insurance company, both to become active in Eisenhower's presidential administrations, were "shocked" by the details of JCS 1067. In 1945, Douglas insisted that it was written "by economic idiots! It makes no sense to forbid the most skilled workers in Europe from producing as much as they can for a continent which is desperately short of everything!"

While most Europeans and many Americans had visions of a disarmed Germany in perpetuity, the administrators of the U.S. occupation insisted on an economically strong, an industrially vigorous Germany. America's long-range economic plans raised the specter of an industrially vital Germany capable of rearming. The decision to base European security on Germany's prompt economic recovery assured French suspicion, Soviet hostility, and the resumption of the Cold War.

Eisenhower's talents as strategist and diplomatist were clearly irrelevant to the governing demands of occupied Europe. Financiers and engineers were required. Before Eisenhower left Germany for his new assignment as Chief of Staff, to replace General Marshall, who had been sent to negotiate peace between the Communists and Chiang Kai-shek in China, he made several last-ditch efforts to fortify the Grand Alliance. In November, Eisenhower went to Berlin to celebrate with Zhukov the twenty-eighth anniversary of the Russian Revolution. In lengthy conferences, the two commanders actually succeeded in ameliorating several issues of discord in the occupied zones. Eisenhower reported to General Clay that Russia's recent order to stop U.S. air traffic between Berlin and Warsaw had been an error. Zhukov promised to protect "reasonable rights and privileges" regarding such issues and "to promote mutual confidence between the two Armies and the countries." Specifically, Zhukov agreed to an exchange of press representatives, and Eisenhower agreed to provide Zhukov with a list of press representatives from which to select, recognizing that the Soviet Union would want to exclude those publications "definitely inimical to their interests."

Eisenhower and Zhukov discussed the crucial issue of reparations at length. Eisenhower noted that the Russian officers "spoke rather earnestly, almost plaintively, about their conviction that while we were concerning ourselves with the economy and living standards in France, Belgium, Holland and even in Germany, no one had spoken up to talk of the living standards in Russia." Eisenhower replied "that we knew about the standards in these countries but that we had no knowledge whatsoever of those standards in Russia. Marshal Zhukov then said that Russia would never place itself in the position of begging but that he could tell me with the utmost frankness that the standard of living in Russia today was deplorably low and that it was his conviction that even the *present* standard in Germany was at least as high as it is in Russia. . . ." Eisenhower assured Zhukov that "nothing would please us more than to get factual data . . . and to govern ourselves accordingly" in terms of the Potsdam agreement, and with "flexibility in making advance reparations . . . in view of [Russia's] deplorable economic ruin. . . ."

In conclusion, Zhukov told Eisenhower that he "could tell anyone in the United States the following as coming from him and as concurred in by Marshal Stalin and all the leaders of their party and government":

> Marshal Stalin and the whole Russian government want nothing so much as peace and understanding between the United States and Russia; that no economic or military move in the Soviet Union should be or could be interpreted as inspired by unfriendliness toward the U.S. He said that the great desire of the Russian government and people was to be treated as intelligent human beings on the basis of equality in every respect.

> . . . He asked that we exert ourselves in every possible way to carry out the spirit and the letter of the Potsdam agreements, and as a concluding remark said in a half-choking manner: "When reparations really start flowing from your zone into the Russian, you will find that a lot of difficulties you are experiencing will probably disappear. . . ."

Eisenhower encouraged Clay "to follow these things up . . . and move instantly to meet them always at least half way."[13] Three days later, on 11 November 1945, General Dwight Eisenhower left Germany suddenly, with little fanfare and few farewells. Apparently he had planned to return, but a temporary illness rendered that impossible and Eisenhower's farewells were made by mail. On 2 December, General Clay wrote that he carried out Eisenhower's "wishes, paying your respects to all of the commanders. . . . Marshal Zhukov was particularly affected and said . . . that he, Zhukov, wanted to carry out anything which you had requested." Clay then reported on the results of Eisenhower's last conference with Zhukov:

> We have been given the air corridor route to Frankfurt, and we have had no further incidents on the Berlin–Warsaw route.
>
> We were able to give Zhukov the plants which he desired and also to agree to a 50% allocation from the list to the U.S.S.R. This pleased Zhukov immensely as it evidenced the result of your good faith.
>
> The news correspondents exchange has been reaffirmed in principle and Zhukov renewed . . . his intention to carry it out in detail. . . .
>
> By and large our relations with the Soviet have improved in recent weeks, and your visit to Marshal Zhukov turned the tide. . . .[14]

On 11 December, Eisenhower wrote Clay that he was "delighted that you are finding some fruitful results from my visit to Marshal Zhukov. The fact is, of course, that I like him and so it was never any real chore for me to try to do business with him." On 6 December, Eisenhower had written directly to Zhukov in detail: "I truly feel that if the same type of association that you and I have experienced . . . could be established and maintained between large numbers of Soviet and American personnel, both military and civil, we would do much in promoting mutual understanding, confidence and faith between our two peoples. I know that during the entire period my own admiration, respect and affection for the Red Army and its great leaders, and for the Russian people all the way up to the Generalissimo himself, constantly increased." Eisenhower wrote to Zhukov, "I truly hope you feel the same. I hope you will always permit me to call you 'friend.'" Zhukov replied that he did feel the same, that he would "ever hold the warmest memories of the time we spent together in Berlin and during our trip to Moscow and Leningrad" and that he hoped "we shall remain good friends as we have been, and therefore I agree beyond all doubt to your calling me your friend, and I trust that you will likewise allow me to call you my friend."[15]

Much of Eisenhower's subsequent correspondence with General Clay involved Eisenhower's plans for Zhukov's projected trip to the United States. They included all manner of journeys and entertainments Eisenhower believed Zhukov would enjoy. When, in March, Bedell Smith was named ambassador to Moscow, Eisenhower wrote again to Zhukov: "I consider General Smith one of the finest and most able men that we have in this country. He is absolutely honest and believes, as I do, in the promotion of Soviet-American understanding and friendship. I hope you will have many opportunities to see him in Moscow and to encourage him along the lines you and I have tried to follow. . . ." Zhukov assured Eisenhower that he welcomed General Smith and would continue "to collaborate in the further development, and strengthening of the friendship and mutual understanding between our peoples, continuing to abide by those high principles which guided you and me in our mutual combat efforts. . . ."

On 13 March, Eisenhower wrote Zhukov again, to thank him for his "latest present of delicacies from Russia." Eisenhower noted that Zhukov, too, was to leave Berlin for reassignment in Moscow. He hoped it might free him to make his long-planned visit to the United States. But Eisenhower wondered about the effect of the fact that Allied wartime personnel, experienced in dealing with each other no matter the differences, were now fully dispersed: "Frankly, with so much misunderstanding in the world, so much inability on the part of people to understand and appreciate the viewpoint and problems of other peoples and so much readiness to accuse others of bad motives, I feel that warm personal friendships between officers of different nations is one thing that offers some hope for the future." On 11 April, Eisenhower wrote to Bedell Smith in Moscow about Zhukov's "hope that he could visit the United States." Eisenhower believed that "much good" might still result from such a visit. "Entirely aside from visiting military installations, I know of a number of people in the industrial and agricultural fields who would like to show him some of their unusual developments. Naturally I would personally do everything humanly possible to make his trip an enjoyable one. . . ."[16]

Zhukov never did get to visit the United States. The Eisenhower-Zhukov correspondence of March 1946 coincided with great changes in Allied relations. On 5 March 1946, in Fulton, Missouri, with President Truman sitting behind him, Winston Churchill's words rang clear: "From Stettin in the Baltic to Trieste in the Adriatic, an iron curtain has descended across the Continent. Behind that line lie all the capitals of the ancient states of Central and Eastern Europe. Warsaw, Berlin, Prague, Vienna, Budapest, Belgrade, Bucharest and Sofia, all these famous cities and the populations around them lie in what I must call the Soviet sphere, and all are subject in one form or another, not only to Soviet influence but to a very high and, in many cases, increasing measure of control from Moscow."

Few Americans knew, although many Europeans did, that a similar speech had been made by Joseph Paul Goebbels, Hitler's chief propagandist, the master of the twisted word. On 23 February 1945, Goebbels had denounced the Yalta agreements that acknowledged Russia's right to military security along its western frontier. At Yalta, the Allies had agreed that the *cordon sanitaire* created at Versailles after World War I was to be denazified, demilitarized, and dissolved. Astounded that the Allies had agreed to regroup the Nazi satellite countries, Goebbels declared that an "iron curtain" had descended over the area. "Behind this curtain," Goebbels warned, there "would begin a mass slaughter of peoples, probably with acclamation from the Jewish press in New York."[17]

Unlike Goebbels, Churchill accepted Russia's "need to be secure on her western frontiers from all renewal of German aggression." But in March 1946, Churchill called upon the English-speaking world to reconsider its wartime agreements; to reconsider the Central European territories British and United States forces had withdrawn from "in accordance with an earlier agreement . . . in order to allow our Russian allies to occupy this vast expanse of territory which the Western Democracies had conquered." At Fulton, Missouri, in March 1946, Churchill called for Anglo-American unity in the decision to discard wartime treaty commitments. "The agreement which was made at Yalta," Churchill argued, "was extremely favorable to Soviet Russia. . . ." It resulted in Russia's physical presence throughout Central Europe and ensured the activity of Communist Party and "fifth column" movements "far from the Russian frontiers," notably in Italy and France, "and throughout the world." Everywhere except Britain and the United

States, "where Communism is in its infancy," these parties "constitute a growing challenge and peril to Christian civilization." This, declared Churchill, "is certainly not the Liberated Europe we fought to build up. Nor is it one which contains the essentials of permanent peace."

Permanent peace, Churchill said, depended upon the creation of "a new unity in Europe, from which no nation should be permanently outcast." This call for the restoration and reintegration of Germany was compounded by Churchill's reference to "the quarrels of the strong parent races in Europe." But Churchill did not call for renewed warfare. He called for the abandonment of the wartime alliance, and a strengthened Anglo-American partnership involving a fraternal military association featuring "joint use of all naval and air force bases in the possession of either country all over the world." That partnership would ensure "the highlands of the future . . . not only for our time, but for a century to come." Churchill did not believe that his proposal would result in war. "I do not believe that Soviet Russia desires war. What they desire is the fruits of war and the indefinite expansion of their power and doctrines." According to Churchill, "the permanent prevention of war" required a show of "strength." "From what I have seen of our Russian friends and allies during the war, I am convinced that there is nothing they admire so much as strength, and there is nothing for which they have less respect than for military weakness." Since the United States stood at war's end "at the pinnacle of world power," and nobody knew what Russia intended to do, "or what are the limits, if any, to their expansive and proselytizing tendencies," it was, Churchill said, "a solemn moment for the American democracy." It was the moment for the United States to assume the challenge of its destiny, its "awe-inspiring accountability to the future." Churchill's speech went far to erode whatever vestiges of trust had remained in the Grand Alliance.

After March 1946, attitudes hardened, negotiations stalled, and specific antagonisms emerged. In Moscow, Churchill's speech infiltrated every moment of Ambassador Walter Bedell Smith's first conference with Stalin. It was not the first time that Churchill had been belligerent, Stalin told Smith: "He tried to instigate war against Russia, and persuaded the United States to join him in an armed occupation against part of our territory in 1919. Lately he has been at it again." Stalin regarded Churchill's speech as "an unfriendly act; it was an unwarranted attack upon the U.S.S.R. Such a speech," Stalin noted, "if directed against the United States, never would have been permitted in Russia." Smith asked if it were possible that Stalin "really believed that the United States and Great Britain are united in an alliance to thwart Russia?" Stalin replied, simply, "*Da*." Smith assured him that that was not the case and that he held "no brief for his Fulton speech." But it did represent, Smith acknowledged, a commonly held "apprehension" in both Britain and the United States. While the United States "could appreciate and understand the desire of the Soviet Union for security," there were questions that needed to be answered: "What does the Soviet Union want, and how far is Russia going to go?"

Smith assured Stalin that the United States "knew and deeply sympathized with the suffering that the Soviet people had endured at the hands of the German aggressor. . . . We understood the desire of the Soviet Union for security and for a share of the world's raw materials, and consequently, our people did not strongly criticize what seemed to be some of the Soviet objectives." But one issue, Smith repeated, was uppermost "in the minds of all the American people: 'How far is Russia going to go?' " Looking directly at Smith, Stalin replied, " 'We're not going much further.' " Smith then asked him about Russian intentions in Turkey. Stalin said, " '. . . the Soviet Union is very conscious of the danger of foreign control of the Straits. . . . The Turkish government is unfriendly to us. That is why the Soviet Union has demanded a base in the Dardanelles. It is a matter of our own security.' "[18]

Turkey and Greece were still embattled. Civil wars that had begun during the war continued to rage—and continued to involve extensive British participation with U.S. military support. The first line of defense to Britain's oil interests in the Middle East, these countries were key to Britain's continued imperial status. But in fact by 1947 Britain could no longer afford to administer or secure its empire. Churchill's call for an upgraded Anglo-American partnership represented more than a statement of ideological unity. The American Century was brought fully into being when Britain admitted its incapacity to defend its extensive international interests. It is possible, therefore, to date the resumption of the Cold War very specifically: 21 February 1947, the day "Pax Britannica" ended and the United States agreed to pick up the crumbling pieces of Britain's empire in the Middle East.

That day was, by all accounts, a cold, dreary, wet day in Washington. On 21 February, the First Secretary of the British Embassy, H. M. Sichel, telephoned Loy Henderson, Assistant Secretary of State for Near Eastern and African Affairs, with a "rather important" message from the Foreign Office. George Marshall, now Secretary of State, had left for the weekend. Henderson met with Sichel. It appeared, Sichel calmly, but plainly, told Henderson, that Britain could not afford the 500 million dollars it would take immediately to defend Greece and Turkey against communism. The United States could either fill the vacuum or let it go.[19] The future of the Middle East was at stake. In fact, the future of the entire colonial world was at stake. The American Century, for so long in some circles a dream, had suddenly become a command performance.

Britain's imperial abdication coincided with the first international conference to negotiate a treaty on Germany, one of the major issues left unresolved at Potsdam. U.S. representatives George Marshall, Lucius Clay, John Foster Dulles, and the ubiquitous Robert Murphy traveled to Moscow for the conference, which began on 10 March. Deliberations at the Moscow conference were deeply influenced by events in Washington. On 12 March, Truman asked Congress to assume British obligations in Greece and Turkey. The President's request for the first of the United States' "mutual assistance" plans became known as "The Truman Doctrine." Truman's 12 March 1947 speech was rhetorically the first fully developed statement of the United States' Cold War vision:

> . . . The United States has received from the Greek government an urgent appeal for financial and economic assistance. . . .
>
> The very existence of the Greek state is today threatened by the terrorist activities of several thousand armed men, led by Communists. . . .
>
> Meanwhile, the Greek government is unable to cope with the situation. . . .
>
> Greece must have assistance if it is to become a self-supporting and self-respecting democracy.
>
> The United States must supply that assistance. . . .

There is no other country to which democratic Greece can turn. . . .

The British government, which has been helping Greece, can give no further financial or economic aid after March 31. Great Britain finds itself under the necessity of reducing or liquidating its commitments in several parts of the world. . . .

To ensure the peaceful development of nations, free from coercion, the United States has taken a leading part in establishing the United Nations. . . . We shall not realize our objectives, however, unless we are willing to help free people to maintain their free institutions and their national integrity against aggressive movements that seek to impose upon them totalitarian regimes. . . .

I believe that it must be the policy of the United States to support peoples who are resisting attempted subjugation by armed minorities or by outside pressures.

I believe that we must assist free peoples to work out their own destinies in their own way. . . .

In helping free and independent nations to maintain their freedom, the United States will be giving effect to the principles of the charter of the United Nations. . . .

I therefore ask the Congress to provide authority for assistance to Greece and Turkey in the amount of $400,000,000 for the period ending June 13, 1948. . . .

In addition to funds, I ask the Congress to authorize the detail of American civilian and military personnel to Greece and Turkey, at the request of those countries, to assist in the tasks of reconstruction, and for the purpose of supervising the use of such financial and material assistance as may be furnished. I recommend that authority be provided for the instruction and training of selected Greek and Turkish personnel. . . .

The seeds of totalitarian regimes are nurtured by misery and want. They spread and grow in the evil soil of poverty and strife. They reach their full growth when the hope of a people for a better life has died.

We must keep that hope alive.

The free peoples of the world look to us for support in maintaining their freedoms.[20]

The Moscow conference was a six-week failure. There was little agreement among the Western Allies on the question of the economic restoration of Germany, and increasing Russian intransigence in the light of the United States' new international commitments. There was in fact never to be a German peace treaty. According to Murphy, the "abortive Moscow Conference . . . really rang down the iron curtain." But the Moscow conference was only one step in a long spiral of enmity between Churchill's speech and the announcement of the Marshall Plan. According to Murphy, the Moscow conference was the "birthplace of the Marshall Plan." Murphy was less disingenuous by far when he pointed out that the basic principles of the Marshall Plan derived from the work of Henry Stimson, John J. McCloy, and Lewis Douglas—and their insistence on the rapid economic restoration of Germany began in May 1945.[21]

When, on 5 June 1947, the Secretary of State spoke at Harvard University's commencement and formally introduced the Marshall Plan, the contours of the renewed Cold War had already solidified. Marshall emphasized the enormity of Europe's economic dislocation:

Under the arbitrary and destructive Nazi rule, virtually every possible enterprise was geared into the German war machine. Long-standing commercial and private institutions, banks, insurance companies and shipping companies disappeared, through loss of capital, absorption through nationalization or by simple destruction.

In many countries, confidence in the local currency has been severely shaken. The breakdown of the business structure of Europe during the war was complete. Recovery has been seriously retarded by the fact that . . . a peace agreement with Germany and Austria has not been agreed upon. . . .

The truth . . . is that Europe's requirements for the next 3 or 4 years of foreign food and other essential products—principally from America—are so much greater than her present ability to pay that she must have substantial additional help. . . .

. . . It is logical that the United States should do whatever it is able to do to assist in the return of normal economic health to the world, without which there can be no political stability and no assured peace.

Our policy is directed not against any country or doctrine but against hunger, poverty, desperation and chaos. Its purpose should be the revival of a working economy in the world so as to permit the emergence to political and social conditions in which free institutions can exist. . . .

Any government that is willing to assist in the task of recovery will find full cooperation. . . . Any government which maneuvers to block the recovery of other countries cannot expect help from us. . . .[22]

Although George Marshall insisted that U.S. policy was not directed "against any country or doctrine," his warning that any effort "to block the recovery" of another country excluded participation in the Marshall Plan specifically concerned the Soviet Union. Russia refused to support the Anglo-American intention of rebuilding Germany in order to restore Europe's traditional balance of power. The Moscow conference was a failure, because the United States never was prepared to move toward a definitive settlement of the German question. On 10 December 1947, during a subsequent conference held in London to negotiate an agreement on the future of Germany, Walter Bedell Smith wrote Eisenhower a secret letter explaining the nature of the problem: "The difficulty under which we labor is that in spite of our announced position, we really do not want nor intend to accept German unification in any terms that the Russians might agree to, even though they seemed to meet most of our requirements." The core of the difficulty lay in Russia's refusal to accept an economically refortified Germany. Their intention "to prevent the resources of Germany from contributing" to Europe's recovery precluded any agreement. Smith wrote to Eisenhower that "this puts us in a somewhat difficult position, and it will require careful maneuvering to avoid the appearance of inconsistency if not hypocrisy." The United States position was that there were "vital economic decisions which have to be made during this winter, and if they are not made on a four power basis they will have to be made unilaterally or bilaterally. What happens," wrote Smith, "after that God only knows."

Ambassador Smith concluded his letter to Eisenhower with information of more personal interest—information that reflected the new international concerns of former military officers whose views and perspectives were expanding as rapidly as world conditions were changing. Smith had talked with their mutual friend "Ronnie Weeks, who is now about to take over the complete directorship of Vickers, which is apparently doing a booming business." Weeks had assured Smith that Britain's Labour government would "be forced to take a more restrained line" regarding its nationalization program in order to "encourage foreign, and particularly American, investors to put their money into British interests. The major project on which he is working, however, as are a number of other friends of yours, is the decentralization of industry, and to a certain extent, of the population of the British Isles to the other sections of the Empire. He is particularly interested in Australia and South Africa, in both of which places Vickers have begun to locate factories."[23]

Eisenhower had nothing to do with the Truman Doctrine or the formulation of the Marshall Plan. Whether or not he disapproved, as he had disapproved of the use of the atomic bomb as "a supreme provocation to other nations, especially the Soviet Union," to use his brother Milton Eisenhower's words, is unclear. But it is clear that by 1947 Eisenhower was out of step with his countrymen. And he knew it. As chief of staff, he called for universal military training and continued Allied unity. American public opinion called for rapid and complete demilitarization and demobilization. And Allied unity had become a historical abstraction. Britain's Labour government was impoverished, dependent and largely irrelevant to America's new international interests. France was in disarray and overextended. The United States had resumed the Cold War with Russia. Eisenhower did not like being out of step. He was a team player.

The hero of World War II seemed somehow misplaced as chief of staff, somehow out of focus in the background of Washington politics. His public pronouncements were disregarded. His enormous popularity was wasted. A variety of people converged on the general, intent on polishing his image. People of power had powerful plans for Eisenhower. But first he required political guidance, social exposure, better-developed economic principles, a more useful public forum.

Forever mindful of history, Eisenhower kept a running river of documents explaining his distaste for politics. He never wanted to be a politician. And he wrote to everybody telling them so. He kept copious notes in his diary reaffirming his disinterest in politics. All his friends, all his brothers, all his associates received letters of heated denial regarding his alleged political ambitions. A paper mountain many feet high exists to prove Eisenhower wanted nothing to do with politics. But Eisenhower wanted to serve his country, to pursue his vision of the future, to fulfill his vow to help the world avoid renewed warfare. Eisenhower was a man of deep conviction. If not overtly political, he was profoundly ambitious. He believed he could help to keep the peace. He believed in the mission of America. And he agreed that he needed a new forum from which to influence public opinion. When Thomas J. Watson, head of International Business Machines, offered him the presidency of Columbia University, Eisenhower accepted.

Bedell Smith wrote to congratulate Eisenhower: "You have certainly made an excellent choice, as this will place you in a dignified position where you will exercise a great deal of influence while removed from the political mess which seems to me to be boiling up stronger all the while. . . ." Eisenhower explained to Smith how difficult his Columbia decision had been for him. It was, after all, his first entirely free personal decision since he chose to go to West Point. Despite the fact that he "loathed" the idea of living in New York City, he was under terrific pressure for over a year to accept the post. He finally did so in June 1947 almost as "a duty."[24] To Swede Hazlett, the recipient of his most detailed letters, Eisenhower wrote fully about his alternatives. "Regardless of my regular response that I did not care to think of such things," Eisenhower was regularly encouraged to consider the most extraordinary proposals. His acceptance of the Columbia position made it finally clear that he "would not consider anything commercial in character; the offers I have received of this type at times appeared to me fantastic."

Eisenhower considered going to Columbia merely a change in "the location of my headquarters." More accurately, he wrote, "I am changing the method by which I will continue to strive for the same goals." Eisenhower wrote to Swede Hazlett that he believed "fanatically in the American form of democracy." For Eisenhower, that meant a system that protected the rights of the individual, affirmed the dignity of individuals because they are created "in the

image of a supreme being," and that was based on "free enterprise." Beyond that, Eisenhower believed "that world order can be
established only by the practice of true cooperation among the sovereign nations and that American leadership toward this goal
depends upon her strength—her strength of will, her moral, social
and economic strength and, until an effective world order is
achieved, upon her military strength." "If by living . . . and
preaching" these "simple conceptions" Eisenhower could "do some
good," he would stay at Columbia "indefinitely."[25]

Having dined with presidents and kings, having shared power
with the most powerful rulers in the world, Eisenhower was neither
humbled nor awed by learning or status. He was aware of his own
talents, proud of his achievements, entirely secure emotionally and
intellectually. He delegated authority easily, and had a celebrated
capacity for long-lasting and deep friendships. There was, however, one group that Eisenhower seems to have relegated to a special place. Men of finance, business leaders of untitled but vast
power, were, for Eisenhower, in a class by themselves. While he
was more pleased than flattered that they seemed to court him, to
provide him with rare opportunities for new society and economic
advancement, Eisenhower accepted their self-appointed role as his
tutors. And he accepted their pressure to assume the presidency of
Columbia University and begin to move thereby into a more public
environment.

Eisenhower's recent biographer Peter Lyon argued that it was
"cruel" to burden Eisenhower with the presidency of Columbia.
Lyon considered Columbia the most ill-fitted job of Eisenhower's
long career. But Eisenhower's years at Columbia were necessary.
His friends thought so; and he thought so. During the last years of
World War II, Eisenhower acquired a new set of friends. They
were loyal and supportive and believed that he would play a great
role in the future of America. They set out to teach him the rules,
the subtleties and nuances of public service. They invited him to
join their clubs and the policy sessions at the Council on Foreign
Relations. They helped him select new clothes and invest his
money. They provided him with a new career in the nation's financial and cultural capital. Daily they underlined and clipped articles
from a variety of papers and journals. Eisenhower read everything
that was sent to him and commented at length. He began to write

about capitalism and Marxism, about labor and management, about war and peace in theoretical terms. Eisenhower's new philosophy was carefully developed. He received an intense course in the realities of American power from a superb collection of tutors. Columbia was not cruel. It was a rite of passage.

CHAPTER III
FROM COLUMBIA UNIVERSITY TO THE PRESIDENCY: THE POLITICAL EDUCATION OF GENERAL EISENHOWER

Eisenhower's political career began long before his Columbia tutorial. As the president of the athletic club he organized at Abilene High School and during his popular years at West Point, he developed a personal style that marked him for leadership positions. Although he forever denied specific interest in politics, and crude partisan politics were in fact of no interest to him, he was widely recognized as a political leader. President Roosevelt told his son James, for example, that while he "thought Marshall the wisest of the generals," he selected Eisenhower as commander in chief because "Eisenhower is the best politician among the military men. He is a natural leader who can convince men to follow him. . . ."[1]

During the war, Eisenhower's military strategy depended on his ability to secure the trust of both Churchill and Stalin, negotiate with all the bitterly contending French factions, coordinate the frequently opposing political and military interests within his own command, and convince all the delicate personalities of the international anti-Fascist forces that he was sensitive to their specific and personal needs. By war's end, he seemed an Olympian talent. His reputation as one of the greatest statesmen of the twentieth century was well established. Eisenhower was compared with George Washington and Benjamin Franklin. While his rivals and detractors criticized him as a politician, his supporters sought to enhance and direct his skills. They encouraged him to do public work. They involved him in public activity. And they went to great lengths to refocus his international vision and direct his domestic perspectives. Eisenhower responded at first unevenly to their efforts. They increased their efforts. They flattered him, pursued him. They talked endlessly of the contribution he would make, should make, must make for America, for the future of America in the world.

Self-assured and dedicated, Eisenhower never doubted his capacity for service to those ideas, those principles he believed in. He had, after all, just commanded the international anti-Fascist armies against the most sinister forces ever assembled or imagined in human history. On the other hand, he believed—long after it was advantageous to do so—in the possibility of continued amity with Russia. Even after Churchill's "iron curtain" speech, announcing that Russia and not Germany represented the world's primary threat, Eisenhower continued to speak as if the Grand Alliance survived, and continued to acknowledge Russia's geographic "sphere of influence" as established at Yalta. Moreover, even while McCarthyism increased throughout the United States, demeaning all New Deal programs, naming all New Deal ideas socialist and un-American, Eisenhower spoke against unlimited privilege that deprived "so many girls and boys" of opportunity. Although Eisenhower did in fact fear that certain features of the New Deal might lead to socialism, he had absolute faith in the power of opportunity in America. Born poor, he believed that if he could achieve fame and fortune, anybody could. The little boy from the flats of Abilene who had wanted to become a railroad conductor to get out of Kansas believed that there should be no barriers to the kind of opportunities—public education, access to work—that had benefited him.

He was not a "rugged individualist" Republican. Over time, his views became more conservative. But between 1945 and 1952, many Republicans considered him too progressive. America's most celebrated hero persisted in opinions that were beginning to make him stand out like a bright red thumb. It was untenable. Naïve. All his friends, all his associates, told him so. And, sometime between 1948 and 1950, Eisenhower joined the proper line of march: the Russians were transformed into the Reds, and he adopted the habit of calling New Dealers "socialists."

The disintegration of New Deal liberalism was a necessary corollary to the revival of Cold War fervor. Keynesian liberalism, considered by many the salvation of capitalism in crisis, was now attacked as Communist-inspired. The WPA and the demands for full employment, fair wages, and safe workplaces were denounced as Communist plots. New Deal values would lead to Soviet domination of the United States. To pursue America's expanded interests throughout the world, it was necessary to destabilize New Deal attitudes toward change, to roll back "creeping" socialism—at home and abroad.

The Cold War was, and remains, about power and influence, resources and place. But it has been fought in terms that have tended to distort its real purpose. The terms of United States-Soviet rivalry emerged out of a sense of betrayal forged in the cruelest and most bitter fires. The millions of dead and displaced during World War II haunted every postwar decision. Subsequently, Nazism, Communism, Capitalism, the Free World, Soviet Slavery became symbols around which to dance the threat of atomic bombs and thermonuclear missiles. They were used to camouflage the real purposes of the Cold War.

In 1942, Winston Churchill had announced: "I have not become the King's First Minister in order to preside over the liquidation of the British Empire." But by 1945 only the United States was capable of supporting Britain's imperial burdens—as well as those French, Japanese, and German burdens yet to be negotiated.

Only the United States was economically solvent and politically stable. The United States benefited mightily from Europe's economic collapse and geographic dislocations. Russia, far more devastated than the United States and economically exhausted, nevertheless emerged from the war the United States' only international rival. Some have claimed that there were no alternatives to the Cold War after 1945. There could be no peace with godless communism. Others disagree. The debate continues. One historian, Norman Graebner, has put it very simply:

> Why did the United States after 1939 permit the conquest of eastern Europe by Nazi forces, presumably forever, with scarcely a stir, but refused after 1944 to acknowledge any primary Russian interest or right of hegemony in the same region on the heels of a closely-won Russian victory against the German invader? When scholars have answered that question fully the historical debate over the Cold War origins will be largely resolved.[2]

Whatever the resolution, aspects of the crusade against communism seemed capable, after 1945, of galvanizing American public opinion into heights of enthusiasm reserved previously for baseball games, notably during the World Series. Anticommunism began to dominate public life in the United States. Russia became an American obsession. America's historic populist and progressive traditions were heaped into the discard in a frantic search for traitors and spies. Even the constitutional precepts that had designated the United States free and civil-libertarian were now denounced as Bolshevik. Dissent, freedom to speak, the right to assemble were discredited as diversionary Communist tactics. Politicians, otherwise bereft of personal or political charm, became heroes for the most sleazy anti-Communist antics.

In November 1946, an obscure Californian was elected to Congress because he "proved" his New Deal opponent, Jerry Voorhis, a Communist. Thousands of voters in California's twelfth district received anonymous telephone calls: "This is a friend of yours but I can't tell you my name. I just want to tell you that Jerry Voorhis is a Communist." Despite the fact that the CIO's radical Political Action Committee had refused to endorse Voorhis because of his spirited support for anti-Communist legislation, Richard M. Nixon printed leaflets that asserted: "A vote for Nixon is a vote against the PAC, its Communist principles, and its gigan-

tic slush fund. . . . The issue is clear. . . . The people will vote
for me as a supporter of free enterprise, individual initiative, and a
sound progressive program, or for my opponent who has supported
. . . the foreign ideologies of the New Deal Administration."[3]

Richard Nixon was elected to the Eightieth Congress along with
a freshman representative from Wisconsin, Joseph R. McCarthy. It
was the first Republican Congress since 1928. It was one of the
few Congresses in United States history to be dominated by a single theme. Not since the Civil War was there such partisan unity.
There had been "twenty years of treason." The Democrats had become the Commicrats. In 1945, the House Committee on Un-
American Activities (HUAC) was designated a "standing" investi-
gative committee. It was to become an impressive feature of
American life. Left-leaning Americans were hunted out of jobs,
professions, public life, Hollywood. Labor unions "purged" themselves. Civil servants stopped talking politics with friends. High
school and college courses on political economy were canceled.
Political commitment, economic idealism were suspect and went
"underground." America was a two-party democracy. Everything
else was suspected of treason, including one of those parties.

In 1948, Nixon became the chairman of a subcommittee of
HUAC to investigate Communist espionage in government. "The
full story of Communist espionage will not be told until we get a
Republican President who is not afraid of skeletons in the closet,"
declared Richard Nixon in September 1948. But in 1948 Thomas
Dewey was the Republican choice—and he was known to have
had New Deal dealings, if not sympathies. Eastern, "liberal" Republicans such as Dewey and John Foster Dulles, widely believed
to be Dewey's designate for Secretary of State, were tainted by the
broad sweep of Nixon's charges against Alger Hiss. Not only had
Dulles represented Roosevelt and Truman foreign policy, he had,
as chairman of the Carnegie Endowment's board of trustees,
promoted Alger Hiss to his post as the Endowment's president.
Nixon met with Dulles urging him to repudiate Hiss. But as late as
September 1948 the trustees of the Endowment chose to do nothing. They refused to demand his resignation and decided instead to
give him a leave of absence to prepare his defense in the case that
catapulted Nixon to prominence and remains today one of the
most controversial "espionage" cases in United States history.

Hiss's supporters at the Endowment were liberal internationalists. Also Republican, they differed dramatically in vision and style from the Nixon-McCarthy wing of the party. Among others, they included James T. Shotwell, Philip Reed, David Rockefeller, Thomas Watson, Henry Wriston, and General Dwight David Eisenhower. Understandably, the election of 1948 did not highlight the Hiss case.[4]

In 1948, Eisenhower's partisan preferences were as yet unknown. The Republicans were committed to Dewey, and Democrats clamored for Eisenhower. As early as 1943, Eisenhower was urged to think about the presidency. In 1945, at Potsdam, Truman said directly to Eisenhower: "General, there is nothing that you may want that I won't try to help you get. That definitely and specifically includes the Presidency in 1948."[5] Franklin, Jr., Elliott, and James Roosevelt all worked for a Democrats for Eisenhower movement in 1948. Hubert Humphrey recalled that "Eleanor herself called several times to discuss it." He wrote that "much of the pressure" for a draft-Eisenhower movement "came from people associated with Franklin Roosevelt, old New Dealers, now new ADA'ers." According to Humphrey, the Americans for Democratic Action "felt that their politics were purer and their ideas better than those of Truman's people."[6] Such a draft was premature. Eisenhower was adamant. He did not feel ready for presidential politics in 1948. He required an organization of his own. And that was temporarily committed to Dewey.

Professional politicians misjudged public opinion in 1948. Popular anticommunism did not yet mean the end of class consciousness in America. Dewey, fastidious and pompous, failed to stir American voters. Alice Roosevelt Longworth thought Dewey looked like the little groom on the wedding cake. Most people thought he looked, simply, ridiculous. Truman called him a "Fascist" and compared him to Hitler, mustache and all. Truman ran a frankly class-related campaign, a people's campaign that took the wind out of Henry Wallace's progressive sails and maintained intact America's two-party system. He called Republicans "gluttons of privilege" and declared that they would "nail the American consumer to the wall with spikes of greed."[7] Such hyperbole ensured Truman's election.

With Truman's victory and the "loss" of China, the anti-Communist crusade intensified. The years and years of "Commicrat" treason had to end. In 1950, Nixon beat Helen Gahagan Douglas to the Senate. The "Pink Lady" was a Democrat who supported all anti-Communist measures while in Congress, including the Marshall Plan, Point Four, and aid to Korea. Nevertheless, Nixon's public-relations men called her a Communist, a "red-hot." They made much of the fact that her actor husband, Melvyn Douglas, was at birth named Hesselberg. For so long that even his aides became embarrassed, Nixon accepted the support of the notorious Gerald L. K. Smith, who urged Californians to help "Richard Nixon get rid of the Jew Communists."[8] The crusade was getting out of hand.

More and more, Eisenhower seemed the one man capable of healing America's partisan tensions. With Eisenhower at the helm, the fifties might be prosperous, peaceful, apolitical, and televised. Beneficial and good, the American way would seem enviable enough for export. That was not only the American dream; that was, many Americans came to believe, the world's aspiration. For success, Eisenhower would depend on his friends, on his colleagues at the Carnegie Endowment. They were the men on whom he leaned for advice and on whom he depended for the creation of an appropriate and generous political organization.

It would be impossible to exaggerate the influence of these men of business and prominence on the formulation of Eisenhower's ideas, his future policies, his entire presidential vision. Eisenhower's contacts with the world of business, with the men who shaped and promoted that world—with capital and capitalists—had been limited and indirect. Now they impressed him with their erudition, their easy use of power. He admired, among other things, the efficiency of their style and what he believed was their "selfless" attitude toward public events. Eisenhower remarked frequently about how they gave of their time and energy, never themselves seeking political office or personal recompense. And, too, they sought his company. Indeed, they demanded his company.

Henry Wriston, then president of Brown University, chairman of the Association of American Universities, and chairman of the prestigious Council on Foreign Relations, insisted that Eisenhower personally attend the meetings of the university presidents—meetings that Eisenhower as president of Columbia University had planned to delegate to subordinates. Wriston assured the would-be truant that it was necessary for Eisenhower to be seen and heard and known by the academic community of the United States. And it was necessary for Eisenhower to direct one of the study groups of the Council on Foreign Relations. It was in fact necessary for Eisenhower to become an outspoken presence within the mainstream of Cold War America.

Douglas Black, president of Doubleday, contracted for Eisenhower's wartime memoirs, *Crusade in Europe*. William Robinson, vice-president of the New York *Herald Tribune* and president of Coca-Cola, urged Eisenhower to write popular columns, digested and syndicated parts of his book, and promoted it in a variety of ways. The pages of Henry Luce's publications generously featured Eisenhower's activities.

Although Henry Luce was relatively slow to court Eisenhower, he became a vigorous and persistent courtier. They were not on a first-name basis until the spring of 1951, when Luce wrote: "Dear Ike—That's what all us Americans call you anyway, so I guess it will be all right if I step right up and call you that to your face. And since my friends call me Harry, I'd be happy if you would, too." When Eisenhower forgot and addressed Luce as Henry, Luce told one of his associates he would give the man only one more chance. By the summer, Luce sent a copy of *Life's Pictorial History of Western Man* to Eisenhower, "because you are the spearhead of the battle to save western man. . . ." Luce courted Eisenhower very carefully. But Ike was slow to warm to Harry, who never did become part of Eisenhower's intimate circle.[9]

In that circle were Philip Reed, the board chairman of General Electric; Philip Young, dean of Columbia's school of business; Edward Bermingham, one of the United States' leading investment bankers and an executive member of the Republican National Committee; W. Alton ("Pete") Jones, president of Cities Service Oil Company and chairman of the board of the American Petroleum Institute; William Robinson, of the *Herald Tribune* and Coca-Cola; and the administrators of *Joroberts Corporation*, established to market Coca-Cola and other soft drinks internationally: Clifford Roberts, vice-president and treasurer; and Robert Tyre Jones, president and secretary. Eisenhower was a major stockholder in *Joroberts*, and Roberts and Jones were among his closest associates after 1948. In fact, Clifford Roberts, president of Reynolds & Company, was Eisenhower's personal investment counselor.[10]

These men became Eisenhower's golf and bridge partners. They introduced him to important people—to Charles Wilson, president of General Motors, and to Eugene Black, who became head of the World Bank when John J. McCloy resigned to return to Bonn as the U.S. high commissioner for Germany, in 1949. The World Bank, the International Bank for Reconstruction and Development, had been created originally to finance and administer Marshall Plan aid and the Point Four Program. Roberts and Jones understood that it was important for Eisenhower to know these people in the course of his difficult months as commander in chief of SHAPE. Eisenhower's goal was to achieve an international commitment to the NATO alliance, an economic and military commitment. And Eugene Black had access to information about the international business scene that few shared. They considered it important also for Eisenhower to meet a variety of other people. "Pete" Jones and Roberts thought it of the highest consequence that Eisenhower meet E. T. Weir, for example. Roberts wrote that Weir was "a rugged individualist" who had succeeded in keeping all labor organizers outside "his domain," the Weirton Steel Company. "Needless to say, he is actively opposed to a good many people who now reside in Washington. I know 'Pete' will be very grateful for any courtesies that you can extend to brother Weir."[11] Eisenhower ordered his assistant Robert Schulz to "Be on the Lookout" for Brother Weir.

In addition, they sent him articles, reviews, cartoons, reports and statistics. They were a self-appointed clipping service and information bureau. They represented a significant network. They supported each other, publicized each other's views, and worked hard to see that Eisenhower saw the best of their efforts. Rarely a week passed that Eisenhower did not receive, with requests for his comments, such material as W. Alton Jones's October 1951 address to the annual meeting of The Texas Mid-Continent Oil and Gas Association, "Communism Is as Communism Does"; a *Wall Street Journal* article Roberts considered "encouraging": "Capitalist Comeback/France to Fight Nationalization Trend. . . . Millions in Marshall Plan Aid Spark Nationalized Coal, Electricity Industry";

William E. Robinson's protest against government practices such as profits taxes that, he wrote, interfered with needed business expansion by eroding private investment incentives, "Capitalism's Worst Foes Aren't Reds at All." Robinson's point was the same as the one made by Roberts' partner, Frank Willard, chairman of the Industrial Securities Committee of the Investment Bankers Association: ". . . in terms of the purchasing power of the investors' current income from business, a dollar today is little greater than the fifty cents of the prewar era. The investor is today the forgotten man." Robinson's article was couched in more political terms: ". . . the capitalist free-enterprise system . . . has never been so much as scratched by the communists, but it is being bled to death by . . . [those] responsible for the endless expansion of bureaucracy. . . ." But neither Robinson nor Willard stated clearly the targets of their criticism: all those Keynesian New Deal/Fair Deal Democrats they sought to remove from office.[12]

And so they invited Eisenhower to join their clubs. Robert Tyre Jones presented Eisenhower with a new set of golf clubs, was instrumental in improving his game, and invited him to join the exclusive Augusta National Golf Club, over which Bob Jones himself presided. It was at Augusta in 1948 that Eisenhower was introduced to W. Alton "Pete" Jones. Robert Woodruff, of Coca-Cola, arranged the meeting at Eisenhower's request. Before they met, Eisenhower wrote to "Dear Mr. Jones. . . . I would be more than delighted if Bob Woodruff can someday arrange a golf game so that we two can meet. You must expect nothing of my golf. It is of the century variety and is mainly useful in providing opportunity to meet interesting and friendly people." "Pete" Jones was also a member of the "Committee of Morals, Manners and Mayhem" of the Bohemian Grove, an encampment for America's business, entertainment, and social elite. Jones invited Eisenhower to attend a summer encampment. Eisenhower accepted eagerly: "When I see you it will be fun to talk about the trip . . . and to learn whether a man carries his fishing rod or golf clubs with him or whether he merely goes out there to soak up laziness and good comradeship. Whatever it is, . . . I am truly anxious to go."[13]

The Bohemian Grove was, and remains, a somewhat mystical and irreverent place where America's leaders go to negotiate America's future. Although Bohemian Grove rhetoric emphasizes druidical "hijinks," "lowjinks," and general merriment, it is the annual business meeting of America's leadership camp. The club's logo features a learned owl and the message: "Weaving Spiders Come Not Here." While self-advertisement is discouraged, international business is the business of the Bohemian Grove. C. D. Jackson, Eisenhower's chief political-warfare consultant during World War II and the presidential years, noted on his return from one Bohemian Grove encampment that he was back from the summer "jamboree, saturated with sunshine, whiskey and tycoons." Situated seventy-five miles north of San Francisco, at Monte Rio, the Grove consists of three thousand acres of redwood lands and comfortable campsites bearing such names as Stowaway (Eisenhower's cabin), Cave Man (Nixon's and Herbert Hoover's cabin), and Mandalay (the cabin of the Bechtels, Lucius Clay, and many of Eisenhower's closest friends). Eisenhower was not actually invited to join until 14 August 1950, when he was admitted under a clause that permitted "persons of special eminence in Military or Diplomatic affairs, or other public service" to become Honorary members by unanimous vote of the board of directors.[14]

Eisenhower's correspondence between 1948 and 1951 is full of detail about whom he is to meet at these clubs. And whomever he failed to meet at Augusta or the Bohemian Grove he was sure to meet through Edward Bermingham, who hosted "stag" parties for Eisenhower throughout the country. These gatherings of rich and powerful men became models for Eisenhower's political socializing throughout his presidential years. They included a full mix— regional, professional, financial. Eisenhower would, when President, invite an occasional labor leader. Bermingham's invitations were limited to businessmen—and he seemed to know them all.

Independent and committed to his own anonymity, Bermingham preferred to negotiate the future from the background. Publicly unknown and rarely acknowledged, he was one of America's shadow powers. An investment banker first associated with Dillon, Reed & Company, he moved to Lehman Brothers in 1933 in order to devote more attention to international economic activity. Although he formally retired in 1940, he "never lost touch" with business activities. According to Katherine C. Bermingham, who compiled her husband's correspondence with Eisenhower and donated it to Columbia University, Ed Bermingham "believed that the salvation of the United States lay in a Republican victory under the leadership of Eisenhower in 1952. . . ." To ensure the success of his vision, Bermingham arranged stag dinners throughout the United States. The invitees read like excerpts from lists of *Fortune*'s annual "500." The quail dinner at the Chicago Club on 4 March 1949, for example, included David Crawford, president of Pullman; Paul E. Russell, Harris Trust & Savings Bank; Sewell Avery, Montgomery Ward; Merle Trees, Chicago Bridge & Iron; John L. McCaffrey, president, International Harvester; R. Douglas Stuart, president, Quaker Oats; Fred Gurley, president of the Atcheson, Topeka & Santa Fe Railroad; and assorted bankers and officials. A more modest luncheon, in the Southwest, included many of the same people and also Lewis B. Maytag, president, The Maytag Company; Harold Swift, the meat packer; General Robert E. Wood, the chairman of Sears Roebuck; and others.[15]

Despite all the early activities to lure Eisenhower directly into Republican politics, he hesitated. To begin with, many of his personal, loyal, and longtime friends were Democrats. Sid Richardson, for example, was one of Eisenhower's oldest friends—from the early years when he was a young officer based in Texas. An oilman of phenomenal wealth and significant power, Sid Richardson is more popularly associated with Sam Rayburn, Lyndon B. Johnson, and John Connally. But this did not reflect ideological difference. Texas was ruled as a one-party state, and Connally was generally recognized as the manager of Texas Democrats for Eisenhower. Richardson supported Eisenhower vigorously. When Eisenhower was president of Columbia University, Richardson sent large checks for the promotion of the American Assembly and other Columbia programs Eisenhower favored. When Eisenhower returned to Europe, Richardson kept him well stocked with American steaks, cases of lettuce, smoked turkey. What Sid Richardson thought, mattered to Eisenhower. And the future of America mattered to them both. It was not a matter of simple partisan politics.[16]

The truth was that Eisenhower hated partisan politics. Petty rivalries, party rituals annoyed him. His vision was global. He had a wider vision of public life: the mission of America, and his own potential contribution to that mission. He also had a secret ambition: bipartisan citizens for Eisenhower acclaiming his view of the future. If he was to be President, he wanted it to be not for reasons of party, or even state—but for that kind of future he was now in the process of defining. The mountains of letters Eisenhower wrote protesting his disinterest in politics are not to be dismissed. But there is one letter that offers a more complex statement of his attitude toward the presidency. On 18 September 1947, Eisenhower wrote to Bedell Smith:

I do not believe that you or I or anyone else has the right to state, categorically, that he will NOT perform ANY duty that his country might demand of him. You did NOT WANT to become our Ambassador to Moscow. . . . Now in this matter of a political role the question naturally arises, "What circumstances could ever convince you or me that it was a DUTY to become a political candidate?" Certainly I do not see how anyone could obtain a conviction of duty from a deadlocked convention that should name him as a "compromise" selection. . . . Under such circumstances I believe that instead of feeling a call to duty a man would have to consider himself merely a political expediency or political compromise. . . .

On the other hand, if you should assume the occurrence of an American miracle . . . that has never heretofore occurred, at least since Washington, you might have the spectacle of someone being named by common consent rather than by the voice and manipulations of politicians. So-called "drafts," since Washington's time, have been carefully nurtured, with the full, even though undercover, support of the "victim." . . .

Now Eisenhower made his point very clearly. Like George Washington, he, too, would respond if "such an unmistakable call" came from the entire nation. Not to do so would be unpatriotic. It "would be almost the same thing as a soldier refusing to go forward with his unit. . . ." Eisenhower wrote that he "would regard it as the saddest day of my life if ever I should become convinced that I owed it to any considerable portion of the public" to become President. On the other hand, he also "sincerely and honestly" believed that the United States faced "national and international problems of such grave import that little room is left for political maneuvering." And in this perilous time there were "few people outside the armed services and the higher echelons of the State Department that are giving their full attention to American interests as a whole and refusing to color their conclusions and convictions with the interests of party politics. I should like to be numbered among this disinterested group. . . ."[17]

Smith and others were quick to understand Eisenhower's message. Less than a month later, William E. Robinson walked into Eisenhower's office for a ninety-minute interview so intimate that Robinson wrote to his boss, Helen Reid, with evident surprise: "He was completely free, unguarded to the point even of indiscretion. There was no pose, no pretense, no attempt to establish anything for the record, no attempt to build an impression of any kind. He was natural, alive, alert, spirited, and gave the impression of having an intense amount of unloosened energy, both intellectual and physical." Their conversation touched on many subjects. Robinson had visited Eisenhower on the pretext of offering him "the services of the New York *Herald Tribune* Syndicate" should the general intend to write anything "in the future." Robinson encouraged Eisenhower to write his own record of the war and emphasized "that there were only two people in the history of this country who had, as a matter of necessity, to get on with the British and with other Europeans . . . Benjamin Franklin and General Eisenhower. He must find some way to return—in advice, information and enlightenment—the opportunity which the American people had given him."

Robinson noted that Eisenhower "seemed almost to get on fire with his burning, patriotic feeling to be of helpfulness to the country that he loves. He would, every few minutes, arise from the chair in which he was sitting and stride up and down the office, talking about his limitations at one moment, and in the next outlining the manner in which he would like to be of service. . . ." And although they did not discuss the presidency specifically, Robinson believed that it was "apparent that he will not move a finger to promote himself for the nomination. It is also clear that if one of the major political parties could demonstrate a preponderance of opinion in his favor, he would accept the nomination. . . ."[18]

In January 1948, General Lucius Clay and political warrior Robert Murphy were in Washington to testify before a congressional committee. During dinner, Eisenhower showed his friends a copy of a letter he had mailed that day. It was to a publisher that had urged him to become the Democratic candidate for President. Eisenhower said that he had never spent so much time on a letter.

He had drafted it twenty-five times. Since everybody expected
Governor Thomas E. Dewey to win by a landslide in 1948, Eisenhower refused—leaving "sizable loopholes for a different response
at a more favorable time." Although Eisenhower did not seem to
know it at the time, it was clear to Clay that Ike was a Republican
"whether he realized it or not." It was also clear to Clay that,
should Dewey lose, Eisenhower would be the Republican choice.
Clay was to be in the forefront of those who led Eisenhower into
Republican Party ranks.[19]

Others shared Clay's presumption of Eisenhower's essential Republicanism. In June 1948, Robinson wrote a long and detailed
letter to Helen Rogers Reid, the owner of the New York *Herald
Tribune,* outlining Eisenhower's "political convictions and his personal philosophy." In frequent conversations with Robinson, Eisenhower had indicated that he believed fervently in the individual
but that he was not a "rugged individualist" of "the old-fashioned
Republican" school. Rather, he believed in "freedom and independence for the individual with its collateral responsibility for cooperation. Several times . . . he made the statement that 'only the
strong can cooperate.'" For Eisenhower, this meant full "opportunity for every boy and girl in the nation." This, wrote Robinson,
"would always come in conversation about some consequence of
the New Deal which sought to substitute SECURITY for OPPOR-
TUNITY."

On the issue of labor and capital, Eisenhower believed that "no
one group or segment of America should be the prey for any
other." Although, over time, Eisenhower's views on labor and capital came more and more to reflect those of his business supporters,
in 1948 Eisenhower emphasized fairness and a mutuality of interests. Robinson wrote, ". . . any national legislation . . . which is
developed out of pressure from one side or the other, instead of
out of a concept of fairness and equity, is abhorrent to him." On
all other subjects, Robinson emphasized Eisenhower's concept of
liberal moderation. He considered the Democratic Party "a mix-
ture of extremes on the right, extremes on the left, with political
chicanery and expediency shot through the whole business." This
assessment, combined with his abhorrence of the "bureaucracy in
Washington," rendered Eisenhower "a liberal Republican." "He
says," Robinson wrote, "that actually the middle of the road in

America is no narrow white line; it is a broad highway that reaches over to a fanatical fringe on the left and a benighted strip on the right."

Despite Eisenhower's essential Republicanism, Robinson concluded that it was "barely conceivable that in certain circumstances he would not resist an overwhelming draft as a Democratic candidate for the Presidency." With Dewey's defeat in November, the likelihood of those circumstances dried up. Eisenhower was the logical Republican in 1952. The campaign started immediately: After November 1948, great pressure was put on Eisenhower to become more visible—to give speeches, to publish books and articles. Bill Robinson urged him to write a series of articles that would be widely syndicated, nationally and internationally, under a general heading such as "The American Doctrine," "The American Creed," that would be both anti-Communist and positive. Robinson emphasized that Russia's "postwar tactics have resulted in consolidating a strong anti-Communist philosophy among the American people." Since there had been the danger of a "misguided drift in the direction of socialism" in the United States, Robinson concluded that this "was at least one fortunate byproduct of the otherwise unfortunate friction between Russia and America." But there was as yet no "honored and respected voice" to "define and explain the soundness and the high moral value in our doctrine. . . . Our need is a clearly defined positive philosophy to fight for." Robinson assured Eisenhower that if the "trend of our economy" was not reversed in the next half decade, it might become "too late to attempt to create the necessary faith. People without jobs and food are poor prospects for philosophy." More significantly, Robinson wanted Eisenhower to understand that the "fact that there is no respected and unsuspected voice other than yours competent to define, explain, and inspire faith in our doctrine is a constant subject of conversation in any group I meet these days."[20]

Once the campaign began, specific changes in Eisenhower's political philosophy emerged. Washington observers were quick to recognize those changes. In December 1949, journalist James G. Crowley contrasted Eisenhower's immediate postwar speeches, so "thrilling and uplifting," so "informal" and "feeling" about the "rights of men everywhere" to enjoy "the fruits of our industrial genius" and the need for redistribution so that all might enjoy those rights, with his more recent efforts. Now, Crowley asserted in a national broadcast sponsored by the American Federation of Labor (AFL), Eisenhower "has taken his stand beside those who would deny to all but a few the most fundamental of the rights he once so eloquently championed: the right of personal and family security, economic security, without which none of us can fully exercise the other rights and other freedoms which are supposed to be inalienable."

Eisenhower had, in a recent speech, in December 1949, referred to the mindless quest for the "illusion called security." In one of the most unfortunate speeches of his career he had actually said: "I have seen many white crosses in many parts of the world, and the men under those crosses are there because they believed there was something more than merely assuring themselves they weren't going to be hungry at the age of 67." He asserted: "We think too much of luxuries." "We want to wear fine shirts, have caviar and champagne, when we should be eating hot dogs and beer." Many hard-working Americans were appalled. Smiling, open Ike, the enlisted man's hero, seemed to have become a Republican politician. Eisenhower, now so frequently feasting on champagne and quail, was content to condemn Americans to hot dogs and beer. Crowley and the AFL thought it "indecent," "tawdry and smug," especially considering Eisenhower's own income security—the pension of a five-star general, which amounted in 1949 to a very grand $18,761 in base pay plus additional money for quarters ($150 a month "when they are not provided"), and $5,000 additional per year—an extra "personal money allowance," and a government-furnished aide assigned as Eisenhower's personal valet, free hospital and medical services for the rest of his life—all guaranteed and in addition to whatever work he might choose to do in the future. A tasteless statement on security, all things considered. And Crowley gave some of those considerations. In 1949, two thirds of all families in the United States had incomes of less than four thousand dollars. From his public education at West Point to his government pension, the general was, concluded Crowley, an authority on security. But he knew nothing about insecurity. And that fact enabled him, Crowley asserted, to be used by "others of ignoble purpose," who were merely "capitalizing" on

Eisenhower's "esteem, cajoling the General into fronting for them, leading him up to the top of the mountain."[21]

Actually, Eisenhower tended to regard workers much the same way as he regarded troops in wartime: They had a job to do for the good of the nation. The reality of his disregard for workers' aspirations is unclear. But it is clear that he was not merely fronting for others of "ignoble purpose."

Although both Eisenhower and his brother Milton served the Roosevelt administrations loyally, they disagreed about the wisdom and implications of New Deal legislation that seemed to promise so much hope for genuine economic security. As early as 1934, Milton, who worked closely with Henry Wallace in the Department of Agriculture, defended the New Deal, while then-Major Eisenhower questioned its constitutionality and feared "creeping socialism." This fear hardened after the war, as did his fear of international socialism.[22]

During the war, Eisenhower's commitment to the future of the Grand Alliance with Russia depended largely on his belief in an alliance arrangement in which he was commander in chief and in which his orders were faithfully, earnestly followed. After the war, no longer in authority—under vastly different circumstances—his attitudes began to change. Writing in 1948, Eisenhower looked back to the end of the war in Europe as "the peak of postwar cordiality and cooperation that we were ever able to achieve" with Russia.

The years of growing tension since the war "shattered" Eisenhower's "dream of rapid progress toward universal peace and the elimination of armaments. . . . Fear, doubt, and confusion are the portion of those who fought and won the war with the fervent prayer that at last this was the war to end wars." In 1948, Eisenhower concluded his book on World War II by calling for renewed "military preparedness" and an aggressive psychological war against communism. Armaments were insufficient, he wrote, to "annul Communist appeals to the hungry, the poor, the oppressed." Communism, Eisenhower wrote, appeals to "human beings who become desperate in the attempt to satisfy common human needs. Therein it possesses a profound power for expansion." To counter that expansion, he advocated "practical measures untiringly prosecuted for the elimination of social and economic evils that set men against men."[23]

His views on this theme were entirely contradictory. He increasingly condemned as socialistic all New Deal/Fair Deal legislation to eradicate the worst evils of poverty and unemployment. He called New Deal/Fair Deal legislators socialists. He applauded the vast sums of Marshall Plan and Point Four money sent overseas to ensure profound social change internationally. But he dismissed all calls for such programs domestically. The citizens of the United States, it seemed, were not to benefit from the crusade against communism. Eisenhower's economic understanding was limited, and his emphasis—economic and political—was and remained international. The war in Korea, the revolution in China rigidified his vision. Eisenhower, the man who in 1945 had seemed most committed to permanent peace with Soviet Russia, came by 1950 to regard communism at home and abroad as America's leading threat. Abroad, communism was to be contained by social change, the achievement of economic security. At home, all social change and programs for economic redistribution were to be dismissed as communistic.

On 4 January 1950, Eisenhower noted in his personal diary: "Today the New York *Sun* ceases to exist as a separate paper." For Eisenhower, that incident had great significance, because the former owner of the paper had listed the reasons why the paper died, emphasizing his inability to meet labor-union demands and explaining what the *Sun* had "stood for during its existence." Eisenhower wrote that "These are the things in which I believe":

> . . . constitutional government, sound money, reasonable protection for American industry, economy in public expenditures, preservation of the rights and responsibilities of the several states, free enterprise, good citizenship, equality before the law. . . . It has opposed indecency and rascality, public and private. It has fought Populism, Socialism, Communism, governmental extravagance, the encroachments of bureaucracy, and that form of governmental paternalism which eats into the marrow of private initiative and industry. . . .

Eisenhower was deeply troubled by the demise of the New York *Sun*. If "a paper that has preached these things cannot secure enough support to operate successfully," there was only one question to be asked: "Are these principles, as guides to American action, now to go into the discard? If they are I am wasting a lot of energy—but I'll go down fighting."[24]

It was a difficult time for Eisenhower. The presidency of Columbia University was a political stopgap, a temporary removal from the center of activity. He was reluctant and uneasy. He recognized the significance of the contacts to be made, the new roles to be played, the expanded horizons. He wrote in his diary that he believed he could do more at Columbia "than anywhere else to further the cause to which I am devoted, the reawakening of intense interest in the basis of the American system." He would, while at Columbia, publicly reject political affiliations. He did not believe it appropriate to proclaim a loyalty to a particular party—since "we have here men and women of all parties" and to participate in one "would certainly antagonize some." By 1950, Eisenhower had become restive and impatient. He wrote in his diary on New Year's Day 1950, "Columbia is the place I THINK I can do the most good for all—even if that most is a rather pitiful amount."[25]

Isolated at Columbia while the Cold War escalated, Eisenhower's needs began to change. With his political and financial support base largely solidified, it was necessary to have his position clearly understood—publicly and widely disseminated. As president of Columbia University, Eisenhower considered the creation of the American Assembly to be his most substantial contribution. It was also his most significant public forum. On 29 September 1950, Eisenhower wrote to Bermingham that the most important issues before United States citizens were foreign relations, taxation, "proper medical care for the entire population," school aid, unemployment insurance, and old-age pensions. Since they were "discussed only by people seeking elective office," Eisenhower's conference plan was to assign a professional staff to research each of these areas for intense discussion with business, labor, professional, government, and media representatives who would then debate and analyze them in a suitably quiet country atmosphere. For Eisenhower, "informal small groups" meeting in "friendly cooperation" was "the real key to the whole project." When Averell Harriman donated the magnificent atmosphere of Arden House, in Harriman, New York, Eisenhower was delighted. The site featured comfortable accommodations, a fishing lake, a driving range, softball grounds, and abundant woodlands for contemplation and conversation.

The American Assembly was to become the agency through which Eisenhower communicated his developing political positions. In a memorandum sent to the supporters of the Assembly, Eisenhower systematically presented his conception of America's future. He wrote that when he returned from Europe in 1945, he had a "profound conviction that America was in danger" for two reasons: international communism, which menaced American values "from without," and a "creeping paralysis" that involved "indifference and ignorance," which threatened "the basic values of democracy . . . from within." Eisenhower wanted it understood that he was not resigned to the triumph of socialism in Britain, Australia, Western Europe, and the United States. He was committed to the "future of our democracy and individual freedom based upon a competitive enterprise." "The Columbia conference plan has been designed," he wrote, to address the concerns of American citizens who "sense that politicians are leading [us] down a primrose path whose end could be . . . a socialized form of economy, with resultant regimentation. . . ." International communism was not the only threat to America's future. Elements of the New Deal and the Fair Deal were equally threatening: "Bureaucratic controls, deficit spending, subsidies, and just plain hand-outs" might on occasion "be required," Eisenhower wrote. But they might also produce "a stagnated economy," the "commandeering of property, and finally, dictatorship."

In a fund-raising letter Eisenhower sent to his Texas friend Amon Carter, a letter to be shared with Sid Richardson, Eisenhower wrote of his fear that certain social and economic changes in the United States would destroy America's traditional values. Today, Eisenhower lamented, "too many essentially humanitarian" people were so "fuzz-minded" that they threatened America with "economic as well as political slavery." Eisenhower wrote that he had become president of Columbia University in large part to combat this trend in American society. When Bermingham told Eisenhower that Sewell Avery wanted nothing to do with the American Assembly, because Avery's experiences as a former trustee of the University of Chicago had left him with a "violent distaste for socialism in the colleges," Eisenhower replied that it was that very concern that had influenced him "to enter the educational world." He asked Bermingham to assure Avery that he had embarked on his presidency at Columbia with the vow to rid the university of any Communists he might encounter. Eisenhower wrote in specific detail about his activities in this regard: "So alert—and I might say, so allergic—was I to the possibility of finding Columbia honey-combed with socialistic teachings that I made it my first business to acquaint myself well with operations in Teacher's College, previously reported to me as practically a hotbed of this kind of indoctrination. . . ." Eisenhower was "happily able to disprove" many of the rumors about suspect faculty, and he introduced a program, funded by a $1.5 million foundation grant, to improve the teaching of citizenship training in America's secondary schools.

The American Assembly was to be in part a service center for the business community. Eisenhower was concerned about the businessman's limited horizons: "Most businessmen are so busy meeting payrolls and paying taxes that they have little chance for study and contemplation." The Assembly would enable them to deal in depth with those serious questions which "bother the businessman" and which "office-holders are bungling." For example:

> What rates of taxations are we able to support without mortally wounding our economy? . . . What is the effect of unlimited Federal authority to tax upon the independence of the several states and therefore finally, the freedom of the individual?

What about the crucial and "bewildering" issues of foreign policy —of "Berlin, Spain, Yugoslavia, Formosa, Korea, Japan, Germany, Atlantic Pact, and the rearmament of Europe?" Regarding "our military forces," with "their terrific cost, how do we find the proper dividing line between tragic unpreparedness . . . and unconscionable cost . . . ? What about outlawing Communism? Hunting out subversives? How do we correlate peace-time economic considerations with security requirements"—specifically relating to imports, tariffs, stockpiles? Eisenhower, in preparing for the future of the American Assembly, listed all the issues that would become the major themes of his public life, the focus of his presidential years.[26]

On the eve of his return to military service as commander of NATO forces, Eisenhower considered the future of the American Assembly linked to the future of America's assumption of "Command responsibilities for the defense of Western Europe." On 6 November 1950, he wrote Clifford Roberts that the "concept of the American Assembly will increase in importance according to the duration and intensity of the tensions under which we live." As he contemplated his return to uniform, Eisenhower hoped that the first Assembly would be devoted to America's "responsibilities in Western Europe." The years at SHAPE, years of intense international diplomacy dedicated to the creation of a European military and economic alliance to combat communism, were also years of total political immersion for Eisenhower. And his only official point of contact was the American Assembly.[27]

The great political reality was that Eisenhower while at SHAPE was running for President. It was a tense and thoroughly complicated time. Eisenhower was, above all, a man of specific principle. In uniform he was not, he would not be partisan. His primary concern was the future of the United States. And that future, he believed, depended entirely on creating a military and economic unity among all European nations not yet lost to U.S. interests. He was dedicated to the creation of an international alliance that involved the remilitarization and economic reconstruction of Germany. Implicit in that program was the restoration of former Nazi officials to positions of power. Eisenhower, who had refused to meet with Nazis in 1945, who had refused personally to accept the surrender of German forces in Tunisia in 1943, declaring, "I won't shake hands with a Nazi!" was now in charge of their return to power and authority.

International politics had changed dramatically between 1945 and 1950. And in some circles, Eisenhower was held largely responsible for some of those changes that favored the Soviet Union. Eisenhower's critics condemned his decisions to honor the diplomatic agreements made by Roosevelt, Churchill, and Stalin, condemned his wartime faith in Russian honor and military accord. He was criticized as soft on Russia and weak-spirited, if not weakminded. Eisenhower's denazification orders of May 1945 had been discarded within weeks of Germany's defeat. The economic reconstruction of Germany was immediately adopted as the central fea-

ture of Europe's defense against communism. By 1948, the year of
the Berlin blockade and the airlift, enthusiastic adherence to the
precepts of the Cold War was the only acceptable position for men
in public life. Eisenhower would have to overcome his reputation
as "soft" on Russia.

Eisenhower critics were quick to point to the first postwar
Eisenhower-Zhukov meeting in Berlin as the moment when all
went wrong with the joint occupation of Germany. It was at that
meeting, in June 1945, Robert Murphy would write later, that Eisenhower gave it all away, that Eisenhower allowed the Russians
to have "everything they wanted."[28] Eisenhower had agreed to acknowledge the Yalta accords in practice. He had failed to understand that the engineers of containment were dedicated to the
demise of those accords. Eisenhower had been out of step. It was a
temporary condition. After five years of political obscurity, years
of economic and social growth, his public exile at Columbia was
over. He accepted fully the implications of the European Recovery
Program (the Marshall Plan) and NATO, over which he would
now preside. Jarred by the revolution in China and the war in
Korea, United States interests mobilized vigorously. Once again,
Eisenhower was handed the reins of a major mission. He was
mandated to negotiate America's economic, political, and military presence in Europe's future. Russia's wartime sphere of interest was once again up for grabs. Everything was renegotiable.
Nothing was settled, Yalta and Potsdam notwithstanding. And Eisenhower would not repeat those errors committed out of his military respect and enthusiasm for the Grand Alliance.

The Grand Alliance had been dead for five years. The primary
enemy, the primary threat to the United States, to Western civilization, to world prosperity and harmony was again the Soviet
Union. That Russian diplomats were now jumping up and down
calling the creation of NATO abusive, belligerent, and warmon-
gering was of no concern to the former commander in chief of the
Grand Alliance. His primary concern was now to convince European leaders that America's policy served European interests. He
considered his task of the utmost significance—and believed he
had little time to fulfill it before communism spread throughout the
continent.

Eisenhower was pleased with his new assignment. He recognized that it was one of the most significant and delicate of his career. On 1 November 1950, he wrote to Swede Hazlett that Hazlett had "astonished" him by hoping Eisenhower would not be "talked into that Atlantic Pact job." In high anger, Eisenhower replied that he considered the creation of "Atlantic Union defensive forces the last remaining chance for the survival of Western civilization."[29] Eisenhower agreed with Henry Wriston, chairman of the Council on Foreign Relations, that without an effective allied force in Europe, "all the Russians needed to march to the Channel was shoe-leather."

Eisenhower worked closely with Henry Wriston in this period. Wriston monitored Eisenhower's reluctant attendance at the Association of American Universities and in 1948 he had appointed Eisenhower to chair a study group on Western Europe at the Council on Foreign Relations. In 1950, with Tracy Voorhees, former Undersecretary of the Army; James B. Conant, president of Harvard University; and several others, Wriston had founded a Committee on the Present Danger. Their first activity was to meet with George Marshall on 24 October to offer their services to build "public support of such stern measure as may be necessary" for the defense of Western Europe. Encouraged by Marshall, now Secretary of Defense, the Committee on the Present Danger held a press conference and issued its first public statement, calling for a significant military buildup in Europe. This statement coincided with Eisenhower's appointment to NATO and the twentieth meeting of Eisenhower's study group on the future of Western Europe, on 12 December.

During that meeting, a major policy statement, written largely by Eisenhower and signed by the members of the committee, to be sent to Truman, triggered an American remilitarization campaign. According to Wriston, the letter, which represented the fullest statement of Eisenhower's international philosophy as it had evolved since 1945, was an accident of history. Wriston had chanced to notice Eisenhower's somber expression as he climbed the stairs to the meeting, and remarked: "I don't think you're very happy." Eisenhower's famous temper flashed: "What the hell do you know about it?" Eisenhower's fury related to his new assignment. He was to lead a phantom international army that was not yet established and might never emerge. Not only was the United

States' commitment in troops and equipment neither specific nor guaranteed, but vigorous congressional opposition to universal military service and training, which Eisenhower had recently toured the United States to popularize, threatened to obliterate his vision of a militarily secure future. Moreover, not one European country had yet committed itself to a single issue relating to this entirely hypothetical force. NATO was, in sum, an American dream. NATO was created, financed, and promoted by the United States and presented for participation to a reluctant and begrudging Europe. On 28 October, Eisenhower had written in his personal diary that there was "one major obstacle" to making his "assignment effective and public." In Europe, the Council of Defense Ministers was awash in controversy. France objected to German rearmament, and all other decisions seemed to be suspended. Eisenhower wrote that he appreciated and sympathized with France but considered "vigorous" German participation essential. He believed that France's responsibility was to "get busy on the job of educating public opinion in France to accept" German rearmament. Eisenhower wanted such a commitment from France before he would agree to assume "responsibility for command." Later, Eisenhower would pen an addendum to this entry. On 1 February 1951, he added that Britain's Air Chief of Staff "came to my office . . . and said this idea belonged to American Chiefs of Staff only; that the British were confronted with a package which they did NOT like!" With only the United States in favor of German rearmament, it did not occur until 1955.

But Eisenhower had never really paused to wait for a European commitment. By December 1950, he sought only a United States troop commitment to meet what he referred to as "a world crisis." As he addressed the members of his committee at the Council on Foreign Relations, he became more and more intense. To promise to defend Europe "without troops would be in the nature of a bluff." He considered the situation preposterous and dangerous. "We were," he said, "dangling by a thread over the edge of the cliff." The members of the Council agreed with Eisenhower, made a few changes in the draft of the letter he wrote to Truman, and signed the document that called for the return of United States troops to Europe. Eisenhower wanted to "mobilize up to twenty divisions" but agreed to leave the number of divisions vague. Allen

Dulles agreed to get the letter to Truman by breakfast the next morning, through Averell Harriman, then special assistant to the President. During the cocktail hour, Eisenhower went off by himself to a corner to write the following document, and Allen Dulles went off to call Harriman to set up the meeting with Truman. All present (except Eisenhower)—Hamilton Fish Armstrong, Percy W. Bidwell, William Diebold, Jr., Allen Dulles, Edward Mead Earle, George Franklin, Jr., Walter Mallory, Stacy May, Arthur S. Nevins, Philip D. Reed, Lindsay Rogers, Henry M. Wriston—signed the letter.

A disunited free world is certain to fall, piecemeal, under the tyrannical power of Soviet imperialism.

There is today in the nations comprising the North Atlantic Union such pitifully inadequate military force that it is fair to assume that only our possession of atomic weapons and a Russian economic and political unreadiness to risk the consequences of a war of attrition against the U.S. have maintained an uneasy peace.

The only way in which our peaceful intent and moral purposes will be respected by the Soviets is the rapid production by us, and by our friends, of powerful military forces. To this effort the only limit should be national solvency, and we should recognize its price as sacrifice by all in the whole free world to include definite recessions in our standards of living through payment of taxes, longer work hours and military service as an obligation of citizenship. . . .

The following sentence was added to the final version sent to Truman:

With this must go a satisfactory understanding among the North Atlantic Pact countries and with the authorities in West Germany for the use of West German military potential in the common defense of Western Europe. . . .[30]

Eisenhower left for a fact-finding tour of the twelve capitals under his European command on 6 January 1951. This initial meeting with the signers of the North Atlantic Pact, to assess "the sincerity of their resolve," convinced Eisenhower that there was serious support for the "collective defense of Western Europe against possible Communist aggression." On 2 February, he reported to an informal joint session of Congress and testified before the Foreign Affairs Committee and the Armed Services Committee. In 1968,

Wriston remembered that because of Eisenhower's persuasive performance, "Eisenhower had troops to command as quickly as they could be sent after he took over the command of NATO."[31] But Wriston apparently forgot the tensions of a bitterly divided Congress, the acrimonious battles that raged within the United States between Eisenhower and his supporters on the one hand and the isolationists—Senator Robert Taft and his supporters—on the other.

Congressional opposition to Eisenhower's call for troops was well organized and bipartisan. Taft was outraged by Truman's dismissal of constitutional precept. The senator resented Truman's usurpation of congressional authority when he failed to consult Congress before he dispatched U.S. troops to Korea. Taft argued that if Truman's unconstitutional precedent were allowed to go unchallenged, a President might in the future order troops to Indochina or Tibet "or anywhere else in the world, without the slightest voice of Congress in the matter."[32] Eisenhower dismissed Taft's objections as self-serving artifice. After a lengthy meeting with the senator, Eisenhower's "disappointment was acute." He wrote that he resented those who played politics with vital issues and believed that Taft's primary purpose was to cut Truman "or the Presidency down to size."[33]

Whether partisan politics, constitutional interpretation, or basic differences between isolationism and interventionism were involved, Congress withheld America's troop deployment to NATO for months. Not until April, during the height of the crisis over Truman's removal of MacArthur from Korea, did the Senate agree to the promised four divisions. Even then, the House failed to concur. Finally, Truman sent troops to Europe without congressional authority.

Eisenhower and his associates were appalled by the behavior of the "isolationist" members of their own party. They feared that Taft and MacArthur might "create a paralysis of government" that jeopardized Eisenhower's efforts "to unify the coalition." All of Eisenhower's friends were "bitter" that Republican politicians used "such an important question as our European policy as a means of repudiating Truman." They were also dismayed that a considerable group of their own business and political associates questioned the significance, the necessity, the wisdom of Eisenhower's mission and all it represented: economic aid to, political involvement in, and military support for Europe.[34]

But Eisenhower, a committed internationalist, was convinced of the wisdom of his position. Isolationists, he insisted, failed to understand the economic base of American prosperity. The demands of America's "national security" required international cooperation. He also rejected the notions of such interventionists as MacArthur, who sought to "carry the world" alone. He insisted that "enlightened self-interest" demanded international cooperation.

> I sincerely wish that I knew of some way we could possibly sustain our economy, our prosperity, and indeed our very existence in a world where all other countries that are important to us have fallen, one by one, under Soviet domination. I wish I could believe that we could . . . secure adequate supplies of manganese, uranium, and a number of vital materials without the need for assisting in the defense of countries other than our own. I wish I knew how to ignore the menace that would arise for us if the western European industrial complex and its enormous pool of skilled labor would fall under the domination of a dictatorial government. . . .[35]

Eisenhower had accepted Truman's offer of renewed military leadership at a politically perilous time. His years of most recognized activity had been under Democratic auspices, by Democratic appointment. Eisenhower's tasks had been to fulfill the mandates of the bipartisan foreign policy established by Roosevelt and Truman. They were policies with which he largely agreed. Yet Eisenhower was not a Democrat. The Republican Party, on the other hand, was dominated by Robert Taft, Herbert Hoover, Charles Halleck, John Bricker. They opposed continued military intervention in European affairs. They rejected the need to invest unlimited billions of dollars for Europe's military defense and economic reconstruction. And they opposed unlimited presidential control over foreign policy. While they shared Eisenhower's dread of Communist expansion, they preferred to oppose the spread of socialistic tendencies within the United States, and in that area they considered America's primary center of resource supply—the Pacific and the Far East.

Eisenhower wrote a long letter to Bermingham—for distribution at Bermingham's discretion—that carefully explained his position. He wanted it fully understood that his work in Europe implied no "approval of governmental policies in other parts of the world" or at home. "You are quite well aware," he assured Bermingham, "of the extreme degree in which I differ with some of our governmental foreign and domestic policies. . . ." He was not a Trumanite. He was not a progressive internationalist. He would not "trust America's welfare to an international Congress of any kind." He approached international questions "from only one angle," from a position "of America First." America's role as "the chief of a capitalistic economy" renders America the "chief target" of communism. That was the only reason he returned to Europe. He agreed with all those who understood that "bankruptcy for us would be a tremendous, if not a decisive victory for the Kremlin. One of the things communism tries to prove . . . is that our system is weak, inefficient, and unfair. I violently disagree with any plan or program that ignores this basic principle. . . ." Eisenhower wanted it clearly understood: He was a Republican. To William Robinson he was even more specific. There were "far greater areas of intellectual agreement" between Eisenhower and Herbert Hoover than there were between Eisenhower "and so-called New-Dealers." There was, in fact, only one disagreement between Eisenhower and Hoover, Hoover's contention that the United States need not embroil itself militarily all over the planet, that the United States might become a "military Gibraltar," an independent island of strength. Eisenhower dismissed as absurd the idea that the U.S. "could dwell peacefully and happily no matter what happened to the rest of the world." But he resented partisan efforts to classify Hoover and himself "as very great intellectual antagonists," when they disagreed only "on this one issue."[36]

As the United States approached 1952, that issue was in fact the crucial one. It was the subject of "the Great Debate." The entire future of the United States' role in the world depended on decisions made around differences well represented by Eisenhower and Hoover: Should the United States, alone or with allies, assume the burdens of empire? Could the United States afford the economic and social costs of empire? All nineteenth-century imperial structures were beginning to fall. All over Asia and the Middle East, British and French colonial possessions were collapsing. Would the United States pick them up, piece by piece? Were endless American lives and infinite American dollars to be invested around the globe? Or was the United States to let it all go?

Eisenhower had been tucked away on the Columbia campus while many of the features of the Great Debate had been designed by Truman, Marshall, and Dean Acheson. In partisan America's terms, it was a Democrat's design. Now Truman restored Eisenhower to a position of international influence and prestige, to the center of activities Eisenhower believed in. Partisan subtleties notwithstanding, Eisenhower did in fact represent Truman's foreign policy as commander of NATO forces. Assigned to Supreme Headquarters Allied Powers Europe (SHAPE), Eisenhower took a leave of absence from Columbia University and directly challenged isolationist opposition to Truman's foreign policy.

Isolationists during World War II were part of a broad coalition of "America-firsters" that ranged across the partisan spectrum from Democrats like Joseph Kennedy to socialists like Norman Thomas and independent militant pacifists like the former publisher of *The Nation,* Oswald Garrison Villard. But Republicans like Taft and Hoover dominated. Members of "The America First Committee," World War II isolationists, were insufficiently impressed with Nazi and Fascist dangers to risk U.S. lives or spend American money in any European coalition. They tended to regard Britain as the primary threat to America's international economic interests. Their hatred of communism precluded an alliance with the Soviet Union. Taft, for example, considered Communist ideology "far more dangerous to the United States" than fascism. And they were vaguely unconcerned about the future of countries already on the decline. After the war, the "isolationists" bitterly attacked the internationalists, whom they called "liberal interventionists," at every opportunity.[37]

In the beginning, Taft and Hoover and the "isolationists" argued that the United States could not afford the staggering costs of the Truman Doctrine, the Marshall Plan, and the Military Assistance Program (MAP). With the revolution in China and the war in Korea, their emphasis changed. The "isolationists" became individualistic interventionists. Taft, for example, preferred an expanded Monroe Doctrine whereby the United States would unilaterally lead the anti-Communist movement. He deplored entangling alliances. Taft and his colleagues called for unlimited use of air superiority and atomic bombs to smash communism. By 1951, "isolationist" policy meant splendid isolation for U.S. decisions and activities wherever the Communist menace arose. "Isolationists" sought freedom from the traps, the costs, and the haggling associated with a complicated alliance system that involved impoverished, reluctant, and unstable nations.

In 1949, "the isolationists" challenged the wisdom of the Organization of European Economic Cooperation and its administrative office, the Economic Cooperation Administration (ECA), erected to fulfill the goal of the Marshall Plan to finance the economic recovery of Europe. Paul Hoffman, the president of Studebaker-Packard Corporation and a director of Time, Inc., was named director of ECA. Later chairman of the Advisory Committee of Citizens for Eisenhower, Hoffman celebrated the ECA as the "first example . . . of the deliberate integration of economic resources among free peoples." Convinced that "war is the great despoiler of all resources" and that "prosperity is a powerful antidote for communism," Hoffman was an early designer of the international economic recovery program. In 1942, he became the first chairman of the Committee for Economic Development (CED), an independent research group of businessmen, educators, and economists that planned for the creation of a "high-production postwar" economy. At the first session of ECA, Hoffman explained its primary objectives: "To keep our America strong and prosperous, to help the free nations of western Europe regain their strength and prosperity, and to bind the free, strong, prosperous nations of the Western World together into a union so firm that no aggressor will dare to march against it." The "isolationists" disagreed. Taft, for example, thought that Stalin, a man of "oriental cunning," might himself promote the ECA to "bankrupt" the United States. Taft argued that the aggressive economic policies promoted by the ECA would give the Soviet Union a "basis for the charge that we are trying to dominate the countries of Western Europe."[38]

"Isolationists" also opposed the Atlantic Pact, which created the North Atlantic Treaty Organization (NATO), comprising twelve nations: Belgium, Canada, Denmark, France, Great Britain, Iceland, Italy, Luxembourg, the Netherlands, Norway, Portugal, and the United States (subsequently Greece, Turkey, and the Federal

Republic of Germany were included). NATO was to be the military arm of a new union for prosperity and peace. A reluctant, war-weary, impoverished Europe relied completely on the United States to finance the operation.

NATO, a "binding alliance" whereby an attack on one of the signatories was considered an attack on all, was approved by the U. S. Senate on 21 July 1949, by a vote of eighty-two to thirteen. Taft was among the thirteen who voted against it. He also opposed Truman's 27 July request for $1.5 billion for the Mutual Defense Assistance Program (MAP), which was to include the NATO nations as well as Greece, Turkey, Iran, the Philippines, and South Korea.

These sweeping and costly programs involved abundant weapons and sufficient resources to create, supply, and fortify an international "will to resist" subversion, revolution, and invasion. Assistant Secretary of State Ernest A. Gross was very clear about the nature of MAP, which was to become of ever greater significance especially during the Eisenhower presidency. MAP was to be the key to a long-range strategy "under development" in 1949 to create the capacity for self-defense against "fifth columnists." According to Gross, all of Europe and notably the French, Belgian, and Dutch "people felt completely naked against the possibility of an assault across the border, or of Communist-inspired rioting, political strikes, and all the rest. . . ." It was, he asserted, their fears of social revolution "at home" that inspired General Marshall to develop "this military assistance program."

The fiscal burden for Europe's internal political stability was to be undertaken by the United States. Isolationists occasionally cited Lenin's "prediction" that the United States would "spend itself into destruction." Taft considered Truman's foreign policy aggressive and dangerous, "not a peace program" at all, but "a war program." Senator Bourke Hickenlooper, of Iowa, emphasized Europe's apparent reluctance to become party to the United States' vast plans. It was in 1949 not at all clear that the divided leaders of Europe shared America's enthusiasm for remilitarization and renewed alliances. Hickenlooper feared that it was "the definite plan to try to force this stuff on European countries. There have been people running around with drawing boards and models and contract forms, saying, 'Now we can put all this stuff in Europe.' We are

trying to force this stuff on them." It was, according to Henry
Cabot Lodge, Hickenlooper's thesis that "if we're not careful
they won't take our money."[39]

But events moved swiftly between 1949 and 1950. China was
"lost" to the Communists. Russia ended America's atomic bomb
monopoly. North Korea "invaded" South Korea. Former "isolationists," now foursquare behind Joseph McCarthy, blamed it all
on Truman, Marshall, and Acheson and all those State Department strategists who somehow "lost" China, Korea, and the secret
of the bomb. Taft said that the "greatest Kremlin asset in our history has been the pro-Communist group in the State Department
who promoted at every opportunity the Communist cause in
China." McCarthy was more crude: The Truman administration, a
bastion of "Communists and queers," consisted of "egg-sucking
phony liberals" who "sold China into atheistic slavery."[40]

Such hyperbole was pure opportunism. No respected statesman
in 1949, neither Democrat nor Republican, considered China's
Nationalists defensible. In November 1949, William E. Robinson
sent Eisenhower a *Herald Tribune* column by A. T. Steele regarding the situation in Asia and assuring Eisenhower that Steele "has
the most seasoned and informed mind on this subject." Steele
wrote that Communists controlled two areas of Asia: China and
North Korea. There ". . . we may obstruct and irritate, but nothing short of war will get the Communists out. South Korea would
go under overnight were the props of American policy removed."
In Burma and Indochina, "the problem is dangerous and immediate. In the rest of Asia," Steele explained, communism might yet
be blocked "if energetic measures" were "taken promptly." China
was "lost in the military sense." A devastating idea; and Steele was
very specific:

> The fact is that the Nationalist regime has lost almost completely
> the support and confidence of the Chinese people. On the mainland
> further military help would be useless unless a new force arises capa-
> ble of consolidating anti-Communist feeling. . . . No such force is
> in sight.

> Only on the island of Formosa could American assistance be of pos-
> sible benefit, and even there the uncertainties are great, the govern-
> ment weak and unpopular.

Steele did not consider China irretrievably lost, however. He pointed out that the Chinese Communists "cannot convert China into a great power . . . unless they are able to obtain large quantities of capital goods and essential raw materials from the capitalistic West and especially from the United States. Thus the United States has not lost its power to influence events in China. We retain at least one powerful weapon—the economic one." Steele's recommendation for an economic boycott or blockade was accompanied by his suggestion to refuse or "delay" recognition of the new government. To recognize communism in China would "discourage and demoralize anti-Communist forces . . . and increase Communist prestige at home and abroad." There was, however, Steele observed, another point of view. Some argued that recognition would better serve to protect American investments and stimulate new trade in China. Also, a policy of nonrecognition threatened to expose cracks in the Anglo-American alliance, since Britian and India seemed "eager to establish diplomatic relations" with China. Steele's column substantiated the Truman administration's policy in China. Having spent hundreds of millions of dollars to bolster Chiang Kai-shek's regime in 1948 ($275 million in economic aid, $125 million in military aid), Dean Acheson presented a State Department white paper on 5 August 1949 announcing that the United States would not risk "full-scale intervention in behalf of a Government which has lost the confidence of its own troops and its own people." On 12 January 1950, Acheson announced that both Taiwan and South Korea, where Syngman Rhee had lost the only popular election in that country's history, were outside America's defense perimeter. Everything changed within the year.[41]

The war in Korea revised America's foreign policy and determined our future course toward communism in Europe as well as in Asia. Indeed, Eisenhower's acceptance of the NATO command coincided with China's entry into North Korea, on 26 October, which resulted in MacArthur's retreat from the Yalu. It was the start of an international game of dominoes that was to last for decades. Korea clarified a point kept hazy between 1945 and 1950: To contain communism would require the investment of hundreds of thousands of American troops as well as billions of American dollars. On 24 June, North Korean troops crossed the thirty-eighth parallel. On 27 June 1950, Truman ordered air, ground, and naval forces to Korea.

Korea was not high on the United States or Soviet agenda at Yalta or Potsdam. Bordered by Manchuria, Vladivostok, and the Sea of Japan, Korea was, however, a long-established area of contention between China, Russia, and Japan. Throughout the twentieth century, Korea had been involved in United States commercial negotiations in the area. It was considered basic to America's Open Door policy. In February 1904, Japan launched a surprise attack on the Russian fleet at Port Arthur and declared war. Russia had rejected Japan's demands for "a free hand" in Korea and Manchuria. The Russo-Japanese War was fought exclusively on Chinese soil, and President Theodore Roosevelt feared the loss of America's interests throughout Asia. The future of America's business depended on a balance of power in the area.

In September 1905, Japan and Russia signed the Treaty of Portsmouth, negotiated in New Hampshire by Theodore Roosevelt. Japan agreed to give up its demand for a large monetary indemnity. Russia agreed to withdraw from Korea, agreed to give half of the island of Sakhalin to Japan, and surrendered all special interests in southern Manchuria. Roosevelt received a Nobel Peace Prize for his tactful diplomacy. Although much was made about the fact that an Asian nation had defeated a European nation for the first time, Japan's victory did nothing to diminish the course of empire. Japan joined the imperial ranks and dominated Korea until 1945.

Throughout World War II, Korean nationalists fought vigorously against the Japanese. As in Europe, the anti-Fascist resistance in Korea was largely dominated by Communists. By 1945, a coalition of nationalists claimed control of an independent Korea. The Korean People's Republic was dominated by Communists in Seoul and P'yong-yang but, according to Stephen Pelz, "included a number of prominent non-communists in high positions—the Christian leader Cho Man-sik, the conservative Kim Koo, and most important Syngman Rhee." Several Communist factions were also represented: the Soviet Koreans, who had lived and trained in Siberia, many of them since 1917; a pro-Soviet group of anti-

Japanese guerrillas led by Kim Il-sung; a Yenan group of Chinese-trained nationalists; and a faction of independent Korean Communists.

At Yalta, Roosevelt and Stalin had agreed to a trusteeship for Korea. As United States and Soviet troops entered to liberate the country from Japan, a frantic meeting was held at the Pentagon to divide Korea. Despite protests that Korea was "a social and economic unit," and there was "no place to divide it," a line was found. According to Dean Acheson, Dean Rusk, recently returned from the Chinese Theater, ". . . found an administrative dividing line along the 38th Parallel." With Soviet troops deep within southern Korea, Stalin agreed to the demarcation and the Red Army withdrew from Seoul and Inchon. Joseph Grew predicted, however, that the "economic and political situation in Korea would be conducive" to a popular Communist movement once thirty-five years of ruthless Japanese occupation was terminated.

But the United States opposed an independent and revolutionary Korea. Despite the coalition nature of the Korean People's Republic, United States officials denounced it, determined that "communists advocate the seizure *now* of Japanese property and may be a threat to law and order," and assigned Japanese officials and their Korean collaborators to police the country. H. M. Benninghoff, the State Department's political adviser in Korea, reported that the only encouraging factor of significance "in the political situation is the presence in Seoul of several hundred conservatives among the older and better educated Koreans. Although many of them have served with the Japanese, that stigma ought eventually to disappear." By February 1946, there were separate governments in the North, where the Soviets recognized the Korean People's Republic, and in the South, which was increasingly dominated by former Japanese collaborators and frank reactionaries supported by the United States.

From that time to this, the tortuous history of Korea has been stalemated in violence. While the debate over who started the Korean War continues, and whether or not the United States used biological warfare remains a subject of contention, the United Nations "police action" in Korea resulted in an estimated two million Koreans, North and South, killed during a war that served, above all, to galvanize United States public opinion on behalf of military intervention against communism.

After the armistice in 1952, John Foster Dulles announced: "All free nations, large or small, are safer today because the ideal of collective security has been implemented." Eisenhower did not particularly agree with Dulles' estimation. "It is almost hopeless," Eisenhower wrote in his diary, "to write about the Korea-Rhee situation. Both the Communists and the South Korean Government have raised so many difficulties . . . that it raises in my mind a serious question as to whether or not the United Nations will ever again go into an area to protect the inhabitants against Communist attack. It has been a long and bitter experience, and I am certain in my own mind that except for the fact that evacuation of South Korea would badly expose Japan, the majority of the United Nations now fighting there would have long since attempted to pull out. . . . Of course the fact remains that the probable enemy is the Communists, but Rhee has been such an unsatisfactory ally that it is difficult indeed to avoid excoriating him in the strongest of terms."[42]

Eisenhower's misgivings were recorded in his diary in July 1953. But in 1950 United States foreign policy required the war in Korea. "Communist aggression" in Korea assured the Cold War's future. The Great Debate between Republican isolationists and liberal internationalists ended with a military flourish. The United States was from that moment on committed to a crusade against "communism" no matter how popular and broad-based or nationalist and democratic the independence movement might be, and no matter how repressive, cruel, or generally unsatisfactory the rightwing ally might be. The Korean War committed the United States to a policy of military intervention with or without United Nations support, with or without such regional defense formations as NATO.

Within the context of the war in Korea, a war that seemed to threaten American "interests" throughout Asia, the Middle East, and Europe, Truman asked for six divisions of American troops for NATO and appointed Eisenhower commander. At SHAPE, Eisenhower's tasks were monumental: to persuade Europe that the return of American troops represented a commitment to the economic restoration and peaceful stability of Europe and was not a neocolonial ploy; and to convince the Western allies that their interests lay in the economic restoration and remilitarization of Germany. NATO's future depended on a military alliance with West Germany that was to be costly and dominated by the United States. Eisenhower was to convince impoverished nations not yet dug out from under the rubble of years and years of bombings, such as England and the Netherlands, and such bitter conquered nations as France, that despite their own burdens, Germany was the "key" to their safety and future prosperity—and they should contribute their own resources to the remilitarization of an alliance in which West Germany was designated the pivotal industrial and military area. Five years after V-E Day, Eisenhower was called upon to use his celebrated diplomatic virtues to attempt the fantastic. Britain's Foreign Minister, Ernest Bevin, was appalled. France's Robert Schuman refused even to discuss John J. McCloy's proposal that West Germany provide ten divisions for NATO. West German opinion, moreover, was hopelessly divided on the issue of remilitarization. There was in fact little support in Europe for Eisenhower's mission. And in the United States, isolationist opposition was vigorous.

Initially, the "isolationists" objected to both the war in Korea and Truman's call for troops to Europe. Joseph Kennedy addressed a stunning protest to the Law School Forum of the University of Virginia on 12 December 1950. He called for U.S. withdrawal from "the freezing hills of Korea" and the scarred "plains of West Germany." "What business is it of ours," he asked, "to support the French colonial policy in Indochina or to achieve Mr. Syngman Rhee's concepts of democracy in Korea?" Europe was too weak to resist communism. Germany was entirely reluctant to rearm. Communism was unsupportable and would die, Joseph Kennedy concluded, under the weight of its own overextended burdens. Hoover also called for total troop withdrawal from Korea. A land war against communism, he argued, would be a "graveyard" for "millions" of Americans. Troop commitments would destroy "this Gibraltar of Western Civilization." Hoover adamantly opposed assigning U.S. troops to NATO. Europe disagreed about German rearmament, refused to admit Spain to NATO, and harbored "well-organized Communist parties." Not "another man or another dollar" should be sent to Europe, Hoover insisted, until Europeans committed themselves and their own resources in sufficient amount to dam "the Red flood."[43]

By 1951, however, the "isolationists" rallied behind General Douglas MacArthur. By some mystical logic understood exclusively by isolationists, Taft, Hoover, and even Joseph Kennedy supported MacArthur's call to widen the war in Korea, to initiate a "diversionary" or preventive war against China, to bomb the strategic villages and factory centers of China, and to overrun North Korea. On 9 February 1951, Hoover modified his earlier position on NATO and called for vast quantities of munitions, full air and sea support, and sufficient troop deployment anywhere as needed. Taft called for "atom bombs" wherever they "might be decisive" and full-scale political warfare. His emphasis on "aggressive propaganda, infiltration," and all manner of political warfare represented a significant change in Taft's vision. The United States should "use the same methods which communism has adopted," he explained, "or be swept away." Although Taft believed that the rearmament of West Germany would needlessly provoke Russia, he endorsed Truman's demand for four U.S. divisions to Europe in February 1951. When, on 10 April 1951, Truman removed MacArthur, the "isolationists" went berserk. Herbert Hoover, who had once considered MacArthur an arrogant prig, now called him the "reincarnation of St. Paul." It was election time in America, and the isolationists had supported MacArthur before, both in 1944 and 1948—despite the fact that he represented interventionism, not isolationism.[44]

Republican "isolationist" support for MacArthur unnerved Eisenhower's colleagues. On 13 April, General Lucius Clay telephoned Eisenhower in Paris to express his deep concern and followed his transatlantic call with a letter warning Eisenhower not to be maneuvered into commenting on MacAruthur:

> This we know. The Taft forces are definitely aligned with MacArthur who, because of his age, no longer seeks office but is determined to obtain vindication. Their OFFICIAL strategy (this is not hearsay) is to maneuver you into taking a position on the MacArthur issue, thus aligning you with the President and indirectly with his party and its inept conduct of government. . . .

Although Eisenhower had not yet committed himself in any direct
way to the 1952 campaign, Clay wanted it understood that "conditions at home are so bad, the public so confused," that Eisenhower's future political credibility depended on remaining "aloof"
from the MacArthur crisis. Clay concluded:

> We cannot let the true isolationists gain control of government if we
> are to endure as a free people over the years. This may depend on
> you and, whether you like it or not, you must be prepared to meet
> that challenge. There could be no choice.

Eisenhower promised to "maintain silence in every language
known to man." In the face of the most blatant contradictions between military adventurism and continued calls for isolation, Eisenhower remained silent, unobtrusive, diplomatic. Throughout
this period of intense partisan effort, Eisenhower's chief concern
was European unity. He wrote to Clay that Europe was "torn to
pieces by violent differences of opinion, and by ancient fears, prejudices, and superstitions."

Since it seemed to Eisenhower impossible for the United States
to develop "any reasonable alternative" to NATO, he was committed "to plugging away . . . until we are assured that collective security for the free world is an accomplished fact."[45]

MacArthur's newfound popularity upset Eisenhower's supporters. Clifford Roberts, who wrote Eisenhower to reinforce
Clay's advice, noted that Truman "succeeded in making a popular
hero out of MacArthur—something that the General was never
able to do for himself." MacArthur had become "the Standard
Bearer" of those who opposed the United States' Far Eastern policy
"beginning with Yalta." He was now "the leader" of all who
disliked: "(1) Truman or Acheson, (2) Marshall's report on
China and (3) the British Socialist policy re Chinese Communists." In the political storm generated by MacArthur's statements
to Congress, "Bradley's speech yesterday was lost in the gale." And
the gale continued to blow treacherously in Eisenhower's direction.
William Robinson wrote that the *Herald Tribune*'s report of Mac-
Arthur's popularity was, if anything, understated. MacArthur had
simply "swept the country off its feet." All Truman-Acheson
policies were under attack. And Eisenhower, at SHAPE, repre-

sented one of the basic structures of that policy. According to Robinson, MacArthur had reduced Truman and Acheson in "status and influence to about the lowest point ever reached by men in that high office. . . . This adds up to the fact that the public will be mistrustful of any position Truman and Acheson take, however right and sound it may be. This is an unfortunate and unfair liability for both their Asian and European policies." Robinson therefore urged Eisenhower to say nothing, to do nothing that would in any way involve him in the fray.[46]

Eisenhower's supporters worked vigorously to turn the MacArthur affair to Eisenhower's advantage. If there was to be a public schism between Republican generals and Democratic generals, between the forces of Taft and the forces of Truman, Eisenhower would remain above party; he would seem to transcend party.[47]

It was a political quagmire for Eisenhower. He was an active though entirely unacknowledged candidate. His advisers, who were efficiently campaigning on his behalf, warned him to keep silent on MacArthur but to come out as a Republican. He could hardly do both while the bitter, divisive MacArthur hearings were underway. In May, Clay presented the complexities of the problem. The suggestion "that no comment of any kind whatsoever be made on the MacArthur fracas is repeated, underscored, and re-emphasized."

> The banner headlines given to General Marshall's testimony that General MacArthur's program would handicap General Eisenhower in Europe was elicited and inspired by those who wish to create an embroilment. This should be avoided at all costs by reason of total concentration on the job at hand.

On the other hand, Clay began more and more earnestly to push Eisenhower into making a public political commitment. He believed that although Taft was "fading . . . because of the inconsistency and stupidity of his scatter-brained, weather vane, foreign affairs statements and the fact that he has tied his star securely to General MacArthur," he remained "the only effective, active candidate with organization contacts and delegates." In American convention politics, party delegates counted above all. May 1951 was the time of intense delegate-gathering, and there was, Clay warned Eisenhower, "a natural fear . . . of being left at the post" with no candidate at all, unless Eisenhower acknowledged his intentions.[48]

Eisenhower's ability to say nothing about General Douglas Mac-Arthur represented a Herculean political effort. The relationship between the two had always been strained. Although Eisenhower had never publicly criticized MacArthur, there was little warmth or mutual regard in their relationship. Eisenhower was MacArthur's aide when he ordered tear gas, bayonets, and tanks to advance against the Bonus Marchers, the World War I veterans who had built an encampment at Anacostia Flats, in Washington, DC, to petition for the release of their promised pensions during the Depression. On 28 July 1932, the Army burned down the encampment and routed the veterans and their families. MacArthur claimed they were mostly Communists anyway. Eisenhower had disapproved. But his advice had been contemptuously dismissed. From 1935 to 1940, Eisenhower was MacArthur's aide in the Philippines, where Eisenhower achieved a reputation for international diplomacy and personal tact. Geographically locked in place, the two men never became friendly. During World War II, Eisenhower considered MacArthur "as big a baby as ever," a yelping uncertainty who "likes his boot lickers." Once asked if he knew MacArthur, Eisenhower replied: "I studied dramatics under him for five years in Washington and four in the Philippines." MacArthur was heard to label Eisenhower "the best clerk who ever served under me." When MacArthur was asked what he thought about Eisenhower's presidential possibility in 1948, he snorted that Ike was too gutless "to tackle the job." In June 1951, several of Eisenhower's advisers talked to MacArthur to assess his ambitions and opinions generally. Clay reported that MacArthur was still "what you and I have always thought, which makes him most vindictive."[49]

As political tensions mounted, international tensions escalated. In the spring of 1951, Iran and Bolivia elected "Communist-backed" candidates. Cliff Roberts wrote to Eisenhower, "Even with an ulcer this is going to be an interesting world!" Ending months of self-imposed silence, Eisenhower wrote a long, analytic assessment of the entire situation to his friend Swede Hazlett. Regarding NATO, there were, after six months, "encouraging developments." A "tremendous increase in morale, courage, and determination" was evident throughout Europe. This, wrote Eisenhower, was fundamental: "Morale cannot be imported." And the success of NATO would depend not only on U.S. leadership but on the depth of Europe's commitment to it. For Eisenhower, that was basic:

> If the free world cannot provide for its "collective" security, the alternative for every one of these nations, including our own, is an eventual fate that is worse than any kind of expense or effort we can now imagine.

> Consequently, American leadership must be exerted every minute of the day, every day, to make sure that we are securing from these combined countries their maximum of accomplishment. Where any nation fails, . . . our leadership has been partially ineffective. . . .

> [But] Europe must, as a whole, provide in the long run for its own defense. The U.S. can move in and, by its psychological, intellectual, and material leadership, help to produce arms, units, and the confidence that will allow Europe to solve its problem. In the long run, it is not possible—and most certainly not desirable—that Europe should be an occupied territory defended by legions brought in from abroad, somewhat in the fashion that Rome's territories vainly sought security many hundred years ago. . . .

Eisenhower was also expansive regarding Iran. Swede Hazlett had written that he joined the "Get Acheson" crowd over the "bungling" in a country of such "strategic position regarding oil and control of the Middle East." "The democratic world can ill afford to lose Iran," Hazlett wrote. And, "with this emotional psychopathic, nationalist Mossadegh . . . it looks like we're going to." Eisenhower agreed that the situation was "tragic." He wrote Hazlett that many visitors to his office attached "as much blame to Western stupidity as to Iranian fanaticism and Communist intrigue." But Eisenhower was less concerned about apportioning blame than he was with finding "some scheme or plan that will permit that oil to keep flowing to the westward. We cannot ignore the tremendous importance of 675,000 barrels of oil a day." Eisenhower assured Hazlett that the situation was not yet as bad as it was for the United States in China, "but sometimes I think it stands today at the same place that China did only a very few years ago. Now we have completely lost [China]—no matter how we explain it, . . . we FAILED." Eisenhower deeply hoped that "this calamity" would not be repeated in Iran.

Regarding China, Eisenhower was puzzled by Hazlett's bellicosity. He wrote that General Albert C. Wedemeyer's testimony "bewildered" him. He was unsure what Hazlett meant by "punishing the aggressor." Eisenhower explained his position to Hazlett carefully: "Unless you can get at Mao and the small group of advisers he has right around him, I do not believe we would be punishing the aggressor merely by bombing Canton, Shanghai, or any other place where we would certainly be killing a number of our friends along with the people who are true followers of the Communists."

As for politics, Eisenhower was deeply involved. For the first time, Eisenhower made it clear to a friend beyond his inner circle of advisers and promoters that he should abandon his notion that Eisenhower was "out of the present picture." Evidently, Ike was impressed with a Gallup poll that showed he led MacArthur 51 percent to 27 percent, despite the many "MacArthur for President" rallies and the mammoth parades in his honor. The May Gallup poll had found Eisenhower the "popular choice of the rank and file of both the Democratic and Republican parties."[50]

In addition, Eisenhower was informed by Bill Robinson that not only had MacArthur's tide "definitely receded," the Taftites were thoroughly destabilized. The "aid and comfort" bestowed upon MacArthur by the "Taft-Hoover-Wherry-Wiley clique" had merely confused their isolationist supporters and "put Taft in a peculiarly contradictory position." Now everybody knew that MacArthur's views were fundamentally opposed to Taft's. The entire business had served only to build support for Eisenhower, for Eisenhower's international vision and prestige. Since Truman and Acheson were made to appear feeble and unworthy, and Taft and Hoover were "badly injured" aboard "MacArthur's bandwagon," it was left up to Eisenhower to unify the American public. Eisenhower alone had remained throughout the long ordeal a towering presence of stability and nonpartisan strength.

For Eisenhower, the MacArthur affair became the first phase of a very smooth campaign. Internationally, it offered significant bonuses: America rejected MacArthur's call to "go it alone" throughout the world. The need for alliances, such as NATO, was accepted. At the same time, the State Department's ambivalence toward Nationalist China was discredited. Roberts wrote to Eisenhower enthusiastically: "Formosa will not be handed to Red China. Red China's entry into the UN will be opposed."[51] Eisenhower was ready to go public. On 19 June, he met with a delegation of congressmen and presented a formal statement of his long-contained opinions.

Eisenhower considered the situation "global" and indivisible. Between East and West, he said, there were simply no "isolated, unrelated events." He thought there was conceivably a "relationship between the time that the Marshall Plan was really reaching fruition in Europe and the starting of the Korean War. It was time, I think, the Soviets felt they had to create a diversion. They just didn't like a growing strength and unity here." Similarly, Eisenhower explained, France's activities in Indochina, so strategically placed "on the Southeast Asian sea routes and also at the crossroads of the paths that lead into India," seemed to detract from France's ability to place its military forces primarily in NATO. But it was all connected; a global effort was underway. France's efforts in Indochina, Eisenhower concluded, were essential to the success of NATO. If the French collapsed there, "they [the Communists] would be pushing in through Burma—already a hotbed of unrest and trouble—pushing on down to rubber, tin, tungsten, the Sumatra oil. Then you begin to see a picture that is terrible."

At the end of his formal remarks, Eisenhower made some very controversial statements. When reported to the Washington bureau of the *Herald Tribune,* they were held up for confirmation. Over a month passed before Eisenhower's assistant, General Gruenther, confirmed that "General Eisenhower did say substantially what he is reported to have said." Although the documents relating Eisenhower's political indiscretion were not declassified until August 1976, a very simple statement was involved: Eisenhower considered "the loss of China to the Communists the greatest diplomatic defeat in this nation's history." The problem was that during the Senate hearings on his dismissal, MacArthur had said: "The greatest political mistake we made in a hundred years in the Pacific was in allowing the communists to grow in power in China. . . . I believe we will pay for it for a century." According to the censored press release, Eisenhower's statement raised the question "of his seeming disagreement with Secretary of State Dean Acheson and Secretary of Defense George C. Marshall over the importance of China."[52]

Eisenhower's public statement did not represent a moment of mindless passion. It was a carefully timed, well-aimed announcement of his long-obscured political presence. Since 1948, Eisenhower had been a presidential contender. If he did not admit it to himself, if he denied it to his closest associates, including his brother Milton and his childhood friend Swede Hazlett, he refused no public appearance, no fund-raising party, no opportunity to meet the affluent and influential. The truth was that Eisenhower was surrounded by a political team of financiers and friends who coordinated a masterful campaign to promote a President whose convictions would heal America's distemper, reforge a bipartisan united front against communism, and build an era of fiscal prosperity and international peace through military cooperation. With an amazing circumspection that was at once elaborate and naïve, the early campaign for Eisenhower's presidency involved "top secret" memos and a stunning galaxy of disingenuous disclaimers.

Eisenhower's public statement was followed by a long report from his most trusted political adviser, Lucius Clay. Filled with code names and cloaked allusions, the memo was very specific:

1. G's agents are conducting a very effective campaign in all 48 states, backed by immense resources which are being spent quite without scruple.

2. They are conducting an extensive smear campaign against our friend, which is in accordance with their customary practice. . . .

F came to New York for a meeting with B, L and me last week. It was a frank, useful, and working meeting. The most significant highlight was that he said that he pledged himself "1000%" and with no reservations to the movement so long as our friend was available and said all he wanted was cooperation and orders. . . .

F gave Clay a full report regarding "his friends from around the country" who endorsed Eisenhower with two conditions:

a) that our friend must not under any circumstances be available to the incumbent party or they themselves would be irreparably damaged. Their argument was that if G should succeed within our party and our friend accept the other, all of them would be made to appear ridiculous. . . .

b) they want to know now whether our friend will accept. . . .

F had an interesting conference with M. G's gossip columnists and rumor spreaders had the word out that M would remove himself . . . and announce that no military man should be considered. Of course he did not do so. G's people now claim that he will do so a year from now when it will have the maximum effectiveness and damage.

F reports that he referred to these stories . . . in his conversation with M who rejected them completely and said that he had "the greatest admiration" for our friend. . . . This conflicts with other reports. . . . F said he thought it might be solved if our friend could make a pleasant public reference to the brilliant landing at Inchon or something else to indicate friendship and respect. . . .*[53]

All the while Eisenhower was at SHAPE, his friends in the United States were building a convention base for his support. The election of 1952 was perceived by many as a monumental event that would determine the course of America's future role in the world. But Eisenhower was physically removed from partisan politics. Throughout his tour of duty at SHAPE, he was an undeclared candidate for office, sincerely preoccupied with a diplomatic mission he considered of foremost importance: to persuade Europe's leaders that America's policy served European interests and that those interests would best be protected by a one-uniform European force.

---

* G=Taft, F=Harold Stassen, B=Herbert Brownell, L=J. Russell Sprague, M=MacArthur.

CHAPTER IV
MISSION FANTASTIC: COMMANDER, SUPREME HEADQUARTERS ALLIED POWERS EUROPE (SHAPE); PRESIDENTIAL CONTENDER, U.S.A.

Eisenhower's task at SHAPE was to build a solid military and political foundation for an international situation over which he would soon preside. From the beginning, Eisenhower's international policies depended on the creation of alliances and the expectation of an Anglo-American unity that proved for many reasons elusive. Unexpected antagonisms between Britain and the United

States continually blocked allied cooperation. On 21 December 1951, for example, Eisenhower noted in his diary that Britain's Prime Minister Winston Churchill, the British ambassador to France, and Britain's Foreign Secretary Anthony Eden had visited SHAPE. Churchill continued to oppose all plans for a European army. Recognizing that such antagonism would retard his effort, Eisenhower no longer encouraged Britain to join the projected force. But he had hoped that Churchill would at least support the idea of a continental army and would extend Britain's "moral support" to the project. Eisenhower found it curious that Churchill continued to insist "that men must wear their own national uniforms, wave their own national flags, sing their own national hymns, and serve under their own national officers," given the fact that "he offered to put British soldiers in American uniforms in order to facilitate their entry into North Africa." Convinced himself that a totally unified movement against communism would alone ensure civilization's salvation, Eisenhower refused to recognize critical political realities: the reality of nationalism, the reality of a certain European reluctance to be directed and dominated even by the leading anti-Communist crusaders based in the United States. Instead he concluded that Churchill was simply closed to reason. "My regretful opinion," Eisenhower wrote in his journal, "is that the Prime Minister no longer absorbs new ideas. . . ."[1]

On the other hand, Eisenhower recognized that differences within the alliance were inevitable. United States foreign policy was based, after all, upon very specified and self-serving premises. And Eisenhower recognized the full implications of those assumptions, which he shared. In an angry letter to his friend Earl Schaefer, the president of Boeing, Eisenhower rejected vigorously criticisms Schaefer sent on to Eisenhower from an unnamed friend reputed to be "one of the top business executives of the country." Eisenhower considered the critic ignorant of American law, callous in regard to American life, and positively dangerous to the republic. Eisenhower's response represents one of the best statements of his understanding of the roots of U.S. foreign policy:

From my viewpoint, foreign policy is, or should be, based primarily upon one consideration. That consideration is the need for the U.S. to obtain certain raw materials to sustain its economy and, when possible, to preserve profitable foreign markets for our surpluses. Out of this need grows the necessity for making certain that those areas of the world in which essential raw materials are produced are not only accessible to us, but their populations and governments are willing to trade with us on a friendly basis.

Regarding other points of criticism, Eisenhower denied that he had ever been party to the " 'Roosevelt-Truman socialism game.' " He pointed out that his "single job was to bring victory in Europe as quickly as possible, with minimum loss in lives," and noted that Schaefer's "friend talks about flinging armies around Europe as if he would enjoy incurring American casualties. Frankly, I don't." Addressing the criticism frequently made by cold warriors during this period, that Eisenhower failed to beat Russia to Berlin, he pointed out that "long before the date of this final attack," the division of Germany was fixed at Yalta. Moreover, U.S. troops were 300 miles from Berlin and "back of a great River, the Elbe, while the Russians were less than 30 miles away from the city and with no obstacle between." Eisenhower was appalled that his critic suggested that he should have disobeyed "the infamous Roosevelt" so as not to "betray" his country, much as MacArthur did, or attempted to do. Eisenhower pointed out that MacArthur had in fact obeyed Truman's order not to attack the airfields north of the Yalu, and concluded:

> When the day comes that American soldiers can in war successfully defy the entire civil government, then the American system will have come to an end. If your friend is not bright enough to see this, then . . . there is some remarkably OBSCURE reason for the success he has achieved.[2]

Eisenhower's letter to Schaefer highlighted three elements that were to become hallmarks of his presidential years. Eisenhower would attempt (1) to work within a system of international alliances (2) to avoid, above all, a return to large-scale international warfare and (3) to maintain basic constitutional precepts, notably civilian control over the military, and congressional participation in the decision-making process. On the other hand, any immediate threat to capitalism's hegemony would be checked immediately. Although Eisenhower avoided large-scale international warfare, he experimented with a variety of short-range, quick-shot activities in

Latin America, the Middle East, and Africa. And he was critical of those who recommended more intensive negotiations and long-range cooperation with Communists in Europe and Asia in order to avoid military activity altogether.

Eisenhower was impatient, for example, when any of his own fundamentally dedicated supporters questioned the wisdom of the vast European rearmament program he championed. Although he agreed with his friend Clifford Roberts that the United States had to walk "a tightrope" to avoid military overspending, his own emphasis remained the need to ensure European stability through the creation of a one-uniform European military force. Eisenhower's attitudes regarding the dangers of a military-industrial complex that rested entirely on military growth while ignoring demands for increased productivity and economic development, basic to the war against communism, emerged during this period. He was persuaded by his friends and advisers who insisted that "it would be disastrous to free world unity" if the World Bank's efforts to increase productivity and raise living standards were frustrated by an exclusive preoccupation with rearmament. Cliff Roberts urged Eisenhower to meet with representatives of the World Bank (the International Bank for Reconstruction and Development) and sent him a New York *Herald Tribune* editorial on the need for development and rearmament to continue apace: "The member nations in Asia, Africa, and Latin America must not be told that their progress toward self-reliance, health and economic decency must wait until the end of the West's arms effort." The crusade against communism did not pose an either-or solution. Rearmament and development were equally required. Eisenhower did not disagree but feared that some of his economic advisers were unwilling to face the full implications of what he had come to believe was an imminent Soviet threat of expansion in the absence of any military force or even a clearly visible will to resist.[3]

In an address to the First International Conference of Manufacturers, a meeting of three hundred industrialists from twenty-five nations, Philip Reed, the chairman of the board of General Electric, had declared that businessmen must take the lead for peace by removing such roadblocks to economic expansion as "exchange controls, import quotas, protective tariffs, unconvertible curren-

cies, burdensome and discriminating restrictions on foreign investment or employment of foreign personnel." Since all "the evidence
indicates," Reed said, "that Russia will not deliberately precipitate
another world war within the foreseeable future," the real problem
facing NATO nations was the costs of rearmament. Reed feared
that "if the NATO countries undertake to meet the defense production program as recently formulated and scheduled, serious
economic and political disturbances will result." He concluded that
it was his "own carefully considered view that the peak of the rearmament program . . . is too high and that it comes too soon."
Since he was speaking as president of the National Association of
Manufacturers (NAM) to "the managers of free competitive enterprise," Reed's talk received wide circulation and became the
subject of heated debate. Eisenhower was furious. He wrote to
Reed that he hoped his "conclusions" regarding "Soviet intentions"
were correct and agreed that it was possible "to go broke in the
process of rearming and destroying the very economic and social
fabric we are trying to defend." But Eisenhower feared that Reed's
talk gave too much comfort to those who opposed all rearmament,
and preferred simply "to put off unpleasant chores" and do nothing.[4]

Economically, Eisenhower, like Reed, believed that capitalism's
future depended on its remaining a global system. They agreed that
economic expansion involved the integration of international business interests. They both believed that international peace—a stable world order—was essential to the success of a transnational
economy. But Eisenhower believed that to obtain that goal, communism had first to be destabilized and finally eradicated. To
achieve that without war, without renewed holocaust, Eisenhower
sought a European demonstration of resistance to communism.
Rearmament, military coherence, and security in a defense posture
that directly challenged communism's continued internal growth
and geographic expansion constituted for Eisenhower a first principle. Military resistance was, however, only part of his vision.
Economic solvency and tangible signs of fiscal health and development were necessary to make communism seem unattractive, unnecessary. The rearmament of postwar Europe in fact depended on
convincing millions of doubtful citizens that their interests would

be best served and protected by the expansion of America's economic interests throughout the world. That was no simple chore. But it was basic to Eisenhower's mission.

The success of Eisenhower's mission depended on popular support. Political warfare and psychological strategies to transform public opinion were to become vital realities at SHAPE. Eisenhower's mission did, after all, involve some of the most unpopular postwar ideas imaginable: the military unification of Europe under U.S. domination, the revitalization of widely hated German industrial power, the rearmament of the German behemoth, the notion that world peace could be ensured only by intensive and expensive preparation for world war, and the notion that communism meant slavery while capitalism meant freedom. In Europe, where the majority of antifascist resistance forces had been socialist or communist, where capitalism and the realities of class were widely understood and carefully studied, Eisenhower's ideological crusade against communism was a frequently embarrassing and only marginally successful effort. Throughout Europe for over twenty years, facism had been resisted by communists and supported by capitalists. After the war, practically all Europe seemed to be moving toward socialism. Beyond the Soviet sphere of influence, in Britain, France, Italy, the Netherlands, and West Germany, socialists and communists struggled to gain control of party politics. To convince the people of Europe that business and labor had the same goals, that there was in fact no class division of labor, that capitalism assured freedom and prosperity for all, was an outrageously creative undertaking.

Throughout his public career, Eisenhower was deeply committed to the essential value of political warfare. To sell capitalism, to destroy socialism's appeal meant to introduce new concepts, new meanings, new ideas—to change the very words of public life. In his first speech to the people of West Germany as commander of NATO, Eisenhower introduced the new words of that new system he had come to represent:

I am back in Europe on a mission of peace. We have discovered . . . people that believe in the individual and in freedom. . . . The Western Nations have found and believe that in unity they can develop, first, the moral strength that will allow their cultures to live, and secondly, through that unity of purpose, they can develop whatever material strength, specifically, military strength, is necessary that people living free lives may do so in confidence and tranquillity. . . .

Western Europe is the cradle of civilization as we know it. From this area has spread out over the world a culture, a culture that has been described as a Christian civilization. . . . Its cornerstone has been the dignity of the individual and the result of which has been to produce more things, more intellectual, spiritual and material contentment for people than any other nation or system that has ever existed. . . .

Eisenhower wanted to make it clear that while he had during the war "a very definite antagonism toward Germany and certainly a hatred for all that I thought that the Nazis and the Hitlerites stood for," he bore no resentment "against the German people. For many years," Eisenhower said, he believed one urgent fact: "No people, no people, wants war; there is no such people. The people that have to fight, they don't want anything to do with it. Governments, our national prejudices, our national prides, sometimes just our national ignorance, brings us into conflict, and it is always a pity." Eisenhower concluded that as commander of NATO his role was to ensure peace by creating a united effort against war. Only in unity can the Western world "gain that feeling of confidence and tranquillity that is necessary if we are to continue to develop as free peoples everywhere."[5]

Eisenhower's statement was not particularly eloquent. But his words had been carefully chosen: freedom, the individual, culture, the ability "to produce more things," "intellectual, spiritual and material contentment." The word capitalism never appeared. Free enterprise. The Free World. Free peoples. There were to be new words, key words, in the struggle for men's minds. Capitalism and capitalists would soon cease to appear in public. The point of conflict was remodeled. It was not between capitalism and communism. It was between freedom and slavery. This was neither accidental nor casual. Political warfare was about words. In the beginning, when Eisenhower occasionally forgot and referred specifically to capitalism, his friends, his advisers, were quick to refer to his error. In one letter, for example, Eisenhower called the U.S. economy "capitalistic." In response, he received several letters of correction. William Robinson explained in detail why the U.S.

economy should no longer be "characterized as capitalistic." Thirty years ago, Robinson wrote, the United States was capitalist. Then the sole "motivation was, as it should have been, profit. . . . Then our capitalistic system differed little from capitalism as it was and is practiced in Europe. But in the last 25 or 30 years there has been a quiet but a sure revolution in our economy." Today, Robinson assured Eisenhower, the United States' economic philosophy "is based on the concept of the greatest good for the greatest number; that is, there will always be more customers than stockholders. In actual operation, it can be more aptly and accurately called the democratic system." Edward Bermingham wrote to explain that capitalism in Europe denoted "a system of rigid low wages. Ownership has no sympathy with the idea that participation in profits through a wage scale that spells comfort is to the advantage of the whole economy." European capitalism was, therefore, as different from the United States' form of economics, Bermingham wrote, "as the poles are apart." And the very word capitalism could be "handily used by the communists to damn us and all our works." Bermingham, like Robinson, called upon Eisenhower "to find a synonym for capitalism." Eisenhower agreed that he had perhaps "used that term too loosely," explained that he meant "a system that does yield profit to private ownership," and assured his friends that he would seek alternatives in the future. In 1951 he suggested "we invent a new term and call it a 'customer economy.' "[6]

Later, as President, Eisenhower thought the word capitalism might be reintroduced if it were designated a "people's capitalism." But that idea never became very popular. And so, for years, for decades, the United Satates became a country without workers and without capitalists. Everybody was classified as middle class. Proletarians lived abroad; and they were un-American. Without workers or capitalists, there were no classes, and there was no class conflict. "Labor-management" tensions and issues of race relations, segregation, unemployment, and poverty had nothing to do with class; and little to do with Eisenhower. As one of the key architects of the American Century, Eisenhower, by 1951, had very specific goals: greater international prosperity would alleviate the side issues of the American Century. The truth is that regarding certain domestic issues, Eisenhower's interests were barely engaged. "Frankly," he wrote to Lucius Clay in May 1952, "I do not consider race relations or labor relations to be issues." Prosperity was an issue, because greater prosperity would erase labor and racial tensions and obliterate all interest in socialism.[7]

Eisenhower's public career was devoted to the fight against socialism. Marxism, distorted by McCarthyite hysteria in postwar America, had a long and deeply rooted tradition throughout Europe. After World War II, many of the popular parties were Marxist parties, although they differed widely in emphasis, membership, and style. There were democratic socialists, parliamentary socialists, communist-anarchists, and an amazing number of Marxist-Leninist parties (communist)—all with different perspectives, some allied to the Soviet Union, some aloof from the Soviet Union. The idea that deep nationalist impulses might spawn and sustain differences among communists, the idea that communism was not a monolithic system, engendered confusion among political warriors in the United States. Eventually, however, a compromise was reached. While all things Marxist seemed to disappear from the United States, a double standard began to emerge regarding Europe. To recognize reality meant to recognize that some forms of socialism would prevail against all the promises of the American Century.

There was little American unity about how to deal publicly with America's conditional acceptance of socialism in Europe. In March 1952, Averell Harriman, for example, agreed with critics of the Marshall Plan that in nonsocialist countries workers had not benefited from the aid program. Harriman then referred to Europe's moderate left as simply "new deal or fair deal groups." The United States insisted on confusing social democracy with communism. John J. McCloy, former head of the World Bank, then U.S. high commissioner in Germany, cabled an angry message to Harriman demanding a retraction. Harriman's statement caused SHAPE in Germany "considerable embarrassment" because of vigorous opposition to Konrad Adenauer. McCloy insisted that "Marshall Plan Aid did get down to the workers in Germany. . . . It gave them food, jobs and a stabilized currency." But in Germany the socialist opposition to Adenauer, led by Dr. Kurt Schumacher, the head of the Social Democratic Party, was nationalist and bitterly anti-communist, and far too popular to be ignored by American statesmen seeking allied unity against the

Soviet Union. Eisenhower and McCloy both courted Schumacher in an unsuccessful effort to win his support for a European Defense Force.[8] In 1952, Schumacher died. Adenauer, related to McCloy and Lewis Douglas by marriage, was strengthened by the United States over a period of time. United States policy toward socialism in Europe evolved slowly. A hierarchy of preference was established: from antisocialist supporters of U.S. policies, to socialist allies of the United States, to communist enemies of the Soviet Union.

Regarding socialists in Europe, the United States would be flexible, pragmatic, and liberal. Good socialists would be nurtured and supported. Good socialists would, over time, with careful guidance and bountiful U.S. aid, become social democrats. It was a compromise strategy for an unbalanced situation. As early as 1945, even Henry Luce, the chief American Centurion, when faced with the temporary triumph of the Labour Party, deemed "socialism" in Britain, called for such a compromise. In a memo to his staff, "A Personal Comment on the News," Luce called for compromise. "Yes," he wrote, "there can be a great deal of socialism in a liberal society. . . . While I remain frankly skeptical as to how much more socialism you can have on top of all we've got, . . . I guess I am forced to confess error at last and personally consent to alliance with socialists—with all such at least who sincerely believe in compromise."[9] Cooperative, independent socialists willing to compromise were to become essential to many political-warfare operations. In Europe, social democrats were among the most vigorous anti-communists, and because their anti-fascist record rendered them politically more acceptable than monarchists or collaborators with fascism, they were to become a key element in the creation of a massive anti-communist movement. The support of friendly socialists and such independent communists as Yugoslavia's Tito was reluctantly considered necessary to long-range political-warfare plans that sought to undermine popular support for socialism altogether. U.S. political warriors tended to judge socialists trustless and inimical, and preferred to support and work with known and visible fascists, monarchists, and collaborators. That tendency reduced the credibility of America's political-warfare efforts for many years.

United States political-warfare strategies were, as a result, crude and unsophisticated. A historical contempt for East Europeans, belittled as barbaric; a widespread and unsubtle racism that distorted understanding and limited empathy for Asian, African, and Latin American peoples; an assumption of power and inviolability that seemed arrogant when not bullying, marked all early efforts in the "psychological" field. On the other hand, Eisenhower both as statesman and as personality was one of America's leading political-warfare assets. His ease with people, his celebrated smile, his nonaloof manner and warm, man-of-the-people style coupled with his proven antifascism, covered him with a mantle of assumed concern, benevolence, honesty, and wisdom. Eisenhower believed in political warfare and for many purposes would become its chosen instrument.

Eisenhower's presidency was devoted to the task of undermining popular support for socialism, and the hidden weapon—long obscured and generally denied—was carefully planned political warfare. Until a policy of secrecy erased the traces, Eisenhower's commitment to political warfare was known. He had never been vague about his intentions or his chosen methods. During a public address in San Francisco in October 1952, he spoke precisely:

> Our aim in "cold war" is not conquest of territory or subjugation by force. Our aim is more subtle, more pervasive, more complete. We are trying to get the world, by peaceful means, to believe the truth. That truth is that Americans want a world at peace, a world in which all people shall have opportunity for maximum individual development.
>
> The means we shall employ to spread this truth are often called "psychological." Don't be afraid of that term just because it's a five-dollar, five-syllable word. "Psychological warfare" is the struggle for the minds and wills of men. . . .[10]

From 1950 onward, Eisenhower worked with Bedell Smith, Lucius Clay, and C. D. Jackson to develop America's political-warfare strategies. Smith, Clay, and Jackson directed America's entrance into those experimental battlegrounds. While the Marshall Plan, Point Four, the ECA, and NATO represented the economic and military institutions of the Cold War, Radio Free Europe and the Crusade for Freedom were erected to win the war for "men's minds." General Walter Bedell Smith, Eisenhower's former chief of staff and the United States' first postwar ambassador to Moscow, reluctantly agreed to become the director of the Central Intelligence Agency (CIA) in October 1950. He wrote to Eisenhower that he had wanted "to avoid" the job, "but in view of the general situation, and particularly the Korean affair, I did not feel I could refuse for a third time."[11]

General Lucius Clay, one of Eisenhower's closest confidants and oldest friends, retired from the military to become president of Continental Can Company. In 1950, he agreed to preside over the organization of and set the direction for the Crusade for Freedom. Clay and Eisenhower had first worked together in the Philippines, where as a member of the Corps of Engineers, Clay built dams and analyzed the potential for hydroelectric power. During World War II, he worked with the War Production Board and in 1945 was appointed deputy military governor of the United States' occupation zone in Germany. Clay, with Robert Murphy and John J. McCloy, were in large part responsible for the creation of Bizonia, the economic fusion of the U.S. and British zones that emerged as the Federal Republic of Germany, and the popularization of the decision to rebuild Germany as the pivotal center of anticommunism in Western Europe. As Murphy wrote, "Bizonia really laid the foundation for western Europe's most powerful state, West Germany, destined to make possible a vigorous non-Communist Europe."[12] Throughout Eisenhower's tour of duty at SHAPE, he relied heavily on Clay for advice and political analyses. Clay, the son of Georgia Senator Alexander Clay, grew up in political Washington, knew and understood the principles of politics, and ran political interference for Eisenhower in the United States. As President, Eisenhower appointed Clay to engineer the United States' massive interstate highway program.

C. D. Jackson, although one of the most significant figures in U. S. Cold War history, has remained strangely unknown, his activities largely unrecognized. Vice-president of Time, Inc., Jackson organized the Council for Democracy in 1941, "to combat all the nazi, fascist, communist, pacifist" antiwar groups in the United States. The Council was a limited affair that served mostly to highlight Jackson's talents as a propagandist. After a short assignment to Turkey on behalf of the State Department's Bureau of Economic Warfare, Jackson was selected to improve the Office of War

Information (OWI) in North Africa in 1942. It was the moment of the Darlan Deal, when the OWI was dominated largely by independent journalists critical of Eisenhower's policies in the area. Jackson wrote that until his mission, the chief preoccupation of the OWI staff seemed to be "to spit in Eisenhower's eye." Jackson's task was to weed out the unfriendly members of OWI, which featured, he wrote, "enough long hair . . . to stuff the mattresses for an entire invasion force."[13]

From North Africa, Jackson traveled with Eisenhower to Sicily and then to England, where he was chief of the Psychological Warfare Division. In that post, he prepared for D-day and was then assigned "to appraise the reactions and ideas of liberated and conquered peoples toward the Allies in general and the U.S. in particular." After the war, he returned to Time, Inc., and in 1949 was appointed publisher of *Fortune* magazine. During the postwar years, he spearheaded a variety of organizations to establish America's preeminence throughout the world. If there were a hierarchy of American Centurions, C. D. Jackson would surely be in the first rank. With Nelson Rockefeller, who had prepared a survey of "all old and new organizations in the promotion of exports and imports," he participated in the activities of the World Trade Foundation, which led the movement to globalize America's international business interests.[14]

Jackson was also one of the early proponents of an "institute for democratic leadership," which he first suggested to Princeton University in 1941. Based on Germany's "Fuehrer Schule" concept, it was conceived "not in slavish imitation of the Nazi idea, but in order to turn out young men with the knowledge and emotional drive to act as 'pro-Consuls of democracy' in the course of their careers. These young men must be ready to devote two years of their lives to a serious and intensive course in democratic leadership, with the earnest devotion of the zealot rather than the casual interest of the dilettante." Although Princeton University seemed not to pick up the idea, The Johns Hopkins University did—creating the School for Advanced International Studies (SAIS), which absorbed the Foreign Service Educational Foundation, which had been sponsored by Jackson under the direction of Christian Herter. After the Foreign Service Educational Foundation was incorporated by The Johns Hopkins University, on 30 June 1950, SAIS became one of the leading centers for the training of urbane and erudite "Americans for World Careers."[15]

The establishment of "Enterprise America" was one of Jackson's most outstanding contributions to the ideology of the postwar period. Enterprise America was to transform private domestic business, long suspicious of and inimical toward government, into a cooperative effort involving international expansion, military defense for international business expansion, government support, and interchangeable business-government personnel practices. This global feat was to be popularized by a massive public-relations campaign. Enterprise America involved a complex operation based on a very simple theory.

For Jackson, the world was crudely simple: The United States was the "all-important part" of the world. Business was the "all-important part" of the United States; and "businessmen are the important men in the U.S.—Q.E.D." America was "a business nation" and, according to C. D. Jackson, everybody—farmers, workers, philosophers, artists, buyers, manufacturers, sellers—were all part of that fact. They were all united by the business of America—now "involved all around the world." But in 1949, despite that unity, Jackson observed a "power vacuum" that represented "the greatest single challenge that has ever confronted the U.S. businessman." It was not only "the greatest opportunity on Earth," it was the most urgent. Because of increased "communist competition," it might be the businessman's "final challenge!"

To meet that challenge, private enterprise needed to do the unusual, the outrageous: ally itself with the State. In a speech entitled "Who Will Win the Cold War Between Free Enterprise and Statism?" delivered to a group of conservative businessmen who had for the past twenty years opposed all New Deal/Fair Deal legislation that extended the concerns of government, C. D. Jackson proclaimed:

> One thing that private enterprise cannot do abroad is to create a favorable climate for U.S. investment—that's a job for the U. S. Government, and it's a job that it is today honor-bound to do. . . .

"To create a favorable climate for U.S. investment" throughout the world was the goal. The shift into Enterprise America was the means. Jackson's vision involved more than an alliance, it involved the takeover of the machinery of government by the interests of capital. And Jackson was very specific about that: Given "the challenge of the power vacuum . . . WHO shall assume the responsibility for a functioning America . . . ? Shall it be the State, eager, plausible, and prepared—or shall it be Enterprise, the businessman, who by his works has shown . . . that he is the most competent administrator of the welfare of this country." Jackson then presented a three-part plan that actually became a blueprint for that takeover. Through ECA, the Point Four Program, and participation at all levels of the Washington bureaucracy, business would merge with the State, and Enterprise America would be affirmed.

Regarding ECA, Jackson urged "the leaders of American business enterprise [to] participate in the thinking, the planning, and the acting. . . . Both as individuals and as members of committees and associations, machinery exists for you to be heard. Paul Hoffman has a willing ear, and Washington can no longer afford to turn a deaf one." Regarding Point Four, Jackson agreed that there were "many ways of thinking." Point Four could be dismissed as another "Operation Rat Hole," or it could be used to build up consumer demands and raise the world's standard of living. "There are," Jackson explained, "two billion people on this globe, and 50% of them have a sub-marginal standard." To increase that by even "a fraction of a percent created a demand" for production beyond all contemporary capacity in the United States and Western Europe, and Jackson pointed out it would be unwise to "exclude from that billion-plus of sub-standard human beings those under Russian domination," who were surely about to demand more material bounty. All those demands, Jackson concluded, could be answered by the Point Four Program only by an extension of the productive capacity of the United States that involved the "export of private capital, the export of private enterprise knowhow, the export of plant. . . ." Without Washington support, without state involvement, such a vast international operation would be impossible. And that brought Jackson to his final, crucial point: The Washington bureaucracy was dramatically "understaffed." There were, he asserted, "untold key jobs in Washington going begging because private enterprise has not supplied the men. To be sure," Jackson acknowledged, "the rewards, material and otherwise, are meager. . . . But if enterprise were to organize itself to furnish Washington with a rotating panel of high-level, experienced businessmen for a 12 or 18 month tour of duty, with a salary differential taken care of in whole or in part by industry . . . , a healthy and effective working relationship between Washington and industry could be brought about."

In this remarkable 1949 speech, Jackson did more than describe the task. He named Eisenhower as the man of the future who would work to see it realized. Eisenhower's Labor Day speech, his plea for "Middle of the Road" statesmanship, had signified him the banner carrier. "General Eisenhower," Jackson asserted, had chosen "the path of heroes, leaving it to the sheep to fall for the thoughtless attraction of the extremes." That path led to Enterprise America, which, Jackson concluded, was a "frontier that puts all previous frontiers in the shade." It was unlimited. For Jackson, it was "the frontier of the minds, the hearts, the lives of the 2 billion people who inhabit the world." "Enterprise America" meant "Liberation." It meant infinite opportunity, and psychological warfare.[16]

Jackson and his associates understood that communism was not merely a rival economic system eager to secure its own supply zones for raw materials and industrial growth. It was also "an idea." And "a very dynamic idea" that "has reached well beyond the limits of Slavic desperation." To counter that idea, C. D. Jackson urged "America at mid-century" to embark on "the American Crusade," a Crusade for Freedom. Financed by and directly affiliated with the CIA, both the National Committee for a Free Europe (NCFE), which C. D. Jackson became the president of in February 1951, and the Crusade for Freedom, chaired by Lucius Clay, were organized as private, independent agencies. The Committee for a Free Europe created the Crusade for Freedom to establish "a spontaneous movement" to promote the idea of freedom, raise money, and "build up the prestige" of Radio Free Europe, NCFE's most important operation. The Crusade was to wrap a protective cloak around the activities of NCFE by enabling it to appear a popular movement that involved all virtuous American citizens. It was also considered "extremely important that Negroes and women" participate in the Crusade's international events.[17]

For success, psychological warfare in the United States depended on its ability to appear independent from government, to seem to represent the spontaneous convictions of freedom-loving individuals. In addition, C. D. Jackson wrote, for "maximum effectiveness," psychological-warfare organizations in peacetime required "adequate funds," "the freedom to operate on a 'no-holds-barred' basis," and "to be in a position" to have "no questions asked."[18] Conversely, government agencies required the freedom to deny a variety of bizarre activities undertaken by the National Committee for a Free Europe that served over time to escalate international tensions. Since NCFE was undercover as a private, independent corporation, the government could claim ignorance and lack of responsibility for its wide-ranging programs.

The National Committee for a Free Europe and the Crusade for Freedom were organized "to liberate" the people of those countries in Central Europe that had been created after World War I to isolate the Soviet Union. Conquered and named "satellites" by Hitler, liberated by Russia during World War II, they were regarded as essential to Russia's defense against a rebuilt and rearmed Germany, by Churchill, Roosevelt, and Stalin at Yalta and by the Allied representatives at Potsdam. Now, the Crusade for Freedom brochures explained, the Nazi yoke had been replaced by the Communist yoke, and "80 million sturdy people living between Germany and Russia are still in bondage."

The NCFE began its operations by supporting anti-communist exiles "materially and spiritually" through the Division of Intellectual Cooperation. This division provided "constructive work" for exiles until that day when they would resume "once more their democratic leadership" in Central Europe. In cooperation with the Library of Congress, the division created a Research Center in Washington to analyze and index new Soviet laws and do other research for members of Congress. East European study centers were also created, notably the Mid-European Studies Center, in New York, supported in part by New York University and the Carnegie Endowment for International Peace. It also sponsored the Free University in Exile, in Strasbourg, to prepare "young exiles . . . to take over the leadership of their liberated countries." The Free University was incorporated under the Education Law of New York State in 1951. A. A. Berle was chairman of the board. A second committee, the American Contacts Division, was responsible for lecture tours and informal meetings with exiles throughout the United States.

The National Councils Division represented associations of politicians in exile. Exiles from "each imprisoned country" provided "the formal basis of cooperation" and contact between the United States and democrats "now submerged" in their homelands. C. D. Jackson considered the National Councils not quite governments in exile but power centers capable of filling the power vacuum that would follow liberation. The council exiles represented "symbols of hope" and courage for the millions who might choose also to pass through the iron curtain and join the NCFE "To Halt Communism and Save Freedom."

Radio Free Europe, the most important part of this program, was to pick up where the official U.S. propaganda broadcast network, Voice of America, left off. "Relieved of official limitations," RFE was to be "harder hitting." According to its creators, RFE promised to preserve "the Western democratic tradition in Eastern Europe."

It was a thorough and expensive enterprise. To raise money and popularize NCFE activities, the Crusade for Freedom called upon American citizens to join this effort "to recapture our traditional faith in the dynamic power of an ideal—in order, to paraphrase Lincoln: 'THAT THIS WORLD UNDER GOD, SHALL HAVE A NEW BIRTH OF FREEDOM.'" Crusade for Freedom literature announced "The Struggle for the Souls of Men" in immediate terms: "At this very moment it is being decided what kind of a world your children and grandchildren are going to live in. It is not a question of whether industry is to be more or less nationalized. . . . The alternatives before us are extreme and one of them revolting. Are your children's souls going to be crushed under the tyranny of a Communist totalitarianism? . . ."[19]

Radio Free Europe inaugurated its broadcasting transmitter in Munich on May Day 1951. The first international transmitter of freedom broadcast only to Czechoslovakia. By the end of the summer, additional transmitters broadcast to Hungary and Poland. The radio was chosen as "the great psychological warfare weapon" to stimulate revolt in the Communist countries. Radio Free Europe was to become the psychological front line of counterrevolution through seduction (the prospect of American material culture, fashion, commodities) and through fear (the prospect of an enslaving, death-dealing communism). Radio Free Europe featured music and news, "skits," "satires," and "talks by exiled leaders." In the beginning, it was on the air for eleven and a half hours a day. In addition, RFE monitored the broadcasts of all Central and Eastern Europe, and managed—through careful timing and political emphasis—the use of information derived from the intelligence community.

In April 1951, for example, RFE discovered that Czechoslovakia planned to devalue its currency. For seven months, intelligence operatives watched the currency situation. Finally, in January 1952, RFE warned the inhabitants of the situation, stimulating "a nationwide buying panic in Czechoslovakia." Radio Free Europe also participated in a variety of psychological-warfare stunts that exacerbated tensions not only between the United States and the Soviet Union but between the United States and its allies. According to C. D. Jackson, one of RFE's major goals was "to sow confusion among the local communists, to warn them that a day is coming when even their Russian masters can't save them." That involved a wide range of personal criticism, tawdry and slanderous attacks ranging from rumors of brutality and torture, to corruption, and to madness, perversion, and vice. Everything was used that could be imagined in order to make communists, whether in England or in Poland, look silly, undignified, and insignificant.

These activities were part of America's official Cold War effort. The CIA and the State Department were directly involved in the planning and the programs of the NCFE and the Crusade for Freedom. When C. D. Jackson resigned from the Committee for a Free Europe to return to *Fortune* and, subsequently, join Eisenhower's official campaign team, he wrote a letter thanking both CIA director Walter Bedell Smith and Allen Dulles for their support. This exchange of letters, only recently declassified, goes a long way toward demystifying the long-guarded secret of the relationship between the CIA and RFE. Jackson's "personal note of thanks" to Smith was written on his return from "a ten-day blitz of our European installations." The trip enabled him to see and assess "the entire operation," and he "was tickled silly at what we have all been able to do in one year." Jackson wrote to Smith, with a copy to Dulles:

We would never have been able to create these things . . . had it not been for the attitude that you and your organization had toward us. The freedom you granted us, which could have been only an illusion, was so skillfully and tactfully handled that in our minds it became a fact—and thanks to that fact we were able to do a lot of things more quickly, and with a greater sense of responsibility, than would have been the case had we constantly felt tugs at the reins. I know just enough about official and semiofficial organizational relationships to appreciate how nearly miraculous our relationship has been, and I can't tell you how grateful I am to you, and Allen, and Frank, and Gates, and Tom, and many others, for the way you have handled us.

In response, Smith thanked Jackson for "the tremendous contribution" Jackson as president and "directing genius of the National Committee for a Free Europe and related enterprises" had personally made. He assumed that Jackson's resignation did not mean the end of his contacts with the agency and anticipated "the benefit of [his] wise advice" in future activities. Regarding future activities, Smith assured Jackson that "the status and present effectiveness of the National Committee for a Free Europe and Radio Free Europe" now numbered "among the most potent and effective weapons at the disposal of the West in its struggle to withstand the Communist onslaught." Smith congratulated Jackson on his ability to forge weapons with the capacity to "strike through the enemy's outer armor and reach his vitals." Radio Free Europe was now "one of the most critical" weapons in the U.S. arsenal. And one of the finest features of RFE was that it seemed for so long to be an independent operation, a private, tax-deductible corporation, free of government regulation or control. There were many benefits to that arrangement.[20]

When Communist governments officially protested RFE's invasion of their national airwaves, the State Department pointed out that the United States believed in freedom of speech and had no jurisdiction over private, independent groups. One can only speculate about what the official U.S. response might have been had the situation been reversed on, for example, the "balloon" invasion that carried millions of pieces of propaganda deep inside Poland and Czechoslovakia in August 1951. C. D. Jackson noted that everybody involved with the operation was delighted over "the helplessness of the authorities to do anything about it." Jackson,

Harold Stassen, and Drew Pearson released the first balloons on 19 August. Allegedly, Soviet planes attempted to shoot them down. But it was impossible. There were eleven thousand balloons carrying 13 million leaflets to "boost the morale of the entire non-Communist population" and to fortify "spiritual resistance" until "the day of liberation" arrived.

Imaginative and rambunctious, Jackson introduced a note of caution. All the United States had to offer, really, was hope. It was a dangerous game:

> We in America have a romantic penchant for thinking that everything will be all right if we can drop 10 million cigarette-pack-size radio receivers behind the Iron Curtain. . . . [While] the central handicap . . . is that all we have to sell today is HOPE, when conditions are rapidly approaching a point where radio listening endangers life. . . . And yet . . . thousands of people are doing just that, for just hope—which is the supreme reason why we must not toy with that brave listenership. . . .[21]

Although Eisenhower never publicly repudiated a Crusade activity, he wrote to Clay that he questioned the "effectiveness" of the balloon event. Balloons were not actually Eisenhower's style. On the other hand, he agreed with Clay that by the "full use of our native salesmanship . . . we can avoid full-scale war." Eisenhower worked closely with the Crusade for Freedom. He was a member of its corporate board and one of its most robust supporters. On Labor Day 1951, he launched the Crusade's first fund-raising campaign with such a dramatic radio broadcast that, according to Clay, he persuaded Americans to contribute $1.3 million to RFE. In August 1951, he launched the second fund-raising appeal with a message to America taped in Paris:

> Ladies and Gentlemen:

> You have just heard the great bell of Notre Dame in Paris. From its towers for nearly eight centuries bells have carried forth a message of hope and of eternal faith in the future.

> Tonight the bell of Notre Dame carries hope across the Iron Curtain to lands and peoples deeply rooted in the heritage of western civilization. Though they are marched and countermarched in the lockstep of totalitarianism, those unhappy people yearn for a better day when freedom and natural rights of man are theirs again to enjoy.

They hunger also for truth, to sustain them under the crushing weight of a godless dictatorship. You can help bring them the truth through the Crusade for Freedom. I trust that every American will support wholeheartedly its campaign to use truth as our most powerful weapon against Communistic domination of the world.[22]

In October 1951, General Walter Bedell Smith informed Eisenhower of new activities to be sponsored by the CIA, directly within Eisenhower's domain. Because of the rapid and demonstrable success of the National Councils and Radio Free Europe work based in New York, it was judged "desirable for us to shift our focus in émigré work . . . to Europe." Smith was enthusiastic about the idea. "If properly sustained and used, it is our belief that the psychological and operational contribution of these groups to all overt and covert propaganda activities throughout Eastern and Western Europe can be immense." Specifically, Smith sought to cooperate with a French committee to promote a national Emigré Council, originally conceived by General Marie-Émile Béthouart, former French high commissioner in Austria, and to be headed by Paul Reynaud with "the support of high French officials, including Robert Schuman and the Quai D'Orsay." But there was little unity among the émigrés.

Political differences were widespread. Conflict and animosity marked the entire NCFE operation. Smith sought to avoid the kinds of struggles that pervaded the New York council and wanted Eisenhower's reaction to his idea that "European unity might be successfully injected as a goal. . . . We would like even to explore the possibility of having the new committee formed as a European group, rather than as a purely French committee." Unfortunately, in 1951 there was little support for European unity of any kind. Smith pointed out that "domestic political issues" had, despite significant effort, blocked British support for "any tripartite policy" regarding "the émigré question." He concluded "that the present situation can only lead to disastrous disunity and bickering among the émigrés and to the negation of the useful role which the émigrés can play in European unification and in the ultimate conduct of their national affairs." Smith wanted Eisenhower's support for his idea to link the councils of émigrés with the movement for NATO:

If, through Reynaud and the French government and with tacit support of the U.S. government and, eventually, of the NATO Powers,
an émigré committee inspired with a genuine common goal—a
united Europe embracing both Western and Eastern Europe—can be
made the rallying point of all émigrés, such a committee may also
ultimately succeed in receiving the British cooperation which is a
prerequisite to attainment of our common objectives in the émigré
field.

Moreover, we believe that such a committee of proper stature might
act as a galvanizing force to bring public opinion in Europe more
firmly behind the NATO concept. . . .[23]

There is no evidence that Eisenhower received Smith's plan with
enthusiasm. Despite his general support for the Crusade's projects,
Eisenhower was unwilling to jeopardize the NATO alliance for
NCFE's more uncertain escapades. His entire mission was, after
all, to create a defensive force against the possibility of communist
aggression. NATO was to be an international military force to
"contain" communism. RFE emphasized "liberation." RFE's
theme troubled some of the NATO allies, as did balloons and the
prominence in NCFE of former fascists, collaborators, and such
unpopular monarchs as King Michael of Romania. Although
serious efforts were made to select exiles for broadcasting and public appearances who represented "positive" and not "negative" images, each national group was largely responsible for its own staff.
There were bitter national rivalries, political differences, factions,
cultural animosities, and a great range of delicate problems: how
to use, for example, deposed and despised monarchs who were
eager to serve the cause but were hardly captivating or seductive
figures. Psychological warfare was a very subtle and complicated
business. And for many years, tactical errors continued to be
made.

Well into Eisenhower's presidency, psychological warriors
persisted in ignoring the entire significance of Russian history in an
absurd effort to stimulate "partition" or secession movements
among Turkestan, Georgian, and other national groups. Elements
of a crude Anglo-Saxon racism limited the effectiveness of many
aspects of the psychological-warfare program. Germany was not
alone in its national conviction that high culture—Western civili-

zation—ceased as one traveled east beyond Vienna. The attitude that designated Eastern Europe the land of Slavs and all things barbarous gave rise to tired political jokes about Russia as a land of crude peasants, unpolished merchants, and diplomats who went out the window as frequently as the door. These attitudes existed even within Eisenhower's circle. William Robinson, for example, wrote to Eisenhower that he had lunched with Clarence Dillon. Knowing that Eisenhower shared his respect for Dillon's "astute and well-balanced mind," Robinson sent a full report of their conversation. Dillon, Robinson wrote, had "a well-founded knowledge of Europe" and was certain that Eisenhower could create a "European army . . . to guarantee peace. He pointed out that, after all, there are 250 million Western Europeans from an industrial and intelligent atmosphere with a great variety of skills who can produce an army that will give pause to one created from 190 million heterogeneous and sometimes barbaric peoples."[24] Hardly an attitude guaranteed to "win" hearts and minds. And Eisenhower knew that.

Eventually Eisenhower placed conditional limitations on his continued support for the Crusade for Freedom: that there be no activities that "could be inimical to the policies of the twelve governments making up NATO," and Lucius Clay's continued personal direction as chairman. When, in March 1951, Clay informed Eisenhower that he would continue in his position for another year, Eisenhower wrote: "Since it appears . . . that you are to belong to it for one year only, I would not want to engage myself for a longer term."[25] Eisenhower's reluctance to be officially connected with the Crusade and its parent body, the NCFE, in Clay's absence was well advised. While C. D. Jackson called for "skilled and fanatical personnel" to staff public programs, Eisenhower was busy trying to convince his war-weary allies that the psychological warfare between the United States and the Soviet Union did in fact somehow involve their immediate interests. At SHAPE, he achieved only modest success on that score. Britain refused to join the European defense alliance. France refused to accept German rearmament. The Netherlands was vigorously disinterested. Germany had no particular desire to rearm, and moreover, a considerable proportion of the citizenry wanted the "foreign" forces to "go home." In a stunning public-opinion survey made by a West

German agency in March 1952, Eisenhower was informed that "no favorable public opinion toward NATO has yet developed in West Germany. . . ."[26] In addition, Italy, Britain, France, the Netherlands—indeed all of Western Europe was tilting toward socialism. It was a mess.

By 1952, Eisenhower had accepted the arguments of his associates. Only with all the power and prestige of the presidency behind him did Eisenhower's vision stand a significant chance for success. Cut off, alone, in Europe, at SHAPE, responsible to such an "isolationist" as Taft or such a "socialist" as Truman, his vision would be truncated, twisted, distorted. It would not be his vision at all. Too much was at stake. Eisenhower agreed. Noting that "in Britain they 'stand' for office," while in the United States they "run," he decided that if he could stand perfectly still and be nominated he would, after the convention, run for the presidency. His terms were very specific, and his first public statement, released on 7 January, was very limited. He acknowledged merely that he was, after all, a Republican.

Eisenhower's announcement coincided with the fall of the French Government on 7 January 1952. The next day, he wrote to Henry Luce that "yesterday" he "finally felt forced to make a statement to clarify certain points of fact . . . relating to my past record and present leanings." He wanted Luce to know that his *Life* editorial about Eisenhower's potential for "political service" "was one of the factors" that persuaded him "to break my policy of complete silence." That same evening, the French Government collapsed over what Eisenhower considered "a question of internal detail." Such evidence of international "irresponsibility" helped persuade Eisenhower that the United States did in fact have the burden of world leadership, if only because the "American people today are the most politically mature of any in the world."[27]

There was a great deal of pressure on Eisenhower from his NATO associates to remain in Europe. He was widely perceived as the only individual capable of persuading twelve dissonant governments that America's commitment to NATO was neither partisan nor mercenary. Eisenhower alone seemed to placate the conflicting, even inimical NATO personalities. Eisenhower alone seemed steady, steadfast, reliable. He seemed genuinely concerned about Europe's future. He had not returned to Europe to create a new American dependency, nor to prepare the United States' chosen battlefield against the Soviet Union. Eisenhower seemed committed to Europe for what it represented—the seat of Western society, high culture, civility, freedom. He might be about to become a politician in the United States. But in Europe he was still a hero—a noble warrior who appreciated the human sacrifices of war. Eisenhower honored his alliances and seemed throughout the continent genuinely a man of peace.

France's Marshal Alphonse Juin, for example, lunched with Bermingham to convince him that Eisenhower "was the only man living who could handle his present position and that under no circumstances should he be tempted to accept any other offer." Bermingham left Juin wondering "if perhaps he was not a Democrat!" The task, Bermingham wrote Eisenhower, was to persuade the United States' allies that "the ultimate and complete success of [our] endeavors lies with your directing it from the White House."

Eisenhower's commitment to NATO was absolute. He was deeply convinced that collective security "among the free nations" was "a must for the future of our type of civilization." And, he wrote to his brother Milton, without strong U.S. support—moral, political, economic, and military—such security will not be brought about. Eisenhower believed that to do anything to divide America's attitude on this question, to divert America's attention away from this question for a domestic political campaign, would be "nothing less than calamitous."[28]

Eisenhower seemed to waver on the brink of politics for months. Clay was among the first to persuade him to make a definite public statement. Uneasy about Taft's unchallenged position within the Republican Party, Clay wrote Eisenhower in May that it was time "to move." Throughout the spring and summer of 1951, Eisenhower was bombarded with advice to acknowledge at least his "partisan preference." He was continually warned that Taft could be nominated but could not win—"a fatality" that only Eisenhower could prevent. Clay wrote: "Please remember that no matter how badly you may be needed in Europe you are needed even more here, and perhaps if you do not return nothing accomplished there would have any real permanency." Bermingham was even more persusaive. He wrote in September that a statement at least was required to "unloose the activities of your friends all over America who want to get the delegate machinery moving in your behalf." That statement was needed urgently to "offset" the "already well-oiled" Taft machinery that might give him the nomination "by default." Bermingham became impassioned: "Your mission abroad . . . can be completed as you envisaged it by that unity of purpose which only you can create and preserve, and there is only one spot from which you can inspire and direct it. At the top. The indispensability of yourself in Europe—preached by many—can stem only from personal motives, and is just plain rot."[29]

Eisenhower was not unmoved by such appeals. Nor was he unmoved by favorable public-opinion polls, which showed that while in September 1947 Eisenhower had 48 percent of the votes to Truman's 39 percent, in August 1951 Eisenhower's support was an "unprecedented" 64 percent. Nevertheless, for months his response to such pressure remained the same: Western civilization depended on his work at SHAPE. In September he wrote: "With weak governments the rule on the continent, and the possibility of having new governments in both Britain and France, continued momentum . . . will depend entirely upon American leadership." The United States was "the keystone of the entire structure," and U.S. "unity before the world must be unassailable." Eisenhower did not "want to overestimate" his "own contribution" but believed that his continued influence depended on the fact that he represented "no faction, group or party in the U.S. or in any other country. . . . Until we are definitely past the shoals, I could not jeopardize this position of non-partisanship, even by so much as a sneeze. . . ." As late as December, Eisenhower refused to budge toward a public statement: "The future will have to take care of itself," he wrote Bermingham. "I have plenty to do in the present."[30]

The pressure continued to escalate. Sid Richardson sent Eisenhower the Texas "Chuckle a Day":

"What kind of car you driving?"
"An Eisenhower."
"An Eisenhower?"
"It's one of those you don't know if it's going to run or not."

Bermingham sent Eisenhower information about "a secret analysis" made by a research department at Columbia University regarding voting trends for 1952. "If the conclusions reached could be published (which of course they never will be) it would shock the conservative element into a realization that an avalanche of voters never before recorded will go to the polls in 1952, all voting in classes for the New Deal (or whatever will be the new pattern)." Just anybody running Democratic, Bermingham wrote Eisenhower, "will soundly trounce anyone other than yourself." And President Truman, apparently still unaware of Eisenhower's Republicanism, sent the general a personal, handwritten letter:

> Dear Ike:—The columnists, the slick magazines and all the political people, who like to speculate are saying many things about what is to happen in 1952.
>
> As I told you in 1948 and at our luncheon in 1951, do what you think best for the country. My own position is in the balance. If I do what I want to do, I'll go back to Missouri and MAYBE run for the Senate. If you decide to finish the European job, (and I don't know who else can), I must keep the isolationists out of the White House. I wish you would let me know what you intend to do. It will be between us and no one else.[31]

Eisenhower's letter was just as specific. He wanted to live "a semi-retired life with my family, given over mainly to the study of, and a bit of writing on, present day trends and problems." He felt no "duty to seek a political nomination, in spite of the fact that many have urged to the contrary." He assured Truman that this "answer is as full and frank as I am able to devise." Eisenhower, in fact a man of principle, felt obliged to acknowledge the possibilities of "unforeseen circumstances of the future." He insisted, however, that because of his "determination to remain silent . . . the possibility that I will ever be drawn into political activity is so remote as to be negligible."[32] That letter, disingenuous in substance and tortured in style, goes a long way toward explaining the frigid relationship that developed between two formerly cordial public men after January 1952.

As early as October 1951, Eisenhower had agreed to the creation of an informal study group organized by Cliff Roberts and William Robinson, who with "Pete" Jones had "agreed to meet the expenses of the project." The study group would collect all "basic data" on significant issues "in concise and easily digestible form" should Eisenhower have "occasion to use it." At the same time, Eisenhower was informed that the *Herald Tribune* "came out so early" for him because Taft was getting too far "out in front." Eisenhower requested that his brother Milton be on the team, because, he wrote, "he is not only a very wise and understanding person, but . . . in many respects, we think exactly alike." Eisenhower was informed that the original list consisted of men who qualified "on the basis of (1) Unselfish devotion to you, and (2) Civic mindedness." None were politicians: L. B. Maytag, R. T. Jones, Jr., B. F. Peek, W. A. Jones, Philip D. Reed, W. E. Robinson, E. D. Slater, Barry T. Leithead, Douglas M. Black, Milton Eisenhower. Ike requested that Clay, Dave Calhoun, Whitney, Aksel Nielsen, and Phil Young be added. Cliff Roberts assured Eisenhower that all the members of "The Gang" were "free of ambitions" and "would want no public recognition hence the existence of the committee would never need to be known."[33] Eisenhower's supporters shared one purpose: the chance to steer the United States through its moment of unrivaled primacy.

Despite all the activity, Eisenhower promised only not to "repudiate their efforts." He would not "participate" in any way. To do so, he wrote Roberts, would only confuse twelve governments, "to each of which I have preached incessantly the paramount importance of NATO," and "divide, along partisan lines, American support" for NATO. To Robinson and his brother Milton he sent a detailed paragraph for use in any way they might see fit:

> For me to admit, while in this post, a partisan political loyalty . . . would encourage partisan thinking, in our country, toward a job in which the whole nation has already invested tremendous sums. . . .[34]

Even after his January statement affirming "a party allegiance coinciding with that of so many of my friends" and acknowledging that he "would regard nomination as a CALL TO DUTY TRANSCENDING THE ONE I AM NOW PERFORMING, . . ." he insisted that he would do nothing to pursue that nomination. "More than this," he wrote Bermingham, "I shall not do." The United States, he repeated repeatedly, had "already invested billions" for NATO. He would not "be false to the trust" assigned him. If his statement of party allegiance and nonrepudiation was insufficient, then his supporters could forget the whole thing and this "plan of theirs should be forthwith abandoned." In one post-script Eisenhower suggested, without much conviction, that they find somebody young and vigorous "and forget old soldiers!"[35]

Eisenhower's entire preconvention campaign was therefore a limited and most unusual affair. Eisenhower never did become a politician in any ordinary sense. He was and remained supreme commander. There was a devoted, if motley, staff pulled together by his trusted lieutenants. Clay was chief liaison officer, who reported faithfully to Eisenhower all the activities of his complicated network of advisers, supporters, businessmen, and politicians who developed his campaign strategies and his position papers. They held forums, meetings, and public events. They drafted speeches and wrote public letters, private letters, and newspaper editorials. They acquired convention support and wooed delegates. And they held massive, moving rallies. Eisenhower himself was profoundly moved by the demonstrated extent and intensity of his popularity.

After all his friends reported with vigorous enthusiasm on a February rally at Madison Square Garden that was filled to capacity despite the fact that the rally was also televised, Eisenhower wrote an intimate, atypical letter to Ed Bermingham:

> I hope I don't get emotional, because I must confess that it is difficult for me to understand that so many thousands of American people genuinely want to put me into a position where my views, convictions and instincts could be so influential in determining the future of America. It is a thought to fill any citizen with great pride, just as it should send him to his knees in front of his God in deepest humility.
>
> I don't mean to be pontifical—and certainly I would not like . . . to appear to be hypocritical. My feelings are very genuine.[36]

When Jacqueline Cochran flew to Paris to show Eisenhower the pictures of the rally, he wrote to Reed that he "could not completely conceal the emotion" he felt. That thousands of Americans were "turning confidently toward" Eisenhower filled him with "a deep sense of overpowering pride." He thought that anybody who could fail to feel "pride in such confidence . . . would be scarcely human."[37]

After that rally, Eisenhower became more involved in his transatlantic campaign. He wrote to Lucius Clay that he would "try to be cooperative" and more "understanding" of the increasing demands his supporters would make. He met with Spyros Skouras and "listened very carefully" to all the media possibilities. He wrote a long philosophical "screed" to William Robinson for possible syndication of his views on varied subjects. He designated Henry Cabot Lodge his campaign manager. That was a profoundly political act. Ike began to recognize the significance of and the need for political acts. His advisers required a political machine. They were grateful for the support of Dewey's reliable Republican machinery, "the framework for Cabot Lodge's efforts." They created a public-relations bureau directed by Sigurd Larmon, the head of Young & Rubicam, "an organization genius in this field."[38]

There was money to raise (over $4 million was needed by July), tempers to assuage, personality differences, ideological differences, and differences in emphases to coordinate. Eisenhower wanted his organization "to keep everybody feeling good." It was up to his liaison officers (mostly Clay) to keep everybody "harnessed so as to pull generally in the same direction." No small task for Clay. There were "mutual prejudices," petty "jealousies." Many considered Lodge, now named leader, a lightweight who threw his weight around too heavily. Bermingham supposed he was "doing the best" he could "with the tools he possesses." But he upset Clay. And, Clay wrote, Lodge made Herbert Brownell "squirm." Then there was Paul Hoffman, who came "in like a hurricane." Clay considered "his values great," but "he likes to be the bridegroom at each wedding, the corpse at every funeral." Moreover, he warned Eisenhower, "do not be OVERSOLD on him." Hoffman did "not have the complete confidence of the business world, although he has a large public following." Then there was Stassen—a total "enigma." Clay wrote Eisenhower: Be "careful in talking to him. He can be very valuable, but no one, I repeat no one, of your group trusts him fully." And Dewey was "irritated" by Senator Duff. And then there was a flap over a finance manager named Talbot, who, it seems, was "dumped rather unceremoniously." Eisenhower was appalled. He demanded unity, coherence. He insisted that all those who supported him understand that there were "major problems to worry about." There was a world to win. "We cannot," he wrote

Robinson, "all mount our horses and ride off in different directions together."³⁹

Rapidly after the New Hampshire primary "landslide," in March, Eisenhower's team pulled forcefully together. Personality tensions eased, and staff problems dissolved with the addition of Sherman Adams and C. D. Jackson. Bermingham brought Adams to Eisenhower and recommended him as an efficient doer, "an Al Gruenther." And Henry Luce released Jackson to run political interference for Eisenhower's staff. Eisenhower sent Luce a handwritten note thanking him for Jackson, who was "a Godsend" who saved his "sanity—such part as is salvageable—and is giving us all a lift."⁴⁰

It was, most days, a smooth campaign. There was, after all, only one significant scandal. "The Poor Richard Show," featuring Nixon's "Millionaire's Club," and his self-punishing response by way of cover-up, which severely limited Pat Nixon's wardrobe: "I'm proud of the fact that Pat Nixon wears a good Republican cloth coat, and she's going to continue to." Eisenhower apparently had not known that he had the responsibility for selecting his Vice-President. He thought that would be done through convention rituals. According to Herbert Brownell, Eisenhower selected Nixon on the recommendation of Clay, Dewey, and Brownell, based on several requirements: youth, western constituency, political experience. After the scandal, Clay and Dewey wanted Nixon to step down. Dewey telephoned Nixon to request his resignation. Bill Robinson was enraged. He urged Eisenhower to dump him, and he attempted to persuade Nixon to remove himself. The New York *Herald Tribune* editorialized that "the proper course of Senator Nixon in the circumstances is to make a formal offer of withdrawal from the ticket." Eisenhower did nothing, and Nixon refused to step down. Instead, he made a speech—the most famous speech of his career. "My fellow Americans, I come before you tonight as a candidate for the Vice Presidency whose honesty and integrity have been questioned. . . ." He was not a rich man. He and his family lived modestly. Yes, there was a dog, a gift, named Checkers. Nixon loved that gift, named Checkers. But he was patriotic, a veteran. He bought government bonds, did not own stocks, and banked his earnings. His daughters loved the dog. And there could be an independent audit to prove his financial moderation. Besides, Stevenson had slush funds too. But the point, the real point, was that Nixon would not step down; not for reasons of his own interests or ambitions—but out of respect and caring for Dwight David Eisenhower:

> And now, finally, I know that you wonder whether or not I am going to stay. . . . Let me say this: I don't believe that I ought to quit, because I am not a quitter. . . . [And] I would do nothing that would harm the possibilities of Dwight Eisenhower to become President of the United States. . . .

Nixon submitted to the Republican National Committee the right to make the final decision, and urged TV America to "wire and write" the committee "whether you think I should stay. . . ." Stunning. Breathtaking. Richard M. Nixon had, somewhere between "I Love Lucy" and the Milton Berle show, transformed himself forevermore into "Tricky Dick."[41] Eisenhower's failure to act on behalf of his own principles in October 1952 saddled American politics with Richard Nixon for decades. In retrospect, that was undoubtedly the lost political opportunity of the postwar years.

Adlai Stevenson's response to the issue of campaign and personal finances and slush funds was to disclose his own income tax. That really infuriated Eisenhower's advisers. Bermingham wrote Eisenhower that he must not respond to Stevenson's "mouse-trap." To acknowledge in any way "this socialistic demand" to publish the personal finances of public figures would, Bermingham assured Eisenhower, "bedevil" him for years. It would become impossible to get "men you will want" to "accept a position of high office should that become a requirement." Eisenhower's own campaign funds were never discussed. Bermingham assured Eisenhower that "the American people know generally your financial picture." Besides, in his travels throughout the United States, Bermingham wrote, he had simply "found no interest" in the subject.[42]

Eisenhower's campaign was devoted to international peace. Very early, Eisenhower had attempted to define his political philosophy fully. In February, he sent Bill Robinson a detailed essay, full of broad theoretical generalities, emphasizing the historic "task of the progressive in human relationships." Eisenhower wanted it understood that he was "dedicated to the idea" that every individual "be assured . . . the greatest possible opportunities for self-development and advancement" and "be protected against injustice and unnecessary domination, of whatever origin." "Power concentrations," Eisenhower acknowledged, "can be basically political," as in "the Kremlin politburo," or they "can be largely financial"—even when "dedicated otherwise to personal liberty, as was the case in practically all industry of the Western World during portions of the 19th century." Eisenhower opposed "the influence of concentrated wealth" and considered it "needful . . . to stand watch to see that new financial despotisms do not arise." He concluded on this subject that "weak government favors the predatory; too strong a government (dictatorship) regiments us all."

Eisenhower here developed at length his notions of a financial middle ground. He laboriously discussed the need to control, diminish, and diffuse "the power of concentrated wealth" so that it does not "menace . . . the self-respect, opportunities, and livelihood of great groups of ordinary citizens." He also opposed "too much government," "unwise government," and "extravagance in government spending." He opposed high taxes and socialism. He believed there were connections between "a prosperous free enterprise and freedom—national solvency and individual freedom. Worthless money and bankruptcy lead to nationalization of property; a development that compels bureaucratic control, which must finally give way to autocratic control." High taxation. Vast government debt. Inflation. "Our money grows cheaper and cheaper; and . . . the victim is not the wealthy man—one who could . . . live out his days, if he so chooses, in idle comfort. It is the workman, the mass of America, that is to pay the price; regimented labor is the inescapable basis of the socialized or planned economy!"

The document went on for pages, twelve single-spaced pages. Eisenhower considered himself a progressive, and he warned against the use of labels. The "same individual who is labeled by the radical theorists as a reactionary will often be himself called a radical by the extreme reactionaries." Eisenhower was sincere about these things. He had been asked for his political theory. He wanted it to be fully understood: *"The true progressive must refer again and again to the axiom that liberty is not possible for one except as it is defined and limited by equal liberties for others."* (Eisenhower's italics.) Although he did not have many alternatives, he

wanted to demonstrate that he understood some of the complexities. This was true about the issue of "socialized medicine," which
particularly disturbed him in a moment when the United States
had to win the battle for men's minds. He wrote on another occasion that while he was "as violently opposed" to socialized medicine "as anyone," he was also disturbed by the fact that "many of
the doctors were quite self-centered in their attitude and were of
no help at all in suggesting ways and means of meeting the obvious
needs of the population in medical care." He urged the medical
profession to develop "a middle-of-the-road solution" that main-
tains our "basic conceptions and principles and still provides decent medical care regardless of the economic status of the individual or family."

These were issues that never would receive his full attention.
And they were issues about which he felt uncertain, more reliant
on the views of his advisers, his Columbia tutors who remained to
the end of his life the source of his economic understanding and
determined the extent and nature of his activity in this area. He
had written a bold document, expressed his views positively, and
was shy about the possible reactions of his friends: "I make no
claim of profundity in these observations so hastily set down.
There is little of organization or coherence in this composition, but
I think that here and there you will find at least some basic truths
to which you will readily agree." He hoped Robinson would send
him "the results of your combined criticism." Cite "page and paragraph." "I'd like your most 'radical' friend to go over it, as well as
the conservatives. Of course, you'll say it's too long and wordy;
will you give me a short version?"

Eisenhower had searched his soul. The paper was entirely sincere and heartfelt. His advisers, however, rejected his "composition" as profoundly naïve. Robinson wrote there were "several paragraphs" that would be lifted to fit "beautifully" into the *Tribune*'s
series on the Eisenhower creed. He encouraged Eisenhower to
write a speech on peace. They never referred to it again.[43] But Eisenhower wanted to be understood. He wanted his views represented. He wrote Clay that his essay to Robinson apparently "was
not exactly what he was looking for." He would make another
effort, this time addressed to Lodge. "Of course, such a document
would not be published," he now agreed. But "it would allow the

several members of the Committee to make verbal quotes with absolute assurance that there is no misinterpretation." Eisenhower
thought "such a paper might occasionally be useful." He also
thought his return to the United States on the pretext of attending
a "ground-breaking" ceremony of the "Eisenhower Foundation,"
in Abilene, Kansas, rang false. It was to be the occasion for Eisenhower's long-awaited political entry. And he would deliver a
speech on peace. He hated the entire idea. He also hated to disagree "with loyal and devoted friends." In fact, he wrote that he
scarcely believed that he had the right to disagree. But he felt pressured. And he could not "shake free of an instinctive feeling that
the proposal has a glaring appearance of artificiality."[44] He was
being pressured. He had become a politician. He would go to
Abilene.

Peace was, after all, the area of his particular competence. And
his advisers were very forceful. Robinson wrote that his first public
address on his return to the United States should emphasize only
one theme: peace. It was the only unfulfilled aspiration of the
American people. "You know," Robinson wrote Eisenhower, "no
one in my lifetime ever made a great speech on peace." Nor did
anybody throughout history—"no one was equipped to do it,
. . . no one but you." "I can hear you saying at Abilene that you
are dedicating your life to the proposition that this Abilene memorial will be the LAST WAR memorial that anyone will dedicate."
"The cynics will cry politics—but the people won't. Candidate or
not the people need your leadership—not on the 'issues' (to hell
with the issues)—on their greatest unfulfilled ambition,—peace."[45]

The *Herald Tribune* introduced the keynote of Eisenhower's
campaign. "The Eisenhower Movement," Walter Lippmann editorialized immediately after the New Hampshire primary, was a
"mission in American politics." Its sole purpose was to "re-unite
the American people, to heal their divisions, to assuage the bitterness of regions, of interests, of classes and of sects. . . . We cannot carry the burden of protecting and leading the free nations of
the world if every policy and every measure we have to take must
be dragged through the stinking mess of shyster politics." The Eisenhower movement was "about raising the standard of public life
to a level where these conflicts" of class, of race, of differences and
antagonisms, "would cease to be irreconcilable."[46]

Whenever Eisenhower became tempted to debate questions of politics, the domestic economy, or the fiscal future, his friends reminded him to return to the primary principle. Cliff Roberts wrote simply: "The chief reason that people want to vote for you is because they think you have more ability to keep us out of another war." Eisenhower's "outstanding asset" was his training and confidence that he could steer the United States "on a course designed to prevent the third world war, keeping the country strong both economically and militarily while the program is being developed and executed."[47] That was all. Eisenhower would end the war in Korea, end all war.

As the nineteenth-century imperial world shattered into many independent pieces, as Britain and France lost their colonial grip, only the United States was solvent and dedicated to the task of reconstructing the planet into its own image. That opportunity for reconstruction, Eisenhower proclaimed in October, represented the greatest opportunity history had ever given to one nation. It was an opportunity for global change, and it could "bring peace on earth." For Eisenhower, the use of peace as a major rhetorical theme throughout his campaign and during his presidency was neither sham nor artifice. But it was very complicated.

Frequently, it was the press that rendered Eisenhower's views on peace simplistic. And he resented it. He would go to Korea. But he had no secret plan "for the decisive winning of the Korean war." Yet in June those were the headlines. All he actually said was there was "no easy way out of the Korean war." He wrote Roberts that "the only program" he could imagine might even "be in operation": To "organize and arm the necessary number of South Koreans to defend their own front lines and withdraw our troops into reserve positions." Eisenhower considered it "far from satisfactory," but he had concluded that there was no possibility of settling tensions in Korea "until we can establish a better understanding with the Russians on the whole front."[48]

Eisenhower's quest for peaceful solutions was, in part, limited to Europe and, moreover, limited in scope. Eisenhower did not want to see the world ripped apart by atomic warfare. He was dedicated to the prevention of World War III. He preferred political warfare, psychological warfare, to military battle. But he would, over time, involve U.S. troops in military activities of defined scope and lim-

ited duration. To preserve U.S. and allied interests in Latin
America, the Middle East, Africa, and Asia, Eisenhower presided
over the creation of entirely new dimensions of political warfare:
the "secret war," the countervailing force. To destabilize Communist advances throughout the neocolonial world, Eisenhower introduced a new, counterrevolutionary strategy. Subsequently called
"counterinsurgency" and credited to John F. Kennedy, whose activities in Laos, Cuba, and Vietnam received far more attention,
Eisenhower-era counterinsurgency activities were less publicized,
less understood. Obscured for decades, Eisenhower's operations in
Iran and Guatemala became the models for all of America's subsequent activities in the neocolonial world.

CHAPTER V
MISSIONS OF
PEACE AND
POLITICAL
WARFARE

I believe that the people in the long run are going to do more to promote peace than any governments. Indeed, I think that people want peace so much that one of these days governments had better get out of their way and let them have it.

EISENHOWER TO HAROLD MACMILLAN, LONDON, 1959

In Lincoln's language: "With public sentiment on its side, everything succeeds; with public sentiment against it, nothing succeeds." Lincoln could not have foreseen the power of a modern police state. Yet in the long perspective of history, he may be proven right.

WILLIAM H. JACKSON, CHAIR, EISENHOWER'S COMMITTEE ON POLITICAL WARFARE, 1956

Ike's election meant different things to different people. His Republican campaign staff had a formula, $K^1 C^2$—Korea, Communism, Corruption. Ike would go to Korea, halt the Communist tide, and remove all corrupt Democrats and assorted New Deal fellow travelers from influence and public life. To the millions of Americans who voted for Ike instead of Adlai Stevenson, Ike meant more: He meant honesty and goodness and peace. Americans liked Ike, and trusted him. So did the rest of the Western world. So did the Soviets. They despised Dulles. But they liked Ike. His smile could melt the Soviet snows. He would work toward peace on earth.

In the White House, Eisenhower remained supreme commander of allied, if disparate, forces. Always the general, Eisenhower's staff formulations were designed to maximize responsibility in each department. He surrounded himself with bold and forceful talents he admired, and sought vigorous participation and debate at cabinet and staff meetings. Eisenhower abhorred yes-men. There were no toadies or lackeys on his staff; and his chief advisers frequently disagreed with each other. Sources recently made available reveal the extent to which Eisenhower courted advice and sought conflicting opinions—the extent to which he wrote his own speeches and made his own decisions. The traditional image of Eisenhower as bullied by John Foster Dulles and awed by George Humphrey is simply incorrect.

John Foster Dulles was Eisenhower's first certain appointment. Dulles visited Eisenhower at SHAPE and, at the general's request, sent him an essay detailing his political and international views. Correspondence between Clay and Eisenhower, although critical of Dulles' essay as vague and insufficiently substantial, reveals that by April 1952 Eisenhower would select Dulles for Secretary of State, because he so nearly replicated his own views. For a time, Dewey seemed to be a possibility, and Henry and Clare Boothe Luce promoted his qualities. But Eisenhower was impressed by Dulles' learning,* dedication to principle, heritage, and determi-

---

* One curious lack in Dulles' educational preparation for the job of Secretary of State has been described by C. L. Sulzberger, who was invited by Maurice Schumann to lunch with French diplomatic officials in honor of Foster Dulles in Paris in May 1952: "I was able to eavesdrop, sitting, as I was, across the table

nation to be a great Secretary of State.[1] Dulles' maternal grandfather, John W. Foster, had been Secretary of State under Benjamin Harrison. His uncle Robert Lansing, Secretary of State under Woodrow Wilson, appointed both John Foster and Allen Dulles to the American delegation of the Versailles Peace Conference in 1918–19. As an attorney, Dulles specialized in international economics, and as senior partner with Sullivan and Cromwell he represented international business interests based in the United States as well as in Belgium, Sweden, Germany, and Latin America. But his entire public life was devoted to his ambition: to become Secretary of State, and unlike his uncle Robert Lansing, who lost Wilson's attention, to retain the confidence of the President.[3]

Subsequently, Dulles met with Eisenhower daily. The day began and ended with their conversations. Although the public differences in their emphasis and style were dramatic, since Dulles introduced "brinkmanship" while Eisenhower seemed to pursue peace with greater determination, they represented aspects of one, agreed-upon policy. Eisenhower assured Swede Hazlett in 1954 that despite their apparent differences, Dulles "never made a serious pronouncement, agreement or proposal without complete and exhaustive consultation with me in advance and, of course, my ap-

from the guest of honor. Schumann speaks excellent English but made the mistake of saying to Dulles that, of course, the latter spoke French. Dulles smugly agreed and from there on a crisscross of misunderstanding developed with conversations like: 'Do you think German rearmament is a good thing?' being answered with observations such as 'I am sorry she isn't here.' I was sitting next to André Maurois who was equally fascinated."[2]

proval." In 1958 Eisenhower again assured Hazlett that he and Dulles were in accord and, Eisenhower wrote: "I admire tremendously his wisdom, his knowledge in the delicate and intricate field of foreign relations, and his tireless dedication to duty." Although Eisenhower recognized that "with strangers his personality may not always be winning," he wrote Hazlett that "with his friends he is charming and delightful."[4]

Dulles was only one of many friends and associates who influenced decisions during Eisenhower's presidency. George Humphrey, the Secretary of the Treasury, was a penny-pinching conservative with ties to congressional "isolationists." Although Eisenhower did not meet Humphrey until after the election, they became close personal friends. They vacationed, fished, and hunted ducks together. Cabinet battles between Dulles and Humphrey were frequently rousing, and frequently limited activities that Dulles wanted. But Eisenhower believed in cabinet and staff controversy, in compromise and a "middle way." He assured Humphrey's detractors that his Secretary of Treasury's determination "to save money, balance the budget and cut taxes" was mitigated by his sense of responsibility for the kind of "legislative-executive team" Eisenhower demanded.[5]

Eisenhower was pleased with the team he had assembled. He wrote in his diary that his two "slight worries" were Sinclair Weeks of Commerce and Martin Durkin of Labor. "The former seems so completely conservative in his views that at times he seems to be illogical." And Durkin, who soon resigned, seemed to represent labor too vigorously and "to carry a bit of a chip on his shoulder." As for congressional and media criticism that Eisenhower's Cabinet comprised many millionaires and one labor leader, Eisenhower wrote that such opposition, in practice, would result in America's inability "to get anybody to take jobs in Washington except business failures, college professors [crossed out and replaced by 'political hacks'], and New Deal lawyers. All of these would jump at the chance to get a job that a successful businessman has to sacrifice very much to take."[6] Eisenhower relied also on the advice and input of close personal friends such as Walter Bedell Smith, Lucius Clay, his brother Milton Eisenhower, William Robinson, and General Alfred Gruenther. Gruenther, Eisenhower's successor at

SHAPE, was widely recognized as one of the most brilliant and caring analysts of European affairs. Although his role has been largely ignored, few decisions were made without Gruenther's perspective.[7] C. D. Jackson, who considered Dulles the activist in the Cabinet, complained that Eisenhower's determination to get all possible views and his "exaggerated desire to have everybody happy" prevented him from making "clean cut decisions."[8] But Eisenhower's seeming vacillation was part of his style. During press conferences when he was cornered by unpleasant controversy, he would seem to bumble in order—as he once told his press secretary, James Hagerty—to "confuse" the situation. To suspend a crisis was generally to defuse it, so as to negotiate it over time and with consideration. For Eisenhower, the mandate of his office required careful negotiations that depended on contradictory opinions—in order to meet the long-range challenge of the Cold War.

For Eisenhower, the mandate of his presidency was a global mission. It was a complicated, if not contradictory, crusade. He would promote economic expansion, extend political democracy, and maintain international peace. He would destabilize communism and "liberate" the satellite countries "enslaved" by the Communist empire. By vigorous anticolonial activity, the United States would rally to its side the newly emerging states of Asia, the Middle East, and Africa. The resource-rich nations now called the "third world," colonized originally because of the value of their raw materials, would be transformed by United States economic aid into partners for world progress. Europe would be economically restored, politically resurrected. A world economic policy led by the United States would dissolve tensions. France and Britain would be content to release their imperial advantages and unite their interests in a vast international economic development program. For defense there was first the rejected European Defense Community and then the extension of NATO, both dependent on the remilitarization of the Federal Republic of Germany.[9] Global. Imaginative. Ambitious. It was Eisenhower's blueprint for the Cold War.

Peace would be ensured by determination, wisdom, and morality. On 30 May 1951, Eisenhower noted in his diary that "another Decoration Day finds us still adding to the number of graves" to be decorated in the future. "Men are stupid." He was convinced that good will, fairness, and patience would, over time, end international war. Peace would be ensured between the United States and the U.S.S.R. by a balance of strength. After "Hydrogen," or thermonuclear, bombs were exploded, peace would be ensured by a balance of terror. But, Eisenhower insisted, World War II must be the last civil war to tear civilization apart. World War III would mean that the United States had lost the Cold War. With the "new super weapons now available the world could well exterminate itself." Ike told Bulganin and Molotov during a private conversation at dinner in Geneva on 18 July 1955, "Whereas once it was said that wars began where diplomacy fails, diplomacy must now begin because war has failed." They agreed. It was the 1955 Summit Conference—the conference that introduced the hopeful "Spirit of Geneva." It was a spirit that survived many trials, because for eight years the President of the United States repeated over and over again that international war had become—simply—unacceptable.[10]

Eisenhower's political philosophy remained constant throughout his presidency. He considered himself politically moderate. But he rejected the notion that "the middle way" was a fence-sitting operation. It was difficult to maintain, he acknowledged, but it could "in itself be a revolution." He understood that his position incited "the hatred and enmity" of all "extremists."[11] One of his brothers, known as the reactionary Edgar, frequently railed against Ike's "New Deal," "socialist" policies. On one occasion, Eisenhower responded with an angry letter. If a "rule of reason" was "not applied," the United States would "lose everything."

> Should any political party attempt to abolish social security, unemployment insurance, and eliminate labor laws and farm programs, you would not hear of that party again in our political history. There is a tiny splinter group, of course, that believes you can do these things. Among them are H. L. Hunt (you possibly know his background), a few other Texas oil millionaires, and an occasional politician or businessman from other areas. Their number is negligible and they are stupid.[12]

When Dr. Gabriel Hauge, Eisenhower's economic adviser, wrote the President that he was convinced that the "extreme Right Wing" was out to "recapture" Republican party leadership, Ike had "only one remark: If the Right Wing really recaptures the Republican

Party, there simply isn't going to be any Republican influence in this country within a matter of a few brief years. A new Party will be inevitable."[13]

Contrary to traditional assumptions about Eisenhower's political philosophy, it was based on a thoughtful, earnestly acquired set of principles. Whether or not he ever actually read Karl Marx or Lenin, he had come to very specific conclusions about capitalism and communism. He deplored the fact that so many Americans failed to understand "that our political and economic life are so intertwined that we cannot separate them." In a conversation with Dr. Hauge during the controversy over the vetoed 1956 gas bill, Eisenhower declared: "Now you have a situation where the whole life of the United States can be affected by a corporate decision. . . . This sort of thing can be very dangerous unless people act with the greatest wisdom and concern for the nation." When Hauge replied that "business must have an honorable place" in society, Eisenhower said, "I want to give businessmen an honorable place, but they make crooks out of themselves."[14] Eisenhower despised crooks. He feared unbridled power and self-indulgent arrogance. He deplored opportunists and reactionaries. But, above all, he scorned communists. His scorn was based on his conviction that they rigidly adhered to a theory of political economy that was no longer operative.

Eisenhower analyzed Lenin's "contradictions of capitalism" and decided they were all false: "The capital-labor contradiction" depended on a society wherein "there were no restraints on the power of the capitalists—the great corporations and the syndicates. . . ."

The contradiction of "conflict between separate groups of capitalists, each struggling for the sources of raw materials and other means of production," "meant capitalistic wars between capitalistic states for the domination of the world's surface."

But, Eisenhower concluded, Lenin's analysis was plausible only under "extremist" conditions. "All human experience," he wrote, involved "progress," which was "possible only as extremes are avoided and solutions to problems are found in a great middle way that has regard for the requirements, desires, and aspirations of the vast majority. Consequently, the inevitability of the results of the so-called contradictions in capitalism is open to question. In fact, we flatly deny that they have to become so serious as to cause the destruction of [a] competitive form of enterprise and a free government based upon it."

Eisenhower acknowledged that there were events in history that appeared to "give a certain validity to some of these communistic arguments." But he believed that all the principal contradictions within a democratic system occurred "because of the inability of men to forego immediate gain for a long time good." Convinced that "capitalistic—that is to say, self-governing nations have long ago foreseen that any kind of war is too high a price to pay for the hope of a piece of additional territory," Eisenhower counseled long-term economic planning, international assistance programs, "world trade and world cooperation" based on the requirements "of the long-term good of all." If that occurred, "we could laugh at all the other so-called 'contradictions' in our system, and we could be so secure against the Communist menace that it would gradually dry up and wither away." On the other hand, Eisenhower feared "the danger [which] is very real and very great that even the so-called enlightened areas of Western Europe, Britain, United States, and the other English-speaking peoples will, by stubborn adherence to the purpose of achieving maximum immediate gain, actually commit suicide." To avoid suicide, "men should attempt to devise a religion that stresses the qualities of unselfishness, cooperation, and equality of men."[15]

He dedicated his presidency, therefore, to creating the world's "finest advertisement for freedom." In November 1953, he wrote to his brother Milton that he wanted "to establish clearly that the concern of this Administration is for *all* the people, and that we recognize that there are more people of low incomes than there are of high incomes." "Specifically and concretely," he wrote to John Foster Dulles, "this Administration is committed to the development of policies that will bring the greatest good to the greatest number. This means that there must be lifted from the minds of men the fears of disaster, poverty, and old age." Admittedly, Eisenhower wanted Dulles to add those words to his talk before the CIO. But Ike was adamant: "Further, this means that appropriate governmental connection with our entire economy must be so adjusted as to develop and sustain a prosperous agriculture, manufacturing, and services, and above all such an equitable distribution of the resulting products that 160 million people will constitute always the finest advertisement for freedom." Rhetoric aside, Eisenhower wanted his Cabinet to initiate legislation "for a vast expansion in unemployment insurance" and "expanded activity in the business of providing housing of decent standards for every American citizen."[16]

In the worldwide competition against communism, Eisenhower believed that the United States could not remain the only industrial power without a national health program. In July 1954, Congress rejected his national health reinsurance bill. It was defeated by a coalition of Democrats who wanted a stronger measure and forty Republicans who wanted no federal health program at all. In a telephone conversation with HEW Secretary Oveta Culp Hobby, the former commander of the Women's Army Corps, Eisenhower and Mrs. Hobby agreed that unless such a bill was passed, they would be saddled with "socialized medicine." Eisenhower said "America just had to have better health." Mrs. Hobby said she had been talking with "someone who was proposing [a] foundation to defeat communism." She told him that Americans "had to have hope" so that "communism cannot gain a foothold." There were 25 million Americans who could not afford health insurance. In a subsequent meeting with congressional leaders, Eisenhower was told that a coalition of private insurance companies and the vigorous opposition of the American Medical Association had helped defeat the moderate bill. The President exploded: "How in the hell is the American Medical Association going to stop socialized medicine if they oppose such bills as this. I don't believe the people of the United States are going to stand for being deprived of the opportunity to get medical insurance. . . . I refuse to admit defeat on this one." Although medical-care programs did expand under Eisenhower, notably for the aged, the United States remains virtually the only industrial country without a national health insurance program and without socialized medicine.[17]

Throughout Eisenhower's correspondence and diary entries, there are numerous criticisms of "demagogues" and reactionaries who shortsightedly refused to recognize issues that concerned the well-being of American citizens. He believed they contributed to communist propaganda, and to communism. For Eisenhower, America stood for a "partnership" between labor and capital. But the defeats of such legislation as the health reinsurance program imperiled his creed. When he was told that some American workers had adopted "the Marxist thinking" of inevitable class war, Eisenhower declared that that was "the most evil thing [he could] think of."[18]

Communists, who seek "to divide and conquer; to set class against class," would be uprooted, isolated. Eisenhower intended to create national unity in "public opposition to Communism."[19] His anti-Communist crusade was not to be confused with McCarthyism. Eisenhower deplored McCarthy's tactics and style. He was aware that the mayor of Berlin had told Adlai Stevenson that "McCarthy had done more to hurt America abroad in eight months than Soviet propaganda did in eight years." During his European tour, McCarthy and his associates had antagonized many of our allies and insulted almost all United States Foreign Service diplomats. Eisenhower was informed that McCarthyism had destroyed the morale of the United States diplomatic corps. Embassy officials were quitting, right and left. They felt unprotected by the State Department hierarchy and ignored by Eisenhower.

In Tokyo, Jakarta, New Delhi, Beirut, throughout the cities of Turkey, in Rome, Vienna, and Athens, American diplomats seemed to talk of little else. In Rome, for example, a member of the staff was refused an assignment he sought "because he had kept company with Lillian Hellman in 1932." In Athens, the highly regarded Ambassador John Peurifoy complained to Stevenson that he was being transferred to Latin America because he had "clashed with McCarthy over some files." Peurifoy's aggressive activities in Greece were known to have helped destroy the communist danger, and his work in Guatemala was later highly praised by the State Department. But in 1953 he was "unhappy about what was happening" and asked Stevenson to keep it secret. It was "the sort of news that would further depress the already shaky morale of career officers."[20]

R. W. Scott McLeod, former FBI agent and well-known McCarthy associate, had been appointed to "clean out" the State Department. McLeod believed that New Dealers, "queers," "drunks," and assorted "perverts" had kept the State Department both "soft on communism" and "limp-wristed." As a result of his activities, morale and initiative disappeared. On 8 April 1954,

A. A. Berle noted in his diary: "Jane and Andrew Carey back from Ethiopia because, may God forgive us, the Security Service of the Foreign Operations Administration decided that Andy was a security risk because he had married Jane. The real reason was that they had invited Adlai Stevenson to dinner. . . . These are two conservative Republicans, who had behaved approximately like human beings. It makes you a bit sick."[21]

In 1954, Alexander Makinsky, whose reports to the CIA and to C. D. Jackson, Eisenhower's special assistant for Cold War planning, were highly esteemed, wrote a detailed analysis of the political-warfare errors of Eisenhower's first year. Above all, Makinsky wrote, the United States failed to "appreciate that"

> the European Continent, ever since 1914, has been undergoing a social revolution. The Nazi regime, in the majority of the countries which the Germans occupied from 1940 to 1944, was, tacitly or openly, supported by various elements of the big bourgeoisie who saw therein a defense against Communism. The defeat of Nazism was therefore interpreted as the defeat of the big bourgeoisie. In our attempt to find reliable supporters against Communism, we have had, on a number of occasions, to back up some groups who, as a result of the Second World War, would have normally disappeared from the political scene. Thus we find ourselves talking to some of the former Nazi elements in Germany, to some of the former pro-Vichy elements in France, and to similar circles in Italy, Greece, and elsewhere. In the eyes of a great many people in Europe, we are identifying ourselves with "lost causes," whose only hope of survival lies in American support. Our association with those elements, however, brings grist to the Communist mill, especially in France, in Italy, in Holland, and in some of the Scandinavian countries like Denmark and Norway, [which] haven't as yet forgotten the horrors of Nazi occupation. . . .

Makinsky suggested that, instead of supporting "reactionaries," the United States identify itself with more "representative" leaders.

> Our general tendency is to bet, throughout the world, on individuals and groups who are, rightly or wrongly, considered "reactionary," and whom we select or support simply because we feel at home with them: we find we and they speak the same language. . . . (I say this with regret, since I am probably myself a "reactionary!") I do not think it is a secret to anybody today that Bao Dai has no following whatsoever in Indochina; that the Vietnamese "army" (whom we were so anxious to train and equip) existed chiefly in our own imagi-

nation. We fail to realize that we are powerful enough and that we still enjoy sufficient prestige . . . [to] steal the thunder from our opponents by ingratiating ourselves with the more liberal element. . . .

Makinsky considered our "safest bet" in France the "Mendès-France Cabinet." "Only a statesman with a 'left-wing' reputation can succeed in selling a right-wing policy to French political circles and public opinion." Presumably, Makinsky referred to the EDC, which was not to pass the French legislature despite Mendès-France and weeks of intense negotiations. In Germany, Makinsky saw wisdom in an alliance with the Socialists. In Italy, he urged support for "Fanfani, who recently replaced DeGasperi as Secretary General of the Christian Democratic Party, whose left wing he represents, and who might possibly succeed in detaching a variety of left-wing elements away from Nenni and his fellow-travellers." In Indochina, Makinsky thought we should "encourage the French to establish satisfactory relations with Ho Chi Minh," in order to "detach" him "from Red China." Makinsky recognized that these proposals would sound disloyal in some circles, but they were "what the Germans term 'Realpolitik.' " He believed "we must be realistic and opportunistic; we must bet on those who have a following in their own countries and who can deliver the goods—and this regardless of our own personal sympathies and ideologies."[22]

Over time, many of his suggestions were followed. Political warriors stationed everywhere agreed with them. McCarthyism had nothing to do with political warfare, and for years McCarthy's extraordinary domination of American life damaged self-interested international activities. Eisenhower accepted McCarthy's premises. And he refused to criticize his tactics publicly. Eisenhower's unwillingness "to get into the gutter with that guy" led to confusion about the nature of Ike's call for moderation. Old friends would never understand, and some would never forgive, Eisenhower's campaign bow to McCarthy in which he removed a paragraph from his Wisconsin speech that defended the patriotism and integrity of General George Marshall against McCarthy's vicious slander. Since Eisenhower said nothing, it was widely assumed that he approved.† Later, America's political warriors became pro-

† In light of new evidence, one might hazard the theory that Eisenhower, while campaigning in Wisconsin, did unto George Marshall what General Marshall urged he do unto Kay Summersby after World War II. According to Summersby

foundly distressed when he continued what C. D. Jackson called Eisenhower's "Three Little Monkeys act." Jackson believed that to continue to appease McCarthy for his seven congressional votes was "poor tactics, poor strategy, and poor arithmetic." Evidently, Eisenhower's closest friend, his brother Milton, agreed with Jackson. But the President refused to budge. He wrote his brother: "Only a short-sighted or completely inexperienced individual would urge the use of the office of the Presidency to give an opponent the publicity he so avidly desires. Time and time again, without apology or evasion, I . . . have stood for the right of the individual, for free expression of convictions, even though those convictions might be unpopular, and for uncensored use of our libraries. . . . I have no intention whatsoever of helping promote the publicity value of anyone who disagrees with me—demagogue or not!"[23] Whatever Eisenhower's motives, McCarthy's style was not his style. But McCarthyism was advanced and intensified by Eisenhower's determination to ignore it, and his own relentless activity against communists.

One example of Eisenhower's zealous anticommunism shocked world opinion. His decision to execute the Rosenbergs was based on their failure to accept "deals" for their pardon and on his conviction that to pardon them without their public repentance would mean a major political-warfare victory for the worldwide communist movement. He rejected, therefore, all domestic and international appeals for clemency from private citizens and world leaders, including Pope Pius XII, who urged Eisenhower to match "justice with mercy." C. Douglas Dillon, the United States' ambassador to France, wrote that the execution of Julius and Ethel Rosenberg would be a public-relations disaster throughout France. Dillon assured Eisenhower that "we should not deceive ourselves by thinking that this sentiment is due principally to Communist progaganda." The fact was "that the great majority of French people of all political leanings feel that [the] death sentence is completely unjustified . . . and is due only to [the] political climate peculiar to the United States." Even those who accepted the "guilt

---

(and Harry Truman), General Marshall threatened to break Eisenhower politically and "see to it that the rest of his life [would be] a living hell" if he married his wartime driver and companion. Eisenhower never saw her again. See Kay Summersby Morgan, *Past Forgetting: My Love Affair with Dwight D. Eisenhower* (Simon and Schuster, 1976), p. 13.

of [the] Rosenbergs are overwhelmingly of the opinion that [the] death sentence is unjustifiable punishment . . . particularly when compared with [the] prison terms meted to British scientists Allan Nunn May and Klaus Fuchs." In addition, Dillon wrote, there were the "latest doubts" as to David Greenglass' reliability, not only because of the "family connection" (Greenglass, the Rosenbergs' accuser, was Ethel Rosenberg's brother) but because of the charges of perjury, which had "not yet [been] denied."[24] Dillon referred to widely publicized documents that indicated Greenglass lied when he said Julius Rosenberg sent Harry Gold to him. He later admitted he "didn't know who sent Gold to me." Also, Ruth Greenglass allegedly told her attorney that her husband was "an hysteric," who would "say things were so even if they were not." Columbia University Professor Clyde Miller sent Eisenhower a flyer containing these perjury charges. The flyer also contained a photograph of the Rosenberg children, six-year-old Robby and ten-year-old Michael, and a letter addressed to the President written by Michael: ". . . Please let my mommy and daddy go and not let anything happen to them. . . ." Eisenhower was not moved. He wrote to Miller that he failed to appreciate the propaganda value to the communists if the sentence were commuted. Not only would these "arch criminals" be subject to parole after fifteen years, America would appear "weak and fearful" in the face of subversion. "The action of these people has exposed to greater danger of death literally millions of our citizens." And now, Eisenhower wrote, "they have even stooped to dragging in young and innocent children in order to serve their own purposes."[25]

Recently declassified records reveal that a deal to reunite the Rosenbergs with their children was offered to the Rosenbergs. On 22 January 1953, Allen Dulles proposed that their sentence be commuted if they would agree to "appeal to Jews in all countries to get out of the communist movement and seek to destroy it." The first step would be to persuade the Rosenbergs that the Soviet Union persecuted and was "ultimately bent on exterminating the Jews under its sovereignty." The "advantages" of this scheme, Allen Dulles wrote, could "scarcely by overstated from a psychological warfare standpoint."

> The Communist Parties throughout the world have built up the Rosenbergs as heroes and as martyrs to "American anti-semitism."

Their recantation would entail backfiring of this entire Soviet propaganda effort. It would be virtually impossible for world communism to ignore or successfully discredit the Rosenbergs. The couple is ideally situated to serve as leading instruments of a psychological warfare campaign designed to split world communism on the Jewish issue, to create disaffected groups within the membership of the Parties, to utilize these groups for further infiltration and for intelligence work. . . .

Allen Dulles estimated that the "likelihood of success" was doubtful. But, he wrote, "new developments in Soviet policy vis-à-vis the Jews open new possibilities." He also "believed that people of the sort of the Rosenbergs can be swayed by duty where they cannot be swayed by considerations of self-interest. They should not be asked to trade their principles for their lives—for one thing, such an appeal to cowardice would almost certainly fail." They should be, therefore, "offered two things psychologically: (1) an opportunity to recant while preserving their self-respect and honor; (2) a new purpose in life." Dulles suggested that the "ideal emissaries" to introduce his proposal to the Rosenbergs "would be highly intelligent rabbis, representing reformed Judaism, with a radical background or sympathetic understanding of radicalism, and with psychiatric knowledge. . . . The emissaries do not need to be armed with a formal promise of clemency," since, Dulles affirmed, "the Rosenbergs already understand that they can obtain commutation if they cooperate with the United States." "Should the operation succeed," Dulles concluded, "generous commutation appears indicated—both to encourage others to defect and to utilize the Rosenbergs as figures in an effective international psychological warfare campaign against communism primarily on the Jewish issue."[26]

The facts of the Rosenberg case, the nature of America's anti-Communist crusade, the role of COINTELPRO—the FBI's "counterintelligence" program that began in 1956 and involved entrapment and dirty tricks—are now beginning to be declassified. To date, there are an estimated one hundred thousand pages of documents relating to the Rosenberg case still entirely unavailable. Whether or not the Rosenbergs "stole" the secret of the atom bomb, their execution served as a demonstration and a warning: unrepentant communists were traitors and spies, and they might be executed.

The psychological-warfare campaign against communism took many forms. Eisenhower introduced religion, for example, into new areas of public life. He would insert into his Christmas speech of 1953, and into many speeches thereafter, a return to religious faith. Charges that America was merely materialistic and utterly selfish (as Zhukov had once argued) would thereby be dissipated. "More precisely than in any other way," Eisenhower wrote, "communism and freedom are placed in opposition by prayer." On Nelson Rockefeller's recommendation, he agreed to stamp America's paper currency with the motto "In God We Trust." Although he did not want to appear to be "conducting a crusade in this matter," he considered it a noble touch.[27]

During his administration, communists and communist "sympathizers" were removed from public life. He intensified the Employee Security Program, introduced in 1950, and extended it to all government agencies. Between 1953 and 1956, an estimated fifteen hundred civil servants were dismissed for "security" reasons and six thousand more resigned from governmental agencies.

Eisenhower did not "want the issue of Americanism to become a partisan matter." Once the Communist Control Act of 1954, an Act to outlaw the Communist Party, passed, civil liberties in America would protect Democrats and Republicans alike. Eisenhower announced "as a broad policy measure, that any vacancy created by the removal of any person in the government below the policy-making level . . . will be filled by a Republican, if the present incumbent is a Republican, or by a Democrat, if the present incumbent is a Democrat. In other words, I do not intend to use the issue of Communism to build up one party and tear down another. . . ."[28]

Domestically relentless but internationally cautious, Eisenhower was committed to fighting communism without international war. His military career had persuaded him that "any military task" was "largely negative in character." The purpose of military operations was "to protect or defend, not to create and develop."[29] The technology of World War II and the advent of nuclear weapons convinced Eisenhower that war had become unthinkable. At the time of the fall of Dien Bien Phu, he wrote to his friend Earl Schaefer, president of Boeing, that it seemed to him humanity "ought to be intelligent enough to devise ways and means of avoiding suicide."[30] Eisenhower was impatient with and dismayed by associates who seemed ready to embark on "preventive" wars. Congressional "hawks" like Senator William Knowland infuriated him. Frequently, Knowland criticized the Administration for indecisiveness and lack of policy. Eisenhower described his policy as "security through strength, alertness and allies." Knowland's alternative was "preventive war." Eisenhower asked Dulles: "Do you suppose that Knowland would actually carry his thesis to the logical conclusion of presenting a resolution to the Congress aiming at the initiation of such a conflict? Of course I don't believe this for a second." Actually Knowland's only policy, Eisenhower wrote Al Gruenther, was "to develop high blood pressure" whenever he says, "'Red China.'"[31]

Eisenhower's own policies regarding China were uncompromising. Nonrecognition, "massive retaliation," "brinkmanship." Many missiles were waved in his determination to secure Formosa and the offshore islands of Quemoy and Matsu. Deterrence. He did not go to war against China. He restrained Syngman Rhee, of Korea. He did not agree to French and United States military pressure to drop 1-2-3 little atom bombs to defend Dien Bien Phu. Adamantly opposed to the recognition of China and to the admission of China to the United Nations, at least as long as U.S. airmen were held hostage, he was also against a congressional resolution to end United States support for the UN should China be seated. Eisenhower wrote to Vice-President Richard Nixon: "My opposition is based solely on the unshakable conviction that the threat to withhold funds from an organization which we have solemnly obligated ourselves to support . . . is neither becoming to, nor in the interest of, the great nation which is the United States." Eisenhower would refuse to admit China so long as it "is subservient to Moscow and does not abandon its aggressive actions and policies." But Eisenhower considered the impending legislation dangerous and foolhardy:

> Legislation such as this surely would not serve the cause of our leadership of the free forces in the United Nations. Leadership of these free nations . . . is something the Soviet Union can never take away from us. But we can give it away, or lose it if we are careless. And, in my opinion, a hostile, punitive measure such as this . . . would be

a priceless gift to those who would see us weak and alone. Because of the example of irresponsibility it would set for all countries, it could well set loose reckless forces which would level the United Nations before our eyes. . . .[32]

By 1956, Eisenhower's policy of deterrence, from which he never withdrew, created doubts about the future for which he had only one answer: Avoid war. He wrote frequently and specifically about this issue:

I have spent all my life in the study of military strength as a deterrent to war, and in the character of military armaments necessary to win a war. The study of the first . . . is still profitable, but we are rapidly getting to the point that no war can be WON. War implies a contest; when you get to the point that contest is no longer involved and the outlook comes close to destruction of the enemy and suicide for ourselves . . . then arguments as to the exact amount of available strength as compared to somebody else's are no longer the vital issues.

When we get to the point . . . that both sides know that in any outbreak of general hostilities, regardless of the element of surprise, destruction will be both reciprocal and complete, possibly we will have sense enough to meet at the conference table with the understanding that the era of armaments has ended and the human race must conform its actions to this truth or die.

Eisenhower specifically excluded from his discussion "the usefulness of available military strength in putting out 'prairie fires'— spots where American interests are seriously jeopardized by unjustified outbreaks of minor wars." Those should be dealt with directly—as in Iran, Guatemala, Lebanon, the Congo, Cuba.[33]

Eisenhower's convictions on the subject of nuclear warfare were absolute. He was amazed when, in 1956, Field Marshal Bernard Montgomery sent him a paper in which he attempted to describe a nuclear holocaust unleashed by "8000 nuclear weapons," that the Soviets would initiate knowing they would lose, "in order to promote Communism." Eisenhower, in a very polite letter—all things considered—replied that Communists were "avid for power" and "ruthlessly ambitious"; but they were "not early Christian martyrs." Moreover, he wrote Montgomery, "you made no attempt to visualize the true nature of the holocaust . . . and I believe you have far underestimated the degree of destruction that would re-

sult. . . . I believe there would be literally millions of dead. . . .
In such circumstances what does a nation do; what can it do?"[34]

Eisenhower knew just how absurd Montgomery's document was,
because for years he had been reading top-secret reports that described what nuclear war would actually do to the United States, to
its allies, and to its enemies. In a conversation with Senator Styles
Bridges, Eisenhower referred to annual "net evaluation studies"
that indicated what would result from "some catastrophe," even if
we were to emerge "as the acknowledged victor":

> I will give you just one figure. . . . On a single attack—and it was
> not a complete surprise, . . . we figure something like 25 million
> killed, 60 million had to go to hospitals, and there were not enough
> hospitals. When you begin to think of things like that, you know
> there must not be war.[35]

Eisenhower also believed that there was no protection against a
surprise attack. "Blast shelters" were not feasible. There was no
technology to save fragile life against the kind of awesome power
that had blown up the United States' test site in the Pacific. Although the details were long kept secret, he also knew about the
radiation poisoning caused by Project Bravo. Bravo, the code
name for the United States' first hydrogen bomb detonated in the
Pacific, had sickened residents throughout the Marshall Islands.
Twenty-three Japanese fishermen aboard *The Lucky Dragon,*
twenty-eight United States military personnel, and hundreds of
islanders were hospitalized.

The Eniwetok Proving Grounds belong to the United States as
part of the "Pacific Trust Territory" given to the United States to
"administer" after World War II. The sixty thousand people of the
Marshall, Caroline, and Marianas islands were under United States
"protection." When their homelands were designated nuclear test
sites, they protested to the UN Trusteeship Council. India and the
Soviet Union also protested, questioning the legality and morality
of America's chosen sites. The Soviet Union called for a test-ban
agreement. The United States denounced the effort as propaganda
and promised greater protection against fallout "accidents" in the
future. For years, Lewis L. Strauss, head of the Atomic Energy
Commission, insisted that radioactive fallout caused only minor
and temporary discomfort. Americans were fearful but tended to
trust the men of science. The people of the Pacific knew better.

They had witnessed the effects of Hiroshima and Nagasaki. On the other hand, the full significance of radiation, its real effects, its long-term properties, its cancer-producing nature, its global transit on the winds of earth were not fully understood in the 1950s. In 1955, the Killian Report, issued by the President's Science Advisory Committee, acknowledged limited understanding but insisted that, in all future civil defense programs, "The public will need indoctrination to accustom themselves to the fact that low levels of radiation can and must be lived with. Radiation must be a phenomenon that is universally accepted and understood."[36]

The Killian Committee, chaired by Dr. James A. Killian, of MIT, recognized that the hazards of radioactive fallout were insufficiently understood. Nevertheless, it concluded that plans "for the military use of nuclear bombs should not at this time be restrained because of the long-term radiological hazard." The Killian Report, *Meeting the Threat of Surprise Attack,* called for "a sense of urgency without despair" in order to "survive . . . the years ahead . . . in the contest of ideologies to enlarge and strengthen the free world as a cohesive community of nations." The committee's general conclusions were awesome:

> The threats which exist now may continue for many years. They are primarily nuclear weapons carried by intercontinental aircraft, by mine-laying vessels and submarines, and by missiles launched from seaborne platforms. Refinements of the air-borne carriers, and ultimately intercontinental ballistic missiles, must be expected in the future. We must also be alert to other still more obscure dangers—to clandestine introduction of nuclear bombs, to covert or windborne attack by biological agents. . . .[37]

Sufficiently frightful, it was an early, modest, and even optimistic report. Subsequent studies were to be more shrill. The Gaither Report, of 1957, projected the possibility of total annihilation and introduced the subsequently disproved "missile gap" thesis. Submitted four days after Sputnik was launched, the Gaither Report condemned, by implication, Eisenhower's entire foreign policy and especially the economic limitations he had placed on the military-defense industry. H. Rowland Gaither, of the RAND Corporation; Robert C. Sprague, a military-electronics industrialist, head of the Sprague Electric Co.; and William C. Foster, of the Olin-Mathieson Chemical Corporation, directed the project. Although the report was sealed and even refused to Congress, leaks about its contents resulted in the most dire headlines: SECRET REPORT SEES U.S. IN GRAVE PERIL; ENORMOUS ARMS OUTLAY IS HELD VITAL TO SURVIVAL. The report emphasized the need "for offensive power as the best defense" and called for a massive, $5-billion-a-year program to build radiation shelters throughout the United States. The committee compared U.S.-Soviet missile strength and concluded:

> If the U.S.S.R. continues to expand its military expenditures throughout the next decade, as it has during the 1950s, and ours remain constant, its annual military expenditures may be double ours, even allowing for a gradual improvement of the low living standards of the Russian peoples.

The report noted that this "extraordinary concentration of the Soviet economy on military power and heavy industry" transformed the world situation as it existed after World War II. Then they "had no atomic bombs, no productive capacity for fissionable materials, no jet engine production, and only an infant electronics industry. This situation was compatible with a then-backward country, so much of whose most productive areas had suffered military attack and occupation. Their industrial base was then perhaps one-seventh that of the U.S." The detailed estimate of new Soviet missiles, long-range submarines, long-range and short-range jet aircraft and jet bombers, the spectrum of A- and H-bombs, "produced fissionable material sufficient for 1500 nuclear weapons," and new launching pads for surface-to-air missiles was of course staggering. It was certainly a long way from that humble moment, which Khrushchev referred to frequently, "when we were embarrassed to land [at the 1955 summit meeting in Geneva] in a two-engine plane while all the other leaders arrived in four-engine ones."[38]

Eisenhower and his closest advisers judged the report irresponsible. Secretary of State Dulles rejected the idea that it would be worthwhile to spend $22.5 billion for fallout shelters. Such a level of spending acknowledged a level of danger the author of deterrence found repellent. It was impossible to sustain both "an offensive and defensive mood in a population. For our security we have been relying above all on our capacity for retaliation.

From this policy we should not deviate now." Eisenhower remarked, "'You *are* a militant Presbyterian, aren't you?'" Clearly delighted, Eisenhower "decided that we would not embark on an all-out shelter program."[39]

George Humphrey, former Treasury Secretary, returned to Washington to campaign against raising the military budget, as demanded by the Gaither Committee. He argued that the basis of Soviet strategy, the meaning of Khrushchev's economic ploy "we will bury you" was—insisted Humphrey—to get us to "spend ourselves into bankruptcy." At the National Security Council meeting that discussed the Gaither Report, Humphrey demanded: Do you "know how much money you're asking for?" He pointed to the Washington Monument and declared that if the money requested were paid in thousand-dollar bills, "the pile would reach up to the top of the monument and fifty-six feet beyond." "As long as I'm here, you're not getting one of those bills." Eisenhower's current Treasury Secretary, Robert B. Anderson, continued to consider a tax cut of between two and seven billion dollars. The committee's adherents thought the Eisenhower administration outrageous, conservative, and dangerous. The Eisenhower administration thought them adventurist, opportunist, and dangerous.[40]

The Gaither Report, and its companion Rockefeller Report, *International Security—the Military Aspect,* drafted by Henry A. Kissinger, were, in retrospect, the first steps on the campaign trail of 1960. They argued that Eisenhower's stringent Republican financing imperiled the nation. Something more bold, more liberal, was needed for the future. John F. Kennedy would say so. And Rockefeller would say so. The real split in Republican Party ranks in 1960 occurred when Rockefeller, or Nixon, told reporters that Rockefeller was writing the platform and that it would indicate a specific "repudiation" of Eisenhower's position. Rockefeller insisted that the current "Defense operation was inadequate and $4 billion needed to be added immediately." It never happened. And when "the press unwittingly conceded a great victory to Rockefeller, he could hardly repudiate it by saying he didn't win after all." William Robinson wrote Eisenhower: "Whether Nixon or any of his aides leaked to the press the fact that Rockefeller would dominate the platform will never be known—but if they did, it was the neatest political trick of the century." For, so long as he was

President and insofar as he controlled the Republican Party convention of 1960, Eisenhower refused to permit billions and billions of dollars to be added to the already engorged stockpile of deterrence. In 1962, he assessed the Kennedy defense budget and declared that it "should be substantially reduced."[41]

The Gaither Committee also argued that because the United States was in imminent and grave danger, a total reorganization of the defense establishment was required—in order to prepare for many limited wars, "especially in the Middle East and Asia. This reorganization was in addition to the billions of dollars needed for new and elaborate thermonuclear programs and fallout shelters. Members of the financial community Eisenhower had always admired, notably John J. McCloy and Robert Lovett, pledged the "complete backing" of American business. But Eisenhower believed that United States citizens would "balk at paying the bill." Besides, the fiscal conservatives he trusted—George Humphrey, Dulles, Robert Anderson—considered the whole report overstated. It focused only on the issue of industrial-military growth. They feared that the nongrowth, nonproductive spending called for would bankrupt America. Eisenhower's Bureau of the Budget refused to raise the ceiling on military spending, $38 billion, as agreed to before the Gaither Report was submitted.

The Gaither Report unleashed the uniquely American controversy about whether earth's inhabitants would be better off "dead than Red." Rockefeller's fallout-shelter program engendered endless discussions about the quality of life in a survival shelter.[42] Would neighbors be admitted? Relatives? If they died, who would be morally responsible? Schoolchildren were lined up in corridors or were ordered to cringe beneath their desks during air-raid drills. They had thermonuclear nightmares. During Eisenhower's administration, all efforts to agree on a test-ban treaty failed. Security depended on an equality of strength. Parity was everything. We could not be surprised. There needed to be on-site inspection or Eisenhower's "Open Skies" inspection program. The Soviets would not agree. They did not have parity, or equality—the Gaither Report notwithstanding. Although nobody wanted the future to be mortgaged to a nuclear unknown, there was, on balance, no trust. There were efforts at unilateral test suspensions initiated by both the United States and the U.S.S.R. They did not last long. There were always technological breakthroughs that required new test series. Deterrence was not disarmament. But it was practiced in good faith, and it was not war.[43]

In a conversation with Senator Styles Bridges, Eisenhower detailed his program for security through a collective defense system. He considered international preparedness short of nuclear war "part of a great broad program" that involved mutual aid and military assistance throughout the world. The long-range, large-scale mutual security program that Eisenhower sponsored was expensive. But he considered it a better investment over time than a policy that depended on nothing more than greater and greater expenditures for armaments. He told Bridges that his program had two points: nuclear deterrence, and a many-layered international economic program to "keep the rest of the world from going Communistic."

> It is that simple with me. And I want to wage the cold war in a militant, but reasonable, style whereby we appeal to the people of the world as a better group . . . than the Communists.[44]

Eisenhower's long-range program was not only a better investment, it was necessary to block a transition to communism that would result in the withdrawal of the world's resources from United States investment potential. It would be impossible to maximize profits should that occur.

Although nobody used the term any longer, it was Eisenhower's blueprint for the achievement of the American Century. It involved a determination to pursue political warfare, psychological warfare, and economic warfare everywhere and at all times. It was occasionally subtle, occasionally strident, and occasionally violent. For years, Americans were involved in covert activities, conducted by people whose names they had never heard, all over the globe.

Eisenhower's commitment to globalism was announced during his inaugural address. Eisenhower worked hard on that speech. He wanted it to communicate his essential philosophy. He wanted to inform the Soviets that the United States was up for the race. But he also wanted "to warn the free world that the American well can run dry." And he wanted to "tell the American people that internally we are entering a new phase."[45] The President of the United

States now considered himself the unrivaled leader of the free world. On 21 January 1953, Eisenhower explained that his commitment to the Cold War meant a relentless fight for freedom, for the liberation and security "of all the world . . . the grower of rice in Burma and the planter of wheat in Iowa, the shepherd in southern Italy and the mountaineer in the Andes." It meant an equality of dignity for "the French soldier who dies in Indochina, the British soldier killed in Malaya, the American life given in Korea."

World leadership meant that Americans would have to begin to think in worldwide terms about freedom, equality, and justice. The United States would lose access to the diamonds and gold, uranium and oil in Africa, Asia, and the Middle East unless American citizens accepted personally the challenges of Eisenhower's global commitment. That required some fundamental changes that Eisenhower himself only slowly, and very reluctantly, accepted. America's historic racial bigotry was a considerable handicap in the race for world leadership. To persuade over 80 percent of the world's citizens that United States race practices and attitudes did not include them was no easy task.

Integration became a front-line battle in the Cold War. On one occasion when visiting African dignitaries were not served in a southern restaurant, Eisenhower invited them for breakfast at the White House. He assured his southern friends that he shared their feelings, but white racism was bad politics—from a global point of view. Nevertheless, Chief Justice Earl Warren believed that Eisenhower always "resented our decision in *Brown* v. *The Board of Education*." Before the 1954 decision was announced, Eisenhower invited Justice Warren to attend one of the President's famous "stag dinners," a regular White House event that combined social informality (although the dress was formal) with political activity. Warren was seated nearby attorney John W. Davis, counsel for the segregation states. "During the dinner, the President went to considerable lengths to tell me what a great man Mr. Davis was." En route to after-dinner coffee, Eisenhower took Justice Warren by the arm and said, "These are not bad people. All they are concerned about is to see that their sweet little girls are not required to sit in school alongside some big overgrown Negroes." According to Warren, after the Supreme Court's decision, the President never spoke to him again.[46]

On the other hand, Eisenhower was sensitive to the nuances of the global imperative. The Soviet Union monitored and publicized pictures of children who were cursed, struck, and spat upon trying to get into school. America's racial customs represented wretched political warfare. By executive order, Eisenhower integrated the armed forces, veterans hospitals, the District of Columbia, and Red Cross blood plasma. He appointed Nixon to head a commission to investigate withholding government contracts from companies that blocked civil-rights efforts. He assigned Maxwell Rabb, secretary to the Cabinet, to improve public relations in this area. Rabb worked hard at his job and was responsible for significant changes in America's official race relations. His efforts on behalf of voting rights for black Americans prompted Eisenhower's 1957 Civil Rights Act. Although Eisenhower was persuaded by FBI director J. Edgar Hoover that sit-ins, bus boycotts, and public protests were unjustified, illegal, and the work of communist terrorists, Eisenhower did send the troops to Little Rock to enforce the law.[47]

Eisenhower's attitude toward "the race issue" remained entirely ambiguous. To Justice Warren's chagrin, the President never once said a public word to support school integration:

> With his popularity, if Eisenhower had said that black children were still being discriminated against long after the adoption of the 13th, 14th, and 15th Amendments, . . . and that it should be the duty of every good citizen to help rectify more than 80 years of wrongdoing . . .—if he had said something . . . , we would have been relieved, in my opinion, of many of the racial problems which have continued to plague us.[48]

On the contrary, in 1956 Eisenhower called Attorney General Brownell during the Republican Party convention. Ann Whitman monitored the call:

> His quarrel was with efforts to insert the words "The Eisenhower Administration . . . and the Republican Party have supported the Supreme Court" in the desegregation business. He wanted the words Eisenhower Administration deleted.

Eisenhower reminded Brownell that he had consistently "denied that the Administration took a stand on the matter." He pointed out that "it had never come before the Cabinet" and asked if Brownell could "imagine what a storm Mrs. Hobby would raise, had it?" The United States' Secretary of Health, Education and

Welfare was, after all, president of the Houston *Post* and a proud Texan. Eisenhower told Brownell "to talk to Bush and Dirksen and if they did not come around, he would refuse to 'go to San Francisco.'" Subsequently, Eisenhower refused to accept the word "concur" but agreed to "the Republican Party accepts."[49]

Every racial outrage was publicized around the world. It was hard to lead the free world when so many instances occurred that enabled Soviet propaganda agencies to highlight the "inhumanity of the American system." The U.S. embassy in Moscow urged the United States Information Agency to be more aggressive about "American Negro progress." Eisenhower carefully observed all public statements that might be noticed abroad. In March 1957, he corrected a speech to be given by his brother Milton:

> You speak of the "Judaic-Christian heritage." I would suggest that you use a term on the order of "religious heritage"—this for the reason that we should find some way of including the vast numbers of people who hold to the Islamic and Buddhist religions when we compare the religious world against the Communist world.[50]

When Nelson Rockefeller replaced C. D. Jackson as Eisenhower's special assistant for the Cold War, Eisenhower specifically instructed him to work to overcome America's dysfunctional reputation in this area:

> It is my conviction that all the peoples of the world share the same human cravings for freedom and for opportunities to win economic and social advancement. In keeping with our heritage we seek to join with all peoples in a common effort to achieve and sustain the basic essentials of human dignity. . . .
>
> So that these matters may have the increased degree of attention they deserve . . . I hereby appoint you as Special Assistant to the President. I shall look to you for advice and assistance in the development of increased understanding and cooperation among all peoples. . . .[51]

Rockefeller was to attend meetings of the Cabinet, the National Security Council, the Council on Foreign Economic Policy, and the Operations Coordinating Board.

The National Security Council and the Operations Coordinating Board were fully developed during Eisenhower's presidency to administer political, economic, and psychological warfare. To become the key institutions of the Cold War, they were to oversee the activities of the CIA, the USIA, and all cabinet departments. During Eisenhower's presidency, C. D. Jackson, Nelson Rockefeller, General Robert Cutler, chairman of the Old Colony Trust Company of Boston, and Gordon Gray, political warrior and college president, were the most notable special assistants to administer national security strategy. Their purpose was to destabilize communist leaders; liberate communist countries; encourage defection, dissension, and upheaval in the enemy camp; defend the nation's security; and in every way feasible enlarge the "free world." The national security establishment defined and designated the target areas for Eisenhower's missions of peace and political warfare. It was responsible for the globalization of America.[52]

These agencies absorbed the work of the Psychological Strategy Board, established in 1951. For Eisenhower and his national security staff, psychological warfare was "more than the use of propaganda to win over . . . minds and wills." According to General Robert Cutler, appointed executive of the National Security Council, "Every significant act of government should be so timed and so directed . . . that it will produce the maximum effect. All agencies and departments must be brought together into concerted action under an over-all scheme of strategy. We must adapt our foreign policy to a 'cold war' strategy that is unified and coherent. We must realize that as a nation everything we say, everything we do, and everything we fail to say or to do, will have its impact in other lands; it will affect the minds of men and women there."[53]

To develop that effort, Eisenhower created the International Information Activities Committee, chaired by William Jackson. Known as the Jackson Committee, its recommendations would influence United States foreign policy for decades. "The United States as the center of power in the free world is the principal obstacle in the path of the Soviet drive."

> The Kremlin will intensify its efforts to isolate the U.S. and to promote dissension within and between the free nations by political warfare methods, including propaganda, subversion, and penetration, economic pressures and inducements and the instigation of violence. . . .
> In the face of this Soviet drive the U.S. and allied nations must continue to strengthen their military capabilities until . . . the Soviet

Union is unwilling to risk general war, has abandoned its goal of world domination, and will live up to . . . the Charter of the United Nations. . . .

Specifically, the committee pointed out that there is a "psychological" element "to every diplomatic, economic, or military policy and action." " 'Cold War' and 'psychological warfare' are unfortunate terms. They do not describe the efforts of our nation and our allies to build a world of peace and freedom. They should be discarded. . . . New terms are needed to express the solidarity of freedom-loving men and women everywhere." "The efforts of all media—radio, press, and publications, motion pictures, exchange of persons, and libraries and information centers—" should be used to persuade "the peoples of other nations that their own aspirations for freedom, progress and peace are supported and advanced by the objectives and policies of the U.S."[54]

C. D. Jackson was the first political warrior appointed to administer this task. He was delighted with the job; and delighted with Eisenhower's enthusiasm for and "understanding of the art" once called psychological warfare. Jackson wrote that Eisenhower believed it was "just about the only way to win World War III without having to fight it." "He is convinced that psychological warfare should not be the pet mystery of one or more Departments of the Government, but should be the entire posture of the entire Government to the entire world." That, wrote Jackson, all added up "to The Great Opportunity."[55]

It was for Jackson the culmination of many years' work to develop "an integrated United States psychological warfare program." In May 1952, representatives of the State Department, CIA, National Committee for a Free Europe (Radio Free Europe), the Psychological Strategy Board, and members of MIT's Center for International Studies (CENIS), a CIA think tank created by Truman, met at Princeton to establish "overall policy" and present a "blue-print" for activity to Eisenhower. The conferees agreed that the Truman-Acheson policy of "containment" or "holding the line against further Soviet expansion" had outlived its time, "and should be replaced with a more dynamic and positive policy. . . ."[56]

For C. D. Jackson, the "three big ingredients of psychological warfare are (1) money, (2) no holds barred and (3) no questions asked."[57] There were, from the beginning, disagreements and tensions between his approach to problems and the State Department's. At the Princeton Conference, Jackson and members of Radio Free Europe made suggestions regarding the "ultimate liberation of the enslaved nations" that the State Department feared might create "a dangerous crusade" situation the United States "might not be prepared to honor." The State Department and Jackson were more in agreement when it came to his ideas about recapturing the "peace offensive" from the Soviet Union. In December 1952, Stalin's peace proposal was hailed throughout the world and received front-page coverage in the New York *Times*. Jackson was appalled by "the shocking stupidity and/or irresponsibility of Scotty Reston, aided and abetted by the high priests of the New York *Times,* who should know better, which permitted the front page of that paper on Christmas morning to be given over to a photograph of Stalin and his phoney peace proposal." But Jackson was sanguine that with Eisenhower in the White House the situation would change. After all, Jackson wrote, we finally have "a Head of Government who grasps the concept of political warfare" and who "appreciates that practically every other golf club in his bag is broken."[58]

In March 1953, Stalin's death provided an opportunity to introduce America's own peace offensive. It was part of a larger package that included a careful study of the key areas of Soviet "vulnerability created by Stalin's death and suggestions for prompt American action to exploit that vulnerability." Among the guidelines were the following:

> To foster any and all divisive forces within the top hierarchy. . . .
> To stimulate divisive forces between the Kremlin and the statellite governments, including Communist China.
> To maximize the disaffection between the peoples of Soviet Union and Malenkov.
> To maximize the division between the peoples of the satellites, including Communist China, and Malenkov.
> To maintain and increase the unity between the peoples of the free nations. . . .[59]

The CIA introduced a note of caution: "The death of Stalin removed an autocrat who, while ruthless and determined to spread Soviet power, did not allow his ambitions to lead him into reckless courses of action in his foreign policy. It would be unsafe to assume that the new Soviet regime will have Stalin's skill in avoiding war."[60]

Eisenhower's "Chance for Peace" address to the American Society of Newspaper Editors, on 16 April 1953, was hailed as a serious bid for international harmony. Carefully prepared by his psychological warriors, it was also the opening gun of the post-Stalin phase of the Cold War. The speech was written by W. W. Rostow, C. D. Jackson, and *Time-Life* journalist Emmett J. Hughes. Eisenhower monitored every word of every one of the many drafts. But he was committed to his wartime "staff" principle. Over time, he delegated a great deal of authority. On this occasion, he was persuaded to delete two paragraphs he very much wanted. Emmett Hughes wrote that he had omitted "The U.S.-Soviet exchange of radio-and-TV time," because it savored "too much of a publicity stunt"; and "Your renewed offer to travel to meet Soviet leaders," because it tipped the "balance between *firm* and *conciliatory*" and might "suggest an over-anxiety far from our intentions."[61] It would not be the last time his own efforts at greater détente would be short-circuited by his staff. In any case, the speech was, in many ways, the most important statement of his presidency:

In this spring of 1953, the free world weighs one question above all others: the chance for a just peace for all peoples. . . .

It weighs the chance for peace with sure, clear knowledge of what happened to the vain hope of 1945. . . .

In that spring of victory, the soldiers of the Western Allies met the soldiers of Russia in the center of Europe. They were triumphant comrades in arms. Their peoples shared the joyous prospect of building, in honor of their dead, the only fitting monument—an age of just peace.

All these war-weary peoples shared, too, this concrete, decent purpose: to guard vigilantly against the domination ever again of any part of the world by a single, unbridled aggressive power.

This common purpose lasted an instant—and perished. . . . [It was followed by] . . . fear and force.

What can the world—or any nation in it—hope for if no turning is found on this dread road? . . .

The worst is atomic war.

The best would be this: a life of perpetual fear and tension; a burden of arms draining the wealth and labor of all peoples. . . .

Every gun that is made, every warship launched, every rocket fired signifies . . . a *theft* from those who hunger and are not fed, those who are cold and are not clothed.

This world in arms is not spending money alone.

It is spending the sweat of its laborers, the genius of its scientists, the hopes of its children.

The cost of one modern heavy bomber is this: a modern brick school in more than 30 cities.

It is: two electric power plants, each serving a town of 60,000. . . .

It is: two fine, fully equipped hospitals.

We pay for a single fighter plane with a half million bushels of wheat. . . .

This is not a way of life at all. . . . It is humanity hanging from a cross of iron. . . .

Now, Eisenhower said, "an era ended with the death of Josef Stalin." Now, a "new leadership has assumed power." It "has a precious opportunity," with "the point of peril reached," to "help turn the tide of history." Arms control, truce in Korea, peace in Asia, a free and united Germany, freedom in Eastern Europe. "What is the Soviet Union ready to do?" "We welcome every honest act of peace." "None of these issues . . . is insoluble." "The peace we seek . . . can be fortified . . . by wheat and by cotton; by milk and by wool; by meat and by timber and by rice." Eisenhower listed all the essentials for future negotiation. A world economic policy; renewed and accelerated trade; "international control of atomic energy to promote its use for peaceful purposes," his "Atoms for Peace" proposal, which envisioned "the prohibition of atomic weapons." "If we failed . . . to seize this chance, the judgment of future ages would be harsh and just. . . ."

A stunning speech. It "literally blanketed the globe." It was translated and recorded. Every agency participated: radio, TV, the United States Information Service, the CIA, the State Department, RFE, and VOA. In Germany, the text was distributed to 921 newspapers and magazines; in Hungary, a window display at the United States Legation attracted over a thousand people to request a free pamphlet; in Belgrade, nine thousand people "lined up at the U. S. Information Center" for translations. Three million pamphlets were prepared for distribution throughout Europe and Latin America. In New Delhi, over a hundred thousand handbills were

distributed in eight languages. Radio Free Czechoslovakia, Free
Poland, and Free Hungary presented summaries of the speech
every hour on the day it was delivered. Bulgarian and Romanian
newscasts talked of nothing else.[62]

Eisenhower's speech represented the top side of political warfare. Then there was the underside. In December 1954, the National Security Council introduced a "Basic National Security Policy" for Eisenhower's administration. It assessed the world
situation and projected America's future course of action. "The
stability of the U.S.S.R. and its hold over the European satellites
are unlikely to be seriously shaken . . . , despite measures which
the United States may find it feasible to take to weaken Soviet control. . . ." There will be serious strains in the U.S. alliance system,
"resulting from growing fears of atomic war . . . , differing attitudes on China, and greater receptivity by the allies to Soviet overtures. Our allies will probably be more reluctant than the U.S. to
participate in actions which appear to them to involve appreciable
risks of war. . . ." "Underdeveloped countries will continue to be
a major source of weakness in the position of the free world . . .
political instability, economic backwardness, extreme nationalism,
and the colonial issue. . . ." "If the Soviet 'soft' line is not
reversed, our allies will be eager to explore it seriously, and will
probably wish . . . to go to further lengths than the U.S. will find
prudent." The factor of public opinion presents a major challenge:
"to maintain the necessary [allied] unity and resolution" despite
"the talk of 'coexistence.'"

Therefore, the NSC concluded, "the basic problem confronting
the United States is how, without undermining fundamental United
States values and institutions or seriously weakening the United
States economy to meet" this challenge. The "general strategy" involved "a prolonged period of armed truce," combined with nuclear deterrence, and increased "ability to apply force selectively
and flexibly" throughout the world in order "to resist aggression."
It involved rejecting "the concept of preventive war or acts intended to provoke war," but an increased ability to respond "to
local aggression" wherever it might occur. "However, the U.S. cannot afford to preclude itself from using nuclear weapons even in a
local situation, if such use will bring the aggression to a swift and
positive cessation. . . ." Politically, economically, militarily, the
United States "should place more stress than heretofore on build-

ing the strength and cohesion of the free world . . . , creating cohesion within and among all the free nations . . . , and destroying
the effectiveness of the Communist apparatus in the free world."
"Direct action against the Communist apparatus must rest largely
with the local governments concerned, although the U.S. should be
able to help significantly, [portions deleted to the end of this
paragraph]."[63]

To fulfill this policy, the United States introduced a variety of
undercover activities. In March 1954, the NSC determined that
"in the interests of world peace and U.S. national security, the
overt foreign activities of the U.S. Government should be supplemented by covert operations." The Central Intelligence Agency's
mandate to conduct "espionage and counterespionage operations
abroad" was now extended to:

a. Create and exploit troublesome problems for International Communism, impair relations between the U.S.S.R. and Communist
China and between them and their statellites, complicate control
within the U.S.S.R., Communist China and their satellites, and retard the growth of the military and economic potential of the Soviet
bloc.
b. Discredit the prestige and ideology of International Communism,
and reduce the strength of its parties and other elements.
c. Counter any threat of a party or individual directly or indirectly
responsive to Communist control to achieve dominant power in a
free world country.
d. Reduce International Communist control over any areas of the
world.
e. Strengthen the orientation toward the United States of the peoples and nations of the free world, accentuate, wherever possible, the
identity of interest . . . as well as favoring . . . those groups genuinely advocating or believing in the advancement of such mutual interests, and increase the capacity and will of such peoples and nations to resist International Communism. . . .
f. . . . develop underground resistance and facilitate covert and
guerrilla operations and ensure availability of those forces in the
event of war. . . .

All "covert operations" were to be planned and executed so that
"U.S. Government responsibility for them is not evident . . . and
if uncovered the United States Government can plausibly disclaim
any responsibility for them. Specifically, such operations shall include . . . propaganda, political action; economic warfare; preven-

tive direct action, including sabotage, anti-sabotage, demolition; escape and evasion and evacuation measures; subversion against hostile states or groups including assistance to underground resistance movements, guerrillas and refugee liberation groups; support of indigenous and anti-communist elements . . . ; deception plans and operations. . . ."64

All-inclusive. Secret. Costly. Worldwide. To "counter any threat of a party or individual directly or indirectly responsive" to communism in a free-world country. Elections in Italy, West Germany, France. To "develop underground resistance . . . and guerrilla operations." Vietnam, Laos, the Congo, Iran, Guatemala, Cuba. To "strengthen the orientation toward the U.S." The doctrine of "plausible" governmental deniability.

NSC 5412 ended all pretensions about territorial integrity, national sovereignty, and international law. Covert operatives were everywhere, and they were active. From bribery to assassination, no activity was unacceptable short of nuclear war. Named a moral crusade against communist tyranny, America's commitment to lead the free world was a life-and-death contest for access and control of the earth's resources.

There was nothing simple about that contest. The United States perceived itself in a race for influence and markets with the Soviet Union to replace the declining colonial powers in Asia, the Middle East, and Africa. The declining colonial powers—notably the United States' closest allies, Britain and France, were not at all pleased to be replaced by United States-dominated capital investment programs that challenged their privileges and possessions. Furthermore, nationalist leaders were not easily persuaded that such programs would end their colonial status.

In an effort to persuade George Humphrey that the costs of his foreign-aid and mutual-security programs were fully justified, Eisenhower wrote that "few individuals understand the intensity and force of the spirit of nationalism that is gripping all peoples of the world today. . . . It is my personal conviction that almost any one of the new-born states of the world would far rather embrace Communism or any other form of dictatorship than to acknowledge the political domination of another government even though that brought to each citizen a far higher standard of living."65

The United States was theoretically the leading anticolonial power. But when Britain's oil fields in Iran were nationalized, theory and practice collided over the earth's precious resources—which is, after all, what colonialism has always been about.

Eisenhower was not naïve about America's anticolonial dilemma. "Self-determination" was an American tradition. Ho Chi Minh was said to have a picture of George Washington and a copy of the Declaration of Independence on his desk. When Nasser told *Newsweek* publisher Malcolm Muir that the United States had lost its "prestige" because it supported France in Indochina and Britain's "colonial ambitions," Eisenhower told Muir that he agreed with Nasser on the issue of colonialism. He had in fact just written to Churchill to encourage independence combined with a "commonwealth" situation such as the one that connected the Philippines to the United States. "'That's the way this situation must be handled,'" Eisenhower wrote Churchill. "'We must work with these people and then they themselves will soon find out that we are their friends and that they can't live without us.'"[66] When, however, nationalists failed to perceive the benefits of "mutual interests," when they continued to believe they could "live without us," they were called Communists.

The United States' first successful covert operation occurred in Iran, where the Shah-appointed Prime Minister, Dr. Mohammed Mossadegh, actually attempted to "live without us," that is, without the Anglo-Iranian Oil Company. In 1951, Mossadegh nationalized Anglo-Iranian properties, canceled its concession, and seized the huge refinery on the Gulf of Abadan. The British threatened to call in the 16th Parachute Brigade, stationed on Cyprus. Truman sent Averell Harriman to mediate. Eisenhower, then at SHAPE, watched the situation closely. He released his assistant, General Vernon A. Walters, a much-valued translator, to Harriman for the negotiations. Walters' description of Harriman's effort, of the complexities of the Iranian political situation, of the deep nationalism among the right-wing and religious supporters of Mossadegh, of the complex man who was Mossadegh, is stirring and informative. According to Walters, Mossadegh was trapped by the demands of the left, the right, and the religious leaders. Nobody wanted Iranian oil to be drained away by Britain.‡ There was nothing to negotiate unless Harriman accepted nationalization.

---

‡ Between 1913 and 1951, Anglo-Iranian grossed $3 billion; $624 million went to the Iranian Government, and $2.4 billion was transferred abroad as profit.

Both Harriman and the British negotiated with Mossadegh for months.* At one point, Dr. Mossadegh said to Richard Stokes, the British mediator, " 'The reason why we can't come to an agreement is because you are a Catholic . . . in your religion you don't have any divorce, whereas in ours all you have to do is say three times to your wife, "I divorce you," and she is divorced. What you don't understand is that we have divorced the Anglo-Iranian Oil Company.' "

On one occasion, Harriman, "aware of the intense pressure which the ultra-nationalists and fanatics were bringing on Mossadegh," visited Ayatollah Kashani. The *mullah* denounced the British as "the most evil people in the world." When Harriman disagreed, Ayatollah Kashani asked: " 'Have you ever heard of Major Embry? . . . He was an American who came to Iran in 1911 or 1912. He dabbled in oil, which was none of his business, and aroused the hatred of the people. One day, walking in Teheran, he was shot down in the street, but he was not killed. . . . The enraged mob followed to the hospital . . . and butchered him on the operating table.' " Harriman was enraged by the implied threat. The interview was over. The ayatollah accused Mossadegh of British sympathies and warned, " 'If Mossadegh yields, his blood will flow like Razmara's.' " It was widely believed that Ali Razmara, Mossadegh's predecessor, was assassinated by religious nationalists and that this threat had been made to Mossadegh—which, wrote Walters, "was one of the factors" that made agreement impossible.[67] Despite millions of dollars in Point Four aid, the United States' effort to mediate failed. Harriman had not been able to persuade Mossadegh that the United States would be a better business partner than Britain had been, since he had not accepted nationalization. Iran was the only Middle East country in which the United States did not directly participate in petroleum operations. After World War II, Mossadegh had led the movement against a proposed Soviet concession. He threw the British out. And now he refused to let the United States in. The situation was untenable.[68]

In 1953, Kermit Roosevelt, the CIA chief in Iran, prepared and

---

* Dr. Mossadegh was a fragile, aged man, reportedly over eighty, who generally conducted negotiations from his bed. He wept frequently and occasionally fainted. They were difficult negotiations.

organized Mossadegh's overthrow. He dismissed the influence of the religious leaders, considered the Shah to be "growing in stature and acceptability," and believed that, for a few million dollars, a popular movement against Mossadegh could be organized. Kermit Roosevelt wrote that the mullahs were supported only by "the Moslem 'clerical' class and religious students, both of whom had followers among the more superstitious elements of urban workers." They refused to support his coup. He did not consider them "worth the time, trouble and . . . money that would be required. So we decided to go ahead without them." Finally, despite Mossadegh's popular vote in a recent referendum, a vote of 99.4 percent, he assured Washington that Iran's Communist party (the Tudeh Party) represented Mossadegh's main support.[69]

Eisenhower's version of Mossadegh's overthrow fails to mention Kermit Roosevelt. His was, after all, a covert operation. Eisenhower did refer to Mossadegh's plebiscite—in a most extraordinary way: "Mossadegh got 99.4 percent of the votes. Iran's downhill course toward Communist-supported dictatorship was picking up momentum." But then, "suddenly, and dramatically, the opposition to Mossadegh and the Communists—by those loyal to the Shah—began to work. The Iranian Army turned against officers whom Mossadegh had installed. The Army drove all pro-Mossadegh demonstrators off the streets. . . ." The details of the coup are still unavailable. Classified.† Eisenhower tells us: "The Shah returned in triumph." Mossadegh was placed under house arrest. Ambassador Loy Henderson met with the new Premier, General Zahedi, and agreed that the United States' technical-aid program, of $23.4 million, which had been suspended by Eisenhower, would be restored and increased to $85 million for emergency economic assistance. Eisenhower was delighted. He recognized in the Shah "a profound respect for constitutional processes, a sense of responsibility and obligation and an enlightened purpose to further the Iranian people's welfare. . . ." He was informed that Mohammed Zahedi, who was known to have collaborated with the Nazis during the war, "had no love for the British." But he was

---

† For analysis of the coup in Guatemala, which followed this formula, see Chapters VI–VII.

willing to negotiate "an oil settlement as soon as possible." This was, wrote Eisenhower, "good news, indeed."[70]

America's intervention ended the British oil monopoly. An international consortium was created by which British Petroleum received 40 percent, the five United States majors divided another 40 percent, and 20 percent was shared by Royal Dutch Shell and Compagnie Française des Pétroles. Because historically the United States had disapproved of cartels, nine United States independent oil companies were cut into the bargain. And as for Iran, it would be paid in taxes instead of royalties. Iran and the consortium, fifty-fifty.[71] Subsequently, Churchill congratulated Eisenhower. "I am so glad that you recognize the importance of oil from the Middle East. When I was at the Admiralty in 1913 I acquired control of the Anglo-Persian Company for something like £3,000,000, and turned the large fleet I was then building to [oil] propulsion. That was a good bargain if ever there was one."[72]

The salvation of Iran enabled the United States to erect a protective wall across the Middle East's "northern tier," bordering the Soviet Union. In 1955, Turkey, Britain's colony Iraq (which would later revolt and withdraw), Iran, Pakistan, and Britain constituted the Baghdad Pact, a NATO-like alliance. The United States financed the pact but did not formally "adhere."[73]

In December 1954, His Imperial Majesty Mohammed Reza Pahlavi Shahanshah, visited the White House and offered a toast: "But for the grace of God and the help of your country I would not be here today."[74] In 1979, after billions of dollars in armaments, training, and equipment for SAVAK, the Shah's secret, terrorist service created in 1956, and vast sums of economic credits, the Shah was overthrown. The intense opposition to him was constant and well known. From the beginning, the commanding general of the United States Military Mission in Iran, Robert A. McClure, was horrified by the "low" morale and "pitiful" standard of living—even among the military. He appealed for immediate assistance to counter the situation. It was always forthcoming. As C. D. Jackson wrote General McClure: "Having snatched victory from defeat . . . , our Government has a tremendous responsibility to make things work right. . . . This is probably our last chance in that particular country, and possibly in that whole area of the world."[75] That "tremendous responsibility" was upheld throughout three decades of popular opposition to the Shah.

The CIA's success in Iran in 1954 plunged the United States deeply into the most valuable resource centers of the British and French colonial systems. The "Suez Crisis," of 1956, ended that system. In July 1952, Gamal Abdel Nasser emerged as Egypt's leader and a new international power. Dedicated to building a Pan-Arab movement for unity based on "positive neutrality," he met with Tito and Nehru. He called for independence from the Soviets, the French, the British, and the Americans. For years, the superpowers watched, content that traditional regional and religious animosities would continue to divide the oil-rich area against itself. With revolutions exploding all around them, they simply could not believe that the land of Lawrence of Arabia would ever fundamentally change.

Then Nasser ordered Britain to leave its Suez base. The United States courted him. And the Soviet Union courted him. When Egypt was attacked by Israel in February 1956, the United States offered conditional military aid. The condition was a full military-political agreement, on the order of the Baghdad Pact. Nasser refused and accepted arms from Czechoslovakia. He also recognized China. Dulles withdrew United States support for the Aswan High Dam—a billion-dollar project that Eugene Black, president of the World Bank, had so carefully negotiated.

Dulles informed Egypt's ambassador to Washington of the cancellation on 19 July, while Nasser, Tito, and Nehru were conferring in Yugoslavia about the future of a coalition of neutral nations. Dulles considered neutralism immoral. Nasser considered it dignified, anti-imperial, and profitable. The Soviet Union financed the Aswan High Dam. U.S. officials called Nasser a Communist, but communism had little to do with Nasser, or the situation in the Middle East.‡ In a provocative and compelling analysis, former

---

‡ Nevertheless, "The Eisenhower Doctrine," passed by Congress in March 1957, authorized up to $200 million for economic and military aid and a commitment of United States troops to any nation in the Middle East that requested U.S. support against "armed aggression" from "any country controlled by international Communism."

political warrior and oil-company consultant Miles Copeland described the new arrangements Nasser introduced to the old "game of nations."[76] Britain and France lost the game after a final military flourish, with Israel at their side.

On 30 July, Robert Murphy informed Eisenhower that Macmillan's plan was to destroy Nasser and restore British control. Eisenhower would have none of it. Dulles was in the air within two hours. It was not only that Eisenhower was involved that summer in a vigorous election campaign, but reliable sources—including World Bank officials and oil-company executives—considered Nasser an agreeable business partner. They trusted him and could live without British colonial prerogatives in Egypt. They argued that Nasser even ran the canal traffic more efficiently than the British and French had.

Eisenhower determined to oppose the allied effort to restore colonialism by force. From a political-warfare perspective, that was one of his wisest decisions. His opposition to the invasion illustrated for the "emerging nations" America's essential anti-imperialism. On the death of Anglo-French colonialism, United States-dominated oil companies inherited the responsibility to supply its allies with industry's lifeblood: Middle East oil. Britain and France were furious. The tension wrenched NATO. Eisenhower was assailed as weak, incapable of bold action. His hypocritical opposition to violence after his activities in Iran and Guatemala seemed puerile and unworthy. But Eisenhower had acted boldly. The CIA's newest surveillance operation, which combined jet engineering with long-range photography, the U-2, kept him informed of all military activity in the Middle East. He knew that the Israelis were mobilizing and the Egyptians were not. He knew that France had secretly supplied Israel with sixty "late-model Mystères," as opposed to the twelve fighter jets they had acknowledged to Eisenhower. On the advice of the United States' petroleum industry, he ordered the Office of Defense Mobilization to build sixty-thousand-ton tankers to stockpile oil in the event of a "crisis." Russia waved rockets in the direction of Britain and France and invited the United States to join forces to "crush the aggression and restore peace." Eisenhower declined Bulganin's offer, and Dulles presented the United States' resolution for a cease-fire to the General Assembly after Britain and France vetoed it in the Security Council. The world body voted sixty-five to five, New Zealand and

Australia joining the invaders, for the United States' resolution. A major political-warfare victory.

But Eisenhower's boldest efforts were covert. There was an enormous worldwide run on British sterling. The heaviest trading occurred in New York. The value of Britain's reserves plunged. The British Empire ran out of money during its final imperial battle. The International Monetary Fund rejected Britain's appeal for a money transfer. Within one week, Britain's gold reserves were down by 100 million pounds. In New York, British sterling was "offered for sale in huge blocks." Britain's economy evaporated. On the day Ike was reelected, Harold Macmillan announced that he could not "be responsible for Her Majesty's exchequer." As for hypocrisy—it was one of the most reliable weapons in the psychological-warfare arsenal. In Philadelphia, Eisenhower made a speech that C. D. Jackson considered one of his best ever: "We cannot and we will not condone armed aggression—no matter who the attacker, and no matter who the victim. We cannot—in the world, any more than in our own nation—subscribe to one law for the weak, another law for the strong. . . ."[77]

On 3 December 1956, Britain and France withdrew from Suez. Israel refused to leave the territory it had conquered in the Gaza Strip and Sinai. Admiral Lewis Strauss proposed that the United States buy Port Said and the Gaza Strip and internationalize them. The idea "intrigued" Eisenhower.[78] Eventually, a United Nations Emergency Force was sent to enforce peace in the area.

There was, however, no expectation of peace in the area. In 1953, the Operations Control Board, comprising CIA, State Department, and other analysts, had reviewed "Israel's Fundamental Problems." The OCB concluded that the border disputes between Israel and the Arab states reflected Israel's critical "economic and financial plight." Basically, ". . . too many people have been admitted too rapidly into a country which possesses almost no natural resources." Whether Israel could develop "a viable economy" seemed "very uncertain." There "is no coal, iron, or other minerals. The land has not yet produced any oil." Israel's budget depended largely on foreign loans, contributions, and "funds advanced by the United States Government." Only 18–25 percent of Israel's budget was secured from its own revenues. The Arab economic blockade was "relatively effective," and the high cost of

Israeli goods made it "difficult to secure large markets." Peace "with the surrounding Arab states" was judged "extremely unlikely in the foreseeable future."

Israel's response to this situation was to expand. On 25 October 1953, Prime Minister Ben-Gurion called for "complete liquidation of all these problems, within 10 years," and preparations were underway for the "entrance of 2,000,000 more refugees from the Middle East and the [Soviet] satellite states." The OCB projected: "This unrealistic approach can only lead to further economic and financial difficulties, and will probably result in additional pressure to expand Israel's frontiers into the rich lands of the Tigris and Euphrates valleys, and northward into the settled lands of Syria.

> There is a considerable element in the Army, the Government, and among the people who feel that the only solution to Israel's problems is territorial expansion. . . .

The OCB predicted that their numbers would increase over time. The alternative was continued United States "financial assistance over a considerable period of years," coupled with an Israeli determination to "tighten its belt, to restrict immigration rigidly." But even then the country would "not become self-supporting." So long as "realists" like David Ben-Gurion were able to "control the expansionists," there was hope that "Arab hostility" might be "ameliorated," but it would not be eliminated. As for United States policy:

> We would be making a mistake if we attempted at present to force a permanent peace between the Arabs and the Israeli. There are many on both sides who believe the ultimate solution must come by force. The blockade, so painless to the Arabs, will not be easily stopped by U.S. grants-in-aid. Our best chance of success is a steady pressure for a more realistic Israeli approach to their internal problems.

Eisenhower's papers on Israel are still almost entirely classified. There is some evidence that they were determined by the fact that his primary concern was Middle East oil. He thought, for example, that Truman had moved too hastily to recognize Israel. Eisenhower believed in 1955 that in the Middle East the "difficulties of the past 10 years resulted from that decision."[79]

The contemporary phase of the Middle East crisis had, in any case, just begun. In April 1959, the first Arab Petroleum Congress met in Cairo. In September 1960, finance ministers representing the oil-producing nations met again in Baghdad. The Organization of Petroleum Exporting Countries (OPEC) was founded. The oil ministers of Saudi Arabia, Kuwait, Iraq, Iran, and Venezuela sought "stability and predictability" for their oil revenues. The world would not know it for another decade, but the spirit of Lawrence of Arabia had been laid to rest.

While Eisenhower enjoyed some dramatic victories in the Middle East, political-warfare conditions in Europe were more uneven. Europe seemed in fact to be tilting toward stalemate. NATO nations were, despite the United States' continued economic largesse, sulky and dissatisfied. The rearmament and admission of West Germany into NATO, in 1955, offended public opinion. Chancellor Adenauer was to become Eisenhower's most reliable ally. The British wanted to trade with China. France wanted to trade with the Soviet Union. Everybody wanted to trade eastward, including West Germany. And, despite Ambassador Clare Boothe Luce's efforts, Italy continued to vote itself closer to communism. To make matters worse, Eisenhower courted Italy's traditional enemy, Yugoslavia, which was Communist. Luce was mindful of the embarrassing complexities.

In September 1953, Italy moved two divisions to the Yugoslav border at Trieste and threatened to pull out of NATO if a settlement of the contested area with Yugoslavia was not finalized. Luce phoned the White House from Rome to announce that both parliamentary and international conditions were alarming. Eisenhower suggested that the Pentagon's ongoing talks with Tito for military aid be suspended, since Italy "resented them." He asked Dulles to look into the "possibility of another general election."[80] Other people's democratic processes were now monitored carefully in Washington. Indeed, Luce had become deeply, directly, and publicly involved in Italian politics—ignoring the NSC's edict regarding plausible government deniability.

She was widely criticized for her efforts to get Communist auto workers fired by Fiat and was held responsible for heavy losses in "the center coalition" because of an intemperate speech she made in Milan on 28 May 1953. She was accused of threatening Italy with an economic boycott unless it voted right; that is, correctly. She explained to C. D. Jackson that the charges were unfair. "What I actually said was: 'But if—and I am required in all honesty to say this . . . if . . . the Italian people should fall unhappy victim to the wiles of *totalitarianism* . . . *of the right or the left*, there would follow—logically and tragically—grave consequences for this intimate and warm cooperation we now enjoy.' This of course," she pointed out to Jackson, is "a fundamental premise of American policy."[81] In any case, her electoral effort backfired and she blamed it all on Trieste.

In a lengthy report to Eisenhower, Luce analyzed the Italian situation: If the United States were really anti-Communist, and not merely anti-Soviet, why—demanded the Italian voters—does the United States support "Communist Tito [who] is an old-time enemy of Italy?" In addition to Trieste, United States foreign trade policies, which, "while forbidding Italy . . . to trade normally with its ancient customers in Central Europe and Asia and Russia," continues its high-tariff policies, making "it impossible for Italy to trade with America." But the fundamental problem was Trieste. She wrote Jackson, "I know the President likes to have even the most urgent matters summed up on one page . . . :

> For the want of Trieste, an Issue was lost.
> For the want of an Issue, the Election was lost. . . .
> For the want of DeGasperi, his NATO policies were lost.
> For the want of his NATO policies, Italy was lost.
> For the want of Italy, Europe was lost.
> For the want of Europe, America . . . ?
> And all for the want of a two-penny town.[82]

Although Clare Boothe Luce failed to obtain decisive victories for the Christian Democrats, her vigorous activities resulted in as yet classified sums of money and other kinds of support for future election efforts to block a coalition of Italy's socialist and communist leaders. Urgent sums were needed, she wrote Eisenhower, "to give the Center parties time to reform their ranks, regain prestige, and initiate vote-getting programs. . . . [The rest of this paragraph is deleted.]

"The battleground between the Cominform Left and its opposition is political—not economic. . . . In view of the poor physical resources of Italy . . . , *no democratic economic measures* . . .

can be counted on to stop the growth of the Cominform Left. . . . No overt economic measures which the United States can take—unless the sums are vast—can long delay it, either. Since 1945, more than three billion dollars of United States aid have gone to Italy. This overt aid has rehabilitated Italy, but it has not stopped the march of Communism."[83]

Although Luce's recommendations for "covert" aid have been deleted, they are widely known to have involved requests not only for aid directly to the Christian Democratic Party, but for a variety of measures that would have resulted in increased unemployment and isolation of Communist unionists. Records of her meetings with Fiat are now available from Italian sources. Evidently, her effort was sufficiently successful to be recommended as a model for other countries: "Wherever it is possible to apply the policy so painfully achieved by Clare in Italy, of publicly withholding or withdrawing U.S. contracts from Communist-dominated labor unions, this should be done."[84]

Luce's immediate contribution was the successful negotiation of Trieste. On Luce's recommendation, Robert Murphy was sent to Yugoslavia. Eventually, 450,000 tons of wheat were agreed upon, along with, according to Murphy, hundreds of millions of dollars' worth of equipment for the Yugoslav Army.[85] Eisenhower regarded Tito "as one of the greatest assets we have in dealing with the satellite states in Europe." In any case, Trieste was temporarily mediated. It was not actually solved until December 1976, when Italy's parliament ratified the treaty of 1954 and announced, "It is now time for development and collaboration with our Yugoslavian neighbors."[86]

Because Eisenhower's response to Luce's other requests are still classified, there is no record of how much support was actually sent, during his administration, to the Christian Democratic Party. The covert effort to destabilize European socialist-communist unity efforts remains top secret. He was impressed with her statistic that the "Cominform Left" required "only four percent more" to eclipse the Center and Right parties in the next election. But he wrote her a lengthy letter in which he asked: In addition to what the United States might do for Italy "either clandestinely or publicly," what "kind of pressure" could she exert to get "these governments to do something themselves?"[87] Eisenhower was getting impatient with countries that seemed to demand more than he thought they strategically merited. In "Notes to discuss with John Foster Dulles," Eisenhower wrote that Mrs. Luce was having difficulties "in her negotiations for bases in Italy." Eisenhower no longer regarded the bases as "vital at all." He urged Luce to explain that to the Italian Government and the "situation might change." He believed that in "selling the U.S. the idea that 'we cannot live alone' we have also sold the Europeans the idea that we are completely dependent upon their cooperative attitude. In a sense this is . . . true, but if there is not full recognition of a *common* need and because of this the cooperative effort breaks down, it is equally true that they will feel the pinch long before we will."[88]

Eisenhower's attitude displeased Luce. By August 1954, she had become impatient with what she considered Eisenhower's dangerous lack of bold vitality. She complained to James Hagerty that "Italy and Europe" were rapidly moving toward communism. She predicted that "unless we did something to conquer" the situation, communism would overrun Europe "within the next five years." She appalled Hagerty by speaking of both a political and a military victory and pointed to "Formosa and the Chinese mainland" as "the most likely spot" to begin. She promised to send him an outline of her views. He promised to bring it to Eisenhower's attention.[89]

Mrs. Luce sent the President a thirty-seven-page essay, *Russian Atomic Power and the Lost American Revolution*. She also sent a copy to C. D. Jackson, because she feared Eisenhower would never look at it. There is no evidence that he did read her condemnation of the inactivity of his administration, which, she maintained, threatened to doom the world to Soviet domination. In it she called for a preventive war, and questioned why it was "more Christian" for Americans "to be smashed to smithereens" by nuclear weapons rather than for Americans to launch an "attack on Soviet Russia first." A new European policy of "neutralism," led by France, had overtaken Europe. There was Churchill's "obsession with 'going to the summit,'" Alcide DeGasperi's "long wooing of Nenni and tolerance of Togliatti," Europe's generally "laggardly tactics" regarding NATO and EDC, and its reluctance to grant military bases to the U.S. She recommended, therefore, a bold new policy to reclaim America's "atomic supremacy," with "tactical nuclear weapons" for all purposes that could be used from "the steppes to the jungles." Then Clare Boothe Luce, so long identified with the China Lobby, suggested: "The rollback of the Iron Curtain with tactical atomic weapons should begin in Asia." After all,

(a) We still have there two allies eager to fight and able to supply forces—Korea and Formosa.

(b) Western Civilization (the preservation of which is one of our policy goals) cannot be destroyed there.

(c) Unless Moscow is willing to see China defeated, it must come to her rescue. If it does . . . the consequent drain on Russia will ease her military pressure on the European front. . . .

With that done, the United States will have recaptured "the lost American revolution" and "should soon begin to reaffirm in *unequivocal terms* the historic American stand in world politics of being for governments of *free* people, for *free* people, by *free* people everywhere."[90]

There is no evidence that Eisenhower ever responded to Luce's suggestions. There is clear evidence that when "rollback" seemed an invitation to World War III, the United States had nothing to offer the freedom fighters. In December 1956, when Hungarians were being killed by the hundreds in the streets of Budapest, that was a bitter decision. It reeked of abandonment and betrayal. There were, Eisenhower explained, no alternatives. He wondered what he might have done "had Hungary been accessible by sea or through the territory of allies who might have agreed to react positively. . . ." But Hungary was not accessible. Britain and France were preoccupied with their plans to overthrow Nasser and liberate the Suez Canal. "Hungary could not be reached" except by "moving across neutral Austria, Titoist Yugoslavia, or Communist Czechoslovakia." It was impossible. "Sending U.S. troops alone into Hungary through hostile or neutral territory would have involved us in general war."[91]

The origins of the Polish and Hungarian uprisings of 1956 were deeply rooted in national soil, in traditional enmities, in all the complexities that devastated Europe between 1917 and 1945. Revolution. Fascism. Collaboration. Resistance. Anti-Semitism. New

Borders. Communism. Nationalism. Bitter, ugly memories. In Poland, there were the new western territories—including Gdansk (Danzig), the site of Professor Spanner's soap works. During the last battles between the Nazis and the Red Army, a young soap maker boasted to the Russian-born British historian and journalist Alexander Werth, in Danzig, "Now that the Jews are wiped out, we can start on millions of Slavs."[92] Partisans—Catholics, Communists, Gypsies, and Jews—millions of dead. Reparations. Before his arrest in 1951, Władysław Gomułka worked hard to promote settlement in the western territories near Poland's new, Oder-Neisse border. But the area was still contested, and fear of Germany loomed large. He opposed collectivization. He was a hero. He had escaped Stalin's 1937 purge of Polish Communists. He was liberal, a nationalist, and in prison. Stalin said he was a Titoist. Stalinists were in power in Poland and in Hungary. They were suspicious of Titoism, a "national road to socialism." In Hungary, it was the conservatives who had collaborated with Hitler, the conservatives who turned over Hungary's Jews to the Nazis. The Fascist Ferencz Szálasi and his "Arrow Cross" did not come to power in Hitler's last satellite until October 1944, when much of the country was already occupied and Horthy, who was prepared for an armistice, was arrested by Hitler. Szálasi dreamed of "Hungarism," a "Hungarist Corporatist State," dominated by Magyars, racially pure. He sent Hitler a plan for the tribal reorganization of Europe. A passionate nationalist, he vowed to save Budapest from the Red hordes forever. Now Stalinists were in power in Hungary; they were uncompromising, harsh. They perceived "fascist" opposition everywhere. They were suspicious of Khrushchev; they opposed a national road to socialism. Images of "Hungarism." They were Stalinists—and Jews. Mátyás Rákosi, followed by Ernö Gerö, both Jews who had spent the war years in Russia. Some, simplistically, called their opponents anti-Semites. Economic privation and suspicion of all those who did not spend the war years in the East were more significant factors than religion or "race" in Hungary in 1956.[93]

Regarding Poland, however, Khrushchev himself went to great length to explain that his support for Gomułka had nothing to do with anti-Semitism. There was anti-Semitism under Stalin. But the criticism of the Jews in the Polish Communist Party in 1956 was justified, and not anti-Semitism. It was just that there were too many Jews in the leadership. Bolesław Bierut surrounded himself with Jakub Berman, Hilary Minc, Roman Zambrowski. "The unfair promotion of Jews over Poles" created resentment. "Gomułka understood how mistaken—indeed how harmful—it was to let this virus grow unchecked in the Polish leadership. Not only was he a Pole; he was a more mature politician than some of his comrades." Because of Stalin's own anti-Semitism, Khrushchev explained, "you might have thought Stalin would have taken Gomułka's side in the dispute with Berman and Minc, since they were Jews." But Stalin believed the "conflict had nothing to do with the Jewish question." He believed that Gomułka was "pro-Yugoslav," a Titoist.

Now Khrushchev sought a new relationship with Tito, and with the satellite countries. In February 1956, he intensified the "de-Stalinization" campaign he had begun in 1953. In a "secret" seven-hour speech addressed to the Twentieth Communist Party Congress, Khrushchev detailed and denounced Stalin's crimes. He announced the Soviet Union's commitment to "peaceful coexistence." There was, he said, "no fatal inevitability of war." He promised an entirely new economic relationship between Russia and its Warsaw Pact allies.* There would be great economic changes in agricultural and industrial development—more consumer goods, fair market prices for international trade. Moreover, Khrushchev acknowledged there were many legitimate independent roads to communism, including parliamentary victory. An expression of "self-criticism," Khrushchev's speech heralded a new era.[94]

For United States political warriors, it signified a great challenge. For the exiles at Radio Free Europe, it signified potential disaster. The Communist world might now be liberalized and unified—unless it was broken up forever. Poland and Hungary wanted better working and living conditions, new local leadership, and higher prices for their goods. Khrushchev had agreed. But before the changes were made, riots broke out in Poznań and, later, Budapest. Radio Free Europe called for total revolution.

Operation Focus. Operation Veto. For years, the CIA had called, through Radio Free Europe, insistently, constantly, vehemently for the "liberation" of the "enslaved" countries. Radio Free Europe broadcast twenty hours a day, dropped leaflets by balloons

---

* The Soviet Union organized the Warsaw Pact in response to West German rearmament and admission into NATO in May 1955.

at a rate of fourteen million a month. In fact, the Committee for a Free Europe had developed a full-scale plan for the liberation of East Europe as early as 1952. A. A. Berle wrote that the goal was to tie the liberated countries into a united-Europe movement already underway in the West—including Jean Monnet's steel-and-iron community, the EDC, NATO, and the European Payments Union. "This time, at least," Berle wrote, "we will not leave an empire adrift again, as we did after Versailles." Presumably, Berle referred to the fate of the Hapsburg Empire, which, at Versailles, was designated the West's *cordon sanitaire,* the buffer zone to isolate Russia's new revolutionary government. In any case, Berle had misgivings. He was "opposed to broadcasting or starting movements which could only end in the slaughter of the people involved," until the State Department was seriously "prepared to support a liberation." By June 1954, he was assured by RFE Director Robert Lang that RFE was "now the recognized head of the non-communist opposition in great parts of Central Europe and that it can force changes in the governments and the policies both in Czechoslovakia and Hungary." The question remained, for Berle and others, how best to use that power.[95]

The State Department never fully supported RFE's liberation effort. In October 1954, William Griffith, RFE's political analyst in Munich, complained to C. D. Jackson that United States Foreign Service officers sabotaged Project Focus, a major balloon effort, "in every way." "It appears," Griffith wrote, the desk officers "do not believe it is possible to create an internal mass opposition . . .—and admit frankly they wouldn't know what to do with one if it were created." He and Jackson had "always thought it both possible and desirable," and now it was being curtailed. Griffith was furious: "Now I believe we are well on the way to creating one in Czechoslovakia and off to a good start in Hungary. The thought of this being strangled by some third-rate epigones who burn incense daily to the God of Doing Nothing makes me really mad!"[96]

Khrushchev's speech, the "Spirit of Geneva," Soviet withdrawal from Austria, the treaty between West Germany and the Soviet Union, ongoing negotiations regarding Eisenhower's "Open Skies" proposal—all contributed to put great pressure on RFE to cease its antagonistic activities. C. D. Jackson went to see John Foster Dulles and was rebuffed. Dulles agreed with Eisenhower that it was better to be involved in a trade war than a nuclear war. Jackson reported Dulles' position:

> So long as the Soviets under Stalin continued to behave so badly in public, it was relatively easy for our side to maintain a certain social ostracism toward them—and I stress the word social. . . . The man who spits in your eye, puts poison in your soup, has impossible table manners, is the kind of person you don't want around. You don't want him in your house, you don't want him in your community, you don't want him in your club—you just don't want him. And what is more important, everybody else understands. . . .
>
> Now all of a sudden . . . it is becoming extremely difficult to maintain the ostracism—and maybe we should not even want to maintain it. Frowns have given way to smiles. Guns have given way to offers of economic aid. Soviet industry has reached a point where they probably can start producing consumer goods if they want to. . . .
>
> The other thing I know is . . .—with the repudiation of Stalin, with the rehabilitation of scores of officials, scientists, soldiers, dead and alive, with the apparent acceptance of Tito, and therefore of Titoism—with all these things going on, it is very difficult for the U.S. to say to its allies that all of this means nothing, that it is a trick, that the ostracism must be maintained. . . .
>
> I don't think anyone wants to turn the clock back . . . , and furthermore I doubt if anyone could if he tried. We may be in very grave long-term danger because of the Soviets' new economic competition, but I would rather be trying to work out the answers to that one instead of trying to find an answer to H-Bomb competition.
>
> Back in 1950 or '51, I spent $1,000 to build a bomb-proof cellar in my New York house for Janet and myself and my documents. I would not have spent that much money if I had not been convinced at that time it was necessary. Well, today I just would not spend that thousand dollars for that, because I don't think that is the way the struggle is shaping up any more. . . .[97]

While Eisenhower and Dulles, along with Jackson, concentrated on a new foreign economic policy, Jackson also went off in search of allies to reinvigorate RFE. Currently out of power, and rapidly moving out of favor, he refused to accept Washington's unwillingness to take bold advantage of the de-Stalinization campaign. "To oversimplify," he wrote William Jackson, who now occupied his former position, "if Tito is now strictly kosher, Titoism is equally kosher. So what will the Kremlin do if another satellite decided that national Communism or Socialism, is what they would like? And with that as a first step, quite a lot can ensue." Jackson's idea was to create many crises at once. "If," he wrote, "the summer of 1956 passes without our having made some intelligent move toward the Eastern European satellite countries . . . we will really have exhibited the kind of idea bankruptcy for which we are becoming far too famous. . . ." He wrote to Henry Luce that if his "political warfare education" had taught him anything, it was that "international psychological activity" must be accompanied by "little bits of cold, hard action." "We desperately need," he insisted, something that would be visible "to the eyes of the millions of little men around the world": the "detachment of Albania, a successful large-scale raid on the Mainland of China, a lot of bloody Communist noses the first time they try anything we don't like, a 'disabled' Communist submarine caught prowling off the U.S. coast."[98]

Throughout 1956, notes of protest poured in from Czechoslovakia, Poland, Hungary, and the Soviet Union regarding RFE's balloons. In January, the Soviet ambassador, Georgi Zaroubin, requested an appointment "to deliver a personal message from Premier Bulganin." Eisenhower thought it would be a complaint about balloons. But balloons were not mentioned. Dulles "was quite surprised that it had not been balloons, but then laughed and said, 'Maybe that's what you get for having a guilty conscience.'" The message was an offer to extend "the spirit of Geneva" with a twenty-year "Treaty of Friendship with the United States." Dulles thought "we should turn it down politely, pointing out that we want deeds not words." In March, Czechoslovakia charged that a balloon had caused an air crash in which twenty-two people had died. Former ambassador to Japan and Undersecretary of State Joseph Grew, chairman of the board of the Free Europe Committee, denied that balloons that weighed only two pounds could "constitute a hazard to aircraft." In May, the Soviet Union sent a protest about balloons, but it was "a mild protest."[99]

To the staff of RFE, it seemed that seven years of broadcasts and balloons, seven years of "merchandizing hope," of creating "pressure from below," while now at the brink of success, was about to be junked for Soviet promises and smiles.[100] Although Dulles and Eisenhower reacted coolly to all requests for greater support, at no time were RFE activities actually curtailed. As the situation in Poland and Hungary intensified, the tone of their broadcasts intensified.

In June, in Poznań, Polish workers and students rioted during a trade fair attended by many United States and allied industrialists, journalists, and tourists. On 22 October 1956, amid great rejoicing, Gomułka assumed power in Poland. A. A. Berle noted RFE's reaction: "A Titoist Poland is or at least can be an independent Poland. This does not make it a free Poland. Radio Free Europe has been giving the news and generally encouraging the proceedings, but without committing to the Gomułka type of government. Eventually we shall have to have some really free elections there." Gomułka's success was marked by two factors. The entire country united behind him, including Cardinal Wyszyński. And Gomułka ordered Russian troops out of Poland, while at the same time reaffirming his commitment to the Warsaw Pact, and to the Soviet Union.[101]

The situation was very different in Hungary. It was out of control. Workers and intellectuals wanted Imre Nagy. They wanted Rákosi removed. In July, Mikoyan removed Rákosi—to Russia. Gerö was not Nagy, although he promised reforms. There were demonstrations for Nagy. On 23 October, Budapest rioted for Imre Nagy. On 24 October, Imre Nagy became Premier of Hungary. But the riots continued. He called in the Russian troops to restore order. Radio Free Europe called for the overthrow of Nagy; called for free elections—unrelenting revolution. Subsequent denials notwithstanding, RFE called for boldness and courage, implied support, and promised success.

On 28 October, Nagy demanded the removal of Soviet troops, agreed to free elections, and released Cardinal Mindszenty. Charismatic and reactionary, the cardinal's power was divisive. He called for the restoration of church property and the resurrection of a Catholic party. According to Klaus Dohrn, Cardinal Mindszenty was a monarchist, with monarchist pretensions. Dohrn reported to Jackson that the cardinal was not "an internationally and liberally minded reformer":

> He is a fervent patriot, a monarchist . . . although in the historic Hungarian way with more allegiance to the Crown than to the Pretender. It is significant that when he went . . . to the U.S. . . . after

the war his greatest concern was the physical fate of the Crown of St. Stephen. He was also very conscious of his prerogatives as the Primate of Hungary which constitutionally makes him the deputy of the king between reigns or when the king is prevented from exercising his functions. . . .

Dohrn was told that during the only press conference the cardinal held, he declared that "all achievements which serve the interests of the people must be preserved." But when a journalist asked if he intended to take "over the government," Mindszenty "brusquely turned around, snapped, 'I am the Primate,' and left the room."[102]

From 28–30 October, after the Soviet tanks had rolled out beyond Budapest, RFE continued to call for revolution, for opposition to Nagy. Cardinal Mindszenty also opposed Nagy and demanded a Catholic party "on the Adenauer pattern." Then, on 30 October, Nagy declared Hungary neutral and announced its withdrawal from the Warsaw alliance. Repeatedly during this crisis, Eisenhower conveyed to the Soviets that the United States did not regard the Warsaw Pact nations "as potential military allies." But RFE continued to call for revolution. Mysterious supplies turned up in unexpected places. The broadcasts intensified. Courage. Aid. Four thousand Soviet tanks and sixty-eight thousand Soviet troops marched on Budapest. On 4 November, the vapors from RFE Munich became hollow, empty sounds. According to Henry Cabot Lodge, thirty thousand Hungarians and seven thousand Soviet troops were killed and wounded in the bitter conflict.[103] János Kádár replaced Nagy. He promised to order Soviet troops out of Hungary "as soon as order is restored." There were thousands of refugees.[104] Radio Free Europe suspended its call for liberation.

On 19 November, Eisenhower responded to C. D. Jackson's many memos demanding positive action. "I know that your whole being cries out for 'action.' . . . I assure you that the measures taken there by the Soviets are just as distressing to me as they are to you. But to annihilate Hungary . . . is in no way to help her." He sent Jackson an excerpt from a friend's letter, "a particularly moving document on the case of decency versus extinction": "Mothers in Israel and Egypt, sons in England and France, fathers and husbands in the U.S. and in Russia. . . . *After* the event, all of them, regardless of nationality, will be disinterested in the [cause]. . . ."[105] Jackson agreed that bombs over Budapest would not ensure Hungary's liberation. But, he wrote Luce, there was "an awful lot of legitimate theatre sorely needed right now."[106]

Specific changes occurred in Eisenhower's foreign policy after 1956. Political warfare C. D. Jackson style no longer operated out of the White House. Radio Free Europe's freewheeling independence was checked. Independent investigations revealed that Radio Free Europe had indeed been responsible for Hungary's expectation of United States military and material support.[107] The rhetoric of "rollback" was discarded. Ironically, George Kennan, the author of the original containment policy, which had been rejected by the Dulles brothers, was now in part responsible for the change. During the summer of 1958, Kennan visited Poland. Allen Dulles was impressed by his report and recommended it to the White House. Kennan believed that "the best the West can hope for . . . is that the relative liberties and immunities which the Poles now enjoy should continue for so long a time that they come to be considered rights. . . . This will not in itself bring liberation from Russian hegemony in matters of foreign policy; but it should permit a new generation of Poles to grow up in an atmosphere of relative intellectual freedom, and it should create a situation which could scarcely fail to work in western interests." Agitation for "liberation," Kennan concluded, would only embarrass the Polish Government and result in renewed reaction. He suggested a policy of "exchanges of all sorts," "cultural contacts," everything that might "break the rigid patterns of bipolarity, to reduce tensions, and to permit the Poles to play . . . an independent role in international affairs."[108]

C. D. Jackson continued to disagree. But he was increasingly alone. W. W. Rostow, who agreed with Jackson on most issues, wrote a panegyric to liberty that fundamentally agreed with Kennan's view: "The trend in world affairs is rapidly moving towards a diffusion of unilateral power, away from both Moscow and Washington. The postures of Nehru, Nasser, Tito, Gomułka are part of a deeply rooted trend. . . . Americans tend to view this development with pleasure, as they believe profoundly that it is through the diffusion of power that individual and national liberties are preserved. . . ."[109]

The events of 1956 seemed to end a Cold War era. Americans would eat Polish hams again; and the Soviet Union would begin to pay fair market prices for Polish coal and other Central European goods. Although Eisenhower never dismissed C. D. Jackson entirely, his own emphasis was now entirely different. He acknowledged the Soviet Union's western borders and dedicated his last years in office to a serious effort to end nuclear tyranny. Before the advent of thermonuclear weapons, the world had never before been in a state of permanent wartime preparedness. It was economically draining and emotionally exhausting. It constituted a state of global terrorism. Never before had so few men, with so little understanding, possessed so much power. Trustless and inimical, they had no clear areas of agreement or purpose, and no recognized limits to their activities. There were, moreover, no established, easy, or direct means of communication. Only determination kept the distance between the advocates of peace and the apostles of holocaust. Moderate and steady, Eisenhower had avoided war on two continents. His restraint demonstrated that United States policies, despite Radio Free Europe's bluster, did have limits. The Soviet Union, more secure on its western borders, was willing to negotiate economic and political differences with its own allies, and with the NATO countries. After 1956, trade agreements replaced brinkmanship. A period of relative stability and high hopes for international agreements leading to détente, even disarmament, ensued. Summit meetings were planned.

Eisenhower would not accept Communist triumphs in areas where—through covert measures, however heavy-handed—they could be blocked. He agreed with neither the "better Red than dead" pacifists nor their adversaries, and sought, as he had in all other areas, a "middle way." In January 1958, he offered C. D. Jackson the position of undersecretary of state "to head up the Cold War effort." He wanted Jackson's skills. But he wanted them directed toward disarmament.[110] Jackson never took the job. On 22 June 1960, Jackson complained to Henry Luce: "The Dulles-Eisenhower word 'liberation' . . . [was] a perfectly good word." "But from London, Paris, Moscow, and most United States columnists came agonized, dismayed, or furious cries, and the word was formally banned." Now, Jackson continued, "intervention," also a perfectly "useful word," has been banned. With the "Black Africa explosion" and Castro's "bridgehead" in Latin America, Jackson feared for the future. The diplomatic corps, he lamented, "would still like to operate by candle-light and quill pen." And political warfare "is considered 'dirty' and un-American and an unbearable nuisance by the diplomats. . . . And now I suppose I am right back where I started. . . ."[111]

But Jackson was mistaken. By 1960, there were fifteen thousand CIA operatives around the world. There were covert activities everywhere. Surveillance and counterinsurgency. And by 1960, the United States was well along the road to full involvement in Vietnam. In May 1955, France's Prime Minister Edgar Faure had declared that France would not cooperate with Dulles' support of Diem. Faure insisted that Diem was "not only incapable but mad." He would "bring on a Viet Minh victory, focus the hostility" on France. It would destroy the Franco-American alliance. France preferred to "retire entirely from Indochina." By March 1956, the French were out of Indochina, but in North Africa. In May 1956, the United States Temporary Equipment Recovery Mission (TERM) entered Vietnam. The road to America's longest war began slowly: several hundred advisers and a training team; and millions of dollars.

When Diem denounced the Geneva accords and "refused to be bound to them in any way," the die was cast. Ngo Dinh Diem refused to hold free elections. Not in 1956. Not ever. Neither Britain nor the Soviet Union insisted on them. France did nothing. The United States supported Diem. Our only concern, said Dulles, was to halt communism in Indochina. And Diem "was the only alternative to a communist South Vietnam." Indochina would preoccupy American domestic and foreign policy for over a decade. The country's longest and costliest war would sap the United States' economic vitality and moral imagination. Throughout his presidency, Eisenhower refused to commit American troops, on a large-scale and unilateral basis, to what he recognized would be certain tragedy.[112]

On the other hand, he had built institutions that were capable of fighting communism wherever it emerged. Eisenhower introduced covert operations in the Philippines, on Quemoy and Matsu, in Tibet, Indonesia, and Laos. In 1958, there was an overt display of force in Lebanon. Ten thousand marines in full combat dress, with rifles poised, eyes ahead, jaws set, landed—to the amazement of the sunbathers—on Beirut's tranquil and beautiful beaches. The political warriors boasted that Lebanon was saved and not a shot was fired. Of course not. There was no revolution in Lebanon. The revolution was in Iraq. But we seemed to have no welcoming allies in Iraq. So the troops remained in Lebanon, where they had been invited. President Camille Chamoun invited the marines, because he thought it would help him win the election. It didn't. Robert Murphy evidently did not like Chamoun either. Britain had landed in Jordan at the same time. It was an allied and well-orchestrated effort to demonstrate both continued interest in Nasser's unclear ambitions and the fact that the allies come when clients such as Chamoun and King Hussein call. Britain and the United States agreed to pull out whenever the UN ordered their withdrawal. The UN eventually obliged, and the troops returned to their transports; allegedly well tanned and full of soda pop bought on Beirut's beaches.[113]

While the 1958 adventure in Lebanon was little more than a costly psychological ploy, it reflected the attitude that would drive the United States relentlessly into the bitter winds of other landings. Supported by nuclear missiles, thousands of vessels, and seemingly unlimited capital, U.S. troops and U.S. military equipment have been involved again and again in the ongoing effort to protect our preferred candidates throughout the world. The attitude that enabled Eisenhower to dispatch a massive military display of force that seemed so inappropriate to the facts of political life in Lebanon would drive the United States into that deeply destructive war in Indochina. Eisenhower refused to accept the emergence of communism anywhere, in any style, under any circumstances. "Free elections" had become the target of serious American concern and covert involvement. Wherever free elections were in fact an issue, hundreds of thousands of dollars were spent to support acceptable candidates, to deradicalize the trade unions, to destabilize the Communist parties, and to prevent any united-front formation.

In an extraordinary letter to his friend Paul Hoffman, Eisenhower carefully, cautiously defined his position on "free elections." Hoffman had asked Eisenhower a series of questions about how, exactly, Eisenhower proposed to overcome the "difficult obstacles" blocking our "dream of a just peace." Eisenhower answered:

. . . With respect to the fourth question, I think there is no difficulty about defining "government of their own choosing." Obviously we mean any government freely chosen by the majority of its citizens. But in question three you have posed a difficult problem. One of these difficulties comes from an apparent contradiction of terms. Communism could, I think, be defined as a doctrine of complete socialism, but *including the clear determination to employ any means, including force and international war, to bring about a destruction of other forms of government.* Consequently we should not favor on a reciprocal basis giving to proponents a full opportunity to promote Communism, because Communism cannot be divorced from the readiness to use violence. I do not believe this is quibbling.[114]

It was not quibbling. It was honest. Democracy for Eisenhower meant free electoral choice, except for communists. To prevent communists from being elected, the United States would use any means necessary. That was the impossible attitude upon which the 1956 support for Diem was based. That was, and remains, the core of the Cold War. There was then nothing to negotiate except the degree of mutually acceptable violence.

In 1958, Britain insisted on a summit meeting. There was an election in Britain, and Harold Macmillan was adamant. The British people, who knew "they could be exterminated," "jolly well feel that it is only fair to have a go at a conversation on the subject."[115] Macmillan's insistence assured the last summit conference during Eisenhower's presidency. Postponed over and over again, it would result in either something significant, or nothing at all. Tensions were high in 1958. Sputnik was not only a symbol of scientific achievement, it was a Soviet announcement of its ability to launch long-range intercontinental ballistic missiles (ICBMs). On 2 November 1957, the second Sputnik was launched. On 16 December, Dulles shocked the NATO allies with the suggestion that their countries become launching pads for offensive intercontinental nuclear missiles. NATO ceased to be a defensive alliance. The Soviet Union called for a summit conference; a test-ban treaty; disarmament. Macmillan insisted on that meeting.

For a time, Russia went to great lengths to assure the west of its sincerity, its willingness to negotiate faithfully. From January through April 1958, Bulganin and Khrushchev sent many notes with specific proposals for test-ban agreements, nonnuclear zones. A new and congenial ambassador was sent to Washington. Not only congenial, but frank, forthright, and handsome "in the Western sort of way." Eisenhower was impressed. He wrote to his friend Swede Hazlett: "Speaking of personalities, the new Russian Ambassador to the United States, Mr. Mikhail Menshikov, is making quite a splash in Washington. He is extremely affable, good looking (I am told by the ladies of my family) in the 'Western sort of way' (whatever they mean by that), energetic and apparently not impressed with protocol procedures (which break with routine I admit I find refreshing). Only time will tell whether his appointment is in any way indicative of a change in official Russian policy." After Eisenhower had met with Menshikov "for an unprecedented length of time," he told his staff: "He is the only Russian I have ever seen smile outside of Zhukov."[116]

But all the Soviet notes were rejected. No compromises seemed likely. No agreements seemed possible. On 10 November 1958, Khrushchev announced that Russia would unilaterally withdraw from East Berlin. The allies would have to negotiate their access to Berlin with East Germany, which the United States did not recognize. The "Berlin Crisis" of 1958 was on. For the first time, Khrushchev presented Eisenhower with an ultimatum. A specific date. If the United States did not negotiate by 27 May 1959, the Soviets would move out. They proposed a demilitarized "Free City" under UN auspices. The United States had six months to decide. Eisenhower was furious. He phoned Dulles: "Somewhere along the line we have to find a way to say that we are going to do what we want to do." He recalled that he had always known how troublesome Berlin would be. But Roosevelt and Churchill had said, "Oh, we can get along with Uncle Joe."[117]

As the deadline approached, the situation became more tense. W. W. Rostow proposed "hotting up all the satellites at once." It need not be a nuclear war but "a limited war for Central Europe."[118] Although Eisenhower had developed contingency plans (which are still classified) in the event of an emergency, he insisted that we "should not look upon this situation as a 'Berlin crisis.'" We should, he urged his Cabinet and congressional leaders, see this as a long-range problem: "We can anticipate two or three decades of tension." There was no evidence, he pointed out, that the Russians wanted war. "Khrushchev was ready to negotiate within limits" but "had committed himself to turning East Berlin over to the East Germans and to Russian evacuation of East Berlin."[119] Eisenhower urged caution and patience. It was an internal affair.

Eisenhower believed, in 1959 as in 1954, all the evidence that indicated: "Russia is not seeking a general war and will not for a long, long time, if ever. Everything is shifting to economic warfare, to propaganda and to a sort of peaceful infiltration."[120] He was convinced in March 1959, "We should not now go to any sort of extreme military action, such as partial mobilization." This was not a "problem" of "six months, but of forty years." He had "one possible 'ace in the hole.'" He might invite Khrushchev to visit the United States. "We must," he concluded, "conduct ourselves so that the world can believe we are conciliatory." His insistence on conciliation was not shared by many of his advisers. General Nathan Twining informed him, for example, that the Joint Chiefs of Staff recommended more "provocative" action. They were to testify before congressional hearings. Eisenhower instructed Twining "to caution the Joint Chiefs that the military in this country is a tool and not a policy-making body."[121]

At the height of the Berlin situation, Eisenhower declared that it was not only practical but wise to reduce United States forces by fifty-five thousand men. They cost, he noted, $250 million a year. Eisenhower thought that the money would go further in the Mutual Security Program, in the Military Assistance Program—in any of the new programs that were devised during his administration to fight the long-term battle against communism. To fiscal conservatives, to international economic analysts, that made absolute sense. To politicians looking forward to the 1960 elections, it was a perfect target by which to defame Eisenhower's views. The old man. The tired general. The do-nothing President who gave us first the bomber gap and then the missile gap. Ike would be vilified and rendered absurd, frequently by the very people who had supported him: Henry Luce and C. D. Jackson—the entire *Time-Life-Fortune* establishment. The authors of the Gaither Report—and the Rockefeller Report. They had been his friends. But there was an election coming up. And new territories, entire new countries were emerging; the continent of Africa. There was an explosion of opportunity—and Eisenhower urged caution, frugality, fiscal conservatism. He condemned adventures, and adventurists.

His public words were ignored or distorted. It was an election year. But Eisenhower was impassioned. He told a meeting of legislative leaders:

Look at it another way. What would these 55,000 men do if we had them? Certainly they are not going to fight a land war in Europe. How could a land war be fought successfully against the great number of divisions that are available on the other side . . . ? It is perfectly clear, . . . you can't provide security just with a check book. You've got to be prepared to live with a series of Berlins for the next 40 years. If these people decide to put another $3 billion into the budget every time Russia tries to push, they might as well go all the way to a garrison state. . . . Once you spend a single dollar beyond adequacy, you are weakening yourself. . . . Anyone who has read even a little bit on Communism, . . . knows that the Communist objective is to make us spend ourselves into bankruptcy. . . . This is a continuous crisis: Iran, Indochina, Formosa, Iraq . . . it is really a continuing thing that the U.S. has to live with certainly as long as we are going to be here.[122]

His private words, words spoken to his closest confidants and friends in his office during this period were just as specific. During a "serious talk of possible war," Eisenhower exploded: "You might as well go out and shoot everyone you see and then shoot yourself."[123]

On 16 April 1959, John Foster Dulles, dying of cancer, resigned as Secretary of State. Eisenhower was on his own. Christian Herter never really replaced Dulles. Nobody did. The tough guy who snarled was gone. Eisenhower, himself limited by the aftermath of a stroke and a painful intestinal malfunction, carried on. His smile no longer seemed so radiant. But he decided to invite Khrushchev to the White House. Khrushchev agreed to forget the deadline and tour the United States. The ultimatum was withdrawn: 27 May 1959. It turned out to be the day of John Foster Dulles' funeral. The Berlin Crisis was over.

To prepare for Khrushchev's visit, Eisenhower put together several bold proposals to change the very nature of the Cold War. He wanted "to make one big effort to see if the Soviets" would cooperate. He considered a joint effort "to aid the underdeveloped countries," to work with the World Bank and the International Development Association (IDA). But Treasury Secretary Robert Anderson disapproved. The Soviets, he declared, used a "managed currency and would be putting in money of inferior quality while we were putting in hard dollars." They were not "being invited into the IDA." "The President said what he has been trying to do is to hold out before the Russians the possibility of their functioning on the same basis as any other country." Anderson said he was opposed to "a mutual effort with the Soviets." Other countries might withdraw. Russia had already penetrated Africa unilaterally. Eisenhower turned to trade with Russia, and urged a more liberal policy. He was told: "The real problem is that what they have are the things we are now buying elsewhere. A shift would disrupt existing trade relations." Eisenhower insisted: If "we take strategic items off the list, and sell for gold. . . ." He also proposed a massive student exchange program, ten thousand a year. According to Ann Whitman, "he worked on the idea for a long time. J. Edgar Hoover approved, but he was never quite able to sell the State Department." His suggestions were truncated by his staff. Still he persevered. Ambassador Llewellyn Thompson hoped he "might find an opportunity to express awareness that Khrushchev is trying to raise the living conditions of his people."[124]

During the September 1959 meetings with Khrushchev, some advances were made. Some trade restrictions would be removed. Khrushchev acknowledged the need to remove travel restrictions as well, but he "should be allowed to do this by himself, in his own time, without being pressed." Eisenhower agreed that Berlin would not be "the one thing that governs and controls our entire relationship." Khrushchev brought up China, but not insistently. Eisenhower brought up Eastern Europe: "We have no thought of the use of force, but we do hope that the governments there will become more responsive to the will of their people."[125] The arms race, and some agreement toward peace, were uppermost on the agenda. But no agreement was reached. Khrushchev's tour of the United States had created a stir. There was more good will than animosity. It was an opening. But the private Camp David meetings had failed. Still, there was always some good, Eisenhower believed, to be gained by personal, face-to-face contact. There was still the Paris Summit Conference. There was still hope. Eisenhower consistently refused to meet those with whom he had no intention of negotiating: Dr. Mossadegh, President Arbenz of Guatemala, Fidel Castro.

During his last months in office, Eisenhower traveled to Europe, Asia, and Latin America. He spoke of peace and economic development. At the same time, his days were filled with ongoing covert operations, counterinsurgency, and contingency plans. There were the details of a plan to overthrow Patrice Lumumba. The Congo, formerly owned outright by the King of Belgium, was one of the world's richest areas in gold and uranium. The Belgian rule had been brutal. Eisenhower said there were fewer than twenty college graduates in the entire country. Lumumba, a nationalist, was elected President. The CIA said he was a Communist, "a Soviet tool." His days were numbered. A great effort to stop Japan from drifting toward neutralism was underway. Eisenhower ordered massive economic aid to stabilize the United States' most vital Asian ally. In the Dominican Republic, Trujillo had become a burden. Anti-Castro Cubans were being trained in Guatemala. There were military missions and national security training programs everywhere, daily NATO war games, and an ambitious surveillance operation headed by the CIA's U-2 high-altitude spy plane. Khrushchev knew about the U-2 flights over the Soviet Union when he was at Camp David but thought it would be "impolite" to mention them.

On 1 May 1960, CIA pilot Francis Gary Powers failed to do what he was supposed to do in case of trouble. Having been shot down, he neither scuttled the plane nor self-destructed. He and the plane and its sophisticated surveillance equipment were all intact fifteen hundred miles inside the heartland of Russia. Eisenhower did not know that Powers was alive and well and in a Soviet prison. After all, he had been paid thirty thousand pre-1960 dollars for his high-risk activities. Nobody called it treason, precisely. But it was a surprise. Eisenhower's cover-up in the face of the facts was embarrassing.[120] More than that. Eisenhower, the man of truth and dignity, the man whom millions of people in India had just hailed as the "prince of peace," had lied. And then he defiantly said it was his right, his duty to invade the airspace of a sovereign nation.

To justify that aggression with such cavalier disregard for the United States' own principles and traditions seemed to many belligerent, astonishing. The man who above all had raised his hands in hope and friendship, now assumed an entirely different posture. At Geneva in 1955, there were tears around the conference table when Eisenhower, with a sense of timing that was perfect, removed his glasses and said, "'I have sometimes been mistaken, but Marshal Zhukov here knows that as a soldier I have always spoken the truth." According to *Le Monde,* as Eisenhower spoke, his eyes were looking into Zhukov's eyes, and at that moment an extraordinary thing happened: "the psychological and mental Iron Curtain" went up. "With great force, Marshal Bulganin thanked him, saying quietly, 'We believe you.'"[127] The hope engendered by the "Spirit of Geneva" had survived for years. Now he refused to take any of the several exits Khrushchev offered, both before and after the four-day hostilities at the Paris summit. Eisenhower's performance was inexplicable. It contradicted his entire career. Why?

After retirement Khrushchev taped his memoirs, his "Last Testament." His description of the long Camp David conversation that preceded the Summit Conference helps explain Eisenhower's uncompromising stance. According to Khrushchev:

> The primary problem before us during our talks at Camp David was disarmament. I could tell just from looking at Eisenhower how anxious he was to reach an agreement which would create conditions eliminating the possibility of war. . . .

Khrushchev pointed out that it "was our side" that raised the matter of troop withdrawal, the elimination of military bases on foreign territory, the dismantling of both the NATO and Warsaw Pact alliances. The United States rejected that proposal. But, "actually," Khrushchev acknowledged, "we knew that . . . our proposal was premature. In fact, our proposal was intended to serve a propagandistic, rather than a realistic, purpose." Then the United States was "willing to accept a ban on the production and testing of nuclear weapons, but only on the condition that international controls were established." "This condition," Khrushchev wrote, "was unacceptable to us at that time." The U.S.S.R. "lagged significantly behind the U.S. in both warheads and missiles, and the U.S. was out of range of our bombers." The United States was not only "in a much stronger position" but "had us surrounded on all sides with their military bases, including air bases." There was only one point that they could agree on, "the problem of military spending." After they discussed procedures and costs, Eisenhower said: "'You know, we really should come to some sort of an agreement in order to stop this fruitless, really wasteful rivalry.'" Khrushchev agreed that was true. "'But how can we agree? On what basis?'" "That was the problem: we couldn't agree then, and we can't agree now." Khrushchev "could tell Eisenhower was deflated. He looked like a man who had fallen through a hole in the ice and been dragged from the river with freezing water still dripping off of him. . . . He looked so bitterly disappointed." The drive back to Washington, Khrushchev noted, "might have been a pleasant drive" "had we been more satisfied with the outcome of our talks." "But we weren't, and it wasn't. Every sentence was a strain. . . . I could see how depressed and worried Eisenhower was; and I knew how he felt, but there wasn't anything I could do to help him."[128]

The U-2 had been selected by both sides to break up the Paris Summit. Khrushchev and Eisenhower both knew that, for the moment, neither the United States nor the U.S.S.R. had any bargaining chips left to negotiate. At the conference table, the superpowers were deadlocked. Increasingly, around the world, there were upheaval, revolution, counterinsurgency.

CHAPTER VI
ANTICOMMUNISM AND COUNTER-INSURGENCY: THE GUATEMALAN MODEL

Part I
Guatemala's Revolution—Land Reform and Social Change in the Age of McCarthyism

> *When Communism threatened to engulf*
> *Guatemala in 1954 the American people*
> *became uneasy. For the first time we began*
> *to fear that the* backyard *could suddenly*
> *become a path for Communist invasion and*
> *a haven for Communist subversion. We*
> *breathed in relief when forces favoring*
> *democracy restored Guatemala to its nor-*
> *mal place in the American family of na-*
> *tions. . . .*
>
> MILTON S. EISENHOWER, 1963[1]

Eisenhower, not John F. Kennedy, presided over America's first modern "counterinsurgency" operations. Unlike Kennedy's failed effort at the Bay of Pigs, counterrevolution in Guatamala was backed up by air support and a thorough and long-lasting "cover-up." For decades, documents that related to these events were kept not only secret but hidden.[2] For almost thirty years, that cover-up served to obscure and trivialize public knowledge of Eisenhower's activities. Yet the overthrow of Dr. Mossadegh, in Iran, and President Arbenz, in Guatemala, have from that day to this served as models of successful United States intervention. Repeated again and again, the events that occurred in Iran and Guatemala during 1953 and 1954 globalized that aspect of United States foreign policy known as "gunboat diplomacy."

Since 1823, the United States' connections to its Central and South American neighbors were dominated by the Monroe Doctrine. The western hemisphere was the United States' sphere of influence, it's "backyard." The United States considered itself protective and generous. Social and economic changes that occurred in Latin America were viewed through the prism of the United States' national interests. Some Latin Americans called the Monroe Doctrine an "iron-clad umbilical cord." The United States called such Latin Americans "ungrateful traitors" and "communist agitators." In 1954 *Time* magazine called Guatemala the western hemisphere's naughty, "Red problem child."

Even before 1954, Eisenhower committed United States resources to the overthrow of the popularly elected government of
Jacobo Arbenz Guzmán. An intricately planned operation that involved all the tricks of political warfare and featured a military
coup backed by international and economic support of various
kinds emerged to "destabilize" Guatemala. Once Eisenhower
agreed to the operation, he demanded only that it succeed. According to Milton Eisenhower, the President often said, "You don't
just flaunt power." "When you resort to power there is no higher
authority." Although the documents that might reveal Eisenhower's
thoughts on the day-to-day activities against the Arbenz government
remain classified, it is now possible to reconstruct those activities.
The evidence now available indicates that nothing occurred without
Eisenhower's knowledge and approval.

As the operation moved into its final hours and Guatemala City
was being bombed, Eisenhower was at Quantico for a weekend
conference with military officers and White House staff. In an informal, "off-the-record" luncheon address to the senior officers of
the combined military services, Eisenhower emphasized two
themes: the "need for integration and cooperation between the
Services" and the need for silence and discretion when dealing with
"delicate" military and international subjects. "In a country such
as ours public opinion declares war; wages war; wins war." According to James Hagerty, Eisenhower said that "his test of a good
man" was "honesty and imagination" and that "imagination would
bring understanding" to the "problems of the day so that the military may keep the peace, 'which is the only true answer today to
any military problem—the keeping of the peace.'" The President
was very specific about that:

> No matter how well prepared for war we may be, no matter how cer-
> tain we are that within 24 hours we could destroy Kuibyshev and
> Moscow and Leningrad and Baku . . . , I want you to carry this
> question home with you: Gain such a victory, and what do you do
> with it? Here would be a great area from the Elbe to Vladivostok
> and down through Southeast Asia torn up and destroyed, without
> government, without its communications, just an area of starvation
> and disaster. I ask you what would the civilized world do about it? I
> repeat there is no victory in any war except through our imagina-
> tions, through our dedication and through our work to avoid it.

Eisenhower delivered that speech on Saturday, 19 June 1954. Guatemala was in turmoil. But the situation there did not in fact pose the threat of international war. The Soviet Union protested the invasion at the United Nations. Nothing more. There was one small possibility that the bombs that fell upon Guatemala City and selected villages would not be sufficient to smash Arbenz's will. Eisenhower decided to return from Quantico to Washington Saturday evening, instead of Sunday morning "as originally planned." According to Hagerty: "We are saying publicly that he wants to return in time to go to church. . . . Actually, he wants to get back in case anything does happen in Guatemala that would need Congressional action. This is extremely unlikely but there is no use taking a chance. Anything by the President should be done from the White House and not from a military conference at Quantico."

In fact, the joint CIA-State Guatemalan Group had decided the day before, on 18 June, that if Guatemala "attacked Honduras," the United States would defend Honduras "and, at the same time, ask Venezuela and Colombia to join us." As Hagerty noted, that was "extremely unlikely." But no chances were taken. Every detail was prearranged. The overthrow of the government of Guatemala was a carefully timed, finely tuned operation that occurred at all the major crossroads of military and poltical warfare.[3]

The Guatemalan Revolution of 1944 was inspired by Roosevelt's New Deal. Roosevelt's economic and social vision, the introduction of his "good-neighbor policy," combined with increased wartime reliance on Central and South America for bases, minerals, and military services, stimulated a demand for serious reform. The Allied war against fascism enabled Guatemala to confiscate the vast lands of the German coffee barons who had dominated Guatemala's economy since 1914. Although it was called a "banana republic" in the United States, coffee represented 90 percent of Guatemala's export earnings until 1944. Over half of that trade was with Germany. After the German barons were removed, Guatemala's economy was dominated by the United Fruit Company. In 1954, Guatemala harvested $70 million worth of coffee and $12 million worth of bananas. Other exports included mahogany, chicle, and essential oils.[4] If Guatemala's resources belonged to Guatemala, the country would be able to move beyond "feudalism"—to industrialism, independence, and national affluence, or so the revolutionaries of 1944 had reasoned.

In October 1944, a coalition of independent businessmen, intellectuals, and military careerists overthrew the widely hated dictator Jorge Ubico, who was closely identified with the United Fruit Company. The United Fruit Company (UFCO) was more than one of the United States' first transnational corporations. Known as "El Pulpo," "the Octopus that strangled all it touched," the United Fruit Company functioned throughout Central America as an independent government. It dominated the political, economic, and military life of, among others, Honduras, Costa Rica, and Guatemala. Between 1936 and 1937, Ubico consolidated United Fruit's concessions. He enabled the company to control all aspects of the only railway system that passed through Guatemala, the International Railways of Central America (IRCA), which ran from Mexico to El Salvador, from the Caribbean to the Pacific; and turned over Guatemala's electric enterprise to UFCO, after appropriating it from its former German owners. In 1906, the UFCO was granted 170,000 acres of Guatemala's most productive land in return for building the IRCA. In 1936, Ubico extended the UFCO's interests so that it controlled 42 percent of Guatemala's lands. John Foster Dulles, whose law firm, Sullivan and Cromwell, then represented United Fruit, was generally understood to be the author of that 1936 contract. Under Ubico, United Fruit was exempt from all taxes and import duties and entirely in control of all Guatemala's transportation, including its only port, Puerto Barrios.[5] Reasonably, the UFCO resented the overthrow of Ubico.

The Guatemalan revolution was at first acceptable to the United States State Department. A. A. Berle recorded in his diary, 21 October 1944, that the revolution did not appear disastrous to United States interests. The world was, after all, experiencing all manner of upheaval. And 1944 was a presidential election year in the United States. Amid frenzied campaign maneuvers at home and delicate negotiations between Britain and Russia regarding the Balkans and the Middle East, the situation in Guatemala seemed somehow appropriate. Berle wrote: The British have evidently "recognized a predominant Russian sphere of influence in Bulgaria" in return for what "they thought were concessions in Yugoslavia," all of which "took the dreary Polish controversy along another step. . . ." "Just to add to the gaiety," Berle noted, "last night a Guatemalan revolution broke out." The armistice "was signed in our Embassy, which was the neutral meeting place selected by the participants, and the whole Diplomatic Corps, including our man, signed as witnesses. I think this is probably all right."[6]

Francisco Javier Arana, Jacobo Arbenz Guzmán, Jorge Toriello, and Juan José Arévalo led the 1944 revolution. According to Manuel Galich, Arévalo's Foreign Minister, the 1944 junta "had no revolutionary ideology, nor concrete program, nor well planned strategy, simply because the obscurantism we and our parents had lived through over almost a century, had kept us more than a little isolated from the world that surrounded us." Led by teachers, small businessmen, professionals, and several large landowners whose "interests were in contradiction to Ubico's," the movement quickly became a massive, popular effort that involved workers, army officers, and the campesinos—descendants of the indigenous Mayans, who worked in the countryside and earned only three cents a day, when they earned anything at all, under Ubico.[7]

In 1945, Spruille Braden was sent to celebrate Arévalo's inauguration. During Eisenhower's administration, Braden resigned his post as undersecretary of state for Latin American affairs to join the United Fruit Company as "a paid consultant," apparently in charge of political warfare against Guatemala. But, in 1945, Arévalo seemed progressive and popular, having received an overwhelming majority from the adult males eligible to vote in Guatemala's first democratic election in the twentieth century. Arévalo later expanded the voting base to include "literate" women. The fact that both Arévalo and his successor, Jacobo Arbenz Guzmán, were elected under free, democratic circumstances—by United States standards—led Thomas Mann, a senior State Department official later involved in the overthrow of Arbenz's government, to conclude that their elections proved the United States should not "support all constitutional governments under all circumstances."[8]

The United States' attitude toward democracy in Guatemala changed perceptibly in 1947, when Arévalo introduced a work code affirming the right of workers to organize and strike. Bitterly opposed by the UFCO, the IRCA, and the electric company, the work code of 1947 included provisions for compulsory labor-management contracts and minimum wages. Its opponents called it "Communist." Since Arévalo accepted responsibility for the work code, he was labeled a "Communist dictator." The United States sponsored the Inter-American Treaty of Reciprocal Assistance (the Treaty of Rio de Janeiro), whereby a threat against one member of the Organization of American States was regarded as an attack against all. This regional statement of collective self-defense was widely regarded as an effort to isolate and check Guatemala's reforms. In addition to the Treaty of Rio de Janeiro, there were over twenty-five plots against Arévalo's life.

Denounced as a "Communist" in United Fruit circles, Arévalo was virulently anti-Soviet. He refused to legalize the Communist Party and considered himself Guatemala's Roosevelt. Occasionally he referred to himself as a "spiritual socialist." He was a moderate social democrat; an idealist committed to "liberty, justice, and national dignity." He made no effort to analyze the economic base of society. But he supported workers' demands and refused to permit further investments by United States interests. He condemned "Yankee imperialism" and refused to conscript Guatemalans to participate in the United Nations' war against Korea. He also tolerated radical unions.[9]

Only in an environment dominated by McCarthy and loyalty oaths could Arévalo's reforms be considered communist. In addition to the work code of 1947, he introduced a Law of Forced Rental in 1948. Many large landowners (*latifundistas*), who opposed the revolution, had ceased to rent their tenant lands, claiming that they feared expropriation, creating extreme hardship for the campesinos of Guatemala. Since over 70 percent of the country's population were indigenous people entirely dependent on the land for survival, Arévalo's decree represented a major step for the Mayan descendants, whose needs had been in the past entirely ignored and who were largely illiterate and landless. In addition, the new state bank, Banco de Guatemala, provided credit for agricultural diversification, and Arévalo nationalized most of the former German plantations (*fincas*). They became national farms (*fincas nacionales*), to be administered by the government and rented to individuals and cooperatives.

When Jacobo Arbenz, who had served as Arévalo's Defense Minister, succeeded him, in March 1951, he announced the new administration's fundamental objectives: "First, to convert our country from a dependent nation with a semi-colonial economy into an economically independent country; secondly, to transform our nation from a backward past with a predominantly feudal economy, into a modern capitalist country; and, third, to see that this transformation is carried out in such a way that it brings with it the highest possible elevation of the standard of living of the great masses of people."[10]

Arbenz's first act as President was to announce a land-reform program that would transform Guatemala from "semi-feudalism" to modern capitalism. Revolutionary Decree Number 99, Arbenz's Agrarian Reform Law, would:

> eliminate all feudal type property in rural areas, abolish antiquated relations of production, especially work-servitude and the remnants of slavery, . . . to give land to the agricultural workers who do not possess such or who possess very little, facilitate technical assistance, expand agricultural credit for the benefit of all who work the land.

The law specified large fincas "with unused lands," and exempted plantations with all acreage in use. Expropriation was limited to "idle lands" on "holdings over 223 acres." Campesinos would receive lots up to 42.5 acres "in ownership or in use for life," to be paid for at a rate of 3–5 percent of annual production. Compensation to finca owners was to be made in twenty-five-year government bonds at 3 percent interest. The value of the land was to be determined by the owners' own tax declarations for 1952. The law was to be administered by agrarian committees. The campesinos were thereby given power in Guatemala. Land. Literacy. Political power. That was revolutionary.

By 1954, one hundred thousand campesino families had received land, as well as credit and technical aid. One thousand two plantations, covering 2.7 million acres, were affected, of which 55 percent was actually expropriated. The other lands distributed included private farms, municipal lands, and national farms—the former German fincas appropriated during World War II. By December 1953, many cooperatives were cultivated in coffee, sugar cane, cardamon, pasture land, and other crops. The National

Mortgage Credit Banks and National Agricultural Bank extended credit to the farmers, both cooperators and plot owners. The National Agricultural Bank's motto, "credit at the time of sowing," was a major feature of the land reform. Its many branches advanced short-term loans "to increase the yield and seasonal crops" and to finance the purchase of livestock, seed, farm tools, and heavy equipment.

To correct "all kinds of slanderous accusations" about the land-reform program, Luis Cardoza y Aragón, the editor of *Revista de Guatemala,* wrote an article in *The Nation* in March 1953:

> The big landowners, the clerical and conservative elements in the country, and the business interests—especially the United Fruit Company—are doing everything . . . to block implementation of the law and to overthrow the regime that sponsored it. Ignoring the situation described in an official U.N. publication on the urgent need of land reform in Guatemala, they object even to Article 2, which says: "All forms of slavery and serfdom are herewith abolished." Unpaid personal services of peasants, squatters, and agricultural workers, as well as the payment of land rent by labor services . . . are therefore prohibited in any form whatsoever.

The United Fruit Company, Guatemala's largest landowner, lost 178,000 acres. Based on UFCO's own tax return, Guatemala offered $1,185,115 in compensation. United Fruit said, its tax declaration notwithstanding, Guatemala owed the company $16 million.[11]

Arbenz also initiated the construction of a large electrical center to be financed entirely by Guatemalan capital. He planned a network of roads leading to a new Atlantic port, to break United Fruit's monopoly of all transportation and communication into and out of Guatemala. Puerto Barrios, the IRCA, and the electric company would have Guatemalan competition. It was untenable. Arbenz was declared a Communist, a danger to the hemisphere, the entire free world. The United Fruit Company said so. And all United States statesmen agreed. From the moment Arbenz's land-reform program was introduced, United Fruit worked to discredit and destabilize the government of Guatemala. The Guatemalan Government called it colonialism. The United Fruit Company and the United States Government called it containing communism. Arbenz said that, as a result of the agrarian reform, the UFCO, with the assistance of vast sums of United States military and financial aid, sought "to mutilate our existence as a sovereign people and as an independent nation." Thomas McCann, longtime public-relations vice-president of the UFCO, supported that contention:

> The Company operated two divisions in Guatemala, one on the East Coast and one on the Pacific. Together, these two divisions accounted for the lion's share of the company's tropical land holdings. Guatemala was chosen as the site for the company's earliest development activities . . . because a good portion of the country contained prime banana land and also because at the time . . . Guatemala's government was the region's weakest, most corrupt and most pliable. In short, the country offered an "ideal investment climate," and United Fruit's profits there flourished for fifty years. Then something went wrong: a man named Jacob [sic] Arbenz became President.

According to McCann, as soon as the agrarian reform law was published, the UFCO went into high gear. The company's chief weapon was to charge "Communism." Edward L. Bernays, "the father of public relations," a master manipulator who happened to be Sigmund Freud's nephew, directed psychological warfare for United Fruit. In 1951, New York *Times* publisher Arthur Hays Sulzberger accompanied Bernays on a fact-finding trip. While there, "the first 'Communist riot'" occurred in Guatemala. McCann credited Bernays with "a first-class public relations coup." That tour was followed by many others—by the wire services, the national magazines, the electronic networks. Everything the media saw "was carefully staged and regulated" by United Fruit. But, McCann wrote, it is difficult to argue that the press was actually manipulated when it was "so eager for the experience."[12]

Even before Arbenz began legal proceedings to expropriate United Fruit lands, the company with the aid of Guatemalan landlords and exiles and Nicaragua's dictator, Anastasio ("Tacho") Somoza, planned his overthrow. One aborted plan, evidently called "Operation Fortune," failed to get Truman's approval. First "proposed in a conversation between General Somoza and an attorney for the United Fruit Company," the plan "had been to support Guatemalan revolutionary elements who thought at the time they could count on important officers. . . . General Somoza and Col. Somoza had gotten in touch with Peru, Panama, El Salvador, Honduras, the Dominican Republic and Venezuela. . . . Col. Somoza

said that all countries agreed to the plan except Honduras, which
. . . would have nothing to do with it unless it could be certain
that the State Department approved. . . ." According to Guatemalan intelligence, the effort was to have been made in June
1952. But the officers they counted on failed to act. Somoza then
dropped the plan temporarily "as being too risky."[13]

The first record of official United States interest in a coup
against Arbenz occurred on the eve of Eisenhower's election. In
October 1952, Berle was told that a widespread movement was underway and that Arbenz might be toppled by December. The governments of El Salvador and Honduras might lend "direct support." Berle agreed that Guatemala was in the grip of "a
Russian-controlled dictatorship." That was, he affirmed, "perfectly
sound ground for the United States to invoke the Act of Chapul-
tepec and the Treaty of Rio de Janeiro."

Berle noted in his journal that the Council on Foreign Relations
had already "agreed generally that the Guatemalan Government
was Communist." Berle decided to contact Adlai Stevenson
directly and to "see Nelson Rockefeller, who knows the situation
and can work a little with General Eisenhower on it." After Eisenhower's victory, Berle met, on 17 November, with C. D. Jackson.
Eisenhower had appointed Jackson to a task force, which was to
become known as the Jackson Committee, "designed to push the
Russians back rather nearer their original quarters." C. D. Jackson, William Jackson—former deputy director of the CIA, and
Berle were among the original members of that committee.[14]

In February 1953, Berle met at "Cell 13," Nelson Rockefeller's
office-apartment at 13 West Fifty-fourth Street, because Rockefeller was "agitated about the Latin American situation." Although
Rockefeller's particular upset referred to Brazil's difficulties regarding a loan, Berle noted that it was "queer: the Republicans
getting an opposition member to push policy through their own
Administration."[15] Actually, the entire inter-American operation
was remarkably bipartisan. It was, moreover, dominated by longtime intimates of the United Fruit Company.

According to E. Howard Hunt, Eisenhower's willingness to take
on the covert operation in Guatemala was due largely to the efforts
of former New Deal adviser Thomas G. Corcoran. "Tommy the
Cork's" successful influence-peddling as United Fruit's lobbyist

evidently swayed the National Security Council. Filled with vivid details about peeping-tom capers and Watergate-like break-ins, Hunt's breezy book is also filled with facts found—appropriately—nowhere else. On his return from the CIA's Southeast Europe (Balkan) Division, responsible for Albania, Yugoslavia, Greece, Bulgaria, and Romania, "with small bases in Frankfurt, Paris and Rome," Hunt was sent for the second time to Central America. The "National Security Council under Eisenhower and Vice-President Nixon had ordered the overthrow of Guatemala's regime." Hunt was told that "no clandestine project had higher priority." Organized as an independent operation, the "Guatemalan project was set up as a semiautonomous unit within the Western Hemisphere Division. With its own funds, communications center, and chain of command, it was able to operate without the customary smothering attentions of proliferating advisory staffs within the conventional CIA structure." Hunt, who had suggested such an operation to General Bedell Smith in 1951, asked why "the climate was suddenly right." He was told that "the difference had to do with domestic politics," and Corcoran's energetic lobbying.[16]

In his memoirs, Eisenhower noted that he was convinced by the arguments of Assistant Secretary of State for Inter-American Affairs John Moors Cabot, who insisted that Guatemala was "openly playing the Communist game." Guatemala accepted, for example, "the ridiculous Communist contention that the United States had conducted bacteriological warfare in Korea." That, combined with the expropriation of United Fruit lands, were the only evidences for communism that Eisenhower cited.[17]

A roll call of administration-United Fruit connections is not only bipartisan, but startling. In addition to Allen Dulles and John Foster Dulles, who had worked directly with the company, John Moors Cabot was the brother of Thomas Dudley Cabot, a former president of the United Fruit Company who served under Truman as director of the State Department's Office of International Security Affairs. Spruille Braden had been assigned to the embassy in Chile, presumably because he understood Chile, since his family owned the Braden Chilean copper mines. He now worked for the United Fruit Company on the Guatemalan project "in his capacity as a well-known professional anti-communist." According to Braden's memoirs, *Diplomats and Demagogues,* Somoza "was really the man who financed and equipped Castillo Armas" after persuading "Bedell Smith to send the arms to Somoza." As president of the World Bank, John J. McCloy refused Arbenz loans. Later he became a director of United Fruit, as did Walter Bedell Smith. Based in Boston, the company was reputed to be particularly intimate with Massachusetts' former governor Christian Herter and allegedly with the chairman of Boston's Old Colony Trust Company, Eisenhower's National Security Council secretary, General Robert Cutler. Finally, Eisenhower's personal White House secretary, Ann Whitman, was married to Ed Whitman, the head of United Fruit's public-relations department. According to McCann, his boss, Whitman, was one of Bernays' best protégés. McCann recalled that Ed Whitman always said, "Whenever you read 'United Fruit' in Communist propaganda, you may readily substitute 'United States.' "[18]

The effort to destabilize and destroy Arbenz's government existed on several levels. The official, public level involved creating a climate of hysteria against the communist menace in the western hemisphere. Great pains were taken to disassociate political criticism of Guatemala from the UFCO's landed interests. To preserve its image as the anticolonial leader of the free world, the United States could not object to national expropriation. The United States objected only to communism. The United States therefore had to convince the world, and the Guatemalans, that communism dominated Guatemala. In addition, untold millions of dollars were spent in a massive, intricate covert plan that included United Fruit personnel, CIA personnel, and the underground activities of several Central American republics to (1) discover and train appropriate "liberationists"; (2) mount a massive propaganda campaign of suspicion, fear, intimidation, and reprisal; and (3) impoverish, embarrass, and cripple the government at every opportunity. The CIA has yet to release documents that might relate to these activities. The activities are, however, well documented in the Guatemala file at the Library of Congress, in the many *Time* and *Life* articles that boosted C. D. Jackson's less public efforts, and in the recently declassified State Department record.

The Library of Congress's ninety-six-box Guatemala file contains Arbenz's speeches, government publications, and correspondence between government officials. It also contains publications by and correspondence between representatives of right-wing antigovernment groups, communist organizations, and the worker and campesino unions—including the records of the General Confederation of Guatemalan Workers (CGTG) and the National Confederation of Guatemalan Campesinos (CNCG). That collection represents the daily raw data of Guatemala's revolution from 1944 to 1954 and documents the government's effort to survive a massive assault.

That record makes it clear, above all, that Arbenz insisted on his government's right to be self-defined. And he defined himself as a progressive democrat committed to the changes needed to secure the social welfare of Guatemala. When it was "estimated that it would take 667 years to eliminate illiteracy at the present rate," Arbenz encouraged a massive literacy campaign. His wife, María Villanova de Arbenz, worker vigorously with the Alianza Femenina Guatemalteca, the leading women's organization in the country, to create agriculture schools, extend literacy in the countryside, and improve the conditions of women at home and in the workplace. A prominent activist, United States authorities suspected that she was "the real Communist." The Alianza Femenina, like other organized groups dedicated to issues such as international peace, the promotion of literacy, and social change including the National Peace Committee, the student's union, and the Democratic Youth Alliance were all considered Communist or Communist-front organizing groups. In fact, all "mass" organizations concerned with education and public life were considered suspect. "Consciousness-raising" itself was suspect. Literacy would encourage dissatisfaction.

The daughter of a wealthy landed family, María Villanova de Arbenz was frequently criticized in the antigovernment press for her interest in expensive furs and jewelry. In the Library of Congress collection, there are careful notes which were made of her exotic purchases, including a "natural royal pastel mink stole" and a series of books by Freud's contemporary Wilhelm Stekel, including *Cartas a Una Madre, Matrimonio Moderno, La Educación de los Padres, La Impotencia en el Hombre, Onanismo y Homosexualidad,* and *Estados Nerviosos.* She was also criticized for her close association with prominent Latin American intellectuals, notably with Chile's educator Virginia Bravo Letelier and Pablo

Neruda, who was later to be awarded a Nobel prize for his poetry. In the Library of Congress file, where all evidence was collected to prove the Communist nature of the Arbenz regime, evidence to illustrate "Communist Control of Education" included a letter from Virginia Bravo Letelier to Guatemala's Minister of Education dated August 1949. The interpretive headnote, in English, reads: "How Communist propaganda [was] given to virtually all 6th grade teachers by Virginia Bravo." The actual letter describes the extent of illiteracy among elementary-school teachers in Guatemala. A survey had revealed that "of 2,719 teachers, 637," or 24 percent, had not themselves completed the sixth grade. Bravo, therefore, proposed "a two month plan, assigning groups of teachers to various Normal Schools" to receive "an intensive course in elementary and professional education in mathematics, Spanish, natural science, sociology, pedagogy and psychology. . . . Examinations will be held during the last three days." Those who passed would "be obliged to sign up in a teachers' college" for further study. Those who did not "obtain their sixth grade certificate will be separated from the service for not having the minimal preparation that could be asked of an elementary schoolteacher."[19]

Ultimately it did not matter whether or not the Arbenz government was Communist, or whether Arbenz considered himself a Communist. His insistence on independent economic development contradicted all normal relations in the western hemisphere. The United States judged correctly that the Arbenz government was inimical to its fundamental interests. Communism was used, therefore, both as the tool with which to rally Central American support and as the excuse to overthrow the nationalist, anti-imperialist, and naïve government of Jacobo Arbenz. Arbenz and his associates apparently believed, sincerely believed, that they could challenge United States business interests and still be considered acceptable by the United States government. Arbenz evidently believed that the United States would understand and honor his commitment to combine the economic development of Guatemala with the preservation of democratic liberties. He had rejected all pressure to silence the right-wing press (dedicated to his demise) as well as the United States' pressure to silence the Communist press that supported his government. He insisted that charges of anti-democratic communism were mythologies created to confuse the issue. But the label Communist was necessary. It served to obscure the realities and complexities of the government's economic and political experiments and to cover up the United States' role in the government's destruction.

Arbenz's goal had been to close the doors of Guatemala to further foreign investment and to create a developed economy through loans obtained by regular international banking procedures. Undoubtedly it was less obvious in 1954 than it is today that those goals were mutually exclusive. United States and United States-dominated banking agencies would not advance loans for capital development projects from which United States economic interests would be excluded. From 1951 to 1954, Arbenz's efforts were bold, but hopeless. His programs were far-reaching and varied. They ranged from efforts to end the "electric power shortage" to innovative health-care programs to "protect mother and child." But they were frustrated at every level. Since great gains were nevertheless achieved in employment, education, health care, and land distribution, one might well wonder what Guatemala might look like today had Arbenz received those loans and the process of revolution been allowed to develop. But it was not to be.

From the beginning, Guatemalan officials denied communist domination, infiltration, or even significant influence. In a conversation between Dean Acheson and Guatemala's ambassador to the United States, Guillermo Toriello described his government's policy as democratic. The goal was "to avoid dictatorship." Toriello believed that the "best way to combat Communism is to improve the maladjusted social and economic conditions which produce unrest among the under-privileged classes." He opposed repression, "which would drive communism underground." And, Toriello concluded, Arbenz rejected the "methods adopted by El Salvador where the Government had shot some 1400 persons. Guatemala preferred giving the people 'bread instead of lead.' "[20]

Toriello insisted that the number of communists in Guatemala was proportionately fewer than the number in the United States. But the State Department dismissed Toriello's argument and suggested that Guatemala follow the United States' example regarding communists: Ban them from public life. On 23 January 1953, a State Department official elaborated United States policy:

"To contain the influence and power of the communists it was necessary to isolate them from positions of importance. Having recognized the danger . . . of the international communist conspiracy, the people and Government of the United States had adopted vigorous measures to seek out and remove the communists from important positions in Government, labor, industry, education, etc. In the case of Guatemala," the State Department insisted, "it was not always so clear that the Government recognized the conspiratorial character of the international communist movement." Toriello was reminded that high government officials had participated in the anniversary celebration of the founding of the Communist newspaper *Octubre* and asked "if he could conceive of the United States Secretary of Interior and the President of the Senate . . . attending a Communist Party rally in New York." In response, Toriello again insisted that he was not a communist, Arbenz was not a communist, "and no one in the Cabinet was either. His government was merely interested in promoting social reform, raising the standard of living. . . . In the old days of Ubico the peasants and the Indians were put in chains and forced to work for the benefit of a few. President Arbenz's Government aimed at freeing the Indians and the workers. . . . Thus they had promoted the organization of labor unions, developed a social security system, passed an agrarian reform law. . . . This program was not communistic but liberal and progressive." Insisting that there was nothing "Soviet-inspired" about Guatemala's objectives, Toriello concluded: "Guatemala was embarked on a program of full democracy and was intent upon fulfilling the guarantees of the Constitution which permitted any and all citizens to express their own views and ideologies. The Guatemalan Constitution prohibited any discrimination . . . because of race, color, creed, religion or ideology. To move against the communists would require a return to the police state methods of Ubico and the Government would not revert back to Ubicoism."[21]

Ubicoism, or Latin American repression of any kind, did not concern the United States. Communism did. On 31 March 1953, A. A. Berle sent to his fellow Jackson Committee members a detailed outline of a preliminary program on "The Guatemalan Problem in Central America":

The United States cannot tolerate a Kremlin-controlled Communist government in this hemisphere. It has several possible alternatives:

(1) American armed intervention—like that of 1915. This is here ruled out except as an extremely bad last resort, because of the immense complications which it would raise all over the hemisphere.

(2) Organizing a counter-movement, capable of using force if necessary, based in a cooperative neighboring republic. In practice this would mean Nicaragua. It could hardly be done from Mexico, and neither Salvador nor Honduras appears strong enough, though they might help. . . .[22]

Berle's suggested plan, with some modifications, was accepted. It seems also to have been merely the official green light for plans already well underway, highly financed, and largely coordinated. Indeed, throughout March, Toriello visited various State Department officers to protest the increasingly outrageous "calumnies" directed against his government. On 6 March he met with John Cabot and insisted that all the "calumniators" seemed to have one demand: arrest the Communists. Toriello asked how Guatemala could fulfill the mandates of the democratic constitution and "put communists in jail or declare the communist party illegal." Cabot suggested a middle course: Remove the communists from positions of influence. Toriello argued that the head of the Social Security Bureau was opposed as a communist, but "he was married to a landowners' daughter." A man named Fanjul was denounced as a communist, "but he was a wealthy businessman." Even José Manuel Fortuny "used to be a supporter of Ubico and became a communist only after getting mental indigestion by reading Marx." The communists in Guatemala, Toriello declared, were "no danger to Guatemala's stability." What threatened stability was the United States' refusal to respond to Guatemala's offers of cooperation and requests for support. Guatemala had supported the United States on all "major issues" at the United Nations and "particularly in confronting the menace of Soviet imperialism. . . ."* But when Guatemala requested one hundred rifles for the police, tractors to

---

* Subsequently, the United States' compilation of Guatemala's UN vote was kept out of the record of communist activities, because it was so clearly in line with the other American republics. On 2 June 1954, the State Department's study group decided Guatemala's UN record "would not be particularly helpful in our case."

build the Atlantic highway, and airplanes and parts, the United States turned the requests away. Guatemala now agreed to all United States demands regarding the proposed Inter-American Highway, "but there was still no sign that the United States would sign the Agreement."

On 11 March, Toriello met with other representatives of the State Department. Basically the same conversation occurred except that Toriello "professed not to know" whether the head of the CGTG, Víctor Manuel Gutiérrez, was a Communist. Toriello said that while he did not know whether or not he was a Communist, the State Department should, since the FBI worked in Guatemala. To the United States' argument that the "existence of communist influence in Guatemala" was part of a "life and death struggle with world communism," Toriello replied that in his own life he had witnessed the tragedy and severity of dictatorships. Today, he concluded, the opposition, "the reactionary landowners and the United Fruit Company, the Railroad, the Electric Power Company, and Pan American Airways, want to overthrow Arbenz and install a dictator of the old type." Toriello considered the matter clear: the issue of "communism was artificially fostered by the foreign companies, who hired journalists to publicize it in the United States and," he noted, "his government has proof of this fact." The meeting ended as a State Department official suggested that if it was true the United States overestimated the significance of communists in Guatemala, "it should be correspondingly easier for the Guatemalans to deal with them."

Shortly before he returned to Guatemala, Toriello made one final visit to Cabot, on 25 March. Enraged by the "press campaign in the United States," Toriello referred to a series of articles "so mendacious" he threatened to sue. He referred specifically to an "article by a Mr. Toledano" in the *American Mercury* and a "newspaper distributed to school children called *Our Times.*" Cabot assured Toriello that the "paper was not an official government publication." The conversation then turned to such issues as Aviateca's application to fly to the United States, license applications for tank parts, and the Inter-American Highway. Cabot again emphasized the United States' concern about communism. Toriello again reassured Cabot, this time noting that he was certain that the anti-communist campaign against Guatemala would continue until the reform program ended, "even if every Communist in the

country were somehow eliminated." The real problem was unchecked monopoly. Toriello referred to the expropriation of his
own lands and concluded that the payment for his property based
on the "declared tax valuation was just payment." But United
Fruit had a history of "bad behavior." UFCO, for example, paid
seventy-five dollars per car to ship its bananas on the railroad,
while Guatemalans were charged "$575 per car, and that the Gov-
ernment therefore had to build the Atlantic Highway to provide
fair competition." Cabot replied that the highway, like all "subsidiary" matters, would be "settled more or less quickly once the
basic question of Communist infiltration in the Government of
Guatemala was resolved." Cabot noted that the conversation was
"friendly and frank."[23]

The day Toriello returned to Guatemala City, the day before
Berle had submitted his proposal to the Jackson Committee, a premature coup occurred in Salamá, with scattered activity in San Je-
rónimo and elsewhere in Baja Verapaz Department. The United
States embassy in Guatemala City cabled Washington that the rebellion "had no (repeat no) connection" with the anti-Communist
revolutionary group "which is believed to be in touch with Castillo
Armas." Evidently a rival to Castillo Armas, an attorney
"banished by Arévalo in April 1945 for plotting," believed he
would receive support. But he was "reportedly egocentric and not
trusted by other anti-communist leaders." César Izaguirre headed a
group called the "Christian Army," in contact with but evidently
"not united" with the leading antigovernment groups in the capital.
Government troops acted "promptly and efficiently." Because the
rebels had painted "distinctive marks" on an airfield, it was assumed that "they expected re-enforcement by air."[24] On 1 April,
Guatemala's Foreign Minister, Dr. Raúl Osegueda sent a message
to the United Nations denouncing the existence of an international
plot that threatened Guatemala's sovereignty by "external aggression." Guatemala withdrew from the Organization of Central
American States (ODECA) on 4 April in protest. This withdrawal
was later used as evidence that Guatemala aggressively threatened
the security of its neighbors.

Subsequently, parties to the Salamá uprising stated that they had
been "absolutely certain" they would receive "all kinds of aid by
airplanes coming from Mexico and Nicaragua." United States Am-

bassador Rudolf Schoenfeld cabled John Foster Dulles that several conspirators were arrested but others had "better luck": "Disguised as participants in a Holy Week procession," they slipped into the Mexican embassy and, in the time-honored tradition of Latin American politics, were granted "safe conducts" issued by Arbenz's Foreign Office. One leader, Carlos Simons, took asylum in the Honduran embassy "and is understood to be planning a trip to the United States after his departure from Guatemala."[25]

Snafu or betrayal, the conspirators had indeed been expecting air cover. And the United States knew it. On 4 March, the United States ambassador in Nicaragua had sent Dulles the following telegram:

> CONTROLLED AMERICAN SOURCE IS REPORTING . . . THAT REVOLT WILL BE ATTEMPTED IN GUATEMALA DURING HOLY WEEK. FINANCIAL BACKERS REPORTEDLY VENEZUELA, EL SALVADOR, UNITED STATES AND UNITED FRUIT. NICARAGUAN AMBASSADOR TO VENEZUELA . . . QUOTED AS SAYING PRESIDENT OF VENEZUELA REQUESTED AID FROM SOMOZA WHO REPLIED WOULD HELP IN ANY WAY HE COULD. SOMOZA TOLD ME TWO DAYS AGO HE WOULD NOT PARTICIPATE . . . WITHOUT FIRST INFORMING DEPARTMENT GETTING OUR REACTION.[26]

During May 1953, a series of confessions revealed that the Salamá rebellion was in fact supported by United Fruit, Trujillo, and Somoza. El Salvador and Honduras as well as Nicaragua and the Dominican Republic had promised various kinds of aid. The UFCO allegedly provided sixty-four thousand dollars to purchase arms. The movement was to be spearheaded by Juan Córdova Cerna. The leaders were Castillo Armas' rivals. All confessions were later disavowed. Almyr Bump, the UFCO's manager in Guatemala, announced that the charges "were totally false." United Fruit's policy was "to respect the duly-constituted authorities of the countries where it operated." It was not, in any case, the CIA's plan. Actually the State Department was rather chagrined by the independent caper. Coup competition served neither the United Fruit Company nor the United States government.[27]

The official United States plan required more time. It depended on the appearance of popular support and international approval. The United States' plan was to emphasize the survival of democratic virtue in the face of communist violence. A carefully elaborated plan was underway to get international support, especially the support of the Americas in the democratic forum of the OAS. For success, it must seem to have little to do with the particular demands of the UFCO. For success, it must also seem to represent the popular will of the people of Guatemala.

This is not to suggest unconcern for private United States economic interests in Guatemala. They were the United States' primary concern. But they were hardly the stuff with which to coordinate an international rally against Guatemala. The State Department was very clear about that. "American interests" were "under attack." The United Fruit Company was the "prime target." The International Railways of Central America were "also under recurring attack." The Electric Light and Power Company, a wholly owned American and other-foreign-power subsidiary, was threatened "from two sources": Guatemala's hydroelectric power development, which would use water from the same river that supplied two of the company's plants; and a "revision of its concession contracts as a result of actions by a congressional committee dominated by Communists."[28] In addition, Guatemala's long-standing refusal to consider oil exploration contracts with United States companies and its intention to depend exclusively on Guatemalan capital to explore potentially oil-rich areas were irksome.[29]

For three years, therefore, the United States "steadfastly maintained a policy of withholding favors," including World Bank capital development loans, and justified its policy on the grounds that Guatemala tolerated and encouraged communism. At the same time, the State Department noted, "we have not given in to various pressures for direct intervention, which would be in violation of our fundamental Latin American policy and solemn treaty commitments." The State Department believed that the Guatemalan situation required the "most delicate and patient handling and that the dangers to our interests from inadvisable action should be fully weighed against any immediate lure to dispose of the problem abruptly."[30]

Careful, well-planned political warfare was the key to the United States' "delicate and patient handling of Guatemala." Detailed reports were compiled to illustrate "communist infiltration" and "penetration." The State Department noted that the Guatemalan congress "stood in silence in memory of Joseph Stalin, the only government body in the Western Hemisphere to do so." Much was made of the fact that even "independent" newspapers ran articles critical of the United States. Rudolf Schoenfeld cabled Washington that the ordinarily friendly *El Imparcial* carried a UP dispatch that originated from the Communist Party, U.S.A., accusing the United States of complicity in the Salamá uprising and quoting Spruille Braden as saying that Guatemala was "an advance base of international Communism and that suppression of Communism, even by force, by one or more of the other republics, would not constitute intervention in the internal affairs of Guatemala. The fact that this statement by an ex-official of the Truman Administration . . . has not been repudiated by the Eisenhower Administration shows that they are 'coyotes of the same kidney.' " When Guatemala brought its case to the United Nations, the United States decided "to ignore the charges, as Guatemala, at least in the UN, was engaged solely in a propaganda maneuver."[31]

While intensifying its own propaganda effort, the United States decided to "include El Salvador, Honduras and Nicaragua in hemispheric defense plans." Military-assistance pacts were negotiated and arms were shipped. The goal was "to bring home to the Guatemalan military the further disadvantage of noncooperation with the United States." In addition, Washington agreed that Colonel Castillo Armas would lead the CIA's counterinsurgency force of Guatemalan "liberators." According to Hunt, the CIA assembled and trained the insurgents in Honduras. From a clandestine Opa-locka airport, near Miami, the CIA ran airlifts to Castillo Armas' "small band—never more than 140 men." Hunt explained that "Washington" chose Castillo over other contenders, particularly Colonel Ydígoras Fuentes, because he was "a right-wing reactionary." According to Ydígoras Fuentes' account in *My War with Communism,*

> A former executive of the United Fruit Company . . . Mr. Walter Turnbull came to see me with two gentlemen he introduced as agents of the CIA. They said that I was a popular figure in Guatemala and that they wanted to lend their assistance to overthrow Arbenz. When I asked their conditions for the assistance I found them unacceptable. Among other things I was to promise to favor the United Fruit Company and the International Railways of Central America; to destroy the railroad workers labor union; to suspend claims against Great Britain for the Belize territory; to es-

tablish a strong-arm government, on the style of Ubico. Further, I was to pay back every cent that was invested in the undertaking on the basis of accounts that would be presented to me afterwards. I told them that I would have to be given time to prepare my conditions, as theirs seemed to me to be unfavorable to Guatemala. They withdrew, promising to return; I never saw them again.[32]

To isolate Arbenz, to organize public discontent, and to establish conditions for a military mutiny were the primary expectations behind the United States' decision to arm Honduras, El Salvador, and Nicaragua. In an intelligence estimate coordinated by the State Department and "the CIA's Office of National Intelligence and its covert offices," the Division of Research for Latin America concluded:

> Assuming that the external and political and military capabilities of El Salvador, Honduras, and Nicaragua are markedly increased through an effectively initiated and sustained program of military assistance, it is likely (1) that the opposition to Arbenz will become more [critically] militant; (2) that important Army and political leaders now supporting Arbenz will, if they are assured of a place in some alternative regime, calculate that the present regime does not serve the best interests of either the nation or themselves. . . .

The United States calculated that despite "initial resentment against the United States" and a real commitment to Arbenz, Guatemala's military would "eventually" recognize "that military aid to neighboring countries is an expression of United States determination to eliminate Communist leadership and influence in Guatemala." With "increased disaffection among lower echelon officer personnel, emboldened action by elements of the political opposition, an increase in the number of revolutionary attempts against the government, the loss of military position and political leadership in Central America, and new defensive requirements along Guatemala's borders," the United States anticipated "at least a split among top Army leaders, some of whom would be willing to attempt deals with overt and covert oppositionist elements."

United States estimates did not anticipate toppling Arbenz quickly or with assured ease. Intelligence analysts were aware of the widespread support he maintained, "not only from Communist-led labor and the radical fringe of professional and intellectual groups, but also among many anti-Communist nationalists in urban areas, especially Guatemala City." The United States' effort depended entirely on creating sufficient "internal tension and national isolation" to weaken "the Army's loyalty to Arbenz."[33]

The shipment of arms to Guatemala's neighbors created the expected anxiety. Guatemala's Ambassador Guillermo Toriello met with United States officials to resolve what Guatemala believed was the basic difference, the controversy over United Fruit lands. But there was only one issue to discuss: "Communism." State Department officer Thomas Mann was emphatic. The United States "knew that communists the world over were agents of Soviet imperialism and constituted a mortal threat to our own national existence." When Toriello insisted that he and Arbenz opposed Communists but refused to "force them underground with the repressive measures used by his country's hated dictatorships," Mann exhibited the United States' policy toward Communists as the only appropriate model:

> It was not necessary to kill Communists in order to remove their influence from the Government. In the United States the Communists freely printed a daily newspaper and enjoyed the freedoms of other citizens of the country. . . . The U. S. Government, however, did not support Communist candidates in political elections, did not afford them official facilities with which to disseminate international Communist propaganda, did not appoint Communists to important posts in the executive branch of the Government, did not assist Communists to gain key positions in the leading political parties, from where they could wield influence far out of proportion to their numbers, did not issue diplomatic passports to Communists who thereupon traveled to Communist meetings in the Soviet orbit with the immunity of official status under the Government, and did not do a great many other things. . . .[34]

Guatemala refused to adopt the United States' interpretation of civil liberties and political freedom. One year after the Toriello-Mann conversation, the Arbenz government was overthrown. Economic sanctions helped destabilize the economy. While Toriello argued that the "United States could help the opponents of communism by granting normal cooperation and aid instead of leaving them 'perched like birds on the side of a mountain,'" the United

States trained Castillo Armas' forces on a United Fruit Company plantation in Honduras.[35]

But as late as November 1953, municipal elections revealed that all efforts to reduce support for Arbenz had failed. Despite the well-financed creation of an antigovernment United Front, Arbenz supporters held firm. According to the State Department, "Communist-sympathizers" were elected where they had never been elected before. The State Department conjectured that the robust victories for the Arbenz government resulted from the fact that, since the Salamá uprising, leading anti-communists were busy in exile, and the "Opposition as a whole may be said to have given up any hopes of making their views prevail through elections."[36]

The Association of University Students, for example, had been dominated by anti-communists until October 1953. It was now headed by "a member of the pro-Communist student organization," whose first act in office was "to send a telegram to President Batista protesting the detention in Cuba of student delegates returning from the 'peace' congress in Bucharest." In addition, several elected officials who had formerly remained aloof from "communist causes" were now regarded as "opportunists" who moved left to protest, for example, Eisenhower's agreement with Franco to build a United States air base in Spain.[37]

In November, John E. Peurifoy replaced Rudolf Schoenfeld as United States ambassador to Guatemala. Although he could not speak Spanish, the CIA chose Peurifoy for the post and Eisenhower agreed, since Peurifoy was so "familiar with the tactics of Communists in Greece." Known as "smiling Jack," Peurifoy was a tough South Carolinian pleased with his image as the man with a "big stick." He wrote to John Cabot: "I have [the] psychological advantage of being new and [the] government feels I have come to Guatemala to use the big stick. We have been letting them stew."[38]

During his introductory meetings with Guatemalan officials, Peurifoy announced his task: to eliminate Communists from the government, and Communist attitudes from the country. In his first meeting with Guatemala's new Foreign Minister, Dr. Raúl Osegueda, Peurifoy cited Greece, where only 18 percent of the soil was arable, as a country that would soon "produce its own basic foodstuff" without agrarian reform—"thanks to American Technical Assistance." In defense of agrarian reform, Osegueda described conditions in rural Guatemala before 1944, when "farm laborers had been roped together by the Army for delivery to the low-land farms where they were kept in debt slavery by the landowners." Peurifoy replied that "agrarian reform had been instituted in China and that China was today a Communist country."[39]

Charges of communism notwithstanding, Peurifoy and other United States officials knew that Osegueda was not a communist. Raymond G. Leddy had, for example, analyzed Osegueda's politics. He was "a rather typical product of the leftist-liberal depression era in the United States." Leddy hoped that Peurifoy's tough stance would "jar him out of the haze about agrarian reform and his esteemed colleagues," but speculated that his impoverished apprenticeship in California, where he "kept body and soul together . . . by some menial labor which, to a youth of intellectual tastes and educational ambitions, was rankling and proved to him the necessity to change the economic system." Postwar Washington no longer believed in New Deal notions, and such State Department officials as Leddy considered Guatemalans such as Osegueda to be cases of "arrested development." "His ideas on government are an exact parody," he explained to Peurifoy, "of all that we heard up until, roughly, Pearl Harbor—the alliance between capitalism and Fascism, the emptiness of political democracy without economic security, and the deadly danger of military might allied with corrupt politicians." Leddy guessed Osegueda's "mental growth stopped at about that time." He and his associates failed to see that the "'muchachos' they know from boyhood could be any kind of a threat to them or their country for preaching and organizing Communism, just as they refuse to look at the world map and see that Soviet expansion is a relentless and grueling reality."[40]

In a lengthy dinner meeting with President and Mrs. Arbenz, Peurifoy specified the United States' one-issue policy. There was no hope of better relations so long as Communists influenced Guatemala's affairs. To persuade Arbenz of the wisdom of adopting the United States' ultimatum, Peurifoy "reviewed for the President the efforts the United States has made to help free people all over the world." When Arbenz insisted that local Communists like Fortuny were "honest men," Peurifoy questioned their visits to Moscow. María Villanova de Arbenz "said that the Communists here went to Moscow to study Marxism from an economic point of

view, but this had no connection with their political beliefs."
Peurifoy replied that not only the United States, but all Guatemala's neighbors, were concerned about such attitudes. Arbenz
said "most of his neighbors were permitting the Fruit Company to
finance counterespionage and counter-revolutionaries within their
countries against his government." Peurifoy demanded proof,
insisting that the United States had declared in 1945 "that United
States business should not intervene in the internal affairs of nations in the Hemisphere if they expected United States support."
Arbenz promised proof that Castillo Armas had been receiving
money regularly although it was "possible that Trujillo . . . had
been the benefactor." He considered the Fruit Company, however,
"the biggest stumbling block" and believed that it "dominated the
press of the United States." Peurifoy assured him that United Fruit
was "a small corporation by American standards and that . . . no
corporation dominated any of the press in the United States."

After six hours of banter and haggling, Peurifoy concluded that
if Arbenz was not a Communist, he would "certainly do until one
comes along." He was also convinced that Mrs. Arbenz had "extreme and great influence on her husband." "Shrewd and smart,"
she was "a person to be reckoned with." Peurifoy reported to
Washington that "normal approaches will probably not work in
Guatemala. Furthermore, the longer we remain idle and do nothing, the more difficult it is going to be to change the situation. This
very small group of Communists is strongly entrenched and is
strangling the nation day by day. The candle is burning slowly and
surely, and it is only a matter of time before the large American interests will be forced out completely."[41]

"The normal approaches will probably not work. . . ." Peurifoy's mission, therefore, was to involve irregular and unlimited tactics. To destabilize the government of Guatemala, everything was
exploitable. Gossip, aggrieved personalities, "public brawls at the
bull ring," "popular impatience" with "government reform programs," "wasteful experimentation," "disgust at the unfinished,
mismanaged, and disorderly Fair grounds"—a costly public works
project that seemed somehow sabotaged on every level. The 2 November 1953 issue of *Time* magazine described the siutation in
"Oh, Come to the Fair!"

To lure U.S. tourists scared off by its growing reputation as a center of Communist influence, Guatemala this year decided to stage a lavish international fair. Jorge Toriello, a high-powered businessman who backs the regime, was put in charge with $1,080,000 to spend. Promising the republic a gambling casino, horse races, Miami-style dog racing, Ferris wheels, a roller-coaster and a brand-new bullring, Toriello pitched right in. Abroad he laid out $100,000 for publicity, including $30,000 for full-page ads in the *New York Times* ("Guatemala—Panorama of Progress"). In the capital's Aurora park he set thousands of masons and carpenters working to finish the fair for last week's grand opening.

But every difficulty occurred. Nothing was completed. Guatemala's only cement factory "broke down." That made it impossible to complete the bull ring's outer wall. With every ticket sold, and no wall, thousands of "gate-crashers" invaded the bull ring. A riot erupted. According to *Time,* "Soon many choice ringside seats . . . had barefoot occupants" and "8000 angry ticket-holders could not get in." The bullfight was canceled. Bottles and refuse showered the arena. Wooden chairs and debris were set aflame. The toilets were smashed. Many were hurt. In addition, *Time* gloated:

> Toriello's casino attracted little betting, his dog races were put off because of construction fights, and his fellow businessmen showed no interest in the fair's industrial pavilions. . . . And to top it all, the . . . crowds of U.S. tourists failed to show.

All mishaps were reported jubilantly to Washington. All mishaps represented "growing dissatisfaction." Guatemalan reformers were "stripped" of their "glamor," as "promises of 'Revolutionary' progress" were delayed by inefficiency and publicly staged brawls. The mismanaged fair ground would arouse public contempt. And all problems were "accentuated by a series of annoyances, such as the paucity of films in movie theaters due to the government's difficulties with American distributors, an almost total lack of sugar in Guatemala City . . . , and a currently threatened meat shortage."[42]

Those familiar with the destabilization of Allende's government in Chile in 1973 might perceive a familiar pattern. Peurifoy's task was to move "the current phase of ferment and unrest" beyond scattered expressions of petty annoyances to the point of massive public demonstrations of protest leading to the government's overthrow by popular acclamation. There were two problems: There was no unity among the counterrevolutionaries; and there was insufficient opposition to the government.

Castillo Armas complained that Ydígoras Fuentes wanted the presidency "on a silver platter" but was "unwilling to fight for it." Another rival, Colonel Barrios Peña, also had presidential pretensions. But Castillo Armas considered him "erratic, unstable, unreliable," and "by nature" "poco loco." State Department officials complained that there was "no center around which anti-Administration and anti-Communist sentiment can polarize." The exile community of pretenders distrusted each other and sought money for themselves in Washington. One Ydígoras Fuentes supporter, José Luis Arenas, met with Vice-President Nixon, Senator Karl Mundt, and members of the State Department to request two hundred thousand dollars for "volunteers" to participate in "massive popular demonstrations." With sufficient funds he promised to "bring the entire Republic to Guatemala City." No "final decision" was made on his offer, and "no formal memorandum" was kept of the meeting.[43]

Factional disunity and insufficient popular support had persuaded both Somoza and Trujillo that "the only means of overthrowing the Government was through a decision of the United States Government to do so." Trujillo had reportedly complained that "every time something started there were twenty people who wanted to be President after the uprising and none would cooperate with the other nineteen." United States officials were assured that the "United States need not do it itself, but could work through friendly Central American and Caribbean Governments." But organizational leadership was expected. Castillo Armas was, moreover, clear about his own needs.[44] He was a "professional military man" and had specific requirements: "competent direction, substantial resources, and a complete plan of operations." But he informed the United States that the "top echelon" of the armed forces of Guatemala remained entirely "loyal to Arbenz."[45]

On 23 December 1953, Peurifoy outlined the situation and a

fully developed program for its revision: Communists would "gain strength" so long as Arbenz remained in office. All "normal diplomatic procedures" were inadequate. Therefore, to make it difficult for Arbenz to remain in office, Peurifoy suggested a series of measures to be taken prior to the Caracas conference scheduled for the coming spring: (1) Publicize "through press channels Communist developments." (2) Avoid "any overt acts to which Guatemalan delegates at [the] conference could point as evidence of persecution of Guatemala or intervention in its affairs." (3) Avoid "emphasis on fruit company problems." (4) Accelerate "locally overt and covert anti-Communist propaganda." (5) Support the "small Guatemalan free labor organization UNTL" (Unión Nacional de Trabajadores Libres—the National Union of Free Workers)—with "funds for its activities." (6) Establish an environment in which "non-Communists whether now supporting or opposing [the] government would feel forced to coordinate their organizations and take action against [the] government."

In particular, Peurifoy suggested the withdrawal of the United States army and air missions from Guatemala, the withdrawal of personnel from the construction of Guatemala's new Roosevelt Hospital and of its agricultural mission, "not including the Entrerios Rubber Experiment Project, which is important to us"; cancellation of a contract with the United Fruit Company for growing abaca; "denunciation" of the "reciprocal trade treaty"; a vigorous campaign "through columnists and radio commentators for voluntary refusal by American coffee importers to buy Guatemalan coffee." Peurifoy thought the latter might be upsetting even if "purchases did not decrease," since it would "give local growers [an] increased sense of urgency and stimulate their willingness to aid anti-government movement." Impede "issuance of export licenses on shipments of goods from United States to Guatemala," ranging from "delays" to a general refusal to issue licenses especially "for road and port building equipment." "Final or partial suspension" of crucial "gasoline shipments." Peurifoy thought of these proposals as a "starting point for study" that might be applied "progressively" as the situation unfolded. He was not unmindful that these steps could "lead to considerable bloodshed." His plan should, he assured Dulles, be implemented regardless of the "unpleasant consequences since continuance of present regime would also lead to most of them though at a slower pace and at the convenience of the Communists."[46]

In January 1954, several conspirators, including members of the United States-financed labor union UNTL, were arrested as participants in a "well-organized plot." The State Department instructed USIA officers to emphasize that the arrests were "made arbitrarily" and were part of a "campaign to intimidate anti-Communist opposition." The capture of UNTL members "should be treated as forthright government action" against the organization of "a free labor movement outside Communist-dominated CGTG."[47] At the same time, Walter Bedell Smith sent a telegram instructing the United States embassy in Guatemala City to release the statement John Foster Dulles had made before the Senate Foreign Relations Committee during his confirmation hearings the preceding year: He had "no interest or connection" in any "outside organization." He had resigned from his "former law firm" and from all boards of directors and no longer had any "interest" of "any kind, sort [or] description . . . in any foreign government [or] foreign concern. . . ."[48]

Guatemalan efforts to organize a united front for the country's defense progressed slowly. Not until January 1954 did the government organize its own Office of Publicity and Propaganda, "to counteract the insidious campaign" conducted by the United States press, particularly the New York *Times, Life,* and the *Reader's Digest (Selecciones).* Guatemala's Office of Publicity and Propaganda celebrated the country's economic changes and all innovations; it investigated the connections of those who attacked Guatemala in the United States, particularly "their relations with the imperialist enterprises," as well as those "vulgar delinquents" in Guatemala who were implicated in the "repugnant campaign of slander." It monitored foreign newspapers, magazines, and radio stations, and highlighted all international support. The committee introduced a significant and vigorous propaganda factor into Guatemalan politics. Its activities were supplemented by a Committee of Struggle Against the Foreign Intervention, also organized in January.

The State Department was not pleased. The USIS reported that although the government radio station was an "amateur" operation musically, it "combined the best in professional announcing with good technical direction . . . to produce an outstanding emotional appeal to all Guatemalans to unite in making their country 'free, sovereign and independent.'" Its news programs were "slanted," and "excoriated" the United States with such items as: Department of State "refused a passport to a newspaperwoman, Mrs. Beverly Hepburn, 'because of her obvious sympathy toward Guatemala'"; the American Legion "ratified the decision to consider colored affiliates as second-class members." Such reports, the USIS complained, were "impertinently introduced by several bars of the United States national anthem." The station's "special programs" were even more "offensive." One cultural program, for example, denounced the United States Spanish-language contribution to a recent book fair, particularly "comic books," as a "morbid North American invention."[49]

But the most significant act of Guatemala's new Office of Publicity and Propaganda was to release the details of the January plot, the documents of which had been captured and photocopied. They included "a secret unification agreement signed in San Salvador" between Castillo Armas and Ydígoras Fuentes; a 20 September 1953 letter from Castillo Armas to President Somoza asserting that "our friends" informed him that "the Government of the North" now recognized "the impossibility of finding another solution to the grave problem of my country" and had decided "to allow us to develop our plans"; and photostatic copies of the arms and matériel offered to Somoza by H. F. Cordes and Company, of Hamburg, Germany—including unspecified heavy and light arms, machine guns, mortars, napalm bombs, field beds, field telephones, and Vampire jet planes. Since H. F. Cordes did not offer bargain-basement prices, Guatemala understandably concluded that many millions of dollars, "true rivers of money," had been made available to Castillo Armas and his supporters. One used, but guaranteed, Vampire jet was priced at sixty-five thousand dollars (U.S.). Twenty had evidently been sent to Somoza in July 1953 and four in September 1953. One barrel containing one hundred kilos of napalm cost one hundred seventy dollars, not counting the cost of the metal container. The quality of the napalm was designated "According to the specification of the United States."

Guatemala published these documents in a ninety-eight-page

pamphlet in which the tensions among the conspirators were analyzed and the contributions of many public figures, including Somoza, Trujillo, and Francis Cardinal Spellman, were cited. The governments of El Salvador, the Dominican Republic, and Venezuela were also implicated. Jorge Isaac Delgado, a commercial attaché in the Panamanian embassy in Managua, was named responsible for the purchase of planes and ships, "pilots and mercenaries." Clandestine arms had already been brought into Guatemala City and Tiquisate through "various channels," including the use of the International Railways of Central America. In addition, "super-saboteurs, assassins and technicians" were training on Nicaragua's island of Momotombito, "known in the code of conspirators as EL DIABLO"; and Somoza's private ranch, El Tamarindo, served as the communications center. Its code name was "TAP TAP." A Colonel "Carl Studer," allegedly retired from the United States Army and currently employed by the UFCO, was the instructor for the project's personnel.

Guatemalan authorities understood that the key to this "criminal project" was an "extensive and profound" press campaign of "intimidation, calumny, blackmail and defamation." They also understood that the key problem with the project was that Castillo Armas and Ydígoras Fuentes "did not trust each other because they know each other." Guatemalan officials had evidence that the "traitors to Guatemala, sought to betray [each] other." On 7 November 1953, for example, Castillo Armas warned Somoza "to guard the triumph of counterrevolution" and not to give Ydígoras "any information regarding our activities." Other pretenders to leadership, notably Barrios Peña, who was favored by Trujillo, also complicated matters—as did the fact that Castillo Armas mistrusted the Guatemalans recruited for the invasion and the fact that the entire project depended on "world events which exist or will exist elsewhere." The pamphlet concluded with the text of the State Department's press release issued in response to the widespread publicity that resulted from the publication of Guatemala's charges.[50]

A master of the alchemy of twentieth-century political warfare, Walter Bedell Smith transformed the facts of the project into a "Communist-inspired terror campaign." His press release dismissed the charge "that the United States Government had acquiesced in a plot by other nations against Guatemala" as "ridiculous and untrue." He asserted:

It is the policy of the United States not to intervene in the internal affairs of other nations. . . . It is notable that the charge comes as the climax of an increasingly mendacious propaganda campaign and of attacks on freedom of expression and democratic labor organization in Guatemala. This is perhaps connected with the recent change in the Guatemalan Foreign Ministry and with the return from visits to the Soviet Union and Iron Curtain countries of Víctor Manuel Gutiérrez and José Manuel Fortuny, the former a notorious Communist and leader of the Communist-dominated labor confederation (CGTG), the latter the head of the Guatemalan Communist Party, and both closely associated with the leading figures of the Guatemalan Government. The official Guatemalan press and radio offices . . . have a long record of circulating false charges, typically Communist in their technique, against the United States, the United Nations, and particularly those countries which have been actively resisting Communist aggression.

The United States views the issuance of this false accusation immediately prior to the Tenth Inter-American Conference as a Communist effort to disrupt the work of this conference and the inter-American solidarity which is so vital to all the nations of the Hemisphere.[51]

Smith advised the Central American embassies that the United States considered "firmness" in the "face of [the] Communist-inspired terror campaign" vital to hemispheric unity. He applauded Somoza's "equally strong rejection of false Guatemalan accusations" and awaited El Salvador's "acceptance of the United States' military assistance agreements."[52]

In Guatemala, the revelations caused a sensation. Except for one newspaper that headlined "Red saturation has fallen on country," Guatemala's newspapers condemned foreign intervention. Guatemala's parliament formally denounced Castillo Armas and Ydígoras Fuentes. Krieg informed Dulles that Víctor Manuel Gutiérrez accused the saboteurs of receiving money from the UFCO and the Department of State "from $100 million Mutual Security funds." According to Krieg, newspaper headlines representing all factions, including those opposed to Arbenz, seemed to accept the charge of United States complicity. Headlines ranged from "Inter-

national Plot Denounced . . . ," to "Planned Criminal Bombardment with Napalm Bombs." During a five-hour session, Guatemala's congress unanimously opposed international aggression
against Guatemala's sovereignty. Not only did the Communist deputy Gutiérrez accuse Braden, Senator Alexander Wiley, Peurifoy,
and others of "twisting the truth . . . in preparation for the
Caracas Conference and military intervention," non-communist
deputies "referred to the liberties proclaimed by President Roosevelt and said that if the McCarthys, Wileys, Peurifoys, etc., had
forgotten them, the Guatemalan people had not." José Alberto
Cardoza, one of the four Communist deputies in Guatemala's fifty-
six-seat legislature, insisted that a distinction now be made between liberty and the "libertinage" or "treason" practiced by the
anti-government papers and "Radio Success," which reported "any
agrarian, political or labor incident" detrimental to the government
while refusing to report incidents of sabotage. It was time, he
insisted, "to take a new attitude toward this reactionary press."[53]

Subsequently, on 2 February, New York *Times* reporter Sidney
Gruson and Reuters correspondent Marshall Bannell, who was
also Central American correspondent for the National Broadcasting Company, were expelled. Their articles were denounced as "insulting" and provocative. In response, the USIA recommended a
policy of "maximum unattributed press and radio output," emphasizing that the expulsions represented an "undisguised blow at freedom of the press." Information agents were to imply that Cardoza's statement before Guatemala's congress indicated an
"intensification" of the Communist drive against the independent
press and that it was "apparently timed to coincide" with the
expulsion of foreign newsmen and demonstrates, therefore, the
"strength of Communist influence over government."[54]

During Toriello's first meeting with Peurifoy after the publication of the conspiracy details, he told Peurifoy that Eisenhower
had favored a "neutral commission" to investigate the contracts between United States companies and Guatemala to see if they con-
formed with "modern concepts" and if the companies made "adequate contribution to the government and national economy" of
Guatemala. On his departure from Washington to assume his post
as foreign minister, Ambassador Toriello had paid Eisenhower a
farewell visit. Toriello left Washington convinced that Eisenhower

was objective, scrupulous, and open to negotiation. Although there is, to date, no record of that meeting, Eisenhower recalled that he gave Toriello "unshirted hell" for "playing along with the Communists."[55] Toriello, on the other hand, considered the meeting cordial, sincere, and hopeful and complained to Peurifoy that "it was obvious" that the State Department remained "unaware of the contents" of his earlier talk with President Eisenhower. Toriello believed the "bias against Guatemala" was due to Secretary Dulles and John Moors Cabot and considered it lamentable that Eisenhower received "only one side of the story." Toriello hoped that Walter Bedell Smith would attend the Caracas meeting so that there might be a "frank discussion." He also hoped that "nothing would happen at Caracas which would make the situation worse."[56]

The limited information so far available confirms Toriello's suspicion that Eisenhower received only one side of the story. But the bias against Guatemala was not limited to Dulles and Cabot. Walter Bedell Smith had briefed Eisenhower preceding Toriello's visit. Smith considered Toriello "a persuasive apologist for his government." Toriello had tried earnestly to convince Smith that "Guatemalan Communists are different" and without "real influence." But, Smith told Eisenhower, the "facts are otherwise. . . . The Guatemalan Government has abundantly proved its Communist sympathies and toleration of Communist activities. . . ."

> We have repeatedly expressed deep concern to the Guatemalan Government because it plays the Communist game. Our relations are further disturbed because of the merciless hounding of American companies there by tax and labor demands, strikes, and, in the case of the United Fruit Company, inadequately compensated seizures of land under a Communist-administered Agrarian Reform Law.
>
> The Guatemalan situation has attracted the interest of many American journalists who have visited Guatemala and independently reported on their findings. Prominent Congressmen and Senators of both Parties have shown increasing concern with Communism in Guatemala.[57]

Dulles suggested that Peurifoy respond positively to Toriello's inquiry about Eisenhower's plan of a "neutral commission" preceding the Caracas meeting. But he urged Peurifoy to make it clear that it was not of "primary importance in our relations."[58] Communism was of primary importance. And Caracas would settle that issue. Guatemala's liberation would be launched from Caracas.

The Tenth Inter-American Conference, at Caracas, represented for the United States the legalistic call for Arbenz's demise. The Organization of American States voted to protect the continent against Soviet penetration. According to all contemporary accounts, the vote was carefully managed, hard-won, coerced. It was, however, everything the United States wanted. With only Argentina and Mexico abstaining, and Guatemala opposed to the motion, the State Department considered Caracas a major diplomatic victory. But it was an uneven victory, a short-lived and cosmetic victory. Of the twenty nations present (Costa Rica did not attend), only the United States wanted to discuss the "intervention of international communism in the American Republics." The American republics wanted to discuss "trade, tariffs, import quotas, markets, loans, investments." The American republics also wanted to discuss fascism and Peronism. But the United States' determination to focus on communism prevailed—since "fascism and Peronism were not controlled from outside the hemisphere."[59]

The opening of the Tenth Inter-American Conference, at Venezuela's new university center, stimulated serious political analyses by United States journalists. The meeting at Caracas was appropriately regarded as a turning point in United States foreign policy. The choices made there would harness the future. United States journalists noted the wide disparity between the United States' preoccupation with communism and Latin America's long agenda—twenty-eight issues that might take a month to discuss—which had nothing to do with communism. "Our neighbors," *The Nation* editorialized, "were more interested in a reversal of Washington economic policies than in any export of the blessings of McCarthyism to their shores." In March 1954 at Caracas, Latin American delegates represented nations that had average per capita incomes that ranged between two hundred and four hundred dollars a year. They wanted reciprocity for their raw materials. Politically, they demanded reaffirmation of the "doctrine of non-intervention."[60]

Time magazine observed the same situation. The United States could not find "a suitable neighbor" to introduce the anticommunist resolution, and left for Caracas uncertain that there would be sufficient support to take a "strong line against Guatemala's fellow-traveling government." *Time* lamented that, "like many Europeans, the Latinos are not nearly so roused against the dangers of world Communism as people in the United States." In fact, *Time* despaired:

> A large body of non-Communist leftist opinion holds that the U.S. is too upset about the Reds and not bothered enough about right-wing dictatorships. Latin America's powerful nationalist sentiment, moreover, tends to sympathize with Guatemala's Red-led harassment of U.S. companies.

> At bottom the trouble is that any U.S. proposal for strong action against Guatemalan Communism raises the old spectre of U.S. intervention, which scares the Latinos more than Communism. . . .

But, *Time* magazine predicted, should "the situation in Guatemala continue to deteriorate the ultimate possibility of unilateral United States action cannot be ruled out." John Peurifoy had announced in January, shortly before Arbenz published the captured documents, that the United States could "not permit a Soviet republic to be established between Texas and the Panama Canal." He warned, "Public opinion in the United States might force us to take some measures to prevent Guatemala from falling into the lap of international Communism." Peurifoy "declined to say" what measures he recommended, but *Time* magazine pointed out that "Guatemala rarely has more on hand than eight days' supply of gasoline."[61]

Flora Lewis, a vigorous opponent of Guatemalan communism, analyzed the political environment at Caracas in *The Nation*. In "The Peril Is Not Red in Central America," Flora Lewis wrote: "All Guatemala's neighbors are puzzled by the United States' exclusive preoccupation with Reds. Even leaders far on the right, like President Anastasio Somoza of Nicaragua are disturbed. . . . More democratic leaders deplore the single-minded anti-communism of the United States because it bolsters the feudalists in Latin America and heightens the barriers to needed change to the point where only extremism can assault them. . . ." For Latin Americans, Flora Lewis concluded, the real need was economic reform and the real fear was United States intervention. "Everybody agrees," she wrote, "that the United States had better let

Latin Americans work out their own political salvation, but everybody wants better economic treatment. . . ."

Flora Lewis considered the "bickering family" of Central
America largely "backward." "Apathy is great, community feeling
is dim." Real revolution, she concluded, was "still far beyond the
horizon." Given the months and months of regular reports predict-
ing Guatemala's danger to the entire hemisphere, one might well
ask—in the face of "apathy" and "dim" community spirit—what
the fuss was about. Indeed, in another article written in the same
period, Flora Lewis' own "case history" of "Communism in Guatemala," she featured "devoted, angry-tongued Communists"
deeply entrenched and spreading out. Guatemala, she wrote in a
different tone for the New York *Times Magazine*, looked at first
glance "calm and green, tinged perhaps with a rosy glow of
change." But it was actually "red," "blood-and-barricade red." Yet
in her analysis of Caracas she had emphasized the disparity between the United States' preoccupation with communism, and
Latin America's preoccupation with economic change. When Latin
Americans "count up the dollars the United States spends in
Europe and the Far East," they conclude "charity might begin
nearer home." And when Latin Americans are told the United
States decides policy on the basis of whether countries "are with us
or against us, they feel puzzled." Communism, she wrote, is "simply not a real issue" to Latin Americans. "Even in Guatemala the
arguments are about land reform, imperialism, and so on, not
Marxism versus capitalism." Flora Lewis was very specific. She
was writing about "nationalism." Latin Americans were concerned
exclusively with "economic development and national respect-
ability," and not "or—at least not very frequently" with the competition between "Russia versus the United States." Despite all allegations about Russia's penetration into the hemisphere, Flora
Lewis noted that when the Soviet commercial attaché, Mikhail
Samoilov, visited Guatemala, he made only a "half-hearted" effort
to sell cameras and radios. "Tales of Russian plots to soak up all of
Central America's coffee dollars with cheap Soviet exports are,"
she concluded, "jungle fantasies."[62]

From right to left, United States journalists seemed unanimous
about the meaning of Caracas. For Latin America, economic development and not communism would be "the explosive core of

the conference." And on economic questions the United States would be "likely to find itself standing almost alone against a united Latin world" that believed it was time to stop treating the Americas as a "reservoir of raw materials."[63]

Milton Eisenhower's 1953 report to the President on Latin America, so eloquent and hopeful, haunted every detail of the Caracas conference. Although he had declined to visit Guatemala, Dr. Eisenhower's tour of ten nations had persuaded him that:

> Latin Americans hold a persistent feeling that the U.S. could if it wished have made substantial sums for development available to them when it was providing billions for the rest of the world. This feeling is enhanced by the fact that Latin America does not seek financial grants but rather loans . . . for broad and immediate economic development.

On his return, Dr. Eisenhower had written with a sense of urgency: Economic relations were "the key to better relations." "Everything else, no matter how important, must take secondary place, at least in the absence of war."[64] In November 1953, Dr. Eisenhower submitted to the President a lengthy and specific analysis of "the importance of Latin America and the United States to each other":

> As a market for our commercial exports, Latin America is as important to us as all of Europe and more important than Asia, Africa and Oceania combined. Our sales to Latin America encompass the entire range of our national production. As a source of United States imports, the Latin American republics have even greater relative importance, standing well ahead of Europe or the other continents. . . .
>
> The copper, tin, zinc, iron ore, manganese, and other minerals which we obtain from Latin America are vital constituent parts of the machinery which we in turn ship there. The dollars we provide through purchases of coffee, sugar, tropical fruits, and wool, as well as metals, finance their purchases of transportation and industrial equipment and consumer goods. The industrial and military items which the U.S. turns out to help defend the free world, including the American republics, require a continuing supply of a great variety of strategic materials from Latin America. . . .
>
> Almost 30 percent of all U.S. private, long-term foreign investment is in Latin America; this investment of some $6 billion is

larger than the amount invested in any other part of the world except Canada. . . .

But during his June–July 1953 tour of South America, Dr. Eisenhower noticed a disturbing "social ferment." Desperate poverty, widespread illiteracy, "woefully inadequate" health and educational facilities had resulted in greater demands for immediate capital development. "They want," Eisenhower noted, "greater production and higher standards of living, and they want them *now*":

Unhappily, the need for foreign capital is accompanied throughout most of Latin America by a rising tide of nationalism.

In some respects this surge of nationalism is praiseworthy, for it indicates a growing pride in achievement and an impatient desire to raise dramatically and immediately their standards of living.

But ultra-nationalism, with its blindness to true long-term interests . . . leads to laws and practices which prevent the entrance of foreign capital essential to development.

Ultra-nationalism is being fostered by Communist agitators. Sometimes political leaders who in no sense agree with ultimate Communist purposes accept Communist support. . . . Thus, the two may be joined for a time in the fallacious contention that foreign capital investment, private or public, is in reality a form of imperialism. . . .[65]

To counter the dangers of communism and "ultra-nationalism," Dr. Eisenhower recommended tariff concessions, tax relief, expanded stockpiling of crucial minerals "to provide at least some degree of stability in world market prices of raw materials," and greater use of the U. S. Government-funded and -operated Export-Import Bank to guarantee developmental loans. The last two were of special significance to Latin Americans. But in January 1954, Treasury Secretary George Humphrey opposed them both. He was committed to the primacy of the World Bank, which depended for revenue upon the private money market in all international transactions and considered enlarged stockpiling in the interests of fiscal stability and international amity "an unwarranted departure from our basic economic principles."[66]

Just two weeks before the Caracas meeting, a major rift in administrative circles, apparently regarding these two issues, resulted in the transfer of John Moors Cabot as Assistant Secretary of State for Inter-American Affairs to the United States embassy in Sweden, and the resignation of Dudley W. Figgis, the Foreign Operations Administration's regional director for Latin America. Although Cabot assisted Dulles at Caracas, it was widely understood that he "was moved out" because he supported "greater use of Export-Import Bank loans to finance Latin American economic development, and was overruled by George Humphrey."[67] As a result, Dulles went to Caracas with no specific bargaining chips beyond a vague promise to call a meeting in Washington sometime in the future to discuss economic issues. Caracas was in fact an inexpensive victory for the United States. The seventeen to one anti-Communist vote cost nothing and came to symbolize the ease with which the United States might continue to maneuver in Latin America.

Closer attention to details might have warned those concerned with the future that the vote represented an illusory, temporary and entirely unstable phenomenon. Even in its own terms, the State Department achieved only its "minimum objective." The "maximum objective" would have been the adoption of "effective multilateral measures against Guatemala." The "minimum" objective was a resolution to "lay the ground work for subsequent positive action against Guatemala by the Organization of American States."[68]

The resolution called for a "consultative meeting" if two thirds of the hemisphere's nations determined that "the political institutions of any American state" was dominated by "the international Communist movement." That consultative meeting would "consider the adoption of measures" ranging from "admonitions" to "economic sanctions" to unspecified "sterner measures." Dulles was pleased. In the past the Latin American nations had limited its protest against "totalitarian" subversion to a recommendation that each government "examine" its own laws "and adopt such changes as it may consider necessary." At Caracas, Latin America agreed on joint action. After three tense hours, on the fifty-first ballot, following a significant amendment by which Dulles agreed to "dangers originating outside the hemisphere," the United States achieved its only goal at Caracas. Dulles left within an hour of the final ballot. He told newsmen that the "fact that one American nation voted against the resolution shows how necessary it was that the conference should have acted as it did." Now we must be certain that "the enemies of freedom do not move into the breach which has been disclosed in our ranks."[69]

Dulles had left too quickly to appreciate the full extent of the breach "in our ranks." It was a breach into which the economic and political strength of the United States would someday fall. The vote camouflaged deep and widespread discontent. Throughout Latin America, the decision to ignore the real spirit of Caracas intensified the bitterness and violence that has come to dominate hemispheric relations. But Dulles returned to Washington before the "delegates rose one after another to offer 'explanations' of their votes." According to *Time,* "even those who had warmly supported the United States resolution in the debate privately expressed misgivings." One delegate said, "If we did not agree the United States might resort to unilateral action. That would be far worse." There had been no direct pressure, but as one delegate commented: "You don't always see the sun, but you know it is there." Uruguay's delegate explained, "We voted for the resolution, but without joy." Nobody challenged the belief of the Argentinian and Mexican delegates, who abstained because they were convinced the resolution weakened "the principle of non-intervention."[70]

In fact, Latin Americans agreed with President Jacobo Arbenz Guzmán, whose message to Guatemala's Congress coincided with the opening of the Caracas conference:

> The real issue of the Inter-American Conference should be the common Latin American problem of economic betterment, so that we will not continue to be the objects of monopolistic investment and the sources of raw materials, selling cheap and buying dear from one of the countries of the American community.

Arbenz's entire two-and-a-half-hour speech to the Congress challenged the United States' economic and political pretensions over Guatemala's affairs. He mocked the concerted "anti-communist" activities spearheaded by the United States during his predecessor's administration. "It is well known," Arbenz asserted, that "there was not at the time a Marxist party." Yet they organized "the first anti-communist" groups; they invented "the umbrella before the rain." And now, Arbenz affirmed, there were many more reasons for this crusade: a "highway to the Atlantic which will end the transportation monopoly of foreign trade; . . . a truly national port, which will contribute to diversifying this same foreign trade"; a study of alternative and inexpensive "electrical energy for industry and for Guatemala City"; "two governmental interventions were carried out on foreign companies . . . ; and in applying the Agricultural Reform we could not make, nor should we have made, an exception of the United Fruit Company. . . . It happened too that we recovered our independence in questions of internal policies and that we would not participate in any foreign war." "It happened that in Guatemala the doors are not so wide open to monopolistic and voracious investment. All that happened. And, moreover, now, yes, there is a Communist Party."[71]

Before Guatemala's eight-member delegation left for Caracas, they participated in a well-publicized rally to commemorate the twentieth anniversary of the assassination of Augusto César Sandino in Nicaragua. "Bitter anti-United States speeches" against intervention were made. According to the New York *Times,* the "speakers declared that the United States had decided Sandino must be killed and had chosen General Anastasio Somoza . . . as the 'instrument.'" The delegation left for Caracas with printed reports for general distribution of the 29 January white paper "and accompanying photostats" that again associated Somoza with an international plot to overthrow Arbenz that was supported by the "government of the North."[72]

Guatemala's delegation included Estrada de la Hoz, one of the nineteen non-Communist legislators who had charged the United States with using germ warfare in Korea; Guillermo Noriega Morales, a leading nationalist economist of the National Agrarian Bank; and José Luis Mendoza, an expert on Belize—British Honduras. Guatemala considered Belize part of its own territory. The entire delegation offended United States sensibilities. The leader of the delegation, Guillermo Toriello, insisted that Belize and the issue of colonialism be made a priority at the conference. He noted that British Guiana was not Communist and that the recent landing of British troops "on American soil" was "an affront to the Hemisphere." The delegates at Caracas adopted a resolution, introduced by Argentina, that called for an end to colonialism in the Caribbean and South America. The United States abstained, arguing that colonial questions should be considered by the United Nations, "where the colonial powers—Britain, France and The Netherlands" were represented. The conference also condemned racial discrimination; reaffirmed the traditional Latin American principle of political asylum; and presumably as an act of defiant nationalism, voted to hold the projected economic conference in Rio instead of Washington.[73]

Toriello was, moreover, the only "oratorical hit" of the conference. In an impassioned speech, he called the United States resolution "only a pretext to intervene in our internal affairs"; reminded the delegates of "the Big Stick," "tarnished dollar diplomacy," and "the landing of United States Marines in Latin American ports." His speech received the conference's only "ovation." *Time* quoted representative comments: "He said many of the things some of the rest of us would like to say if we dared." But they did not dare. Despite the United States' rejection of a vigorously supported resolution for the establishment of a permanent council to deal systematically with long-term multilateral economic issues of trade rather than "aid," they voted for Dulles' resolution. Dulles considered it a splendid victory. Prescient journalists knew in March 1954 that it would be a "Pyrrhic victory."[74] But, for the present, the United States considered the vote sufficient. In political-warfare terms, Guatemala was isolated, seventeen to one.

CHAPTER VII
ANTICOMMUNISM AND COUNTER-INSURGENCY: THE GUATEMALAN MODEL

Part II
The Overthrow of Arbenz and the Implantation of American Democracy

After Caracas, the United States perceived only one nagging obstacle to the overthrow of Guatemala's elected government: There was no coherent opposition to Arbenz in Guatemala. According to United States intelligence reports, the "adoption of the anti-Communist resolution did not weaken Arbenz's position with respect to the Army or to any other politically important group." Arbenz retained "the loyalty of the most influential elements of the Army." And, despite all efforts to unify his opposition "both at home and in exile," it was still "hopelessly disorganized and demoralized."[1]

The United States' major task was, therefore, to coordinate all political-warfare activities to achieve at least unity of purpose among Arbenz's opponents—in the United States, throughout the Americas, and, of course, within Guatemala. Eisenhower told a meeting of legislative leaders that because of the Caracas decision, "we would have all Latin and South American countries helping us 'whenever the Reds make a move.'" Consistent with the resolution, the United States would, he said, "assemble evidence of a kind that would convince the minds of reasonable men" that communism "controlled and dominated" the political institutions of Guatemala.[2]

To "convince the minds of reasonable men" that "the Reds" of Guatemala "spread their influence" throughout the hemisphere, C. D. Jackson's OCB Special Staff assembled data from "Army G-2 files" and from "the several repositories" of "CIA, State and the FBI." He proposed an "organized, long-term and consistent" plan by which all relevant information would be sent to appropriate individuals throughout the Americas.[3] This plan, among others, was adopted. By the end of April, Henry Holland, who had replaced Cabot, assured Sherman Adams that he could tell Eisenhower, "We are proceeding . . . with resourcefulness and energy." A vigorous media campaign was underway, and congressional support was encouraged. There would be an inquiry by the House Select Committee on Communist Aggression, chaired by Charles Kersten; an inquiry by the Senate Subcommittee on Internal Security, chaired by William Jenner; and other inquiries as "appropriate." Senator Margaret Chase Smith introduced a resolution to investigate the "extent to which Guatemalans imposed unjustified increases in the price of coffee." In addition, speeches by Senator Alexander Wiley, Senator Smathers, and others would be written—with assistance from Mr. Fisher, of the Military Intelligence Division. Smathers, for example, would compare "the Communist problem in Indo-China and the Communist problem in Latin America."

Holland, in collaboration with Peurifoy; Raymond Leddy, of

MID; and Frank Wisner, chief of the CIA's clandestine services, suggested that Eisenhower tell the congressional leaders:

> By every proper and effective means we should demonstrate to the courageous elements within Guatemala who are trying to purge their government of its communist elements that they have the sympathy and support of all freedom-loving people. . . . We know that these patriotic Guatemalans represent the overwhelming majority of the people there. We wish them success.[4]

The effort to build widespread public support was fortified by isolated acts of terrorism and the decision to apply destabilizing economic sanctions. One informer-provocateur, requesting "an intensification of United States psychological operations," reported on the particular success of one "campaign designed to terrorize the Communist leaders." His group harassed pro-Arbenz leaders in Guatemala's congress. After one was shot, "little notes saying 'You are next' . . . were planted in the cars of other deputies and mailed to their homes." This source, considered "excellent" by military intelligence agents, assured his contacts "that these tactics will be continued since they have been proven to be very successful." He also urged the United States to "discuss publicly the possibility of economic sanctions." While he did not urge that they actually be applied, he noted that merely the publication of a discussion of an embargo would "contribute to the fear and uncertainty of the present regime." He did, however, assert that an embargo on gasoline shipments for even two weeks would "allow his group to take over the government."[5]

After a discussion of all the hemispheric "pitfalls" that might result from a program of economic sanctions, the State Department decided to adopt them in May. The fear that an embargo might produce "a state of economic chaos" that only the "Communists would be able to exploit" was dismissed "in view of the worldwide collision course between the U.S.S.R. and the free world." Henry Holland said there was "no alternative but to take action against Guatemala as the situation will only grow worse." And "no one could suggest any better course. . . ." Great efforts would be made to get OAS support so that all activities would not be everywhere regarded as "a David-Goliath struggle between Guatemala and the United States."[6]

The final operation awaited only one usable Guatemalan defector and one reasonable pretext. According to E. Howard Hunt, the plan was "to duplicate" Kermit Roosevelt's "technique" in Iran, which involved "psychologically preparing the minds of the target government and population, then a sudden show of apparently massive force." The necessary opening occurred when a "CIA staff officer, documented and disguised as a European buisnessman, entered Guatemala and achieved the defection of a senior officer on Arbenz's staff." He supplied significant military information and "confirmed for us the expected arrival of the Czech munitions ship." The arrival of the *Alfhem,* carrying arms and ammunition to Guatemala, was the long-awaited pretext. Hunt reported that it "became paramount in all our planning."[7]

On 20 May 1954, Hagerty noted in his diary that at the CIA briefing on Indochina and Guatemala he learned only one "new fact": The "Red arms shipment to Guatemala consisted mainly of field pieces—someone pulled a fast one and we were watching the wrong ship." Whether or not the *Alfhem* bypassed United States surveillance or was allowed to slip through to serve as the galvanizing pretext, United States officials had evidently known about the arms shipment for a long time. A full year before, on 4 April 1953, Frank Wisner asked the CIA chief of the "Western Hemisphere Division" for further information on the subject. C. D. Jackson had asked Wisner for "hard information" relating to "the rumor of some weeks ago . . . that arms from Czechoslovakia were being clandestinely introduced into Guatemala (with or without the assistance of the Russians)."[8]

Not until 17 May 1954 did Dulles have "hard evidence" to present to the press. Guatemala received a shipment of arms "from behind the Iron Curtain." The *Alfhem,* a Swedish ship chartered by a British company, was loaded at the East German port of Stettin with "two thousand tons of small arms, ammunition, and light artillery pieces manufactured in the Skoda arms factory in Czechoslovakia." Eisenhower wrote in his memoirs: "This quantity far exceeded any legitimate, normal requirements for the Guatemalan armed forces." In order "to help counter the danger created by the Czech shipment," Eisenhower explained, the United States airlifted "arms to Honduras and Nicaragua. Our initial shipment comprised only fifty tons of rifles, pistols, machine guns, and ammunition," Eisenhower noted, "hardly enough to create apprehension in neighboring states." The President also assured congressional leaders that the United States would not "sit around and do nothing," but would act to "stop these shipments under the Caracas agreement."[9]

The United States' first direct act was a public-relations flop. It was in fact an international scandal that infringed on the commercial rights and interests of the United States' allies. The State Department decided not only to prevent further arms shipments from Communist countries, but "to prevent the movement of persons traveling in the interests of international communism" and to "stop and examine ships and planes entering or leaving Guatemala where that seemed desirable."[10] It was an extraordinary decision. Even Robert Murphy, generally given to experiment and adventure in political warfare, opposed the decision to violate the principle of freedom of the seas. Murphy wrote to Dulles very precisely:

> Now that the President and you have decided on this action it of course must be seen through, but I would like you to know that I believe the philosophy back of the action wrong and that it may be very expensive over the longer term.
>
> My instinct, and perhaps my ignorance of Guatemalan problems, tells me that to resort to this action confesses the bankruptcy of our political policy vis-à-vis that country. Instead of political action inside Guatemala, we are obliged to resort to heavy-handed military action on the periphery of the cause of trouble. While I do not question the usefulness of a display of naval force in the Central American area under present circumstances, forcible detention of foreign flag shipping on the high seas is another matter. . . .
>
> In our past we asserted our right to deliver arms to belligerents. Our present action should give stir to the bones of Admiral von Tirpitz. . . .
>
> This of course is an important action which seems to have received inadequate staff action . . . , and is grounded on reasoning contrary to an opinion of the Acting Legal Adviser.[11]

The State Department's legal adviser had reported that "there seemed to be no legal authority under which we could detain, say, a Soviet ship, or any other European ship or Asian ship, whether or not the OAS had authorized the step." There was nothing vague about the legal aspects of the situation:

> On the facts now known to this office, there appears to be no basis for concluding that any nation is committing an armed attack against any American state. Guatemala apparently is not committing armed attack against any of its neighbors. Sweden and Finland are not committing armed attacks against any American state. In these circumstances, if the U.S. were to intercept and escort by force any ships in Guatemalan territorial waters or on the high seas to an American port, there would be no legal justification for such action either under the Rio Treaty or under the United Nations Charter. Such action would constitute a violation of international law, and could be considered an act of war. . . .[12]

Britain, a party to the *Alfhem* shipment, was outraged. Eisenhower noted that for success the program required "at least the tacit cooperation of our allies, principally Britain, to avoid placing an almost fatal strain on our relations." To persuade Britain of the wisdom of the United States' decision, Dulles met with Sir Roger Makins, Britain's ambassador, to explain that "he was sure the British would forgive us if we learned some lessons from British blockade practice in the first World War." Dulles made it clear that the United States was "prepared to go further than surveillance in the case of any suspicious vessel." "He invited the cooperation of the British" and "alluded to the serious consequences which might arise from a spread of the infection to British Honduras." Sir Roger noted that London "was fully alive to the situation," and predicted cooperation "in practice." He feared, however, that his government's "reaction on grounds of general principle might not be all that we would wish."[13]

On the eve of sensitive negotiations on Indochina and the future of colonialism, the United States abandoned one of its own most celebrated international policies and historic traditions. Since World War I, the United States had been the major advocate of "freedom of the seas" and had insisted on the primacy of commercial freedom for neutral nations even in wartime. Eisenhower's entire international vision depended on allied cooperation, mutual support, interdependence. Now, without prior consultation with its closest allies involved in Guatemalan commerce, the United States instituted a policy of search and seizure—during peacetime. According to all U.S. conventions, the policy represented terrorism, illegal and belligerent action; and was historically considered an act of war.

Presumably it was intended to destabilize Guatemala's economy so thoroughly that Arbenz would either be forced to step down without more serious acts of war and possibly without bloodshed, or it would result in armed intervention. State Department planners were clear about the alternatives. On 30 May, John C. Hill wrote Peurifoy that the "basic thinking" behind the Department's decision was "to enable us to stop ships including our own to such an extent that it will disrupt Guatemala's economy." That would "accelerate one of two developments: either it will encourage the Army or some other non-Communist elements to seize power or the Communists will exploit the situation to extend their control." If the latter occurred, it would justify vigorous activity by "the American community," or if the American republics refuse to "go along," it would enable "the United States to take strong measures." The plan was not without problems. It looked "odd," for example, for the United States Navy to stop and search United States merchant ships "for arms and Communist agents after they have loaded at United States ports; and there was no Latin American enthusiasm for an OAS consultative conference as envisioned at Caracas.[14]

To avoid the appearance of unilateral aggression, the United States was keen to have OAS support. For three weeks, the United States attempted to persuade Latin American diplomats to "invoke Caracas." Nothing happened. Friendly diplomats temporized and hedged. Beyond Somoza and Trujillo, certain allies in Honduras, and Hunt's 120 mercenaries associated with Castillo Armas, the United States had little support. Early in May, Dulles met with the ambassadors of Brazil, Panama, El Salvador, Uruguay, and other states. He acknowledged that it would "be impossible to produce evidence clearly tying the Guatemalan Government to Moscow." But Dulles insisted that the decision for "joint action" "must be a political one and based on our deep conviction that such a tie must exist." Moreover, if the Soviet Union was allowed to "establish a puppet state in this hemisphere" unsupported by and without a "threat of the Red Army," it would be "a tremendous propaganda victory" for communism. Such a victory would weaken United States "assurances to states in Asia and in Europe that we would support them in their efforts to eliminate communism . . . because of our demonstrated inability to prevent the establishment of a communist puppet state in our own hemisphere."[15]

In a lengthy unsigned report apparently distributed to congressional leaders and all friendly Latin American officials, "Soviet Communism in Guatemala," the "long range" danger of communism outside the Soviet military orbit, outside "the sphere of Soviet influence," was emphasized. If the independent "Guatemalan Way" of communism went "unchallenged by the democracies," it might over the years "be repeated in other countries to the peril of the free world."[16] Still, Brazil's Ambassador Muniz informed Holland: "Throughout Latin America there is apathy on the Communist problem and an unwillingness to face up to unpleasant measures to combat it."[17]

On 7 June, the U.S. political-action officer in Guatemala, John Hill, listed several "economic measures to keep Guatemala off balance" until the United States succeeded in arranging the "proposed OAS meeting":

(1) *Gasoline*. An effort might be made through the American oil companies and/or the Venezuelan and other Governments of petroleum supplying countries to divert tankers away from Guatemala starting now. . . . The diversion of tankers would have a strong psychological effect at once and occupy the Guatemalan authorities in searching for alternative sources of supply. As soon as the Government was forced to rationing, transportation would begin to break down with a consequent rise in public inconvenience and discontent. . . .

(2) *Credit*. Credit supplied by U.S. sources plays an important role in the Guatemalan economy. Coffee [growers] habitually obtain advances . . . from U.S. importers on their next year's crop. Agents and importers of U.S. manufactured goods obtain credit. Special credit arrangements, such as the General Motors Credit Corporation and the Chase National Bank for Ford, underwrite the credit. . . . This credit might be threatened or stopped. . . . For psychological effect, the possibilities of having an official of the National Association of Manufacturers . . . making a speech advising members to stop credit . . . would add to the tension in the country. The disadvantages are that . . . the greater portion . . . of the punishment would be on the affected business interests in Guatemala, including the several agencies run by U.S. citizens.

(3) *Flight of capital.* In 1952, when the Agrarian Reform Bill was passed, some $12 million were estimated to have fled Guatemala in a few weeks as private persons transferred funds to U.S. and other banks. This contrasts with a Guatemalan Government holding of foreign reserves of about $35 million. . . . This condition might be reproduced by the CIA with an intelligently planned out rumor and propaganda campaign. [To stimuate "a business panic"] . . . the line could be "The US is going to put in economic sanctions, the quetzal will be worthless in a few months, and now is the time to get your money out of the country." . . . There should be many channels, including selected U.S. businessmen in such firms as General Motors who could be used to tell their Guatemalan contacts that they have the "inside word" from Washington. Appropriate radio and word-of-mouth agents in Guatemala could be mobilized. If the resulting flight of capital were significant, the Guatemalan Government would be preoccupied with finding ways to meet the problem and perhaps forced into a clumsy and ill-thought-out foreign exchange program. The disadvantages appear to be primarily the ever present danger, we might be caught at it.[18]

The OAS meeting was never held. A CIA-State Department-Defense Department-USIA "Guatemalan Group" met regularly to coordinate the end game. The invasion of Guatemala was political warfare at its most detailed. Rambunctious congressmen were dissuaded from making speeches that called for landing the Marines. When it was discovered that Representative Wingate Lucas, for example, was planning such a speech, the Guatemalan Group offered to help him draft "a more statesmanlike" alternative. To obtain greater Latin American support, Eleanor Roosevelt's cooperation was encouraged. Dismissed by Eisenhower as the United States' delegate to the United Nations, Mrs. Roosevelt's relations with the Administration had remained cold. Prior objections notwithstanding, "it was decided that Mrs. Roosevelt's great prestige in Latin America offsets the problem of her relations with the Administration." A "statement would be obtained from Mrs. Roosevelt"; and efforts would be made to get statements from Ralph Bunche and a "strong follow-up" from the Vatican. The "oppression of anti-communists in Guatemala" would receive "wide publicity throughout LA." The case against Guatemala would include a summary "of all Guatemalan efforts to obtain arms," including "tentative" negotiations with Italy. On 8 June, members of the study group received specific assignments, including: "Publicity and Propaganda," "Economic Measures," "Anticipation and Rebuttal of Guatemala Case," "UN Phase of Problem," "Obtaining Cooperation of Western European Countries," "Pentagon Contacts," "Treatment of Successor Government."[19]

In Guatemala, Peurifoy kept up the tension and did nothing to encourage the urgent requests by Guatemalan officials to negotiate "differences." Officials requested meetings with United Fruit Company representatives "from Boston," as opposed to the abrasive local manager, Almyr Bump; a presidential conference between Eisenhower and Arbenz; and a "neutral non-governmental commission" to be appointed by Eisenhower and Arbenz. Peurifoy urged that Eisenhower announce in his next press conference "that he has made no proposal of any kind for discussion of differences." The "President might wish to add that he doubted [that a] visit by President Arbenz to Washington would be conducive to solution . . . as long as Communists retain their influence. . . . These statements would scotch rumors of possible direct conversations between President Eisenhower and Arbenz and would make it difficult for Toriello to persist in his claim that President Eisenhower had proposed discussion . . . by an impartial board." The Guatemalan Group instructed Peurifoy to "tell Toriello to deal directly" with the United Fruit Company.[20]

On 5 June 1954, Raymond G. Leddy wrote Peurifoy that he could rest assured: "There is 100 percent determination here, from the top down, to get rid of this stinker and not to stop until that is done. For this reason, our morale is rather high and I am sure the Embassy's will correspond as the methods utilized become more understandable."[21]

Throughout Guatemala, the methods were clearly understandable. On 3 June, Guatemala's Minister of Interior Charnaud MacDonald announced the discovery of the "best organized" plot so far. "He said it was superior in equipment and technique and that persons arrested here were only [the] vanguard of others to come from abroad."[22] On 8 June, the flight of retired Major Ferdinand Schupp, the former chief of the USAF Mission, and retired Guatemalan Colonel Rodolfo Mendoza created a stir. Schupp had retired from the Air Force in 1952 allegedly to work "in agriculture" with Prado Vélez, a former mayor of Guatemala City long identified with anti-Communist activities. He had been more recently employed as a pilot for the United Fruit Company. Schupp's career bore a striking resemblance to the unknown Carl Studer earlier identified as a key United States agent officially in the employ of United Fruit. According to the *Tribuna Popular,* "Schupp was picked up by Rodolfo Mendoza at one of the Fruit Company airports in Tiquisate." They flew to El Salvador, where they received "asylum." Newspaper response to the Schupp-Mendoza flight suggested to United States observers that there would be a future "effort to prove United States complicity in anti-Arbenz plots."[23]

In response to press accusations, Dulles sent off aggrieved telegrams to Central American embassies. The cover-up was written in angry language. Guatemala's "extraordinary" measures of "press censorship" and the "suspension of Constitutional guarantees" were "probably preliminary" to the "announcement of phony charges" that United States citizens were implicated in a "revolutionary plot against [the] Guatemalan Government." Dulles recommended that all embassies brief "U.S. news agencies . . . at once" in order to "unmask Guatemalan purposes in advance."[24]

Before the facts about the United States' role in the overthrow of Arbenz were declassified, and particularly during Eisenhower's presidency, United States newspapers or journals that printed Guatemala's charges were considered "un-American." United States citizens so briefed by United States news agencies were convinced that Guatemala's charges were "phony." During the height of the McCarthy years in the United States, democracy had become orthodoxy. To doubt that the United States was the bastion of democracy was to be a "communist dupe." United States citizens were told by President Eisenhower that "Arbenz had declared a state of siege and launched a reign of terror."[25] But the citizens of Guatemala were exposed to another set of facts. From all over the country, Arbenz received petitions for arms and instructions. Entire villages, all the labor and campesino organizations, and countless independent citizens requested equipment and military instructions to defend the country against traitors and foreign invaders.

United States assertions of a "state of siege" and a "reign of terror" notwithstanding, President Jacobo Arbenz Guzmán did not arm the people of Guatemala. He was not a Communist revolutionary. He believed, accurately, that the non-communist officer corps was nationalist and loyal, and saw no reason to challenge its authority. The Army had been demoralized by its inability to obtain arms and strongly supported all Arbenz's efforts to do so. The independent press united with the government press on Guatemala's right to purchase arms for its national defense wherever possible. Arbenz declared that Guatemala's right to import arms to defend its national sovereignty, especially when it faced the growing threat of "open intervention" was "absolutely clear and strictly just." He pointed out that Guatemala made "unfruitful attempts" for several years to purchase "military stores" from the United States; but all overtures were "systematically refused." Even requests for "pistols for police service" and such "munitions of low caliber" as sought by "hunting, shooting and fishing clubs" were routinely rejected. Therefore, Guatemala sought equipment throughout Europe. But repeatedly "pressures of unknown origin" prevented the transactions during the final moments of negotiation. In contrast to the boycott against Guatemala, the United States "apportioned arms and munitions" to various "hostile and aggressive" governments now in collusion with "shameless" counterrevolutionaries who have been preparing an armed aggression against their own country.[26]

From March to June, Arbenz made many speeches, issued many bulletins. A close watch was kept over all activities. Saboteurs were occasionally arrested. Arbenz's own intelligence agents reported the military buildup in Honduras and Nicaragua in full detail. He knew when large shipments of United States munitions landed in Honduras and had a list of thirty-one aircraft that could be used against Guatemala, including nine C-47s belonging to El Salvador, three belonging to Honduras, one belonging to the United Fruit Company, and two belonging to the United States Mission. He knew that, "from time to time," United States Marines arrived in Honduras and Nicaragua, that they were accompanied by "newsmen," and that all military movements occurred publicly —without effort at concealment. He knew that, to isolate Guatemalan officials, the embassy in Honduras was under strict surveillance. Friendly members of the diplomatic community were harassed and dissuaded from attending "any affair here for fear they will be stopped or tagged as communists."[27]

On 1 March, Arbenz had boldly asserted that the "phrase 'intervention of international communism' had lost its effectiveness as a sword of Damocles. The phantom of this phrase no longer frightened those it was supposed to frighten, but only its own inventors." As the Americas met in Caracas, Arbenz insisted that a distinction be made between the "misused" doctrine of "communist intervention," which referred to an abstract idea, and the real intervention that nations may commit. Arbenz demanded precision "according to International Law." "It is obvious," he declared, "that the Soviet Union has not intervened nor is intervening in the internal affairs of our country, nor does it menace us with intervention —contrary to what is happening to us with the dominant circles of other countries."

Later, at the time of the Geneva Conference, Guatemalan officials analyzed the movement against the Arbenz regime in terms of United States economic imperialism. Guatemala rejected the "deformed news" published about Geneva by United States press agencies to "saturate Latin America" with the idea that the conference in Geneva was "a real failure." "This hides the truth" that twenty-five nations were at Geneva to ease international tensions, extend commerce between East and West, and "facilitate the trade of national resources and manufactured products between these areas." At the same time, the Soviet Union proposed commercial relations with Latin America, proposed to buy raw materials "at a just price," offered to accept payment "in the national currency of each country," suggested a "five year" payment plan. Similarly, West Germany held a vast industrial exposition in Mexico, featuring two thousand tons of merchandise. These events, Guatemala asserted, "profoundly affected the United States industrialists, who watch with deep preoccupation the turn of world commerce." These events "threatened the capitalist superstructure of the United States," which is based on "monopoly and trusts." The Monroe Doctrine today is interpreted in an "exclusively economic" manner. The United States' objective, Guatemalan officials concluded, was to prevent the "expansion of European or Asiatic commerce" into Latin America. That is the reason for the "aggressive policy of the United States against Guatemala." It is "solely to intimidate all the Latin American Republics so that no other country shall dare, as we are doing, to extricate itself from the abusive and asphyxiating tutelage of United States economic policy."[28]

Anti-imperialist. Nationalist. Bold. But not Communist. In Marxist terms, Arbenz was not a revolutionary. Arbenz said he was not a Communist, and the United States never directly accused him of being a Communist. Of fifty-six members of Guatemala's congress in 1954, four were members of the Labor Party (Communist). There were Communists in Guatemala. Arbenz insisted on their democratic rights to exist in a country that celebrated its democracy. They dominated the CGTG and the CNCG. Throughout 1954 as they saw their nation imperiled, the unions called for arms, military instruction, active preparations to defend their nation against intervention. To arm the people would have reflected a revolutionary ideology. Arbenz's government was not revolutionary. On 4 June, the United States officially defined its understanding of the state of things. The Guatemalan Group determined: "We do not consider Guatemala dominated by international Communism. Our view is that it is extensively penetrated."[29]

The General Confederation of Guatemalan Workers (CGTG) and the National Confederation of Guatemalan Campesinos (CNCG), in June, issued a country-wide call to prevent the restoration of tyranny:

> The horrible days of the Ubiquista tyranny are still vivid in our memory, when, under the pretext of fighting communism, workers' organizations were not allowed, nor agricultural unions. . . . We have not forgotten that each factory and workshop was a concentration camp, where we were . . . burdened with all manner of punishment for the most insignificant protest or even merely to prevent one. Nor have we forgotten what life was like in the countryside, the forced labor on the roads, without any pay, the unpaid labor on the farms . . . , the theft of the land, . . . the corporal punishment. . . .
>
> The feudal-imperialist reaction makes a mistake if it thinks it can fool us with its dirty lies, with its anti-communist tricks and its divisive tales; it is mistaken if it thinks it can scare us with its threats . . . of an economic boycott . . . and armed intervention. We workers and campesinos already know in our own flesh what tyranny is, . . . what it is to live under an anti-communist regime. . . .

The important thing is to save the country. Everything must be subordinated to this great objective. . . .[30]

United States propaganda notwithstanding, Arbenz failed to respond to appeals for arms to defend Guatemala. As late as 19 May 1954, a military analysis of Guatemala's national defense revealed that all local "militias" were in disarray. The military disorganization of the countryside was considered "unpardonable." The Army had not fulfilled its "basic obligation." It was, therefore, given the urgent task of enlisting, training, restoring, and reorganizing the local militias.[31] But it was too little, and much too late.

The invasion of Guatemala began on 14 June. According to Hagerty's diary, the President was engaged in a White House "air raid drill": "The President and his immediate personal staff went to his bomb shelter with Mrs. Eisenhower . . . the new secret two-way television between the bomb shelter and High Point, the Civil Defense headquarters, was used for the first time. It operates on micro-wave and worked perfectly. . . ." Upon emerging from his bomb shelter, Eisenhower was informed by Allen Dulles that it might become necessary to prepare "some statement on Guatemala for his press conference."[32]

For his press conference, Eisenhower prepared to discuss, among other items: the fall of Laniel's government and how the French crisis would affect Indochina; the demise of the Geneva Conference—sixteen nations pulled out; "Army-McCarthy hearings with end in sight"; TVA and Atomic Energy Commission power project; and "Guatemala, anti-Red movement and Army ultimatum to President Arbenz to get rid of Communists in his government."[33] Beyond the press conference, Allen Dulles had prepared a memorandum that "had the President backing 'their form of activity in Guatemala.'" Secretary of State John Foster Dulles rejected his brother's memo "because he was afraid if the President supported the CIA, it would lead to charges that the President and this country were supporting revolutionary activities within Guatemala and would place the President in the dangerous position of appealing to citizens of a foreign country to revolt against their leaders." Eisenhower agreed with his Secretary of State, and the distinctly United States doctrine of "plausible presidential deniability" went into effect. The President would officially know nothing about the CIA's covert activity in the Americas. Instead Eisenhower would say there was upheaval in Guatemala: "A wave of arrests of anti-Communists." "Strict censorship." People "are fleeing the country." "There have been a number of killings." All activity is "typical" of the well-established "pattern" of "Communist takeover and is not in response to any external threat." The situation "was being studied by the Foreign Ministers of the American states."[34]

Secrecy was basic to the project. Every phase of the operation was marked by intricate misinformation. On 19 June, Hagerty noted in his diary that Allen Dulles called to protest that the United States press "greatly exaggerated" the situation. "Bombings" were reported. Hagerty was told: " 'There are no such planes in that part of the world. There have been a few homemade bombs dropped by Piper Cubs but that is about all.' " Also on 19 June, Robert Murphy issued a joint State-USIA circular to demand "correct handling" of the Guatemalan situation. All United States embassies were to brief correspondents to "stress internal, repeat internal, nature Guatemalan uprising. Stories, principally AP, UP past two days [have] been especially damaging to United States position. . . ." Theodore Streibert, the head of the USIA, issued a more detailed message to United States officials: "Deplore bloodshed and violence. Make plain this [is an] uprising of Guatemalans against terroristic Communist-dominated government." "Avoid use of word 'invasion.' "[35] The messages were clear: Above all, the United States press was to minimize the factor of air support, and bombings, by United States planes piloted by United States officers.

In part, Arbenz's failure to arm even the organized unions can be explained by his conviction that Guatemala's defenses were sufficient for ordinary military exigencies. The Army was loyal. The people were committed. He feared neither invasion nor popular uprising. From March to June, the statements made by Arbenz and Foreign Minister Toriello indicate that, for all the evidence they had, they never fully anticipated that Guatemala would be invaded and bombed. This was, after all, the United States' first major counterrevolution in Latin America since World War II. It involved new tactics, new strategies, new munitions. Guatemala represented a new level of political warfare, including a fully orchestrated cover-up and significant aerial bombardment.

Even after Guatemala appealed to the United Nations Security Council to take action to stop "the international crime that is being committed against Guatemala" and detailed the situation, Dulles sent a circular to all "American Diplomatic Posts" denying the "sensational newspaper stories" that exaggerated a "large scale 'Battle of Guatemala.' " Dulles insisted that there was "no evidence of bombing of capital or strafing of civilian population." He noted that press reactions had been "slow," but "leftist newspapers reported to be slanting reports in favor of Communist-oriented groups" eager "to put [the] blame on [the] United States."[36] But Guatemala's case was so persuasive that even the United States' closest allies, Britian and France, wavered.

On 19 and 20 June, Toriello presented the following petition to the United Nations:

On May 26 [1954] unidentified planes coming from Honduras and Nicaragua violated Guatemalan territory, [flew] over Guatemala City and dropped propaganda which incited the Guatemalan Army to revolt against the legitimate and constitutional Government. . . . On June 14 the planes . . . parachuted arms and ammunition in the Tiquisate Zone, Headquarters of the [Agricultural Company of Guatemala], subsidiary of the United Fruit Company. Such arms apparently are of Soviet and American manufacture. . . . On June 15 the intruding planes again violated our territory. . . . On June 16 there was another incursion, apparently for reconnaissance, in various areas of the country. On June 17 . . . the expeditionary forces . . . captured the Guatemalan frontier post of El Florido, in the Department of Chiquimula, and later advanced about fifteen kilometers into Guatemalan territory. Those forces still remain inside our territory, and we have not ordered that they be repelled, precisely to avoid other pretexts. . . . This morning aircraft coming from Honduras and Nicaragua have attacked the country, dropping explosive bombs on fuel stores at the port of San José and in the City of Retalhuleu. At four P.M. today P-47 planes of American manufacture, also coming from those two countries, attacked Guatemala City, strafing Government buildings and private dwellings, and bombing military bases. Those same planes later attacked the military base at the Port of San José. . . .

In addition, Toriello continued:

I. June 18: (a) During the night, the passenger train from Guatemala to Puerto Barrios was machine-gunned and forced to stop. The attackers, who had previously blown up the bridge at Gualán, compelled the train to take them to the town of Entre Ríos, where they tore up rails, destroyed both national and railroad (IRCA) telephone and telegraph lines, and forced the engineer to cut off the steam. At dawn, the rebels went back to . . . Honduras.

(b) At 11:50 P.M. an unidentified P-47 plane attacked the Guatemalan capital and a few minutes later dropped arms and ammunition by parachute in the area of Nuevo Vinas, Villa Canales, and Palencia.

(c) On the same night, two planes flew over the western part of Guatemala, dropping subversive propaganda.

II. June 19:   (a) At 8:00 A.M. an unidentified plane attacked the capital and three others dropped arms over the villages of Los Mixcos and Potrero Grande. . . . The plane that attacked the capital repeated its act against the military district of Zacapa and then, in the city of Chiquimula, machine-gunned the Girls' Normal School. In the attack on the capital, the plane strafed civilians. . . .

(b) At 11:00 A.M. another unidentified plane dropped bombs on the gasoline tanks at Puerto Barrios.

(c) At 12:00 noon mercenary invasion forces occupied the town of Esquipulas and at 3:00 P.M., the town of Jocotán, both in the Department of Chiquimula. . . .

(i) Several unidentified planes dropped arms and ammunition at different times during the day in different places. . . . This armament was picked up by the towns people and voluntarily turned over to the nearest authorities. . . .

III. June 20:   (a) At 8:35 A.M. an unidentified plane bombed and damaged the Cristina bridge. . . .

(b) At 8:55 the same plane strafed the town of San Juan la Ermita in the same district. . . .

In conclusion, Toriello pointed out that "one of the planes which attacked this capital fell" over Mexico, "that the two pilots are American, and that one of them is wounded." Moreover, contrary to "the false reports published abroad," there "has been no uprising in any part of Guatemala. . . ."[37]

On 20 June, the UN Security Council unanimously adopted a vaguely worded French resolution that called for the "immediate termination of any action likely to cause bloodshed." A United States-backed resolution introduced by Brazil and Colombia would have sent the situation to the OAS. But the Soviet Union vetoed it. Charles Bohlen sent Dulles *Tass*'s editorial from Moscow: "Lodge, having lost self-control, demanded in a temper that [the] Soviet Union keep away from [the] Western Hemisphere." But, *Tass* editorialized, "aggression has no territorial limits." Apart from such commentary, there is no evidence that the Soviet Union made any effort to support Arbenz or interfere with the hemispheric realities of the Americas.

Eisenhower was considerably more rattled by British and French opposition. Even after the United States agreed to Britain's preliminary demand that the OAS send its own peace observers to Guatemala, British officials continued to insist on United Nations observation—as proposed by the Soviet Union. The situation threatened to create a serious and public rift between the allies. Eisenhower's famous temper was aroused. He agreed with Dulles that there were many instances when "the differences between the United States and the U.K. were becoming almost unbearable." The President wanted to get tough with the British and show them that "they have no right to stick their nose into matters which concern this hemisphere entirely." Hagerty reported Eisenhower's conclusion: "The British expect us to give them a free ride and side with them on Cyprus and yet they won't even support us on Guatemala. Let's give them a lesson."

Henry Cabot Lodge told Britain's UN representative that Guatemala "was very close to us, as close as Ireland is to him." And now Britain "undercut our whole effort to maintain an Organization of American States." Lodge, who happened to preside over the UN Security Council during June 1954, said he "would not take any steps whatever to call a meeting" until Britain and France reconsidered. Finally, Lodge informed the British and French representatives that while he did not mean to threaten them "because of course they represented strong independent governments that would do whatever they wanted," he did want them to know that Eisenhower had instructed him to say that

> If Great Britain and France felt that they must take an independent line backing the present government of Guatemala, we would feel free to take an equally independent line concerning such matters as Egypt and North Africa in which we had hitherto tried to exercise the greatest forbearance. . . .

Lodge informed Dulles that his announcement "was received with great solemnity."

But the situation only changed during the Churchill-Eden visit to the White House. All the way in from the airport, Dulles hammered away on the issue. He argued that the very existence of the Inter-American Council, and presumably all regional bodies, was "at stake." He insisted that to put the issue into the Security Council would be "a body blow to the rights of the American States." For two days, Eisenhower and Dulles talked with Churchill and Eden. Although there is to date no record of those conversations, Britain and France agreed, grudgingly, to abstain. The United States' victorious vote, therefore, was five to four, "close but decisive."

Diplomatic difficulties, the loss of supporting aircraft, the absence of popular support for Castillo Armas' "small band," and, as Dulles wrote, the fact that there were "no significant defections from [Guatemala's] armed forces" threatened the entire operation.[38]

Like the Bay of Pigs, the operation in Guatemala was predicated on the assumption that as soon as the "liberationist" troops appeared, the people would rise up and overthrow the hated Communists. According to the CIA, Castillo Armas' movement was not "in any sense a conventional military operation. He is dependent for his success . . . upon the possibility that his entry . . . will touch off a general uprising. . . ." But the appearance of Castillo Armas and his one hundred forty unknown and unappreciated "liberators" did not result in mass revulsion against Arbenz, or even mass hysteria. Instead, campesinos surrounded and occupied United Fruit Company lands; a local civil guard captured a munitions supply ship, the Siesta, which flew the Honduran flag and was filled with machine guns and hand grenades; antiaircraft guns shot down at least two aircraft; and the Army failed to mutiny.[39]

The State Department considered the situation potentially disastrous. Such Latin American leaders as Somoza and Batista were aghast at the lack of popular response. Dismay and panic followed the gloomy reports. The United States ambassador in El Salvador cabled John Foster Dulles that the "lack of substantial progress by Castillo Armas" and the absence of any "uprising against [the] government" have resulted in the fear that Honduras, "already jeopardized" by strikes against the United Fruit Company, may be attacked by Guatemala, and the further fear that Guatemala "will not have to invade other Central American countries as they will each fall one by one through Communist penetration."[40]

Only Guatemala's inability to defend itself against aerial bombardment assured the success of this vastly unpopular enterprise. When Toriello urged Peurifoy to use his good influences to get the United States to "stop the bloodshed," he noted that Guatemala's forces "were completely successful on the ground but could not cope with air attacks." Peurifoy, with the kind of contempt that had made him so famous in Greece, replied that the United States could not stop "Armas without landing [the] Marines."[41] The truth was that the United States could not help Castillo Armas without the Air Force.

On 22 June, the United States decided to send additional fighter-bombers to Castillo. That was the conclusive decision. In his 1963 memoirs, Eisenhower took full credit for it. In a meeting with Allen and John Foster Dulles and Henry Holland, Eisenhower wrote, Holland "made no secret of his conviction that the United States should keep hands off, insisting that other Latin American republics would, if our action became known, interpret our shipment of planes as intervention in Guatemala's internal affairs." But Eisenhower was persuaded by the others, who believed that the bombers were "the only hope for Castillo Armas, who was obviously the only hope of restoring freedom to Guatemala."

> "What do you think Castillo's chances would be," Eisenhower asked Dulles, "without the aircraft?"
> His answer was unequivocal: "About zero."
> "Suppose we supply the aircraft . . . ?" Again the CIA chief did not hesitate: "About 20 percent."

Eisenhower was persuaded. It seemed, he wrote, that to refuse direct support "to a strictly anti-Communist faction in this struggle would be contrary to the letter and spirit of the Caracas resolution." After the meeting, to "break the tension," Eisenhower said:

> "Allen, the figure of 20 percent was persuasive. . . . If you had told me that the chances would be 90 percent, I would have had a much more difficult decision." Allen was equal to the situation. "Mr. President, . . . when I saw Henry walking into your office with three large lawbooks under his arm, I knew he had lost his case already."[42]

Within five days of that decision, President Jacobo Arbenz Guzmán resigned. A victim of a new phase of "psychological" warfare, the chief weapons used against him had been "deception and timing." Minimal air cover and "the massive use of radio broadcasting" created the impression that his enemies possessed awesome, endless power. According to E. Howard Hunt, the CIA transmitter broadcasting from Honduras "overrode the Guatemalan national radio." All messages had one purpose: "to confuse and divide the population." According to Richard Bissell, all communications between Guatemala City and the countryside were cut off because of "some jamming that we did." Guatemala's entire communication system was disrupted. Arbenz "didn't know what was going on in the front. He heard confused rumors . . . wildly different rumors." It was a "time of the greatest uncertainty." And then the wounded began to arrive. Trainloads of dead and wounded mysteriously railroaded from the countryside to the city had, according to Bissell, "a very powerful" impact on Arbenz.[43]

Like State Department spokesmen, CIA spokesman Bissell minimized the extent of aircraft activity. There were, he said, only four "obsolete small aircraft in operation at any given time." They flew over, dropped "a few bombs, and interspersed these . . . with empty Coca-Cola bottles which made the same sound and were about as effective." Presumably these Coca-Cola bottles caused Arbenz's nerves to "collapse." And, according to Bissell, "the breaking of his nerve" ended the fight. Recently declassified documents reveal that Coca-Cola bottles had nothing to do with Arbenz's decision to step down. The survival of his country, the continuation of the revolution in the hands of his loyal military successors, and a belief that by his resignation the people of Guatemala might be spared further bombings, the possible use of napalm and the kind of bacteriological warfare that the Guatemalans believed the United States had used in Korea all contributed to his decision.

On 25 June, Toriello appealed to John Foster Dulles to intercede on behalf of peace:

> I regret to inform your excellency that a savage attack with TNT bombs took place yesterday on the civilian population of Chiquimula as well as strafing of that city and the cities of Gualán and Zacapa. . . .

These planes were flown from Honduras, and Guatemala knew that there were other planes based in Nicaragua. "We have information that from today until Sunday such pirate planes will massively bomb the capital of this republic." Toriello explained to Dulles that Guatemala lacked "modern aircraft to repel them owing to [the] United States boycott," and was incapable of defending itself. Therefore Guatemala

> asks that your enlightened government, always respectful of the human rights of which it has been the standard-bearer, be good enough to intercede with the security council of the United Nations so that its resolution . . . regarding an immediate cessation of all activity provoking bloodshed not be flouted. . . .

Toriello concluded his urgent message with an expression of confidence that "your Excellency's enlightened government and the people of your cultured nation will condemn the inhuman and criminal aggression." Two days later, Toriello was more direct. He told Peurifoy that he knew that the United States could stop the fighting "in fifteen minutes" if it wished. But the bombings did not stop until Guatemala accepted the leadership of Castillo Armas.[44]

By 27 June, Arbenz had agreed to resign and turn over the government to Colonel Carlos Enrique Díaz, chief of the armed forces. Díaz began his introductory conference with Peurifoy by describing the "horrible situation created by the aerial bombardment of Chiquimula and Zacapa." The towns were "virtually wiped out." Díaz said "Castillo could not have obtained these arms without United States acquiescence." Peurifoy "replied sharply" that if Díaz had called this meeting "to make accusations against my government, I would leave immediately." Díaz apologized, and inquired what the "United States would wish in return if it used its good offices to end the fighting." Peurifoy, "constantly emphasizing" that he could speak only as an individual and not for the United States, repeated that there "was only one important problem between our governments: That of Communism."

On 28 June, Colonel Díaz assumed power. He had promised to outlaw the Communist Party, send prominent Communists into exile, invoke martial law, and establish a "pro-U.S. government." But he refused to negotiate with Castillo Armas. Díaz and his colleagues told Peurifoy that they "would rather die than talk with him." He could "never govern Guatemala after [the] massacres his air forces caused." Peurifoy was equally adamant. He "felt very deeply" the "necessity of implanting democracy as far as local conditions permitted and that all sectors of [the] population" should be represented, "including those who have followed Castillo Armas' anti-Communist movement."[45]

Díaz's intransigence extended beyond his refusal to negotiate with Castillo Armas. When Peurifoy brought him a "long list" of Communists to be shot "within 24 hours," Díaz refused. He was replaced the next day by Colonel Elfego Monzon, a "real anti-Communist."[46] For the United States, democracy would not be implanted in Guatemala until Castillo Armas assumed power. Moreover, the bombings continued until the ruling military accepted his authority. Even Peurifoy was displeased by that. On 29 June, he called Washington to ask "if there wasn't some way to get word to Armas to stop it. . . . The new people were being greatly embarrassed and were in a 'flap.'" He didn't know "what was going to happen." On 30 June, he arranged for a meeting between Monzon and Castillo Armas in El Salvador. On 3 July, after difficult negotiations, Castillo flew into Guatemala City in the United States' embassy plane, escorted by "nine army planes and three C-47 transports."[47]

President Eisenhower, with unusual mendacity, claimed that Castillo Armas "enjoyed the devotion of his people." John Foster Dulles asserted: "Now the future of Guatemala lies at the disposal of the Guatemalan people themselves." Counterinsurgency in Guatemala "represented a great triumph for American diplomacy." For the United States, it was all over except for the cosmetics, the cover-up, and the intensified capital investments. According to E. Howard Hunt, "nearly all personnel associated with the successful project received awards or commendations." And the award-winning team, including Hunt and Peurifoy, was reassigned to Indochina.[48]

Dulles ordered all United States embassies to deny "allegations" that United States treaty arms were used in the "rebel action against Guatemala." The United States' "bilateral aid treaties with Nicaragua, Honduras, and eight other republics exist," Dulles explained, "only for the mutual defense of the Western hemisphere."[49] An effort was made to apply a liberal patina to Castillo Armas' style. In political warfare, style was, after all, everything.

To minimize the criticism of influential "non-Communist labor leaders" throughout Latin America, Dulles cabled Peurifoy, "it would be most helpful . . . if President Castillo would publicly emphasize support for free non-Communist labor unions and improved urban and rural living and working conditions." The State Department planned to stimulate the "free labor movement" in Guatemala in every possible and "discreet way." "United States labor organizations and ORIT" were "to give appropriate guidance . . . to insure [Guatemala's] genuine and lasting adherence to the democratic labor movement."[50] To demonstrate that labor's problems with United States companies were due to communism, Peurifoy urged Dulles to persuade the Grace Company and the United Fruit Company to make immediate and congenial contact with the new government and to negotiate new and generous contracts. Acknowledging the difficulties with Bump, Peurifoy suggested that the UFCO send a "high official from Boston" for the "actual negotiations." In addition, the United States resumed support for the Inter-American highway, which had been almost completed when all international loans were suspended; organized a joint U.S.-Guatemalan project to stimulate the "prompt renewal of Guatemala's trade and tourist activity," which the United States had carefully sabotaged for over five years; and helped negotiate a new Petroleum Code, whereby United States companies "received concessions for the exploration of 4,600,000 hectares, which was almost half the national territory."[51]

But all was not well in the Guatemala of Castillo Armas. He did not share Dulles' enthusiasm for democratic affect. All of Castillo Armas' anti-Communist activities were overt. Harvests were burned and an unknown number of campesinos were killed in a frenzy of terror that accompanied the cancellation of the agrarian reform law. Unions were outlawed and the mood of even anti-Communist labor leaders was somber because, according to a State Department report, "of the indiscriminate and uncontrolled action by employers in the guise of 'anti-Communism.'" Hundreds of political and labor leaders went into exile. Over nine thousand people were arrested and many were tortured. To this day, there is no record of the number of Arbenz supporters massacred during the weeks of terror. All atrocities reported were attributed to Arbenz. Thomas McCann, who directed United Fruit's publicity campaigns and claimed that the company was "involved at every level" of the operation, wrote about "some reasonably believable atrocity pictures." There were photographs of bodies, "some had been castrated—about to be buried in a mass grave. The photos got the widest possible circulation and Arbenz got all the credit. For all I know, they could just as easily have been the victims of either side. . . . The point is, they were widely accepted for what they were purported to be—victims of communism."[52]

Under the banner of "God, Fatherland, Liberty," Castillo Armas dedicated his government to the "total and definitive eradication of communism and convinced communists, confessed or concealed, as well as those who hide them." "Communists and Communist sympathizers" would be "purged" from public service and education.[53] Castillo Armas suspended all political parties and disenfranchised the majority of Guatemala's voters. According to a State Department report, Castillo Armas disenfranchised "three-quarters of Guatemala's population which are illiterate, a move which has long been considered necessary by anti-Communists who saw the Arbenz regime manipulate this vote."[54]

On the issue of communist eradication, Castillo differed with Dulles only on the issue of asylum. Castillo Armas insisted on the traditional Latin American custom of political asylum. John Foster Dulles had suggested that Chile, Argentina, and Mexico "refuse asylum to Commies" and that Communist leaders be "captured" so that they "would not be free to plot and direct any remaining Communist cells from abroad." But the right of refuge and exile was honored, and Castillo agreed to safe-conducts for Arbenz, Toriello, Víctor Manuel Gutiérrez, Carlos Manuel Pellecer, and over eighty others, including Che Guevara,* "without prior consul-

---

* Che Guevara credited his experience in Arbenz's Guatemala with revolutionizing his life. When he began his career as a physician, he "dreamed of working indefatigably to discover something which would be used to help humanity, but which signified a personal triumph for me. I was, as we all are, a child of my environment." His travels throughout the Americas, his "close contact with poverty, hunger, and disease" awakened a commitment "to help those people," and he "began to investigate what was needed to be a revolutionary doctor." But it

tation" with the United States embassy. By 27 August, Castillo had issued two hundred safe-conducts. Dulles was appalled. Peurifoy felt "double-crossed." For Dulles, "diplomatic asylum" had nothing to do with Communists, whose "political offenses" were international and who should, therefore, be considered a "class additional to common criminals not entitled [to] asylum."[56]

But Castillo Armas' momentary defection was evidently forgiven over time. In 1963, Eisenhower remembered him as "a far-seeing and able statesman." During Richard Nixon's March 1955 tour of Latin America, he visited Guatemala. He reported that Castillo Armas was "a good President who said" to the Vice-President of the United States: "Tell us what you want us to do and that's what we will do." Although Nixon noted that Castillo was "opposed by both the Left and Right," Nixon believed the new President had "the overwhelming support of the Guatemalan people." Presumably Nixon referred to the 75 percent of the people who remained disenfranchised.[57]

In any case, Castillo Armas was assassinated in July 1957. Eisenhower sent his son, Major John S. D. Eisenhower, to the funeral. The symbolic importance of Guatemala to the United States' political-warfare efforts remained high. Guatemala was the only country that had overthrown "communism" since the Spanish Civil War. Therefore, Major Eisenhower reported, it "takes on an importance far out of proportion to its size." But, he noted, the "long-range prospects for achieving political stability in Guatemala are unfortunately highly doubtful."[58]

They were in fact nonexistent. From that time to this, in Dulles' words, "the future of Guatemala lies at the disposal of the Guatemalan people themselves." Despite enormous sums in direct economic and military aid, estimated to have been as high as $90 million up to 1957, and much more subsequently, neither peace nor

---

was not until Arbenz's government was overthrown that he "realised a fundamental thing: For one to be a revolutionary doctor or to be a revolutionary at all, there must first be a revolution. Isolated individual endeavor . . . is of no use, and the desire to sacrifice an entire lifetime to the noblest ideals serves no purpose if one works alone, solitarily, in some corner of America." Che Guevara wrote that he realized as the bombs helped to topple the progressive but unprepared Arbenz government that a revolution required "the mobilization of a whole people, who learn by use of arms and the exercise of military unity to understand the value of arms and the value of this unity."[55]

stability has been established. The overthrow of the Arbenz government, the return of almost a million and a half acres that had been distributed among one hundred thousand families, the abolition of 533 unions, the general repression—all unleashed a pattern of terror and violence which have over time become more cruel, more deadly. From that day to this, the people of Guatemala have been engaged in continual struggle.[59]

From 1960 to 1963, Castillo Armas' successor, General Ydígoras Fuentes, was under continual attack by rival military leaders, who resented the fact that Guatemala was used as a training base for the overthrow of Castro's Cuba and served as the command post for the Bay of Pigs operation. Throughout the 1960s, rival left groups emerged. Each was dominated by former members of Guatemala's officer corps who defected to organize increasingly revolutionary guerrilla activities. The majority of them had been trained by the United States in the Pentagon's School of the Americas in the Panama Canal Zone or at one of its international war colleges at Fort Benning, Fort Leavenworth, and Fort Bragg. Trained and equipped by the United States, they specifically repudiated the democratic process and condemned Arbenz's parliamentary path to change and his failure to arm and revolutionize the people. In contrast, they took to the mountains to build a mass guerrilla base. In an effort to wipe out this growing movement, a major counterinsurgency operation, called a "pacification campaign," in 1966 resulted in the slaughter of three thousand to eight thousand Guatemalans, mostly in the countryside.[60]

From 1967 to the present, terrorism and torture have dominated Guatemala's political life. In 1967, the United States and German ambassadors were assassinated. In 1970, a state of siege was declared. Between 1970 and 1973, over two thousand people were killed. Amnesty International's 1976 report on *Guatemala* estimated that the number of "deaths and disappearances" between 1966 and 1976 exceeded twenty thousand. Today, Guatemala continues to be enveloped in violence. On 29 May 1978, one hundred Kekchi Indians were massacred. They had peacefully gathered in a public square to protest a forced removal from their traditional lands. Riots occurred in Guatemala City. Over thirty demonstrators were killed. The government fell.

General Lucas' successor government is reported to have the worst human rights record in Guatemalan history. Between July 1978 and June 1979, murder, torture, and mutilation destroyed the lives of thousands of Guatemalans. Death lists are boldly published. Student leaders have been machine-gunned after making public speeches. University faculty have disappeared. Between January and September 1980, thirty-eight students and fifteen professors—the majority of the School of Law—have been murdered or kidnaped. Catholic priests who have criticized the repression have been killed, along with high government officials and political leaders of moderate parties.

Finally, the long-cherished Latin American custom of refuge and asylum, as well as all international traditions of sovereignty and decency, were blown to bits on 31 January 1980, when the Spanish embassy in Guatemala City was attacked. Thirty petitioners, mostly campesinos from El Quiché, in the mineral-rich North, entered the embassy to ask Ambassador Máximo Cajal y López "as a distinguished humanitarian to intercede on their behalf" against the outrages committed by the Guatemalan Army in their villages. The ambassador had accepted the request. Spanish authorities in Spain and Guatemala City specifically demanded that the "inviolability of the embassy be respected." But the building was overrun. Chemical incendiaries were thrown; people were machine-gunned indiscriminately. Thirty-nine people, including seven Spanish embassy employees, were killed. Ambassador Cajal called the action "brutal and indescribable." Spain broke diplomatic relations with Guatemala in protest. When, on 2 February, fifty thousand Guatemalans protested, the demonstrators were attacked. Many were wounded, and two leaders of the "Autonomous Trade Union" were killed.

Since 1978, the campesinos have been the primary focus of the terror. They are once again the main victims of capital expansion. The United Fruit Company, now United Brands, has been eclipsed. Guatemala is a resource-rich land. And in the North, where tungsten and nickel have replaced bananas as major export commodities, campesinos—still largely illiterate and impoverished—are being forcibly removed, and occasionally massacred. In such provinces as El Petén, El Quiché, Izabal, and Alta Verapaz, the people are being removed by the land's new owners. Hispano Oil, Getty Oil, and Exmibal—an affiliate of International Nickel.[61]

For the people of Guatemala, Eisenhower's 1954 legacy has been an endless battle against terror and death. Although the United States has used Eisenhower's Guatemalan model over and over again, for thirty years there have been no final victories.

CHAPTER VIII
THE ECONOMICS OF EISENHOWER'S AMERICAN CENTURY

Counterinsurgency was not meant to be an end in itself. It was not supposed to become the United States' way of life. It was to be an interim policy that would continue to ensure an acceptable political climate for private investment expansion overseas. The goal of the American Century was not, after all, to establish tyrannical and repressive regimes abroad while destroying the domestic economy of the United States. It was to promote the American way of life throughout the world. The American Century would end peonage and suffering. It would thereby eliminate interest in communism and ensure a global marketplace for American goods and services. American strategists were very clear about their goals during the halcyon days of their vision—before and directly after World War II.[1]

In the face of the communist threat to withdraw vast areas from capitalist investment, the traditional United States debate beween "free traders" and "protectionists" began to subside. Postwar opposition to "isolationists" who preferred protective tariffs to reciprocity reflected a growing demand for economic ideological unity within the business community and among U.S. politicians. Although U.S. international economic expansion had been an ongoing process for over fifty years,* the postwar situation created an unprecedented unity of purpose. The Cold War was not merely embraced by the business community, it helped to create an appropriate political climate for self-righteous economic expansion protected by greater government support.

With Europe devastated and the colonial world afloat, the boldest businessmen did not talk about maximizing profits. They talked about all the new worlds to liberate. Their rhetoric was couched in liberal terms of freedom, security, anti-communism, and internationalism. In 1949, General Motors' slogan was, "When better worlds are built, individual enterprise will build them." The organized effort to globalize "individual enterprise" resulted in a newly intensified and odd coupling between big business and big government. "Free enterprise" became more and more dependent on the diplomatic and military services of free government. Building upon long-standing tradition, regular meetings, conventions, and trade missions were increasingly cosponsored by the State Department, the National Association of Manufacturers (NAM), bankers, the National Free Trade Council, and the United States section of the International Chamber of Commerce (ICC). The private sector embraced the public sector, and made it its own. Robert Taft was shocked by the indecency of it all. Such old-fashioned, nationalist conservatives as Taft and George Humphrey failed to appreciate the calculating logic involved in the spectacle of private interests appealing to the public sector for support, legitimacy, and worldwide military protection. The creation of a system whereby the state would expend billions of dollars each year to protect, ensure, coddle, and promote private interests for strictly private profit organized into vast merger-monopolies and international cartels was boldly expanded in the postwar world. Nobody named it imperialism. Nobody named it at all. For years, it was shrouded in cliché, draped modestly in the mystique of free enterprise.

---

* According to Mira Wilkins, the size of "U.S. direct foreign investment in 1914 comprised a sum equal to 7 percent of the U. S. GNP." In 1966 "direct investment abroad by U.S. business" remained 7 percent of the U. S. GNP. Her point is that despite the vast differences in dollars invested ($54.6 billion in 1966, as compared to $2.65 billion in 1914), foreign business has been central to U.S. domestic business interests from the beginning. (See Wilkins, *The Emergence of Multinational Enterprise: American Business Abroad from the Colonial Era to 1914*, Harvard University Press, 1970, pp. 201–2.)

In 1949, members of the United States commission of the ICC met to discuss the "socialization" of Europe, notably Britain, France, and Italy. Members of the ICC decided that "free enterprise will wither in the U.S. if it dies elsewhere." They committed themselves to the expansion of international trade. Private capital would "not survive unless we have free enterprise in other countries." "The best way of supporting and promoting our own way of life is to work toward the expansion of international trade." The United States was "the last stand for the principle of free enterprise." The businessmen of America pledged themselves to "a crusade" to save "economic liberalism" by spreading "the idea of free commercial enterprise around the face of the globe." Their first requirement was to find "somebody to fight for the world we want." Taft refused, Dewey failed, and Truman was judged, somehow and for little reason, a class enemy.[2]

Despite his shabby status with United States exporters, Truman worked conscientiously to improve the conditions of international economic expansion. In addition to the Marshall Plan and the Point Four Program, he appointed William S. Paley to chair a committee to study world resources, and Nelson Rockefeller to chair an Advisory Board on International Economic Development. On 31 March 1950, Truman appointed Gordon Gray to prepare a comprehensive study of the United States' foreign economic policies and procedures. Rockefeller's first task was to appraise the Gray Report. Truman facilitated the postwar call for a business-government partnership for international investment.[3]

Rockefeller was a leading advocate of a world economic policy based on government-business cooperation. His efforts were supported by Roosevelt, Truman, and Eisenhower. Roosevelt appointed him head of the State Department's Office of Inter-American Affairs, which helped to create the Committee for Economic Development in December 1942. A nominally private operation, members of CED worked closely with the State Department's Commission for Inter-American Development. Members of both committees included Jesse Jones, Secretary of Commerce; William L. Clayton, Assistant Secretary of Commerce; William Benton; and Paul Hoffman. After the war, the Rockefeller brothers created the American International Association for Economic and Social Development (AIA) and the International Basic Economy

Corporation (IBEC). At IBEC's founding, in July 1946, Nelson Rockefeller declared that "the sooner all of us recognize the fact that the welfare of the world is indivisible . . . and that our freedom and the freedom of the people of other nations are inseparable, the sooner we will be able to face the gigantic task of raising the standard of living of peoples of all lands."

For Rockefeller it was "a matter of mutual self-interest," and it required a bold new partnership between business and capital. "The United States government can make international agreements, loan funds, and cooperate in innumerable ways." But the government "cannot go abroad and develop the production of goods and services." During the previous century, Rockefeller noted, private enterprise went to those areas that promised the greatest profit. Today that was not enough. "Today capital must go where it can produce the most goods, render the greatest service, meet the most pressing needs of the people. Wherever it goes, it is the function of capital to serve and not to exploit"; to awaken dormant local capital and create an entirely new partnership for growth. To his father, John D. Rockefeller, Jr., Nelson explained the objectives of AIA: to provide leadership in helping people help themselves to combat "poverty, disease and illiteracy"; to strengthen "self-sufficiency and independence of the individual, the basic forces which make possible the growth and development of the democratic system." Nelson Rockefeller was convinced that this was "the hope for future peace and security in the world." Given the magnitude of the problem, it required government support. It seemed to Rockefeller "almost preposterous for a private group to enter this field" unprotected. His "ultimate hope" was that "our government" would "recognize the importance" of international economic development.[4] More liberal than many of his colleagues, Rockefeller, along with America's other leading businessmen, had a fundamental purpose: economic expansion and control.

Rockefeller and his associates distinguished their goals from those that inspired the Marshall Plan. Although the preamble of the Marshall Plan dedicated it to the revival of free trade in Europe, the organized business community deplored its public financial arrangements. It was a government-to-government operation that depended on government-to-government loans. It was a necessary first step, a stopgap measure of minimal value except "to stop civil war in France and Italy." The United States Commission of the ICC and the Committee on Business Participation in Foreign Economic Development surveyed the planet and saw an open door to a free market of endless bounty. There were "one hundred times more jobs to be done abroad than in the U.S. today." Their goal was to replace "bloated" public efforts dominated by "labor" governments with private financing, private profits, private enterprise.

The primary connection between free enterprise and the free world was free trade: the freedom to buy earth's resources at the lowest possible cost and sell manufactured products at the highest possible price. To do that required an appropriate investment climate: stable international relations, agreeable allies, respectful clients. The government could, therefore, be of service to the organized business community. Members of the United States section of the ICC agreed: "We wouldn't like to see our trade under government authority." To use the government's resources and services, and to be free of government regulations, the new international business crusade would begin with "a slow march back" from "statism."[5]

On 9 January 1950, Lowell P. Weicker, president of E. R. Squibb & Sons, explained the U.S.-ICC's position: "For thirty years the world has been moving toward socialism—more government, less freedom; more central planning, less incentive for individual enterprise. Many countries have gone completely overboard. We in America have not done that, but we are well on the way. And we cannot stop the trend unless other countries do." The U.S.-ICC called upon governments and business to forge a united venture that would "break the bonds that shackle individual enterprise." To save the world from communism, government should help to stimulate and expand the "flow" of "private foreign investments."[6]

To save the world from communism, the United States Government should adopt a sound policy to "induce" private investments in foreign countries. Private capital should not, after all, be asked to risk its profits in the dangerous waters of statism and upheaval. The inducements would include tax incentives, dramatic changes in the United States' antitrust laws, "guaranties" against "the risk of loss as the result of war, civil strife, or confiscation." "The United States Government might allow, for tax purposes, a very rapid depreciation of foreign plants owned by U.S nationals." "The United States Government might extend loans for private foreign investments, repayment to be dependent upon profits."[7] The modest and reluctant private sector thus demanded from the United States Government a long and careful courtship, and a dowry.

With sufficient inducements, "men in charge of exports," men C. D. Jackson called the "key Americans," would be able to sell American capitalism "to a not particularly receptive world." Jackson insisted on the word "capitalism" and told the Export Managers Club of New York that "we had better use the word 'capitalism' because that is what this country represents." Jackson and *Fortune* were active on every level of the postwar campaign for international trade. In 1947, Jackson promoted Harold Stassen, a Republican presidential contender, who "was willing to stick his neck out, flatly, for two-way world trade—imports as well as exports." Advocates of world trade were bipartisan, and Jackson applauded them all: Averell Harriman, then Secretary of Commerce; "Scotty" Reston, "a wonderful international economic reporter" who had written that the United States cannot remain "politically internationalist and economically isolationist"; Philip Reed, of General Electric; John Foster Dulles, "that grand old man"; ex-Secretary of State Cordell Hull; Paul Hoffman, of Studebaker; members of the AF of L and the CIO: Phil Murray, Bill Green, Jim Carey; Charles Edward Wilson, of General Electric; Thomas Watson, of IBM—"why, the roster of people who today are willing to stand up and be counted on the side of the angels is absolutely incredible." And they were supported by the Advertising Council, which mounted "a national campaign for world trade and travel"; the Foreign Policy Association, which stimulated "community-level education"; and The Twentieth Century Fund, which produced a movie on world trade. The U.S.-ICC would organize the businessmen. In 1947, C. D. Jackson announced: "You are no longer just merchants. You are businessmen. You are politicians. You are economists. You are statesmen. . . . Because this year the United States is going to assume the political and economic leadership of the world, boldly and honestly, or it is going to abdicate that leadership and force the peoples of the world . . . to look to the East."[8]

To fight for the world they wanted, the organized business community chose General Eisenhower. Their chosen instrument was selected more for political reasons than ideological ones. Eisenhower was popular, globally popular. He studied hard and learned fast. He understood power, and had charisma. But he did not initially share many of the values and purposes of his mentors. At the end of World War II, he naïvely wondered why the world's resources could not be internationalized. He was, for example, overheard to explain that since raw materials represented the world's basic needs, they should belong to and serve everybody. In 1950, he wrote Swede Hazlett: "I likewise thought that we would develop means and methods of producing the munitions of war, including stockpiling, without profit to anyone." "In these assumptions I was, of course, proved quite wrong."[9] One of the more bitter ironies of our recent history is the extent to which Eisenhower's presidency would help to create and to promote the very military-industrial complex he sincerely deplored.

Eisenhower did not create "the warfare state." He did, in fact, more than his successors to restrain the overwhelming growth of that tendency in American economic life. He did not invest endless troops and countless dollars in Vietnam. His first budgetary act in 1953 was to cut $5 billion out of the Air Force's appropriations—creating an uproar that resulted in the fantasized "bomber gap." Eisenhower deplored "crooked" and "selfish" military-industrialists who mobilized America's advertising agencies to lobby sales for extravagant and experimental missile projects. When he curtailed the Nike-Hercules and Nike-Zeus projects, another uproar ensued: the fraudulent "missile gap." Consistently, from 1952 to 1960, Eisenhower warned that it was possible to bankrupt America, destroy the value of the dollar, create an inflationary danger that would ruin the American way of life. Throughout his two terms in office, he gave serious consideration to "a sound currency." The tension between demands for unlimited military spending and demands for the easy outflow of private capital for the development of foreign markets, and Eisenhower's insistence on the stability of America's basic economy, heightened over time.

On the other hand, Eisenhower presided over the formation of every major institutional change that enthroned the military-industrialists. Also, the transnational corporations in their contemporary form were expanded and nurtured during his presidency. Increasingly, the defense industries served to strengthen the world economy. Munificent defense contracts, generous tax policies, and advantageous cartel arrangements stimulated the growth of the transnationals. Rapidly expanding, internationally based conglomerates benefited from both enormous military-industrial profits and such stability as the military-industrial complex could provide.

Eisenhower had insisted on moderation. A middle way. Limits. Once they were unconfined, free of Eisenhower's public admonitions, the military-industrialists, supported everywhere by the imperatives of Cold War militarism, were free to go berserk. And they did so as quickly as possible. Within two months of his inauguration, John F. Kennedy, who had campaigned on the myth of the missile gap,† escalated military spending by billions of dollars. Unprecedented military spending was the essence of the New Frontier. To fulfill his promise to get America "moving again" after eight sluggish years of Ike, Kennedy relied on the military-industrial complex. Militarism was the means by which America would occupy Camelot. Where Eisenhower had negotiated a Berlin crisis, Kennedy exacerbated it. He put the National Guard and reservists on active duty. He added $3.2 billion to the defense budget. He tripled draft calls, increased the military by three hundred thousand and sent forty thousand additional troops to Europe. He revived Rockefeller's moribund family shelter program. He granted a $1 billion contract to Lockheed to design and build one hundred cargo and troop transports. He allocated $808 million for military construction projects in fifty states. Senator Henry M. Jackson, known in the fifties as "the gentleman from Boeing," used the Berlin crisis to revive the frequently rejected and exorbitant program to build Boeing bombers of the future. In his pioneering book, Fred J. Cook documented the facts of "The Warfare State" up to 1962, when the United States was already spending seventy-seven cents out of every federally budgeted dollar "for

---

† Subsequently, the Pentagon acknowledged that there had been a missile gap—two to one in the United States' favor.

past wars, the Cold War, and preparations for wars in the future."[10]

Within ten years, the United States plunged to the status of a debtor nation for the first time since World War I. In 1971 the Nixon administration devalued the dollar and demonetized gold. As the dollar floats, so now do the centers of manufacturing and production. Whenever unpleasant conditions arise, the multinational factory is free to pack up and move. The free market now means freedom from labor unions, health and safety standards, national and local taxes, and antitrust regulations. International free enterprise is free of control, and responsibility. For protection it has United States-financed surveillance, and counterinsurgency.

Eisenhower presided over and accepted each change that mocked many of the values he cherished. In the name of an anti-communist crusade, Eisenhower helped to begin the process of undermining America's economic integrity and transforming the world's economic system. To preserve free enterprise, gunboat diplomacy has been globalized. The United States military has become the largest private security force of a system increasingly dominated by several hundred transnational businesses with corporate headquarters, like military bases, spread liberally about the earth.

While president of Columbia, Eisenhower came to agree, fundamentally, with the precepts of the United States section of the International Chamber of Commerce. After his election, he commissioned Paul Hoffman, then director of the Ford Foundation, to head a committee to "review the international position of the United States in terms of fiscal, monetary and trade policies." Robert Cutler, Milton Katz, and Richard Bissell, who had been chief of staff for the President's Committee on the Marshall Plan, were to analyze America's import and raw-material needs, its international-balance-of-payments position, and its general prospects for economic growth. The Commission operated with a sense of urgency, because Stalin had published a paper, "The Economic Problems of Socialism in the U.S.S.R.," in which he explored the "sharp contraction" of the world market caused by the withdrawal of Russia, China, and their European and Asian allies. The Soviets, Hoffman wrote, were prepared "to exploit" the competitive and divisive tendencies "among the free nations" for the remaining opportunities "in the contracting world market." "Dumping" of surplus Soviet products was anticipated.[11]

During his first year in office, Eisenhower introduced measures to encourage overseas investment through "full diplomatic support," tax incentives for foreign investment, reductions in customs laws and tariff rates, and liberalized tourist allowances. Among his most significant contributions to the international business community was his decision to permit United States oil companies to participate in the international consortium that replaced the Anglo-Iranian Oil Company (renamed British Petroleum) in Iran. In defiance of all United States antitrust rules and traditions against price-fixing and monopolies in restraint of "free trade," the National Security Council determined that the consortium was "in the national interest." The Attorney General therefore provided "clearance" for Standard Oil of New Jersey (now Exxon), Standard Oil of California, Mobil, Texaco, and Gulf to participate with British Petroleum, Royal Dutch Shell and Compagnie Française des Pétroles to obtain 40 percent of Iran's oil profits. To assuage opposition, the Attorney General agreed to modify the terms of the international cartel and permit the American Independent Oil Company, Atlantic Richfield, Continental, Getty, Charter Oil, and Ohio Standard to participate in a minor way—all together sharing five percent of the majors' 40 percent.

The Sherman Antitrust Act, of 1890, was not discarded, however. It was modified to fit the needs of international politics and national security. A long-pending antitrust action against the United Fruit Company, for example, was "postponed on the recommendation of the State Department, Defense Department, and the National Security Council until President Castillo was inaugurated in Guatemala because of the adverse effects upon the foreign relations of the United States which would have resulted from bringing action against an American company during the communist-controlled Arbenz regime." For the same general set of circumstances, the United Fruit Company was ordered to sign a "consent decree" whereby it agreed to cut back its share of the banana market and, within ten years, establish "a competitor of at least one-third its size." On the other hand, the oil consortium was judged necessary and granted immunity. United States business expansion would challenge the nature of United States law and rules of equity, and alter forever the nature of government-business relations. But the Eisenhower administration did not finally settle the antitrust matter. After five years of inquiry and several panels commissioned to study United States antitrust laws, the antitrust question was shelved. Therefore, in practice, if not precisely in law, whenever consortiums and cartels served the interests of national security, they were judged acceptable.[12]

Eisenhower's foreign economic policy was designed to curtail public aid programs—direct government-to-government economic relations "to encourage investment, to facilitate convertibility of currencies, and to expand trade."[13] International trade for national security and private profit was the initial focus of Eisenhower's program. Joint business-government ventures resulted in an ambitious series of trade missions to sell American goods and values abroad. Educational, well-financed, vigorously staffed, the foreign trade missions were coordinated by Clarence Francis and resulted in a "Billion Dollar Bill" to promote tourism and trade on a global basis.[14]

On 30 March 1954, Eisenhower addressed Congress to introduce the expanded contours of the United States' foreign economic program: "The national interest in the field of foreign economic policy is clear. It is to obtain . . . the highest possible level of trade and the most efficient use of capital and resources. That this would also strengthen our military allies adds urgency. . . ." He then detailed America's new tax supports to encourage "the flow of private investment abroad": "Taxation of business income from foreign subsidiaries . . . at a rate of 14 percentage points lower than the regular corporate rate"; "broadening the definition of foreign taxes which may be credited against the U.S. income tax . . ." removal of "the overall limitation on foreign tax credits. . . ." There would, of course, be "full diplomatic support" to promote "the acceptance and understanding by other nations of the prerequisites for the attraction of private foreign investment." Eisenhower considered his program minimal and essential:

Unless we are prepared to adopt the policies I have recommended to expand export and import trade and increase the flow of our capital into foreign investment, our friends abroad may be discouraged in their effort to re-establish a free market for their currencies. If we fail in our trade policy, we may fail in all. Our domestic employment, our standard of living, our security, and the solidarity of the free world—all are involved.

For our own economic growth we must have continuously expanding world markets; for our security we require that our allies become economically strong. Expanding trade is the only adequate solution for these two pressing problems confronting our country.[15]

International economic expansion required the same attention to detail that had marked Eisenhower's political-warfare program. C. D. Jackson proposed a Princeton conference on world economics similar to the one held at Princeton on psychological warfare in 1952. With "no publicity whatsoever," it would be a private conference, sponsored by Time-Life and called by C. D. Jackson in his "private capacity." Eisenhower agreed but insisted that the conference not be another "love feast." He wanted specific, tangible, real answers and programs to deal with the most vital issues of the moment, and he wanted them on "a truly international basis."[16]

The Princeton Conference for a World Economic Plan was held on 15–16 May 1954. Jackson explained to Dulles that the conference was essential to fill a "particular vacuum in our leadership." The United States' emphasis on military reactions to Soviet economic expansion seemed, after all, bankrupt. While the Communists exploited peace and monopolized the symbol of Picasso's peace dove, the United States, wrote Jackson, was "forced to capitalize on the symbols of war." Recent H-bomb developments created, moreover, "a real intellectual and emotional crisis. . . . The curse was almost off the A-bomb . . . when the H-bomb went off, and people said . . . , 'This one we cannot live with; there must be some other way.'" The other way, Jackson concluded, would have to be a really bold economic plan to counter the lure of communism.[17]

Preceding the Princeton Conference, Jackson distributed five key reports submitted to the government since 1950 to stimulate economic expansion. The Gray Report (November 1950), prepared by Gordon Gray and Edward S. Mason, was the first to focus on "the special problems of the world's underdeveloped areas." It introduced the need to develop "democratic societies willing and able to defend themselves and raise the living standards of their peoples." A "fundamental unity of interest" connected all free nations against "Soviet aggressive designs." Western Europe, Japan, and the former colonial nations required "private investment capital" as well as "public loans, processed through the International Bank and the Export-Import Bank."

The Rockefeller Report (March 1951) urged the creation of "a single over-all agency" to administer foreign economic activity and work with "regional institutes." The Rockefeller Report argued that United States private investment "in the critical field of mineral exploitation" could be "quickly doubled" if the United States Government agreed to "help American firms" and (1) exempt overseas income from United States income taxes, (2) negotiate bilateral tax and commercial treaties, and (3) create a $100 million fund to insure American investors against the risk of currency inconvertibility. To stimulate indigenous, local, private enterprise, the Rockefeller Report recommended a new international finance corporation associated with the World Bank to make equity investments and loans to private investors not secured by guarantees of the local government. There would also be a "class of public works investments that cannot be expected to meet the standards of bankability." For that purpose, a new international development authority was proposed. It would avoid "giveaway pressures and leave the administration of the loans . . . to international channels."

The Paley Report (June 1952), "Resources for Freedom," was the most comprehensive "stock-taking of the raw materials base underlying the standard of living and productive capacity of the U.S. and our free world partners." The Paley Commission, chaired by William S. Paley, of CBS, surveyed raw materials from asbestos to zirconium, and projected the United States and free world needs and capacities for the next twenty-five years. A massive, five-volume study, the Paley Report evaluated political as well as market problems and concluded that access to the earth's resources "must be put on a continuing basis and must be shared cooperatively by Government and private citizens." Access should be internationally coordinated "to the ends of common growth, common safety, and common welfare." Specifically, therefore, "the U.S. must reject self-sufficiency as a policy and instead adopt the policy of the lowest cost acquisition of materials wherever secure supplies may be found." The United States' rejection of self-sufficiency as a national policy would over time have far-reaching domestic and international consequences.

The Bell Report (February 1953) dealt with trade and tariff policy. It concluded that all the United States laws "to protect small groups of domestic producers from competition from abroad" had outlived their relevance. America needed a new set of laws that would reflect "the national interest." Basically, the Bell Report proposed to shape tariff law to conform with the Paley Report's recommendations to replace self-sufficiency with easy, low-cost access to foreign raw materials. "In a free trade world, American industry and agriculture 'could expect to have a greater expansion in exports than the producers of any other country.'" In the area of strategic raw materials, minerals, metals, and petroleum, for which domestic supplies are necessary but often at prices higher than import prices, the Bell Report recommended "devices other than tariffs to encourage production," notably "tax allowances" for exploration, and depletion and stockpiling.

The Randall Report (January 1954), submitted by Eisenhower's Commission for Foreign Economic Policy, chaired by Clarence Randall, focused on the world's "shortage of dollars," the immediate postwar "dollar gap." Specific recommendations emphasized the need to terminate emergency aid programs and government-to-government grants. To substitute private investment for public development projects, "everything possible" should be done to encourage the reluctant private sector. Above all, the need was "to encourage favorable investment climates in foreign countries." East-West trade between Western Europe and the Soviet bloc in "peaceful goods" was also encouraged. The Randall Report was controversial. A program, "suggested by the labor member," to protect domestic companies, workers, and communities from the negative impact of increased imports was rejected sixteen to one. "Our tariff negotiators should make no reduction on goods made by workers receiving wages 'well below accepted standards. . . .'"‡ The runaway shops would of course seek just such

---

‡ Significantly, in May 1956, Gabriel Hauge, reporting on tariff negotiations at Geneva, sent Eisenhower this oblique message: "Full account has been taken of your instructions that concessions be avoided which would benefit industries paying substandard wages in the exporting country."

wage scales. A minority report, submitted by Daniel Reed and Richard Simpson, noted that "inadequate" attention had been paid to "the potential injury to domestic interests if a rise in imports is encouraged." The Randall Report was widely criticized for ignoring the factor of Japan, the role of the underdeveloped countries, and the connections between foreign economic and foreign political problems.[18]

These five reports, along with the recommendations that emerged from the 1954 Princeton Conference and a subsequent conference initiated by Nelson Rockefeller and held at Quantico in November 1955, became the basis for what was called a new world economic policy for the United States. The world economic policy intensified a process that began before World War I and emerged clearly in Truman's Point Four foreign aid program. It had been traditionally challenged by such Republican protectionists as Robert Taft, Herbert Hoover, and George Humphrey— who continued to object to government protection for soft, long-term loans subsidized by public funds to attract private investments "in unstable areas." But Humphrey stood increasingly alone. John Foster Dulles objected vigorously to Humphrey's views. "It might be good banking," Dulles told Humphrey, to put South America, for example, "through the wringer, but it will come out red."

By the middle of Eisenhower's first administration, there was bipartisan support to transform the United States' corporate system into a world system. It was not called imperialism, or neocolonialism. It was called a global development project. The interim report of the Princeton Conference, drafted by Max Milliken and W. W. Rostow, announced:

> It is the immediate purpose of the foreign economic policy of the United States to participate in a partnership with the nations and peoples of the free world designed to promote the health and growth of the free world economy. By economic growth we mean a sustained increase in production per head, which gives or promises to give a higher real income to every free world citizen. . . .
>
> The creation and maintenance of an effective free world economic partnership has a particular importance in the struggle against the Communist Bloc:

First, free world success in seeing the underdeveloped countries through their difficult transition to self-sustaining growth would deny to Moscow and Peking the dangerous *mystique* that only Communism can transform underdeveloped societies.

Second, it would provide a foundation for pursuing East-West trade on a basis of political safety, and even political advantage. . . .

Third, an effective free world economy would hold out to the Communist world an open-ended alternative to the present costly struggle, to be taken up whenever they are ready to join. . . .

This ambitious program required, above all, massive doses of protected capital. The Princeton conferees concluded that the United States could "mightily assist in the free world partnership if its actions" had three elements: coordination, "sufficient scale," "continuity."[19]

The United States' new world economic policy was bold. It shocked fiscal conservatives. It dismayed antimilitarists. It was couched in the rhetoric of liberal, anti-imperial internationalism. All those who opposed it were named Communist dupes or mean-spirited. It was the era of McCarthy. And the new plan was specifically anti-Communist. Jackson explained: "Increasing numbers of Free World Citizens" believe that the United States "no longer supports economic and social advance for the benefit of the common man as the bulwark of democracy but rather seeks alliance with any partner, however reactionary, who will pledge military opposition to Russia." America's new world economic plan responds to the "revolutionary expectations" of the world's citizens who "desire to pass from primitive, stagnant economies to steady growth." The plan challenges "the Free World [to] demonstrate that rapid economic progress is possible in societies which respect the individual."[20] To oppose such an effort, one would have to be cruel, selfish, or Communist.

The world economic policy had something for almost every investor in America. Tax rebates, eventual investment guarantees, new levels of contact with the "underdeveloped world," Atoms for Peace, intensified stockpiling of strategic raw materials, surplus disposal—especially agricultural surplus disposal in a "food for peace" project that would help finance a vast international technical assistance program, East-West trade, a new ideology based on "partnership for growth." Eisenhower assigned Clarence Randall, Maxwell Rabb, Kevin McCann, Gabriel Hauge, and General Paul Carroll to coordinate a "bold, far reaching initiative in foreign economic policy." Eisenhower and his economic advisers agreed that American economic growth could not continue except within the context of "an expanding world economy."[21]

On the other hand, several of the proposals directly contradicted Eisenhower's own positions. The entire program was "based on an analysis of persisting dollar shortages in the world which must be alleviated largely by injections of United States Government dollars." The demand for "permanent international pump-priming" suggested the kind of New Deal policies applied to the domestic economy in time of grave crisis. General Carroll warned Eisenhower of the potential opposition: It "would probably convey to many Americans undue concern about foreigners and inadequate concern for U.S. self-interest." Eisenhower was ambivalent. The world economic policy would be "difficult to sell" to the American people, but it represented a real "opportunity."[22]

There was in fact little public enthusiasm for a world economic policy that featured a "Marshall Plan" for Asia, a mutual security program for Latin America, and a "foreign aid" program for every impoverished village in the world except for those with the misfortune to be situated within the continental United States. Costly and unpopular, many aspects of the program got off to a slow start. During Eisenhower's first administration, military agreements for mutual security dominated the economic scene. Eisenhower was enthusiastic about the mutual security program. It would lead to the world's self-defense. It involved a "partnership" for progress. An estimated $2 billion a year in United States funds would protect the world's markets and generate a vast "international flow of private capital in the Free World." In 1956, Indochina would receive $475 million; Korea would receive $480 million; Formosa, $99 million; Pakistan, $95 million; Turkey, $70 million; Yugoslavia, $21 million; and Spain, $25 million. In addition, each nation would receive "military end items." Eisenhower noted that Iran, for example, wanted to use the money to build up a force of ninety thousand troops to "be able to go up into the mountains and hold out if trouble starts." Eisenhower insisted: "We must do all we can to encourage this situation."[23]

"Old Guard" Republicans never did approve the liberal internationalist economic policies that Eisenhower and most of his economic advisers accepted. Within Eisenhower's Cabinet, traditional
fiscal conservatives deplored the entire foreign economic plan. Led
by George Humphrey, cabinet battles raged between Treasury and
State. Eisenhower's staff policies encouraged departmental independence and debate. The long-lasting standoff on foreign economic policy between Humphrey and Dulles delayed any serious
movement toward a well-defined program for four years. In 1953,
Gabriel Hauge attempted to persuade Humphrey:

> The Secretary of State has said, "the Stalin era has ended, the Eisen-
> hower era has begun." We cannot enter that era with what appears
> to be a retreatist mentality. That is presumably what Malenkov
> hopes for and what our allies fear. While there is a great deal of
> truth in the Kremlin's chant that we will destroy our economy by
> overburdening it, I am just as sure that they hope to frighten us by
> that device into a limited security effort that fosters their own
> ends.[24]

But Humphrey was adamant. Even after the National Security
Council had approved Milton Eisenhower's recommendations for
an economic assistance program for Latin America, Humphrey
rejected them. When, in October 1954, Eisenhower urged Dulles
to appoint Milton Eisenhower instead of Humphrey to represent
the United States at the Rio conference of finance ministers, Dulles
refused for protocol reasons. Milton Eisenhower thought it would
be "disastrous" if Humphrey headed the delegation and he himself
did not attend at all. The President was less upset. He wrote his
brother: "Of course it is difficult for George to free himself completely of old convictions to the effect that the U.S. really needs
nothing from the outside world," but, Eisenhower thought, he was
sufficiently considerate of "present day circumstances to overcome
his instinctive reaction." To settle the matter, Eisenhower would
ask Humphrey to invite Milton to join them on a duck-shooting
trip: "You are supposed to have good persuasive powers and your
job is education. This might be a wonderful opportunity." While
Humphrey was not persuaded, Eisenhower was content. He wrote
his brother: "I must say that I don't see that anything is hurt by the
presence in the highest councils of different kinds of thinking. It is
in the combination of these various attitudes that we hammer out

acceptable policies; enthusiasts for or against anything usually go too far."[25]

Committed to moderation, Eisenhower was persuaded of the need for and wisdom of a massive mutual security and development program. In December 1954, he endorsed the Randall Report, which, among other measures, established the International Finance Corporation, under the auspices of the World Bank. According to Hagerty, the Randall Report definitively split "Eisenhower Republicans and the Old Guard, but we are very happy to have this happen."[26]

In June 1955, the House cut $8 million off an $88 million USIA trade-fair project. Eisenhower was furious. On the same day, his economic adviser, Dr. Arthur Burns, protested that the minimum-wage bill had been voted out of a Senate committee. Burns was "concerned about this dollar." Eisenhower was not so stingy about a minimum wage of one dollar an hour but agreed that "inflationary" and popular boondoggles should be curbed. He mentioned specifically Congress' "unrealistic housing bill," passed for "political reasons."[27] The willingness to discount the needs of United States citizens while the security needs of the world were addressed would become a continual theme of the new world economic policy.

United States economic managers argued for years that worldwide economic development programs benefited the United States citizen primarily. Statistics to prove that domestic jobs were created to replace factories on the run to South Korea, Taiwan, Colombia, and the Philippines served for decades to calm protest. But the Cold War—the imperatives of Cold War security—was the ultimate silencing factor. The Soviet economic offensive required American economic expansion. It was supported by McCarthyism, domestic and international political warfare, and "People's Capitalism." Words to calm. Words to confuse. Words to mobilize public opinion for a world economic crusade.

In December 1954, John Foster Dulles told a meeting of wary legislative leaders that the Soviets shifted "from tough warlike gestures" to subversion "through economic assistance." Our allies and friends were uneasy. The United States needed to respond. For example, Dulles explained, in Afghanistan the Soviets are "helping to build roads and factories and in general making a good impression. They could take that country overnight by force if they wanted to but that would be contrary to their peace program. . . . What they are doing economically looks attractive to the peoples of other nations." In Asia, "continual economic aid from the Reds" caused "uneasiness about our position. When we are proposing," Dulles explained, "is a plan of modest aid to Asia so that these countries will feel that the U.S. is doing something, that we are not standing still with our aid while the Reds are going all out."[28]

Speaking before the 59th Annual Congress of American Industry, sponsored by the National Association of Manufacturers, Clarence Randall, Eisenhower's special consultant on foreign economic policy, presented a different emphasis. America's international economic interests involved two elements: "that of military security which requires that we have associated with us in the battle for freedom nations that are economically sound as well as friendly," and the fact "that our own domestic economy requires the world for its market. . . ." Today, Randall assured the NAM, it was possible to restore the three basic principles so vital to the United States economy: "individual initiative and reliance on private resources," "strong, vigorous competition," and "the free market." It was now possible to terminate the Marshall Plan, which was "not well conceived for those purposes." But the world economy still had to be restored to fulfill the United States' economic goals. "The entire world must buy American products but the others have nothing with which to balance their trade budget. Trade must be two way." "The problem," Randall explained, was "how to bring about an increase in world trade and offer hope of a steadily rising volume of production in the world." He concluded that Eisenhower's program was the "answer" and urged the members of the NAM to support it. They should support it not for political reasons only, but because the necessary "outward flow of American private investment capital into the under-developed parts of the world" would result "in gain under the incentive system. Private American capital must do it because we want to and it must be because we will make more money than by investment in the United States."[29]

To popularize a package that would be profitable to the members of the NAM, the Eisenhower administration created a "Foreign Economic Policy Battle Plan." It was an all-inclusive strategy for the media, Congress, and the country. It was "a saturation program" to "create the proper climate for prompt and favorable legislative action." National TV and radio programs, town-hall debates, "off-the-record" press sessions to serve "as a preventive tool in order to avoid negative or disappointing" media accounts—everything was planned, coordinated. Nothing was left to chance. With support from the Advertising Council of America, every government department participated. Major programs, from "Youth Wants to Know" to "See It Now" would feature administration spokesmen to puff America's new foreign economic policy. The Committee for a National Trade Policy was organized to enlist the support of "industrial big-shots." A private Committee on Foreign Trade, Inc., was created to educate the "little guy at the local level." *Time, Life,* and *Fortune* contributed expansively to its success. After all, as Gabriel Hauge said, "Business is one of the most pervasive manifestations of America. It is the way a whole people organizes its economic life."[30]

In addition, Eisenhower appointed Joseph Dodge special coordinator for international economic activity. C. D. Jackson was pleased. Dodge, a Detroit banker with impeccable credentials, considered government-to-government grants for reconstruction, Phase I; Eisenhower's program of military pacts and "massive retaliation," Phase II; and an immediate and effective World Economic Policy, Phase III. According to Jackson, Dodge and Nelson Rockefeller were "very sympatico, and that all will be very useful."[31]

Although Congress was willing, even eager, to spend millions of dollars in excess of Eisenhower's requests for specifically military programs, it was slow to warm to his foreign economic policy of mutual security and foreign aid for international development. In June 1956, Congress cut $1 billion from his program. Observers reported that Congress was "in an ugly mood." The "oratory" had been "violent." "They think that's the way their constituents feel—and this is an election year." Political analysts interpreted the rejection of Eisenhower's foreign economic policy, despite such vigorous public and private efforts, as part of "a strong surge of nationalism all over the world," as well as "in the U.S."[32]

Nationalism became a chief enemy of "our foreign economic policy." Joseph Rand analyzed nationalism's effect: "Economic development by private foreign investment . . . is discouraged by nationalistic expropriation measures." "Nationalistic leaders" stimulate "inflationary forces" by excessive "expenditures for military purposes and unjustified wage increases for political purposes." "Nationalism also creates a receptivity to communist blandishments." Rand explained that nationalists had a "feverish desire to accomplish an overnight transition from a medieval to a modern economy" and might therefore "accept the Soviet argument that aspirations for rapid industrial expansion can best be achieved through communism." Finally, nationalists tended to "make inordinate demands for economic assistance to finance grandiose schemes. Frictions are likely to develop from our unwillingness to accede to such demands."[33] Nationalists abroad, such as Dr. Mossadegh and Arbenz, were therefore labeled Communists and deposed—to assure a suitable investment climate for disinterested American development aid. But before the cycle of antinationalist counterinsurgency to protect worldwide capital investment could triumph, domestic nationalists such as George Humphrey had to be replaced by more appropriate internationalists.

While radical opposition was disregarded entirely, Eisenhower was concerned about the opposition to his program from conservative nationalists whom he admired. In 1956, Paul Hoffman congratulated Eisenhower for his emphasis on the phrase "investment for peace." "Semantics are important," Hoffman wrote, and he "could think of no two words that handicap a program more than *foreign* and *aid*." Gabriel Hauge agreed. He sent Eisenhower a clipping on the debate for foreign trade: "Maybe this is the zenith of Xenophobia." Senator George W. Malone, who, wrote Hauge, "can empty the Senate faster than a fire alarm" when he rises to declaim "on international economics," passed "on to posterity this Maloneism: 'Of the 35 nations now participating in the detested General Agreement on Tariffs and Trade (GATT), all are foreign nations except ourselves.' "[34] In a more sophisticated version, that was basically Humphrey's position. On one occasion, he wrote to Eisenhower that "foreign countries" were building up their gold reserves at United States expense. If it "reaches the point," Humphrey concluded, that "these countries" get "our trade, that would be serious."[35]

C. D. Jackson tried to persuade Humphrey to reconsider his position. He cajoled and flattered Humphrey in a lengthy personal letter. It was an all-out effort:

> . . . . In an attempt to avoid dancing around the problem, may I say that I consider the current Soviet economic offensive . . . as great a danger to our national security and the peace of the world as the Berlin Blockade in 1948, the Czechoslovak takeover, and the Quemoy-Matsu threat. And in a sense, it is an even more serious threat, because so long as the Soviets stuck to their monopoly of sabre-rattling, and we were alone in our monopoly of the use of the economic weapon, it was possible to maintain some kind of seesaw balance between the two. . . .

"Actually," Jackson pointed out, "we are witnessing a vindication" of United States policies. "They are copying us." For Jackson it was the perfect time to "combine our economic might with dynamic diplomacy, coordinated with our military policy, and evolve, at long last, a world economic policy." In conclusion, Jackson wrote, "I would like to add two more thoughts—maybe verging on the personal."

> The first is that it would have been very difficult to write this letter a year or 18 months ago. Today, December 1955, the economy of the U.S., thanks to what Secretary of the Treasury George Humphrey has been able to do, without abuse of federal power, is in such a healthy condition that we may indeed be able to have a world economic policy and eat it too. . . .
>
> The second point is that the George Humphrey who, as head of the M. A. Hanna Company, had the venture vision to do what he did in Canada and Labrador, should be the first one to see what this U.S. venture could do for his country. . . .[36]

Humphrey was not impressed. Economic growth depended on "capital formation." He believed that, above all, we "must accumulate rather than destroy capital to continue our necessary sound growth. This simply means that we must gradually reduce rather than increase military and unessential expenditures. In no other way can we reduce taxes and thereby increase incentives which are essential to both enterprise and savings necessary for the maintenance of a free economy and the support of its continuing growth." Humphrey was aware of the political difficulties, and urged Eisenhower to deal with them directly. Defense costs had to be cut. "I am sure that you and I believe that can be done if we can only overcome the resistance to reductions from all of those who have a vested interest, either politically or financially, in more government spending."[37] Reportedly the richest man in the Cabinet, Humphrey's views deeply influenced Eisenhower. They were close personal friends. Initially, Humphrey's opposition to military spending resulted in the "massive retaliation" doctrine. But reliance on nuclear defense for all situations was impossible even from a political-warfare perspective. With the Soviet Union's "economic offensive," a more pertinent doctrine was called for. Eventually, Humphrey stood alone among Eisenhower's close personal advisers, and resigned.

In the months preceding Humphrey's resignation, an intense exchange of views occurred on the question of fiscal solvency and mutual security. Henry Cabot Lodge and Paul Hoffman, both representing the United States at the United Nations, supported United States participation in the UN's multilateral SUNFED program. The Special UN Fund for Economic Development was a very popular idea, endorsed by most of Europe, the Soviet Union, and the entire "less developed world." United States opposition gave credence to suspicions that United States-dominated aid schemes were insincere and imperialist. To counter a growing anti-American sentiment at the UN, Henry Cabot Lodge issued a press release to support "Multilateral Assistance":

> The seeds of international communism fall on fertile ground when impoverished people see no hope. A hungry man, therefore, is more interested in four sandwiches than he is in four freedoms. . . .
>
> A multilateral program supplies no cover for engaging in political penetration, which is what the communists do and which we are unjustly suspected of wanting to do. . . . A multilateral program conducted in full public view by representatives of the UN will not be misunderstood by those who benefit from it. . . .[38]

Lodge had just returned from a trip to Africa and Asia. He and John J. McCloy had seen the effects of the new Soviet economic penetration. Roads, hospitals, physicians. To counter flamboyant Soviet successes in the Middle East, Africa, and Asia, he and Paul Hoffman had worked hard at the UN. There were nineteen new nations, and there was a desperate need for an international "six year plan" that would emphasize "goods and services, not dollars or gold." Paul Hoffman acknowledged that there were many problems with SUNFED—the amount of money was insufficient, and proposed methods of distribution were dubious; but the United States could not remain aloof from it and win the world's support. Hoffman and Lodge believed that "much of the money would be spent in the U.S. to buy products of American industry." They proposed that George Humphrey "should be put in charge" of the development programs, because he "would think of it in terms of economic health." Moreover, under the aegis of the UN, it would not "look like a cold war move."[39]

Humphrey responded at unusual length. In what Eisenhower considered a paean to the past, Humphrey detailed his political and economic views. He opposed government support for private initiative, and government gifts to "buy friendship." "Discouraging the association of other countries with Russia over a period of time will be determined only by mutually advantageous and sound economic conditions and not by gifts from us. . . . In too many cases we have been building up big governments and government-owned property and more government control of the daily lives of their people." In too many "countries where our aid goes, private investment is disdained." Humphrey detailed the rise of American businesses, including his own. "Governments did not do these things; nor politicians in charge of governments. . . . [America's business pioneers] did not ask, nor did they want, money from government sources or material help of any kind." Humphrey acknowledged the role of government preservation "of law and order"—the appropriate climate for investment, but did not elaborate on the land grants and union-busting involved. In any case, he had concluded: "There are hundreds of energetic people in the world who are better equipped than governments ever can be to risk huge sums in search, exploration, and development" of the "great resources of the world," which, he insisted, "have almost entirely been discovered and developed by private initiative and private capital." Finally, Humphrey noted, he opposed "multilateral ventures because our experience . . . has been that in the end all proposals finally suggest that we provide the money and they provide for spending it. It is far better, more effective, and more useful for us to give by ourselves, whatever we do decide to give, without entangling alliances."[40]

In principle, Humphrey opposed socialism for the rich as well as for the poor. He rejected every major tax-incentive proposal submitted to stimulate capital investment overseas. He objected to tax "amortization," or depreciation allowances for privately capitalized defense industries, that cost the Treasury $350 million a year; and he opposed the Randall Commission's recommendation for a 14 percent reduction in the corporate tax rate "on income from investment abroad." "Tax amortization" had been United States policy since the Korean War. Truman's administration agreed that incentives to encourage private capital investments for defense industries were essential. America's general industrial buildup, stimulated by the Korean War, was "financed by private capital with nothing more than tax amortization as an incentive." By 1955, that fact cost the United States Treasury an estimated $980 million in taxes deferred. Humphrey wanted it stopped. The Administration debated the issue. Since all discussants represented opinions that ranged from industrialist Republicans to industrialist Democrats, there was no spokesman to question the profit motive in national defense spending altogether. It was simply assumed that war, whether hot or cold, was expensive and required industrial expansion which should be rewarded by significant profits and government bonuses.

Among the many arguments for a tax-free future for the defense industry was the amazing notion that industries needed government encouragement to invest despite proven and enormous profits: "Tax amortization must be used as an incentive to persuade new defense facilities to locate outside of targets. . . . Tax amortization must be used to the maximum extent to reduce the concentration of defense facilities. . . ." The government, it was argued, needed to be supportive: "American industry, both large and small, has expanded considerably with private capital to meet essential defense or war requirements. Obviously, this expenditure of private funds was not made for purely patriotic reasons. Every investor hopes and expects to recover his capital expenditure, plus a reasonable profit. The tax amortization program merely permits a quicker return of the capital investment and does not guarantee or increase the return."

Humphrey disagreed: "Tax deferments . . . are a real drain on the income of the Federal Government and consequently a genuine factor to be considered in the process of balancing the budget. The tax deferments are just as much a loss to the Treasury as though they were recorded in expense accounts. The increase in tax revenue which is alleged to be the result of the tax amortization program is in fact due first to the increased demand for war goods and second to the increased demand for civilian goods. If tax amortization had not been involved, the facilities probably would have been built anyway and the loss of tax revenue avoided.

"Certainly at this time, when we are not at war, we should not continue to grant a subsidy to industry in [this] form without specific Congressional approval. The longer it continues the harder it is to stop."[41]

George Humphrey did not oppose capital expansion. He was not an isolationist. But he stood for fiscal solvency and he disapproved of "entangling alliances." He opposed SUNFED because the World Bank, a "large, well financed and active instrument of multilateral lending" already existed and the United States dominated it. Theoretically the United States was to have contributed 30 percent of the World Bank's capital. Actually it provided 80 percent, and 60 percent of the bonds were purchased by Americans. The International Finance Corporation was created in 1954 to supplement World Bank activities with "venture loans" that could be made without the government guarantees required by the World Bank. Humphrey accepted these realities. But new organizations, with "looser" controls, would, he insisted, "undermine" the established facilities. In addition, he considered it "a very wholesome thing" that all funds for international economic activity were part of the annual congressional budgetary process, so that they were "under constant review and subject to the limitations of continuing legislative criticism by the public." If that were not the case, Humphrey warned Eisenhower, the pressure on the President would be "so great that it would be extremely difficult to resist unjustified expenditures."[42]

But the drift of the American economy was all the other way. Between 1956 and 1957, direct foreign investments by United States companies increased by over $4 billion. Over 40 percent of the total was invested in Latin America, and $900 million of that was petroleum investment. In 1957, United States direct capital investments increased in Africa by $40 million; in the Middle East, by $100 million, with an additional $25 million for oil explorations; in Pakistan, India, Indonesia, Japan, the Philippines, Australia, and New Zealand, direct capital investment amounted to $175 million.[43]

To negotiate the differences within the Administration over the world economic policy, Clarence Randall called a meeting of the antagonists: George Humphrey, John Foster Dulles, Sinclair Weeks, Gabriel Hauge, John Hollister, Robert Cutler, True D. Morse (Agriculture), Raymond Saulnier, who replaced Arthur Burns as chairman of the Council of Economic Advisers; Karl Harr, representing Gordon Gray; C. D. Jackson, and the President. According to Jackson, only Randall was prepared to take the bold steps he believed necessary for positive action. He divided the group into "three different types" each forming "an instinctive alliance":

> One type, led by George Humphrey, does not believe that we should do anything beyond strictly military defense unless the proposed recipient country promises to behave like a God-fearing Middle Western businessman.
>
> A second type, led by Foster Dulles, will take no initiative, won't even approve in principle, unless his client, the President of the U.S., tells him to damn well pick up that ball and run with it.
>
> The third type, part Hollister, part Hauge, thinks that actually we have done not too badly, and is mildly irritated that someone should suggest something more, given the difficulties on Capitol Hill, the problems of the budget, and the difficulty of coordinating so many divergent and Departmentally protectionist points of view.[44]

But once Humphrey resigned, Eisenhower told Dulles to run with it, and a world economic policy was promoted vigorously by the Administration. Eisenhower rejected Humphrey's reasoning, his analysis, and his analogies. He pointedly referred to his long rhapsodic letter to the rugged individualist days of America's business boom, and wrote that there were "no conditions left in the world" that would allow "a few men to put a steel plant in a cornfield" all on their own initiative. Eisenhower believed, therefore, in a mutual security program and a foreign development plan, because they would serve to improve conditions, limit nationalist independence movements, and check the Soviet advantage. Without a world market and easy access to raw materials, the

United States would be endangered. The United States, he wrote Humphrey, could not survive "surrounded by a sea of enemies." Eisenhower was convinced "that protection of our own interests and our own system demands and requires" a bold mutual aid program. We "must understand," Eisenhower wrote:

> that the spirit of nationalism, coupled with a deep hunger for some betterment in physical conditions and living standards, creates a critical situation in the underdeveloped areas of the world. Unless we have the fortitude and courage and stamina to meet the situation, we are not going to emerge unscathed from the struggle. Communism is not going to be whipped merely by pious words.

Eisenhower concluded that, with help "at least to some minor extent by the other free nations of the West," the United States must "face up to the critical phase through which the world is passing and do our duty like men." Eisenhower believed that mutual-aid expenditures for national security would ultimately increase the prospects for peace more than "excessive expenditures on armaments."[45]

On 30 August, Eisenhower wrote to Percival Brundage, director of the Bureau of the Budget: "Although I have approved a general policy of holding expenditures to 1957 level, it is necessary to make an exception in the case of mutual aid. Plans in that area should push ahead as required by the world situation."[46]

Humphrey had resigned in April. Eisenhower appointed Robert B. Anderson to succeed him. Anderson represented a different attitude in Eisenhower's Cabinet. Secretary of the Navy and Deputy Secretary of Defense during Eisenhower's first administration, Anderson was a Texas Democrat for Eisenhower, an attorney, head of Ventures, Ltd., a Canadian mining company, and manager of the W. T. Waggoner Estate, "with vast holdings in oil, gas and ranch land in Texas." He was also the director of several large corporations.[47]

Without Humphrey's check on Eisenhower's mutual security program, only occasional congressional cuts curbed appropriations for a vast aid-and-development security program that grew by millions of dollars each year and supplemented in a variety of ways the enormous private fiscal expansion of the world's United States-based businesses. Although a coalition of "diehard Republicans and Democratic representatives of the new industrial south" worked hard to cut appropriations, by 1958 the new world economic policy was well underway. C. D. Jackson was delighted: ". . . everybody who counts is for it." John Foster Dulles spoke eloquently before the UN on behalf of multilateral aid. He announced that the United States was prepared to support expanded capital outlays for the World Bank and the International Monetary Fund (IMF); prepared to "marshal scientific resources"; prepared to intensify support for "regional development institutions" such as the Colombo Plan for Asia, to which the United States had contributed $3 billion since 1951; and prepared to support an international development association.[48]

On every level, and from the beginning, America's new world economic policy was a bipartisan effort. Adlai Stevenson waxed positively rhapsodic. In March 1958, he addressed the National Conference of Organizations on International Trade Policy:

We are the world's greatest traders. Last year our exports were valued at approximately $21 billion and our imports at $13 billion. . . .

The sun never sets on the American business empire. An empire without a capital, colony, or ruler, it flourishes everywhere because it renders its customers greater satisfactions at lower cost than they can receive elsewhere. . . .

Our foreign trade looms over the world. Last year the combined value of exports, imports, and overseas manufacturers, reached the staggering total of $67 billion.

Our total foreign business of $67 billion last year was more than three times larger than the gross national product of India; the India that contains almost one-fifth of the human race.

Our exports range from locomotives to juke boxes. The American movie industry derives nearly half of its revenues from overseas customers. Without them, it would shrivel. . . . In 1956 the H. J. Heinz Company earned 70 percent of its consolidated net income overseas.

In Europe alone the International Business Machines Company [IBM] employs more than 16,000 persons. . . .

Approximately one-tenth of all movable goods manufactured here are sold abroad.

This is the significant tenth; the fraction that spells the difference between profit and loss. . . .

The world takes between 25 and 40 percent of our cotton, wheat, rice, tobacco, fats and oils.

The value of our exports exceeds the value of our house construction.

It is greater than the sales of new cars at home, greater than the farmers' gross income from crops or livestock, or the clothing purchases of all Americans. . . .

Trade makes a bazaar of the whole world; a bazaar where everything is sold to further man's pursuit of happiness and satisfy his needs. . . .

The remainder of Stevenson's speech was devoted to the need for a liberal trade policy to maintain the United States' economic growth. To continue such heady profits, to secure "our overseas investment," the enforcement of one economic rule was essential: "in order to sell you must buy." Tariff reductions, Stevenson acknowledged, bruised some domestic industries. But the harm was negligible when compared with the economic growth rate of $10 billion annually. According to the Department of Labor, the Tariff Commission "found injury or threat of injury from April 1948 to March 1957" in twenty-three industries, in which, Stevenson contended, there was a "maximum total displacement" of only twenty-eight thousand workers. "Moreover, pending legislation contemplated federal assistance to industries, workers and communities seriously injured by foreign competition resulting from tariff reductions."

"Actually," Stevenson concluded, "unemployment is one of the strongest reasons for stimulating rather than stifling trade. The soundest way to restore and sustain full employment and economic health is to expand, to develop new products and new markets.

There are a billion customers around the world who want what we can produce. But they can't buy unless they can sell. Trade with these underdeveloped countries, particularly as we supply them with capital goods, will enable them to increase their capacity for consumption of our products.

And that brings me to the political implications of freer trade, which are more important than its economic aspects. For nowadays trade policy is foreign policy. If we don't understand that, the Russians do.

Ever since the presidential contest of 1952, I have talked about Communist intentions in the field of foreign trade and economic aid. I have often repeated Stalin's counsel to a Moscow conference: "We can win the world peaceably. It will eventually turn upon West Germany and Japan. . . . The stupid, greedy West will hamper their foreign trade. Then we shall draw them into our orbit through overwhelming trade agreements. . . ."

Stevenson emphasized the pivotal significance of Japan. The United States' best customer after Canada, and the "leading market" for United States farm products, "Japan is invaluable to the free world. . . ."

> But Japan can succeed in only one way: through trade. And . . . through trade only by doing much of it with us. With too many people, too little land, too few resources, Japan must import about one-fourth of her food and nearly all the cotton, wool, iron ore and other materials she processes. She can pay for them only with exports. Trade is life or death for Japan.
>
> China with its huge land mass and 600 million population exerts a mighty gravitational pull upon all Asia. It would be a savage irony if the Japan we preserved from Communist aggression by our bloodshed in the Korean war should be driven by American business into the arms of the Communists.
>
> No one in his right sense will any longer laugh off Communist competition in trade and aid or be content with any more assurances that the Soviet Union is about to collapse. . . . So, with the common market on one side of us and the mounting Sino-Soviet economic offensive on the other, any retreat on trade policy will have forbidding and unalterable consequences. It will further weaken our alliances, further enfeeble confidence in our leadership, push the great decisive uncommitted areas into Communist arms, and in the long run isolate, imperil and impoverish us. . . .[49]

America's bipartisan leadership was dedicated, therefore, to the fact that "the sun never sets on the American business empire." There was opposition, there were setbacks. But, by 1960, Eisenhower's foreign economic policy had become America's national way of life. It was divided initially into two parts: a Military Assistance Program and a Mutual Security Program. Both involved international trade and military contracts to international industrialists. Both involved skyrocketing fiscal commitments for widespread intelligence operations, covert operations, and military missions to ensure stability, an acceptable investment climate.

Basic to the entire program was the objective fact that nationalism combined with the Soviet economic offensive endangered the

West's access to valuable resources in Africa, Asia, Latin America, and the Middle East. According to Colonel W. R. Kintner's report to the Draper Committee, "If the natural resources of Southeast Asia—tin, rubber, oil—can be denied to the West or captured by the communists and dumped on Western markets at cut-rate prices, severe dislocations in the economic structure of the Free World Market economy will ensue."[50]

The Soviet economic offensive involved economic credits to the United Arab Republic, India, Afghanistan, Indonesia, and Argentina; and military aid to the UAR, Iraq, Indonesia, Afghanistan, and Yemen. Grants were given to Burma; petroleum development aid was given to Argentina; a steel mill was built in India; a $100 million credit built Egypt's Aswan High Dam. Twenty-eight hundred nonmilitary technical advisers from Soviet-bloc nations had spent a month or more in nineteen developing or resource-rich countries by 1959. Every Soviet economic move was monitored by biweekly "Economic Intelligence Reports of Sino-Soviet Acts in Underdeveloped Areas." These reports included intelligence estimates and projections for potential United States responses by the government and private organizations.[51]

The Soviet economic offensive disturbed the "balance of power" and checked the West's ambitions for undisturbed economic growth. C. D. Jackson urged Eisenhower to consider what the economic consequences of disarmament might be:

> Supposing you were to be successful with the Russians on some form of genuine disarmament. One of the possible by-products would be the release of the Russian equivalent of hundreds of millions of dollars from their military budget, which they could put into either their standard of living, or foreign aid, or both.
>
> Given their history, their temperament, their stated ambition, and the docility of the Russian people, the chances are the bulk of these funds would go into foreign aid in the form of international economic warfare.

Jackson considered the prospect of "a long, tough economic-warfare competition" to be "the scary negative way" Eisenhower could pose the problem to Congress in order to get full funding for the United States' program. He urged Eisenhower to assemble the legislative leaders and tell them:

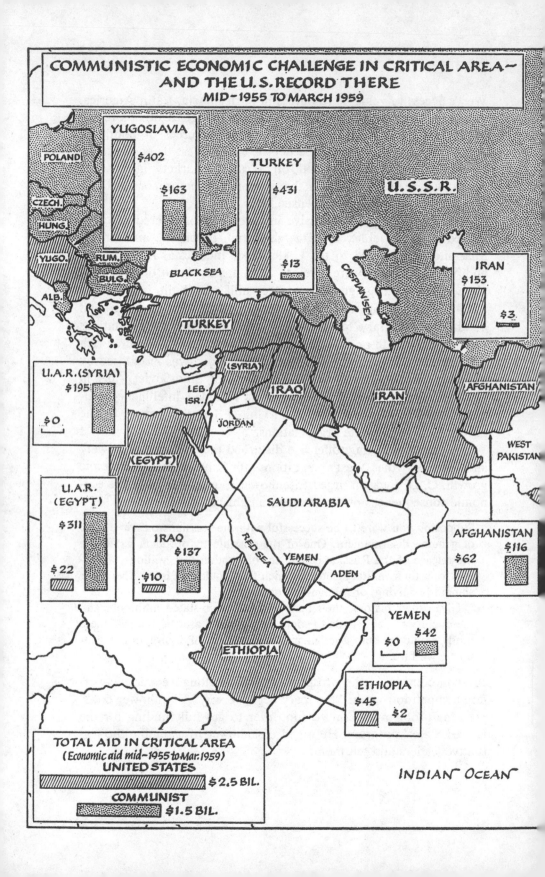

COMMUNISTIC ECONOMIC CHALLENGE IN CRITICAL AREA—
AND THE U.S. RECORD THERE
MID-1955 TO MARCH 1959

POLAND

CZECH.

HUNG.

YUGO.

ALB.

RUM.

BULG.

BLACK SEA

YUGOSLAVIA
$402
$163

TURKEY
$431
$13

TURKEY

CASPIAN SEA

U.S.S.R.

IRAN
$153
$3

U.A.R. (SYRIA)
$195
$0

(SYRIA)

LEB.
ISR.

JORDAN

IRAQ

IRAN

AFGHANISTAN

WEST PAKISTAN

**U.A.R.
(EGYPT)**
$311
$22

(EGYPT)

IRAQ
$137
$10

SAUDI ARABIA

RED SEA

YEMEN

ADEN

AFGHANISTAN
$62
$116

YEMEN
$0
$42

ETHIOPIA

ETHIOPIA
$45
$2

TOTAL AID IN CRITICAL AREA
(Economic aid mid-1955 to Mar. 1959)
UNITED STATES
$2.5 BIL.
COMMUNIST
$1.5 BIL.

INDIAN OCEAN

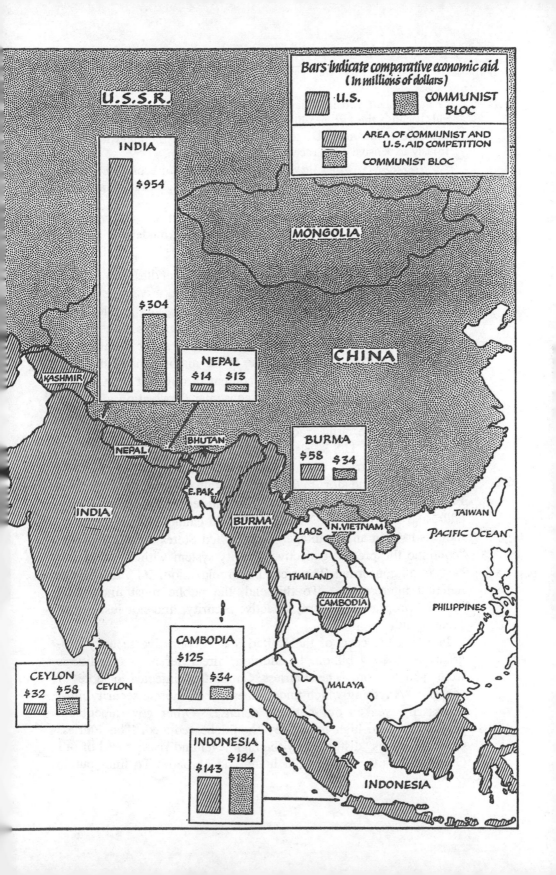

"I have asked you in today to talk about disarmament and foreign aid, because the two are linked. . . . Consistent with the security of the nation, we are all interested in slowing or stopping the disastrously expensive arms race with the Soviet Union.

"We know . . . that they are eager to engage in economic warfare with us—in other words, to compete toe to toe, grant for grant, loan for loan, with the U.S. in foreign aid.

"If you gentlemen are unprepared to meet that economic competition, there are only two other alternatives—surrender, or an ever-accelerated arms race."[52]

Economic competition, combined with an endless arms race, combined with counterinsurgency, resulted in a very expensive package. It was a package that involved the ongoing political-warfare effort to keep the Soviet leadership off balance, so it could not spend in the domestic sector what needed to be spent to satisfy the needs and wants of the people. One of the major aims of the Cold War, after all, was to stimulate discontent throughout the Communist bloc. Scarcity, food lines, and consumer deprivation all served a variety of Cold War purposes, which kept the arms race in perpetual motion. The arms race distorted the Soviet economy and diminished the U.S.S.R.'s ability to compete in the underdeveloped countries. But the costs to the United States were equally high, and for many they remained unacceptable. The Fairless Committee, Eisenhower's Committee on Mutual Security, addressed that problem: "The Free World cannot permit the Communists to gain an advantage." The United States should therefore "continue the present collective security system with its enormous costs to all concerned. There can be no relaxation. . . . It is in our national interest. . . . To this end, the public must understand that the program is one of collective security, and not just a program of aid."

In 1956, the costs of the United States' collective security programs were $7.9 billion. In addition, direct defense expenditures were $38 billion. The Fairless Committee injected a note of caution: "Anything which undermines our economic security must necessarily weaken our national defense." Other government expenditures were high too. They should be reduced. The Fairless Committee was "disturbed by the high level and rising trend of our Government's expenditures at home and abroad." To limit public expenditures, domestic spending should be cut, and increased "private investment with public assistance" was particularly recommended.

The Fairless Committee's influence was felt for decades. Following an eighteen-country trip, the President's "citizen advisers" concluded that the United States, "with only six percent of the world's population, needs the aid of other countries just as they need our assistance." The Fairless Committee announced that, above all, the Cold War was about access to resources, and alliances for their control and development.[53] Its findings were sustained in every major review of the "present conflict" for "power and geographical positions" of the world's "two chief protagonists."

According to the Draper Committee, which Eisenhower appointed to study the purposes and benefits of economic aid and the United States' Military Assistance Program, the objectives of the United States' long-range foreign policy were to assist Soviet evolution, establish a more stable military environment, "moderate the Asian-African Revolution," and maintain our major alliances. "Divorced from U.S. support, Western Europe and Japan would probably be increasingly vulnerable to Communist threats and attractions." The United States' objectives were therefore to avoid nuclear war and hemispheric isolation by "keeping the free world free." To moderate the Asian-African Revolution, United States efforts would "be designed both to help the new and emerging states in their efforts to achieve domestic progress; and to place restraints, as our security requires, on external policies which threaten peace."

To achieve those purposes, Congress appropriated in FY 1957 $250 million for "development assistance" and $1.1 billion for "defense support." Technical aid was estimated at $150 million annually. United States aid grants and soft loans for development ranged between $700 million and $800 million annually and were judged insufficient. For the future, the Draper Committee concluded, United States aid agencies must be further developed; development programs should be separated from military programs and those required "to meet political emergencies"; vast increases in the capitalization of existing banking institutions were necessary; the Development Loan Fund required substantial capital increases; private initiative was needed to finance foreign trade and development. In September 1960, the International Development Association (IDA) was founded to meet some of these needs. Affiliated with the World Bank, its initial purpose was to extend soft loans on flexible schedules.[54]

For years, Americans were told that to protect the United States' vital interests, Americans needed to contribute unselfishly to the defense of the free world. That was not very precise language. The United States did not possess those vital interests. They were leased and developed for profit. Access to the earth's resources depended entirely on governments friendly to the United States' business interests. To secure those governments, the United States supported a variety of political and military leaders who agreed to perpetuate a neocolonial pattern of economic growth and dependency on the United States. They depended, first of all, on United States economic support and military training and assistance for their survival.

The United States began to train foreign military personnel under the Military Assistance Program (MAP) in FY 1950. Between 1950 and 1958, over two hundred thousand representatives of sixty-six nations were trained in the United States, and twenty-five thousand were trained at United States facilities outside the United States, in eleven training missions that were established in Asia, the Middle East, and Latin America. There were also mobile training teams prepared and equipped to cover the world.[55]

Efforts to expand the Military Assistance Program resulted in widespread diplomatic and congressional opposition. In August 1958, eight senators protested to Eisenhower that although they had voted for the Mutual Security Appropriations bill for 1959, they considered the military emphasis "a serious distortion," particularly with respect to the "less developed countries." They believed that Eisenhower's program reflected "little responsiveness" to the Soviet Union's primary emphasis on political and economic competition:

> Overemphasis on military assistance has tended unavoidably to involve the U.S. in situations in which our aid may have contributed to the maintenance in power of regimes which have lacked broad support within the countries we have assisted. It has helped to create abroad a militaristic image of the U.S. which is a distortion of our national character. It has distracted attention, energy and perhaps

economic aid, from more pressing problems. And, finally, we believe military assistance by its very nature tends to create and then to perpetuate military hierarchies which even in the most well-developed countries may endanger the very values of individual freedom which we seek to safeguard.

The letter was signed by Senators Theodore Francis Green, J. William Fulbright, John J. Sparkman, Hubert H. Humphrey, Mike Mansfield, Wayne Morse, John F. Kennedy, and William Langer.[56]

After examining the senators' charges, the State Department concluded that they resulted from Communist propaganda, "uncoordinated and occasionally indiscreet remarks" by various government officials, a tendency of journalists to emphasize conflict, and "the failure of the public to make a clear distinction between defensive measures and a militaristic posture." It acknowledged, however, that "military and strategic requirements sometimes dictate the granting of military assistance to countries ruled by undemocratic regimes. In an ideal world, the U.S. would doubtless prefer to select the recipients of its aid according to standards of ideological purity, among other criteria." Christian Herter, acting Secretary of State, explained that "the actual world" was "so far from ideal" that the United States practice "has been to apply a less refined test: Is the country on our side? Thus, the standards of absolute conformity to American standards of democracy [have] been sacrificed in Latin America and in other parts of the world to achieve what is deemed a more urgent value—security and survival."[57]

The CIA was more precise in its analysis. The agency reported that "there are, indeed, a great many military regimes, of varying vintage and character, which have received MAP aid. . . ." But the CIA believed that they would have emerged without MAP, and argued, for example, that the Dominican Republic received few funds from that particular program. On the other hand, the CIA noted, there was "a category of governments" that is sustained by MAP aid, which enables "the regime to keep power by more or less authoritarian means." The CIA included Jordan, Iran, Thailand, South Korea, Nationalist China, Laos, South Vietnam, Indonesia, and "the old regime in Iraq." Nuri as-Said's regime, for example, "was plainly hated by most of the Iraqi people, but its receipt of United States military assistance was neither a major cause of its unpopularity nor did it help in defending Nuri's government against a military coup."

For the CIA, several notable victories against communist influence were the specific result of MAP aid: "Outstanding examples were Greece, South Korea, Nationalist China and Vietnam. In each instance, it can safely be said that without United States military assistance, the government concerned would almost certainly have gone down to defeat and given way to a Communist or pro-Communist regime." Other cases that warranted a "similar estimate" included the "threats in the late 'forties to Turkey and to the West European states now comprising NATO . . . , and Yugoslavia and Iran could be said to fall into this category. While it cannot be proved that United States MAP aid saved these governments from sure overthrow by the Bloc, it certainly helped in preventing Soviet Bloc takeovers in the states concerned. . . ."

The CIA concluded that MAP, by itself, was not "a major factor" in the establishment of "a trend toward military regimes." Nor did it, by itself, create "a damaging militaristic image of the U.S." "Other factors," the CIA noted, had a "much greater impact"—including "U.S. policies in crisis situations, the network of U.S. overseas deployments and alliances, and the general U.S. military posture." On the issue "of whether military regimes present the best feasible alternative from the standpoint of U.S. interests," the CIA concluded that the question was "complex," but generally "those military regimes which have emerged in Asian and African countries receiving MAP aid, appear preferable to, or at least no worse from this standpoint than the alternative regimes which might have emerged. The case with respect to Latin American regimes is more moot."[58]

Military regimes, with their associated features of repression, brutality, and torture, thus became an approved if unfortunate by-product of the United States' mutual-security and world economic programs. To counter the image of militarism, the United States embarked on a massive public-relations campaign, directed primarily at American citizens. To persuade Americans that the future of the free world depended on military regimes, and that imminent peril demanded personal sacrifice, involved a psychological campaign that depended largely on confusion and fraud. Spyros Skouras, president of Twentieth Century-Fox, offered Eisenhower the services of the motion-picture industry. Skouras promoted a policy of dedication and discipline. The "danger" of the Soviet's "economic aggression" demanded American "self-restraint," stable prices, and ever more stable wages.[59] Americans were to pull in their belts as America expanded its rule.

Opposition was dismissed as unpatriotic. Demands for curbs on international spending and for greater domestic spending were rejected as un-American and flaccid. "Has U.S. Complacency Given Leadership to the Soviets?" became a recurrent and popular theme in a series of radio and TV programs to impress Americans. Dissidents in America were, after all, malcontent, misinformed, or Communists. To win "The Ruble War," America's stagnant obsession for fiscal stability must be replaced with a zeal for economic growth." America's future depended on an orderly world economy: "Freer trade, more foreign investment, and steady support for existing international economic bodies"; more intensive development programs; stable market prices; greater freedom for executive action in "dealing with aid, trade, and economic warfare. . . . Economic war above all requires mobility, flexibility, and freedom to act. Congress must somehow learn therefore to keep its sticky fingers off the steering wheel." The free market required executive freedom. Economic warfare could not afford congressional oversight, congressional restraints, or old-fashioned notions about constitutional law, international law, or commercial practices: "preclusive buying, political prices, export subsidies, even barter" were necessary "to compete successfully." "On Sundays we can go on listening to sermons" that claimed "any departure from the precepts of Adam Smith will doom us to eternal damnation." But these were big business days—and economic warfare required bold departures from economic traditions.[60]

However flamboyant, these were peculiar themes to sell to the American people. Eisenhower was aware of the complexities. He wrote to C. D. Jackson that the problem was to convince "the housewife and her working husband on the basis of 'What am I buying with this amount of money? How important is it to me? What will happen to me if we eliminate this item from the budget?'" Public opposition to the Mutual Security Program did, after all, have an economic base. "Demagogues," Eisenhower wrote, "have appealed to the American people on the proposition of 'Why give millions to Timbuktu when you won't give fifty dollars' worth of cottonseed meal to a distressed farmer in Texas?'" To put "these things into proper perspective before the American people," Eisenhower concluded, "we have to show that the money we are spending on farm programs, school building, road construction and even the health of our people, could all be wasted unless they are supported, in the international field, by policies and procedures that create the proper kind of atmosphere in which America can be safe and prosperous." "We have got to get down to cases and, without calling names, get over to the average family . . . that those who are opposing foreign aid . . . are not only penny-wise and pound-foolish, but are actually risking the security and safety of the country and of all its citizens."

When it came "down to cases," budget cuts would occur in just one sector of the economy. The American people were to pay for the United States' security by enriching America's capital investors all over the militarized and endangered world. Eisenhower was very precise about that. He was proud of an analogy that he had devised to persuade a dubious friend while flying home from golfing at Augusta:

> The U.S., with its budgetary and security problems, could be likened to the individuals in this airplane, if collectively we owned it. All of us pay the costs of its operation and we think that those costs are too high. We want to make savings so that we can have more money for ice cream sodas and ball games. . . .

So all the passengers decided what features of the airplane could be eliminated: First the steward, then the co-pilot, then the radar equipment—were "services we could readily do without." But when one of the engines was to be cut, everybody would agree that that involved a "margin of safety" that could not be cut. The point was, Eisenhower contended, "you simply have got to confine budget cutting to those programs that represent some greater convenience, greater comfort or greater protection against the normal vicissitudes of living; you cannot . . . apply them against the things that keep our ship of state safe and sound in this turbulent world."[61]

Education, hospitals, public transportation, safety and health, clean air, public lands, water supplies, and work. All were expendable. All were to become luxuries to be sacrificed to the globalized ship of state. It is significant that, for a time, housing was considered a useful Cold War weapon. "Every Man a Capitalist—Every Man a Homeowner" was a popular Eisenhower-era slogan. The fifties low-cost-private-housing boom for workers in Peru, Nicaragua, Chile, Puerto Rico, Pakistan, and the United States was part of a campaign to privatize and depoliticize the individual homeowner: "Every time you put a man or a family in his own home you displace a potential collectivist with a capitalist: (1) Economically; (2) Politically; (3) Socially; (4) Creatively; (5) Ideologically."[62]

Conceived and popularized by Willard Garvey, of Wichita, Kansas, the Homeowning Project became a United States interagency operation that involved the Departments of State, Commerce, Treasury, and Agriculture; the Bureau of the Budget; the International Cooperation Administration; the Council of Economic Advisers; the Office of Civil and Defense Mobilization; the Housing and Home Finance Agency; the Federal Home Loan Bank Board; the Small Business Administration; the Development Loan Fund, and the Export-Import Bank. Home ownership was to be financed in large part by United States Government loans, made possible by local land grants and negotiated by United States embassies. An arrangement to use funds from the "Food for Peace" program, PL-480, was also made to finance mortgage loans. In 1959, the Council on Foreign Economic Policy concluded that: "Private home ownership is basic capitalism. . . . As a further bulwark against Communism, expanded private home ownership will help to build a substantial citizenry and more stable political climate. The expansion of private home ownership should also generate much economic activity. . . . And this increased economic strength will mean an economically stronger Free World. . . ."[63]

For "every man" to become a homeowner and thereby a "capitalist," one might imagine that every potential homeowner would be assured a job. But full employment has never been the goal of a capitalist society. Capitalism is defined, simply, as the ownership of the means of production for the purpose of making profit. Healthful food, pleasant housing, and private transportation are luxuries in most countries. But their possession does not render one a "capitalist." On the other hand, those who have argued for full employment so that everybody might begin to have all of those things have been denounced as Communists. As John Maynard Keynes is alleged to have said: "Capitalism is the extraordinary belief that the nastiest of men for the nastiest of motives will somehow work for the benefit of us all."[64]

In the United States, efforts to guarantee full employment have on occasion been made, and specifically rejected. In 1949, the UN introduced a resolution calling for full employment. On behalf of the United States Council Committee to the UN on Full Employment, John K. Jessup, chairman of the board of editors of *Fortune,* denounced the idea as narrow-minded and "unusually dogmatic." The United States Council Committee was "wholly out of sympathy both with the recommendations and the assumption behind the report." The UN report sought to impose a "straightjacket" on the economy. The authors represented "one kind of economic life only —the kind in which a strong government, impelled by the disaster either of depression or war, gathers in its own hands the strings of economic control." Free enterprise had another view: Free-market imperatives were "wage, price, profit and incentive relationships usually termed 'structural,' whose very real bearing on the level of employment" was ignored by the UN committee. Moreover, full employment was "unmistakably inflationary." The implications of this view are clear: a free-market economy depended on a generous portion of unemployment to grow freely, prevent militant unionism, manipulate the market whenever needed to stabilize the cost–profit ratio, and reinforce social control. Finally, Jessup concluded, "quantitative targets," "authoritarian targets," such as full employment, interfere with a free market economy, which "is its own best judge of how fast, and in what directions it chooses to grow," and therefore "endanger both freedom and efficiency."[65]

Today, despite the many billions of dollars spent on mutual security and military assistance, unemployment is one of the "free market's" biggest problems. Today, overcommitted and financially devoured, United States politicians talk earnestly about bringing some of the work back home. They talk even more earnestly about a new generation of submarines, military aircraft, and nuclear weapons to take us, in security, to the year 2000. National security is now to be based, for example, on a missile that "cruises" from place to place so that the Soviets will be denied a "stable" target. It is somebody's $30–100 billion fantasy of the future.

Compared to his successors, Eisenhower had a modest and re-strained relationship to the military-industrial complex. He re-duced the military budget after the truce in Korea. He refused uni-laterally to go into Vietnam. The war in Indochina ultimately cost $160 billion in direct expenditures. In the decade that followed Ei-senhower's presidency, the United States spent $360 billion, ex-cluding Vietnam, in its foreign-aid program. After the war in Viet-nam, the military budget continued to escalate. On the other hand, Eisenhower presided over the globalization of America's military and economic expansion. Although he sought balance between spending and security, he refused to heed the warnings of those who, like George Humphrey, predicted disaster at the end of the economic road Eisenhower chose. Humphrey did not agree with Eisenhower that the transfer of American capital abroad would best serve the interests of the United States. In 1958, he returned to Washington to campaign against the Gaither Report. He wrote letters and gave speeches. America was spending itself to destruc-tion. He called for limits, arms control, caution. He talked about a crisis of "confidence" in the health of the domestic economy.

In November 1958, Humphrey sent an impassioned letter to Neil McElroy, then Secretary of Defense, with a copy to Eisen-hower: "I think our home economic situation is just about as vital to our future freedom as our military posture." Humphrey called for cuts in every area. But since most of the money was spent by Defense, it would have to take most of the reduction: "This coun-try has never before had an enormous entrenched military bureau-cracy. After each previous war, the military has been cut down to size. . . . [Now] we have built up a built-in vested interest in Government spending, and it's going to be hell to cut it down. . . . In fact, I don't believe that with all of its present polit-ical and propaganda power, any civilian could make much of a dent in it even today." But if there was anybody who could, Humphrey believed, it was Eisenhower. His "tremendous personal popularity" gave him "tremendous power." The people of America believed that "he is more qualified than any man on earth to deter-mine . . . what should be the size, the effectiveness and cost of maintaining an adequate military posture." Humphrey appealed to McElroy to team up with Eisenhower to cut military spending be-fore it was too late: "I don't believe we ever again will have the combination . . . that you and the President present . . . to get our sprawling, wasteful, extravagant military machine whipped into shape. . . ." Humphrey concluded that if that was not done, the United States would be "building a burden that no nation can carry, and the Russians won't need military strength, we'll just beat ourselves, economically!"[66]

In March 1959, the popular Washington *Post* columnist Joseph Alsop compared Humphrey's economic ideas with "history's most influential fraud," The Protocols of the Elders of Zion. "The Protocol of Humphrey," wrote Alsop, was "the theory of George Magoffin Humphrey, supported by a wholly unverifiable quotation from Lenin, that the true Communist strategy for the defeat of the West is to force us to spend ourselves into bankruptcy.'"

Humphrey responded that he "could not recall ever having quoted Lenin," but he did believe "that the easiest, most effective and surest way for the Russians to destroy our system is to induce us to destroy it ourselves." Humphrey wrote Alsop that though it might "seem a little odd," he would quote at length from John Maynard Keynes's *The Economic Consequences of the Peace:*

> Lenin is said to have declared that the best way to destroy the Capitalist system was to debauch the currency. By a continuing process of inflation, governments can confiscate, secretly and unobserved, an important part of the wealth of their citizens. By this method they not only confiscate, but they confiscate arbitrarily; and while the process impoverishes many, it actually enriches some. The sight of this arbitrary rearrangement of riches strikes not only at security, but at confidence in the equity of the existing distribution of wealth. Those to whom the system brings windfalls . . . become "profiteers," who are the object of the hatred of the bourgeoisie, whom the inflationism has impoverished, not less than of the proletariat. As the inflation proceeds and the real value of the currency fluctuates wildly from month to month, all permanent relations between debtors and creditors, which form the ultimate foundation of capitalism, become so utterly disordered as to be almost meaningless; and the process of wealth-getting degenerates into a gamble and a lottery.[67]

The remarkable consensus among Lenin, John Maynard Keynes, and George Humphrey extended only in part to Eisenhower's White House. While Eisenhower opposed extravagant missile programs and shared Humphrey's scorn for the Gaither Report, he insisted that billions of dollars invested in mutual security development and military aid programs would save the American way of life. In response to proposed congressional budget cuts for those programs, Eisenhower penned some notes for a speech in a determined and angry flourish: Since 1947, Mutual Security efforts saved Greece, Turkey, Yugoslavia, Iran, Vietnam, and the Middle East. That cost the United States $17 billion, and the Allies $107 billion. Korea alone caused 135,000 casualties. "Do we want to nullify that sacrifice?" Eisenhower wrote that these countries are weak economically, and strong in courage. To assist them "is the business of all Americans." It was not a question of special privilege or special interests. It was "everybody's business regardless of party-race-occupation." What America has "so laboriously and patiently" built in ten years cannot "be allowed to crumble through false economy."[68]

On 14 May 1960, Eisenhower asked C. D. Jackson to "move constructively" to prevent the proposed cuts. The President was about to leave for the Paris Summit, and he could not believe that "at this point in world affairs we should face the possibility of undermining, by our own hand, our buttressing of free nations and our partnerships in defense against Communist imperialism. At stake here are the NATO and SEATO alliance structures, and the defense postures of South Korea, Taiwan, Turkey, Pakistan. Also at stake are the strivings of hundreds of millions of people who look to us for cooperation in making it possible for them to grow in freedom rather than succumbing to an atheistic materialism bent upon domination of the world."

Eisenhower considered these matters "so crucial" that he presumed "once again" to call upon C. D. Jackson's services and to "suggest a crusade for our country." Eisenhower wanted Jackson to make it clear to all congressional opponents that their position, "in these times," represented "the course of retreat and, ultimately, national crisis." The President enclosed for Jackson's use an address he presented to the Committee on International Economic Growth and the Committee to Strengthen the Frontiers of Freedom. It was a long speech. But Eisenhower's theme was persuasive. If the Mutual Security Program was scuttled, "it would be for America and all the free world, a crushing defeat in today's struggle between communistic imperialism and a freedom founded in faith and justice." Mutual Security was a bipartisan program. In 1960, both the Democratic and the Republican platforms solemnly pledged support for collective defense and international economic development.

The point was, Eisenhower declared, "the free world needs America" and "America needs the world." Foreign trade, he noted, was "a $30 billion a year business." "The health of our economy depends upon materials owned by others. Manganese, chrome, tin, natural rubber, nickel are examples. As our economy grows, we depend increasingly upon the others for such materials. Eight years ago we imported only about a twentieth of our iron ore. Today we have to import over a third of it. Yes, America needs the world!" "If nations friendly to us are weakened and imperiled, so are we." "If other free nations prosper, so do we. . . ."[69]

Eisenhower was a victim of his own partial vision. He believed that mutual security and a world economic policy would enable the United States to grow economically, to avoid World War III, to cut purely defense costs, and to be secure. He repeated over and over again that to spend one dollar more than sufficiency was to court disaster. He agreed with Humphrey that "national security and a sound economy are the same thing." He asked a National Security Council meeting: If the economy were destroyed in the process of building military protection, "what is there left to defend?"[70] By 1960, he issued "directives" to restore the United States' balance-of-payments deficit. Between 1957 and 1960, a total of $10 billion more had been paid out by the United States than had been received. "The resulting deficits are settled by sizeable outflows of gold and increases in our dollar liabilities." The United States gold stock declined by $4.5 billion since 1957. The vast "outward movement" of capital occurred because of the number of short-term development projects and the fact of "limited availability of capital in other industrialized countries."[71]

There were many ways to reverse the balance-of-payments deficit. Eisenhower's nine-page memo touched on many of them, including a reduction of troops and dependents abroad, as well as a reduction "by a very substantial amount" in military and military-assistance spending. But, above all, the Eisenhower administration decided that "U.S. private foreign investment" was "not a balance-of-payments drain." Therefore, a "freer rather than a re-tarded flow of capital for industrial development, particularly to the lesser developed and uncommitted areas of the world is a cold war imperative."

Private finance capital would therefore replace government-to-government aid, which was "the largest contributor to long-term balance of payments problems" and tended "to create state-owned and state-controlled economies, whereas private capital development aids in the creation overseas of the kind of modern capitalism that exists in the U.S." The goals of the 1949 United States Council of the International Chamber of Commerce were fully re-iterated by Eisenhower as government policy in 1960:

> If private U.S. firms go to the developed countries, it is because they see a profitable market there which can only be reached by going there. Only a very limited amount of such capital goes for the pur-pose of exporting products back to the U.S., and the vast majority of these imports are minerals, petroleum and other items not fully ob-tainable in the U.S., as has always been the case.
>
> In the case of the lesser developed countries there is an urgent need, not to retard the input of new private capital from the U.S., but vastly to expand it. This is the best way to counter the commu-nist economic offensive, to guard against expropriation and state ownership and to provide private jobs for the growing populations of those regions. . . .
>
> Indeed development of the world through private capital expan-sion offers the best long-range solution to our balance-of-payments problem, our best chance for the reduction and final elimination of ever-increasing non-remunerative government-to-government loans and grants.[72]

These plans required a "re-examination" of direct government aid programs "viewed in the light of an expanded private capital movement." The Eisenhower administration agreed that all gov-ernment agencies would "reduce Government competition with business." Wherever "significant Government commercial and in-dustrial activities" could be reduced by private business, "agencies will start to curtail or end" government enterprise.[73] In August 1960, Joseph Rand suggested to Clarence Randall that the Coun-cil on Foreign Economic Policy discuss the question of whether the United States "should have an *Open* policy of non-interference with U.S.-owned corporations abroad. Wouldn't such an open policy," Rand wondered, "do a lot for us in the underdeveloped countries?"[74]

Today the United States is a debtor nation for the first time since 1917. But a new economic power without flag or loyalty flourishes. The multinationals are the third most powerful economic presence in world affairs. After 1953, their interests began to be coordinated by the "Bilderbergers," representatives of international corporations and private power blocs, who meet secretly and unofficially. Initiated by Prince Bernhard of the Netherlands, their name derives from the fact that they first and then frequently met at the Hotel Bilderberg, in a secluded park in Oosterbeek, close to the German border. From the beginning, their goal was greater economic and political unity between competing European and United States interests. Their purpose was to deal imaginatively with the Soviet economic offensive. The Bilderbergers considered the potential danger of Soviet economic competition "as deadly to Western freedom as nuclear warfare."

Eisenhower worked closely with the Bilderbergers. C. D. Jackson was one of the founding enthusiasts of the group. Members of Eisenhower's administration attended each semiannual meeting. While C. D. Jackson seems to have attended every meeting until his death, in 1964, Richard Bissell, Gabriel Hauge, Paul Hoffman, John J. McCloy, Robert Murphy, C. Douglas Dillon, and Eugene Black, among many others, attended on occasion. In 1976, the United States members of the Bilderberg steering committee were Gabriel Hauge, Henry J. Heinz II, and David Rockefeller. It was at a Bilderberg meeting in 1972 that David Rockefeller first proposed the idea of the Trilateral Commission, to extend the conference formula to include Japan.

Because of the secretive and private nature of the Bilderberg conferences, and subsequently of the Trilateral Commission, it is impossible to assess the impact of these meetings on public policy. There is, however, evidence that all Bilderberg meetings were discussed by Eisenhower's Cabinet and the Council of Economic Advisers.[75] The Trilateral Commission, dedicated to the liberalization of the world economy through economic integration and free trade, emerged in response to President Nixon's 1971 "New Economic Policy," whereby he unilaterally devalued the dollar, demonetized gold, raised U.S. tariffs, and declared a new era of economic nationalism for the United States. After the public debacle of Watergate and the quiet emergence of the Trilateral Commission, Nixon's policies were modified, and the world economic policy was again favored. The Trilateral Commission exists primarily "to make the world safe for interdependence" and to protect international business interests against "the intrusion of national governments" or other nationalist pressures.

Like any self-respecting power bloc, representatives of international banking and business meet frequently to set policy, coordinate goals, and plan strategies for the future development of their interests. That perfectly ordinary phenomenon, combined with the acknowledged presence of the Trilateralists in the Carter White House, has occasioned adverse publicity. On 25 August 1980, David Rockefeller wrote a letter of protest to the New York *Times:* "I never cease to be amazed at those few among us who spot a conspiracy under every rock, a cabal in every corner. . . . Originally, this sort of nonsensical defamation was easy to dismiss. It came from the extreme fringes of the left and the right, and I suppose being called a Communist and a fascist at the same time puts me somewhere near the center of the political spectrum— where I am most comfortable anyway." Rockefeller denied that the Trilateral Commission was involved in the 1980 election campaign and described the Commission for the "conspiracy theorists":

> The Trilateral Commission now has about 300 members from North America, Western Europe and Japan. About one-quarter are from the U.S. and include not only business people, but labor union leaders, university professors, and research institute directors, congressmen and senators, media representatives and others. There are about as many Republicans as Democrats, and most regions of the nation are represented. . . .
> The Trilateral Commission does not take positions on issues or endorse individuals. . . . It holds meetings . . . and assigns task force reports that are discussed. . . . Reports have dealt with different aspects of world trade, energy resources, the International Monetary System, East-West relations and more. . . .

In sum, the Trilateralists are direct descendants of the Bilderbergers and heirs of the international finance capital theorists of the 1949 U.S.-ICC. As the power of their interests expands, so does their need for organization, political coherence, stability, and unity. Economically, they are well coordinated within the structure of the multinational corporations. With corporate headquarters from Brussels to Bangkok, the multinationals are today protected by NATO and counterinsurgency everywhere. Contrary to their frequent advertising campaigns, the transnationals (as they are now called) are not social-work institutions. They exist to maximize profits. Although they present a challenge to the traditional nation-state, they have done little to improve the quality of life. Throughout the free world, now dominated by U.S.- and European-based transnationals, unemployment and underdevelopment prevail. Malnourishment and illiteracy increase. Locked into a phenomenal arms race that even the developed nations cannot afford, the "underdeveloped world" increasingly hosts the transnationals and is increasingly bonded to the military-industrial complex through close ties of dependency, militarism, and repression.[76]

Contrary to Eisenhower's expectations, the flood of private investment capital abroad did not help to balance the budget, reduce inflation, increase employment, minimize defense spending, or revise America's balance-of-payments crisis. During his last years in office, Eisenhower made a heroic effort to balance the budget. His chief target was domestic spending. In June 1961, Milton Eisenhower wrote to his brother:

> It seems to me that if the imbalance in foreign payments is not soon corrected, either by increasing our exports or by other methods, then we must (a) reduce our military expenditures abroad, (b) reduce loans and grants abroad, hoping that other advanced nations will move in to fill the vacuum, and (c) pass measures which will check the outflow of private investment capital. . . .
> It is hard for the people of this country to realize that we, too, can undertake more than we can afford.[77]

But it was too late. John F. Kennedy was President. He inherited the military-industrial package Eisenhower had deplored, had hoped to restrain, and had helped to create. It was, in part, Eisenhower's legacy.

Eisenhower's legacy is complex. He expanded and fortified American capital on a worldwide basis. He loathed demagogues and communists. He feared a "garrison state." He sought international peace. Moderate and cautious, he introduced détente and counterinsurgency. He did not bomb China or Vietnam. He overthrew popular governments on three continents. Since nuclear holocaust was unacceptable, he pursued alternative means to ensure America's dominance in the race against the Soviet Union and in the race to secure access to the world's resources and markets. To Eisenhower and his associates that was a commitment to a free-market economy. Others called it empire. Whatever it is called, to control the world's resources and defend them against nationalists and communists proved to be an ongoing and draining enterprise. It created a military-industrial complex that Eisenhower regretted. His Farewell Address was not a dramatic theoretical departure. It was consistent with one aspect of his entire career. In October 1951, Eisenhower had written to Charles E. Wilson: "Any person who doesn't clearly understand that national security and national solvency are mutually dependent, and that permanent maintenance of a crushing weight of military power would eventually produce dictatorship, should not be entrusted with any kind of responsibility in our country."[78]

On 17 January 1961, Eisenhower "spoke in farewell to the American people." He warned them against the growing might of the military-industrial complex. Drafted by Malcolm Moos, a political scientist from The Johns Hopkins University who had joined the White House staff in September 1958, it was a historic speech. Eisenhower believed it was the most important challenge that he could leave with the people of America:

> During the years of my Presidency, and especially the latter years, I began to feel more and more uneasiness about the effect on the nation of tremendous peacetime military expenditures.
>
> . . . Under the spur of profit potential, powerful lobbies spring up to argue for even larger munitions expenditures. And the web of special interests grows. . . . In the long run, the combinations of pressures for growth can create an almost overpowering influence. Unjustified military spending is nothing more than a distorted use of the nation's resources. . . .
>
> We annually spend on military security more than the net income of all U.S. corporations.
>
> This conjunction of an immense military establishment and a large arms industry is new in the American experience. The total influence —economic, political, even spiritual—is felt in every city, every state house, every office of the federal government. We recognize the

imperative need for this development. Yet we must not fail to comprehend its grave implications. Our toil, resources, and livelihood are all involved; so is the very structure of our society.

In the councils of government we must guard against the acquisition of unwarranted influence, whether sought or unsought, by the military-industrial complex. The potential for the disastrous rise of misplaced power exists and will persist.

We must never let the weight of this combination endanger our liberties or democratic processes. We should take nothing for granted. . . .[79]

In retrospect, one might argue that Eisenhower's middle way was an illusion. It is possible to contend that even the most highly regarded President will succumb to forces stronger than his deepest convictions. The captive President in an unprincipled world might be helpless, hopeless, or assassinated. He might be a charlatan, a puppet, or a fool. But history means nothing if it does not mean individual impact. There are forces—economic and social forces. And there are counterforces. There is the unknown—and the individual. In our time, the power of the individual may be measured by the number of political assassinations—and it may be measured by what we have to remember. Today this violent planet has a memory of one moment in recent history when two statesmen, Eisenhower and Khrushchev, went to the very brink of peace. As we return to the brink of war, to escalated military expenditures that are at once corrupt and grotesque, that moment looms large and significant. Today our enemies are as global as our vital interests.

In a climate of scarcity and unemployment, the citizens of this world, now fundamentally united in an international economic policy, are told to prepare for war and sacrifice. But, to paraphrase Eisenhower, the people of this planet do not want war and sacrifice. People everywhere, under every system, want food, drinkable water, clean air, education, work, pride, dignity, pleasure, leisure, and joy—in short, peace. Indeed the people want that "so much that one of these days governments," and their financial directors, "had better get out of their way and let them have it."

PREFACE NOTES

1. *The Records of Public Officials,* The 48th American Assembly, Arden House, Harriman, NY, 3–5 Apr. 1975. See also B. W. Cook, "The Dwight David Eisenhower Library: The Manuscript Fiefdom at Abilene," in *Access to the Papers of Recent Public Figures: the New Harmony Conference,* ed. Alonzo L. Hamby and Edward Weldon (The Organization of American Historians, Bloomington, IN 47401, 1977). See also B. W. Cook, "Dwight David Eisenhower: Antimilitarist in the White House" (Forum Press, 1974).

2. DDE to Henry A. Wallace, 22 Feb. 1957, DDE diary, Box 12. For Eisenhower's comments about guns and butter and his fear of an American garrison state, see DDE to Frank Altschul, 25 Oct. 1957, Whitman, Administration, Box 30.

3. Ruth Leger Sivard, *World Military and Social Expenditures, 1979* (World Priorities, Box 1003, Leesburg, VA 22075).

INTRODUCTION NOTES

1. Henry Luce's editorial was first published in *Life,* 17 Feb. 1941. All quotations are from Henry R. Luce, *The American Century* (Farrar & Rinehart, 1941).
See also William Appleman Williams, "The American Century: 1941–1957," *The Nation,* 2 Nov. 1957 (reprinted in Williams, ed., *History as a Way of Learning* [New Viewpoints, 1973]).

2. For the activities of the War Policies Commission, see Seymour Waldman, *Death and Profits: a Study of the War Policies Commission* (Brewer, Warren & Putnam, 1932, reprinted with a new introduction by Arthur E. Ekirch, Garland Publishing, 1971). A joint congressional-cabinet committee, headed by Secretary of War Patrick Hurley, the War Policies Commission was created to report on ways "to promote peace, to equalize the burdens, and to remove the profits of war." Instead, the War Department introduced its Industrial Mobilization Plan, by which industry would be guaranteed "full production and satisfactory prices and profit margins in the event of war." As a result, Senators Gerald P. Nye and Arthur H. Vandenberg called for an investigation of the profiteering of the munitions industry during World War I.
See: Paul A. C. Koistinen, "The 'Industrial-Military Complex' in Historical Perspective: the InterWar Years," *Journal of American History* (March 1970), pp. 819–39; Senate hearings, *Special Committee Investigating the Munitions Industry,* Parts 1–37, 74th Cong., 1st and 2nd Sess.; "To Prevent Profiteering in War," *Senate Report,* No. 577; quotations from *Report* No. 944, Part 3, p. 12, and Koistinen. See also Helmuth Engelbrecht's summary of the hearings, *One Hell of a Business* (Robert McBride, 1934); Keith L. Nelson, "The 'Warfare State': History of a Concept," *Pacific Historical Review* (May 1971), pp. 127–43; John E. Wiltz, *In Search of Peace* (Louisiana State University Press, 1963); Wayne S. Cole, *Senator Gerald P. Nye and American Foreign Relations* (University of Minnesota Press, 1962).
Under the general editorship of Blanche Wiesen Cook, Sandi E. Cooper, and Charles Chatfield, several contemporary analyses of the early phase of the military-industrial complex were reprinted in the Garland Library of War and Peace.

See esp.: Helmuth Carol Engelbrecht and Frank Cleary Hanighen, *Merchants of Death: a Study of the International Armament Industry* (Dodd, Mead, 1934; Garland, 1972); *The International Trade in Armaments Prior to World War II,* comprising Fenner Brockway, *Bloody Traffic* (1933), Report of the First Sub-Committee of the Temporary Mixed Commission on Armaments, League of Nations Report A. 81 (1921), and the Union of Democratic Control's *The Secret International* (1932) (Garland, 1972); Richard Lewinsohn, *The Profits of War Through the Ages,* translated from the French by Geoffrey Sainsbury (E. P. Dutton, 1937; Garland, 1972). The above benefit by new introductions by Richard Dean Burns. See also, Paul A. C. Koistinen, *The Military-Industrial Complex: A Historical Perspective* (Praeger, 1980).

3. Eisenhower quoted in Peter Lyon, *Eisenhower: Portrait of the Hero* (Little, Brown, 1974), p. 79; Smith quoted, p. 83.

4. Eisenhower's reflections on his future, his first attempt "to keep some notes of my own in a form I can later read," were subsequently dated 1 Jan. 1950, Eisenhower's Personal Diary, Box 1. Related correspondence includes his letters to Philip Reed, 8 July 1949, Personal Papers, Box 90; Clifford Roberts, 3 Dec. and 18 Apr. 1951; and George Whitney, 27 Aug. 1949, Box 91.

CHAPTER I NOTES

1. See especially Gar Alperovitz, *Atomic Diplomacy: Hiroshima and Potsdam* (Alfred A. Knopf, 1967); Martin J. Sherwin, *A World Destroyed: the Atomic Bomb and the Grand Alliance* (Alfred A. Knopf, 1975); Charles L. Mee, *Meeting at Potsdam* (M. Evans, 1975); Herbert Feis, *Between War and Peace: the Potsdam Conference* (Princeton University Press, 1960); Denna F. Fleming, *The Cold War and Its Origins, 1917–1960,* 2 vols. (Doubleday, 1961).

2. William Appleman Williams, "American Intervention in Russia, 1917–1920," *Studies on the Left* (Fall 1963, Spring 1964), reprinted in Williams, *History as a Way of Learning* (New Viewpoints, 1973), pp. 41–101; Arno Mayer, *Political Origins of the New Diplomacy, 1917–1918* (Yale University Press, 1959); Mayer, *Politics and Diplomacy of Peacemaking: Containment and Counterrevolution at Versailles, 1918–1919* (Alfred A. Knopf, 1967); George A. Brinkley, *The Volunteer Army and Allied Intervention in South Russia, 1917–1921* (University of Notre Dame Press, 1966).

3. On United States diplomacy toward the new Soviet Government, see Daniel Yergin, *Shattered Peace: the Origins of the Cold War and the National Security State* (Houghton Mifflin, 1977). For a critique of Yergin, see Daniel F. Harrington, "Kennan, Bohlen, and the Riga Axioms," *Diplomatic History* (Fall 1978), pp. 423–37. On the Red scare and United States reaction to the Russian Revolution, see William Preston, *Aliens and Dissenters: Federal Suppression of Radicals, 1903–1933* (Harper Torchbooks, 1963); Robert K. Murray, *Red Scare: a Study in National Hysteria, 1919–1920* (University of Minnesota Press, 1955, McGraw-Hill Paperback, 1964); Blanche Wiesen Cook, "Democracy in Wartime: Antimilitarism in England and the United States," *American Studies* (Spring 1972), reprinted in Charles Chatfield, ed., *Peace Movements in America* (Schocken Books, 1973); and Cook, ed., *Crystal Eastman on Women and Revolution* (Oxford University Press, 1978). For Clare Sheridan on Churchill, see Sheridan, *West and East* (Boni & Liveright, 1923), p. 256.

4. Sir Alan Brooke, quoted in Lyon, op. cit., p. 327.

5. *Time,* 2 Jan. 1939; W. A. Swanberg, *Luce and His Empire* (Charles Scribner's Sons, 1972), p. 160.

6. A. A. Berle to Harry Hopkins, 30 July 1941, in *Navigating the Rapids,*

1918–1971, from the Papers of Adolf A. Berle, ed. Beatrice Bishop Berle and Travis Beal Jacobs (Harcourt Brace Jovanovich, 1973), p. 374.

7. For the researchers and their work at Göttingen University, 1923–33, see Robert Jungk, *Brighter than a Thousand Suns: the Story of the Men Who Made the Bomb* (translated from the German by James Cleugh, U.S. ed., Harcourt, Brace & World, 1958). Berle, op. cit., pp. 374–75.

8. Luce's Report, 22 June 1938, quoted in Swanberg, op. cit., p. 57.

9. Robert Murphy, *Diplomat Among Warriors* (Doubleday, 1964), Roosevelt quoted on pp. 206, 70–123; see Lyon, op. cit., pp. 153–76. See also *The Complete War Memoirs of General Charles de Gaulle* (Simon & Schuster, 1964), pp. 349–82. General de Gaulle quotes Roosevelt's reason for the "temporary expedient" of Darlan: " 'Of course I'm dealing with Darlan, since Darlan's giving me Algiers! Tomorrow I'd deal with Laval, if Laval were to offer me Paris!' " (p. 357).

10. Milton S. Eisenhower, *The President Is Calling* (Doubleday, 1974), p. 139; Edward R. Murrow quoted, p. 137.

11. Quoted in Lyon, op. cit., p. 178.

12. For Milton Eisenhower's 1942 tour of Algeria, see Robert Murphy, op. cit., pp. 149–51; and Dr. Eisenhower's very different version of his activities in North Africa, pp. 134–43.

13. M. S. Eisenhower, op. cit., pp. 141, 145.

14. C. D. Jackson to Henry Luce, 12 Oct. 1943, C. D. Jackson Papers, Box 57, DDE Library, Abilene.

15. DDE to William E. Robinson, interview, 20 Dec. 1944, quoted in Robinson to Helen Reid, 21 June 1948, William Robinson Papers, Box 9, DDE Library, Abilene.

16. M. S. Eisenhower, "Psychological Warfare," an address before the Kansas Bankers' Association, 22 May 1943, M. S. Eisenhower Papers, Box 1, DDE Library, Abilene.

17. On the circumstances of Darlan's assassination, see Lyon, op. cit., pp. 180–84. For a theory of political assassinations, see Fletcher Prouty, "The Anatomy of Assassination," in Howard Frazier, ed., *Uncloaking the CIA* (The Free Press, Macmillan, 1978), pp. 196–209.

18. Eisenhower quoted in Lyon, op. cit., pp. 186–87.

19. Ibid., pp. 217–18.

20. John J. McCloy to DDE, 1 Mar. 1943, DDE Personal Papers, Box 67. For Murphy's assessment of Lemaigre-Dubreuil and his activities, see Robert Murphy, op. cit., pp. 116–22.

21. DDE to M. S. Eisenhower, 29 June 1943, M. S. Eisenhower Papers, Box 1.

22. DDE to George Marshall, 24 June 1943, quoted in Lyon, op. cit., p. 218.

23. M. S. Eisenhower, *The President Is Calling,* pp. 143–44.

24. See Robert Murphy, op. cit., pp. 208–9.

25. A. A. Berle, op. cit., 6 Jan. 1944, p. 449; Robert Murphy, op. cit., p. 210.

26. See esp. Alexander Werth, *Russia at War, 1941–1945* (E. P. Dutton, 1964); and Trumbull Higgins, *Hitler and Russia: the Third Reich in a Two Front War* (Macmillan, 1966).

27. Murphy, op. cit., p. 187; Churchill on Operation Husky quoted in Lyon, op. cit., p. 206.

28. Murphy, op. cit., p. 188.

29. Ibid., pp. 194, 198; see also Lyon, op. cit., pp. 223–24.

30. Berle, op. cit., pp. 358, 393.

31. King Victor Emmanuel quoted in Murphy, op. cit., p. 203; for Clark's Italian campaign, see pp. 202–5; see also Lyon, op. cit., pp. 224–26, 233, 245–47.

32. Berle, op. cit., 12 May 1943, pp. 435–36; see also Lyon, op. cit., pp. 208–9.

33. For OWI's effort to undermine the king and Badoglio, see, for example, Berle, op. cit., 28 July 1943, p. 440.

34. Murphy, op. cit., pp. 206–9, 213–14. General Walter Bedell Smith further explained the United States position on Communist participation in the effort "to establish a democratic government with as broad a base as possible . . . and even . . . to facilitate the return" of Togliatti. Smith noted that even if the United States had opposed his return, "it would have been difficult to deny Communist participation in the Italian Government. Disciplined, militant Communist groups, particularly in the industrial areas of Northern Italy, had been the rallying point for Italian opposition to the Germans. The Communists were the hard core of the Partisan movement, and their initial participation in the reconstructed Italian Government was on a cooperative, collaborative basis." Smith, *My Three Years in Moscow* (J. B. Lippincott, 1950), pp. 18–19.

35. This political pattern was repeated notably and tragically in Greece. See Lawrence S. Wittner, "American Policy Toward Greece During World War II," *Diplomatic History* (Spring 1979), pp. 129–49; and Joyce Kolko and Gabriel Kolko, *The Limits of Power* (Harper & Row, 1972), pp. 218–45.

36. Murphy, op. cit., p. 228.

37. On the decision to stop at the Elbe, see Stephen E. Ambrose, *Eisenhower and Berlin, 1945* (W. W. Norton, 1967).

38. Hitler quoted in Lyon, op. cit., pp. 336–37. For details of the Berne incident and a refutation of Dulles' *The Secret Surrender*, see Gar Alperovitz, *Cold War Essays* (Schenkman, 1966), pp. 27–31, 123–25; Daniel Yergin, *Shattered Peace*, pp. 67–68.

39. Herbert Agar et al., *World-Wide Civil War*, a report of Freedom House's Lincoln Day meeting, 1942, C. D. Jackson Papers, Box 45, DDE Library, Abilene.

40. Sir Alan Brooke, quoted in Lyon, op. cit., p. 210.

41. Churchill, *Triumph and Tragedy* (Houghton Mifflin, 1953), pp. 278–80.

42. For a discussion of the economic importance of the Ruhr and the debate over the Morgenthau Plan, see Fred Smith, "The Rise and Fall of the Morgenthau Plan," *United Nations World* (March 1947); Churchill, op. cit., pp. 156–57; Joseph P. Lash, *Eleanor and Franklin* (Signet, 1971), pp. 913–14; and Lyon, op. cit., p. 301. In *Germany Is Our Problem* (Harper & Brothers, 1945), Henry Morgenthau attributed the origins of his plan to a discussion held with General Eisenhower on 7 August 1944. For his denial of Morgenthau's contention that Eisenhower wanted to see Germany "become a pastoral state," see memo No. 1684, to Charles Craig Cannon, 19 Aug. 1947, *The Papers of Dwight David Eisenhower, The Chief of Staff*, IX, Louis Galambos, et al., eds. (Johns Hopkins University Press, 1978), pp. 1877–78; see also *Occupation*, VI, Alfred D. Chandler, Jr., Louis Galambos et al., eds., pp. 424–25, 529–30. For background see Warren F. Kimball, ed., *Swords or Ploughshares? The Morgenthau Plan for Defeated Nazi Germany, 1943–1946* (J. B. Lippincott, 1976).

43. Churchill to Eisenhower quoted in Lyon, op. cit., pp. 333–35.

44. For United States postwar international economic planning, see W. Averell Harriman, *America and Russia in a Changing World* (George Allen & Unwin, 1971), p. 37; see "Past," pp. 2–74.

45. Harriman, p. 31.

46. For Eisenhower's response to Ohrdruf Nord and Buchenwald, see DDE to Gen. George Marshall, 15 Apr. 1945, in Alfred D. Chandler et al., eds., *The Papers of Dwight David Eisenhower: the War Years* (Johns Hopkins University, 1970), Vol. 4, No. 2418; Muphy, op. cit., p. 255; Lyon, op. cit., p. 338.

47. On Eisenhower's military strategy, see Stephen E. Ambrose, *The Supreme Commander: the War Years of General Dwight Eisenhower* (Doubleday, 1969); and *Eisenhower and Berlin, 1945* (Norton, 1967). For Patton's request to move on to Moscow, see Murphy, op. cit., pp. 254, 294; Doenitz quoted in

Murphy, p. 243. See also Forrest C. Pogue, *George C. Marshall: Ordeal and Hope, 1939–1943* (Viking, 1966), and *Organizer of Victory* (Viking, 1973).

48. Eisenhower's 14 June 1945 press conference quoted in Lyon, op. cit., pp. 25–26.

49. Eisenhower, *Mandate for Change: the White House Years, 1953–1956* (Doubleday, 1963), pp. 312–13; see also John Sheldon Doud Eisenhower, *Strictly Personal* (Doubleday, 1974), p. 97; the Eisenhower-Feis conversation is quoted from Memorandum of Conference with Professor Herbert Feis and DDE, 11 Apr. 1960, notes taken by Gen. Goodpaster, DDE, Diary Series, Box 32. For Truman's reaction to the bombing of Japan, *Memoirs of Harry S. Truman: Year of Decisions* (Doubleday, 1955), Vol. 1, pp. 421–26.

50. DDE to Swede Hazlett, 9 July 1945, Personal Papers, Name Series, Box 17.

CHAPTER II NOTES

1. Nikita S. Khrushchev, *Khrushchev Remembers: the Last Testament* (Little, Brown, 1974), pp. 13, 14 n.3.

2. On Eisenhower's visit to Russia, see John Sheldon Doud Eisenhower, op. cit., pp. 100–9; W. Averell Harriman and Elie Abel, *Special Envoy to Churchill and Stalin, 1941–1946* (Random House, 1975), pp. 501–3. On 18 August 1945, General Eisenhower expressed his appreciation to Marshal Georgi Konstantinovich Zhukov: "The warmth of the reception and hospitality we received from you and your comrades at arms touches all of us very deeply. It was indeed a memorable and never to be forgotten occasion." DDE Personal Papers, Box 118.

3. Harriman and Abel, op. cit., p. 503; Marshall quoted by Harriman, p. 503n.

4. W. B. Smith, op. cit., pp. 30–31.

5. Eisenhower quoted in Lyon, op. cit., p. 456.

6. Stalin quoted in Harriman, op. cit., p. 503.

7. Eisenhower's 14 Aug. 1945 press conference quoted in Lyon, op. cit., p. 357.

8. John Sheldon Doud Eisenhower, op. cit., p. 111; Drew Pearson's syndicated column of 15 Oct. 1944, quoted Roy Larsen, president of *Time*, as announcing at a party that Luce planned to "go out against Stalin and his Reds." Larsen implied "that the Soviet Union must be alienated from the U.S.A. and Britain in all matters connected with the Pacific and Asia—at any cost." Bullitt and Chambers quoted in Swanberg, op. cit., pp. 216–17; see also pp. 215–32ff.

9. Murphy, op. cit., p. 283; Lyon, op. cit., p. 361. For a discussion of JCS-1067, the denazification order, see Murphy pp. 250–85 and Alfred S. Chandler et al., eds., *The Papers of Dwight David Eisenhower, Occupation, 1945* (Johns Hopkins University, 1978), VI, especially DDE to George Patton, 23 Aug. 1945, pp. 307–9; DDE to Patton, 11 Sept. 1945, p. 351; and DDE to George Marshall and Patton, 25 Sept. 1945, pp. 374–75. On 11 Sept., Eisenhower wrote to Patton: "As you know I have announced a firm policy of uprooting the whole Nazi organization regardless of the fact that we may sometimes suffer from local administrative inefficiency. Reduced to its fundamentals, the United States entered this war as a foe of Nazism; victory is not complete until we have eliminated from positions of responsibility and, in appropriate cases properly punished, every active adherent to the Nazi party.

"I know that certain field commanders have felt that some modification to this policy should be made. That question has long since been decided. We will not compromise with Nazism in any way. . . . [A]ny expressed opposition to the faithful execution of the order cannot be regarded leniently by me. I expect just as loyal service in the execution of this and other policies applying to the German occupation as I received during the war."

10. Harrison's report, New York *Times,* 30 Sept. 1945; Lyon, op. cit., pp. 358–60; and DDE to Harry S Truman, 18 Sept. 1945, in Chandler et al., op. cit., pp. 357–61.

11. Lyon, op. cit., p. 362. On 20 Sept. 1945, Eisenhower sent a memorandum "To All Subordinate Commanders: 'The burden of providing the means for caring properly for [displaced persons] must be to the greatest possible extent thrown upon the German population. There will be no hesitancy in requisitioning houses, grounds, or other facilities useful to displaced persons. . . .'" *Occupation,* VI, pp. 363–65; see also DDE to Truman, 18 Sept. 1945, pp. 356–61.

12. John J. McCloy to DDE and Gen. Clark in Austria, 10 Oct. 1945, DDE Personal Papers, Box 67.

13. DDE Memorandum to Gen. Clay, 8 Nov. 1945, ibid., Box 22.

14. Clay to DDE, 2 Dec. 1945, ibid.

15. DDE TO Clay, 11 Dec. 1945, ibid.; DDE to Zhukov, 6 Dec. 1945, Box 118; Zhukov to DDE, n.d. Dec. 1945, ibid.

16. DDE to Zhukov re Smith, 4 Mar. 1946, Box 118; Zhukov to DDE, 24 Mar. 1946; DDE to Zhukov, 13 Mar. 1946; DDE to Bedell Smith, 11 Apr. 1946, Box 101.

17. Churchill's Fulton, Missouri, speech, 5 Mar. 1946, in Winston S. Churchill, *The Sinews of Peace: Post-War Speeches,* ed. Randolph Churchill (Houghton Mifflin, 1949), pp. 100–5. Goebbels quoted in David Horowitz, *The Free World Colossus* (Hill & Wang, 1965), p. 62.

18. W. B. Smith, op. cit., pp. 52–54.

19. Miles Copeland, *The Game of Nations: the Amorality of Power Politics* (Simon & Schuster, 1969), pp. 34–35. For Eisenhower on Greece and Turkey, see DDE to Joint Chiefs of Staff, 10 May 1947, "U. S. Assistance to Other Countries . . . ," in Louis Galambos, et al., eds., *The Papers of Dwight David Eisenhower, the Chief of Staff* (Johns Hopkins University, 1973), Vol. VIII, pp. 1700–3; and DDE to William D. Morgan, 4 Dec. 1947, ibid., Vol. IX, pp. 2102–4. See also Wittner, op. cit., and Kolko and Kolko, op. cit.

20. Harry S Truman to Joint Session of Congress, *Congressional Record,* 12 Mar. 1947, Vol. 92, pp. 1999–2000.

21. Murphy, op. cit., pp. 306–9.

22. George C. Marshall's commencement address, 5 June 1947, New York *Times,* 6 June 1947.

23. Bedell Smith to DDE, 10 Dec. 1947, DDE Personal Papers, Box 101.

24. Smith to DDE, 26 June 1947; DDE to Smith, 3 July 1947, ibid.

25. DDE to Swede Hazlett, 19 July 1947, Box 51.

CHAPTER III NOTES

1. James Roosevelt with Bill Libby, *My Parents: a Differing View* (Playboy Press, 1976), p. 167.

2. Norman Graebner, "Cold War Origins and the Continuing Debate," *Journal of Conflict Resolution,* Mar. 1969, p. 131.

3. For Nixon's early political career, see especially: Jerry Voorhis, *The Strange Case of Richard Milhous Nixon* (Popular Library, 1972); William A. Reuben, *The Honorable Mr. Nixon* (Action Books, 1956); Frank Mankiewicz, *Perfectly Clear: Nixon from Whittier to Watergate* (Popular Library, 1973).

4. Alger Hiss was never convicted of treason, or of espionage. He was convicted of perjury on the issue of his relationship with his only accuser, Whittaker Chambers. The Hiss case remains one of the most controversial incidents of this period. See particularly William Reuben, op. cit.; Alger Hiss, *In the Court of Public Opinion* (Harper Colophon, 1972 [1957]); John Chabot Smith, *Alger*

Hiss: the True Story (Penguin, 1977); Edith Tiger, ed., *In Re Alger Hiss* (Hill & Wang, 1979); Allen Weinstein, *Perjury* (Alfred A. Knopf, 1978).

5. Truman quoted by Eisenhower, *Crusade in Europe,* p. 444.

6. Hubert H. Humphrey, *The Education of a Public Man: My Life and Politics* (Doubleday, 1976), pp. 110–11.

7. Truman quoted in William Manchester, *American Caesar: Douglas MacArthur, 1880–1964* (Little, Brown, 1978), p. 534. See also Robert J. Donovan, *Conflict and Crisis: the Presidency of Harry S. Truman, 1945–1948* (W. W. Norton, 1977), Ch. 40.

8. See Ingrid Scobie's forthcoming biography of Helen Gahagan Douglas and the previously cited works of Voorhis, Reuben, and Mankiewicz.

9. Luce to Eisenhower, 24 Apr., 22 Aug. 1951, 7 Jan. 1952; Eisenhower to Luce, 17 Apr. (Dear Henry), 27 Aug. 1951, and Eisenhower's telegram 3 Apr. 1952, DDE Personal Papers, Box 65.

10. Although Eisenhower's financial interests, his personal investments, and his business dealings have been classified "C" and remain closed, several available documents are relevant: DDE to Clifford Roberts, 18 Oct. 1951, Box 91; Roberts to DDE, "to the Stockholders of *Joroberts Corporation,*" 19 May 1952, a statistical report on the operating companies in which Joroberts invested, largely Coca-Cola and soft-drink operations in Uruguay, Chile, Argentina, Brazil, Scotland, South Africa, and England, Box 57. See also Clifford Roberts to DDE, 1 Oct. 1951, 3 Oct. 1951, Box 91; and DDE to Philip Reed, 2 May 1951, Box 90.

11. Roberts to DDE, 1, 3 Oct. 1951, Box 91.

12. W. Alton Jones, "Communism Is as Communism Does," Oct. 1951, DDE Personal Papers, Box 57; Charles Hargrove, "Capitalist Comeback . . . ," *The Wall Street Journal,* 26 May 1951. William Robinson's "Capitalism's Worst Foes Aren't Reds at All," *Clarkson Letter,* Mar. 1948, referred to by Emil Schram, president of the New York Stock Exchange, in his testimony before the Senate Finance Committee and headlined by *The Saturday Evening Post,* 24 Apr. 1948. This article, along with several reports of the Industrial Securities Committee, Investment Bankers Association of America, were sent to Eisenhower by Roberts, 17–18 May 1948. See esp. the convention reports for 25–28 May 1948 and 30 Nov. to 5 Dec. 1947. These materials were prominently featured throughout Eisenhower's 1952 campaign. Robinson's assertion, for example, that " . . . it is all very well to wave the atomic bomb at the communists, but we shall not have much to save if some curb is not placed on those here at home . . . ," was to become familiar indeed to Eisenhower-watchers (Box 91).

13. DDE to W. Alton Jones, 4 May 1948; Jones to DDE, 16 Nov. 1948; DDE to Jones, 19 Nov. 1948, Box 57.

14. On the Bohemian Grove, C. D. Jackson to Paul Smith, 31 July 1952, C. D. Jackson Papers, Box 30, DDE Library, Abilene. See also Norman Loyall ("Blackie") McLaren's correspondence with Eisenhower. McLaren was one of Ike's encampment bridge partners and the president of the Bohemian Grove. Eisenhower was notified of his election to the Club by Holloway Jones, 14 Aug. 1950, Bohemian Club Box, DDE Library, Abilene. For the history and membership of the semi-secret Bohemian Club, see the seventy-six-page pamphlet *Members in Memoriam,* 15 Aug. 1951, in Eisenhower's Bohemian Club Box. See also C. D. Jackson's list of cabin assignments for 1959, C. D. Jackson Papers, Box 30; G. William Domhoff, "Playgrounds of the Powerful: How Fat Cats Keep in Touch," *Psychology Today,* Aug. 1975, and Domhoff's *The Bohemian Grove and Other Retreats: a Study in Ruling-Class Cohesiveness* (Harper & Row, 1974).

15. Eisenhower deeply appreciated these events and the opportunity to meet so many men of "high caliber" in an "atmosphere of friendly intimacy." See Eisenhower's correspondence with Bermingham, 1949–50, Bermingham Papers, Columbia University.

16. For Eisenhower's correspondence with Sid Richardson, see DDE Personal

Papers, Box 90. For a discussion of Richardson's relationship with Connally, Lyndon B. Johnson and Eisenhower, see Charles Ashman, *Connally* (William Morrow, 1974).

17. DDE to Smith, 18 Sept. 1947, DDE Personal Papers, Box 101.

18. William E. Robinson's "Confidential Notes" on his "cold call, without previous appointment," to DDE, 17 Oct. 1947, William Robinson Papers, Box 9. Eisenhower's explanation to Swede Hazlett, 25 Aug. 1947, DDE Personal Papers, Name Series, Box 17, was very precise:

My own deepest concern involves America's situation in the world today. Her security position and her international leadership. . . . Allied to these questions of course is that of internal health, particularly maximum productivity. While there may be little that I can do about such matters, I do have the satisfaction of feeling that whatever I try to do is on a national and not on any partisan basis. Moreover, I flatter myself to believe that the people who listen to me understand that I am talking or working for all, not for any political party or for any political ambition. This is the attitude I hope that I can preserve to the end of my days.

19. Robert Murphy, op. cit., p. 290.

20. Robinson's memo to Helen Rogers Reid, 21 June 1948, William Robinson Papers, Box 9; Robinson to DDE, 5 May 1949, DDE Personal Papers, Box 91.

21. James G. Crowley's speech, sponsored by the American Federation of Labor, was broadcast over the American Broadcasting System; a copy of it is in DDE Personal Papers, Box 91.

22. For an account of the differing attitudes regarding the New Deal held by the Eisenhower brothers, see Steve Neal, *The Eisenhowers: Reluctant Dynasty* (Doubleday, 1978), Ch. 7.

23. *Crusade in Europe*, pp. 474–76.

24. Thomas W. Dewart's final editorial, New York *Sun*, 4 Jan. 1950, and Eisenhower's comments, DDE Diary, Box 1.

25. Eisenhower's New Year diary entry, 1 Jan. 1950, ibid.

26. Memorandum from Eisenhower on the American Assembly, n.d., DDE Personal Papers, Box 91; DDE to Amon Carter, 27 June 1949, Box 20; DDE to Bermingham, 29 Sept. 1950, Bermingham Papers; on antisocialist activities at Columbia, see DDE to Bermingham, 12 May 1951, Bermingham Papers. The American Assembly was supported by many of Eisenhower's old and new friends, notably Amon Carter, president of the Fort Worth *Star-Telegram* and a director of American Airlines; Sid Richardson; Clifford Roberts; Lucius Clay; and several corporations. See L. W. Douglas to Amon Carter, 3 Jan. 1952, DDE Personal Papers, Box 20; DDE to Cliff Roberts, 13 Oct. 1950, Roberts to DDE, 10 Apr. 1951, Box 91; DDE to Clay, 28 May 1951, Box 22; DDE to Amon Carter, 27 June 1949, 22 Dec. 1949, 29 Nov. 1950, Box 20; Carter to DDE, 22 Nov. 1950, Box 20; DDE to Bermingham, 31 Dec. 1950; Bermingham to DDE, 23 May 1952, Bermingham Papers.

27. DDE to Clifford Roberts, 6 Nov. 1950, DDE Personal Papers, Box 91; DDE to Lew Douglas, 28 Nov. 1952, Whitman, Box 13; Bermingham to DDE, 23 Apr. 1952, Bermingham Papers.

28. Robert Murphy, op. cit., p. 259.

29. DDE to Hazlett, 1 Nov. 1950, DDE Personal Papers, Box 51.

30. The quotations are from Eisenhower's original draft, except for the last paragraph. The final version as sent to Truman, editorially recast largely by Hamilton Fish Armstrong, appears alongside Eisenhower's original, in Wriston's document "Eisenhower Study Group Letter to President Truman, 12 December 1950," pp. 8–11. Eisenhower's call for troops was written by Henry Wriston, 22 Apr. 1968, Council on Foreign Relations, DDE Study Group, Box 1, Abilene. According to Laurence H. Shoup and William Minter, the work of Eisenhower's study group was facilitated by a $50,000 grant from The Rockefeller Foundation:

Imperial Brain Trust: the Council on Foreign Relations and United States Foreign Policy (Monthly Review Press, 1977), pp. 35, 54 n 71.

31. See Wriston, p. 13, and Eisenhower, *Mandate for Change,* pp. 12–13.

32. Taft quoted in Lyon, op. cit., p. 417.

33. Eisenhower on Taft, *Mandate for Change,* p. 14.

34. See, for example, Bermingham to DDE, 14 Apr. 1951, Bermingham Papers; Robinson to DDE, 9 Apr. 1951, DDE Personal Papers, Box 91.

35. DDE to Bermingham, 8 Feb. 1951, Bermingham Papers.

36. DDE to Bermingham, 28 Feb. 1951; DDE to Bill Robinson, 6 Mar. 1951.

37. For a full analysis of isolationist policies, see Justus Doenecke, *Not to the Swift: the Old Isolationists in the Cold War Era* (Bucknell University, 1979); Taft quoted in Ronald Radosh, *Prophets on the Right: Profiles of Conservative Critics of American Globalism* (Simon & Schuster, 1975), p. 149.

38. Paul Hoffman's biography and speech "No Man Is an Island" reported in the New York *Herald Tribune,* 24 Oct. 1949. Taft quoted in Doenecke, op. cit., pp. 116–17. For Hoffman's correspondence on the ECA, see C. D. Jackson Papers, Box 49.

39. *The Vandenberg Resolution and the North Atlantic Treaty Hearings,* held in executive session before the Committee on Foreign Relations, U. S. Senate, 80th Cong., 2nd Sess., S.R. 239, and 81st Cong., 1st Sess., *Executive L, Historical Series* (GPO, 1973); Ernest A. Gross's testimony, 12 Apr. 1948, pp. 188–89; that of Bourke Hickenlooper and Henry Cabot Lodge, p. 187. See Doenecke's discussion, op. cit., Ch. 8, of the isolationist response to NATO and MAP.

40. Taft and McCarthy quoted in Manchester, *American Caesar,* p. 535.

41. A. T. Steele, "Asia's Red Riddle," New York *Herald Tribune,* 1 Nov. 1949, attached to Robinson to DDE, 2 Nov. 1949, DDE Personal Papers, Box 91; Acheson quoted in Doenecke, op. cit., p. 173; see ibid., Ch. 9. See also Dorothy Borg and Waldo Heinrichs, *Uncertain Years: Chinese-American Relations, 1947–1950* (Columbia University Press, 1980).

42. Stephen E. Pelz, from Luce Discussion Paper 1, "America Goes to War, Korea, 1943–50: the Incremental Commitment to South Korea," an unpublished paper, East Asian Institute, Columbia University, Spring 1980. Dean Acheson quoted in Manchester, op. cit., p. 539; Grew and Benninghoff quoted in Joyce Kolko and Gabriel Kolko, *The Limits of Power: the World and U. S. Foreign Policy, 1945–1954* (Harper & Row, 1972), Ch. 10; Dulles quoted in Manchester, p. 676; Eisenhower's 24 July 1953 diary entry, DDE Diary Series, Box 5; I. F. Stone, *The Hidden History of the Korean War* (Monthly Review Press, 1952, 1969); Trumbull Higgins, *Korea and the Fall of MacArthur* (Oxford University, 1960); and James Aronson, *The Press and the Cold War* (Beacon, 1970), Ch. 8, "The News from Korea."

43. Joseph Kennedy and Hoover quoted in Doenecke, op. cit., pp. 197–98.

44. Taft and Hoover quoted in Doenecke, pp. 198–99, 202.

45. Clay to DDE, 13 Apr. 1951; DDE to Clay, 6 Apr. 1951, DDE Personal Papers, Box 22.

46. Clifford Roberts to DDE, 18 Apr. 1951; William Robinson to DDE, 20 Apr. 1951, DDE Personal Papers, Box 91.

47. On 30 Apr. 1951, Clifford Roberts sent Eisenhower a Walter Lippmann column, "Taft and Bradley" (New York *Herald Tribune,* 30 Apr. 1951), with the note, "Here is a Lippmann piece you must not miss." Lippmann's theme was that the military schism was provoked by Taft, a "thoroughly confused man" who had abandoned Republican precepts, and the Truman administration, pitifully weak and without "confidence in itself." The situation left only Eisenhower, steadfastly silent in the public arena to represent the American tradition of civilian control over the military.

48. Clay to DDE, 15 May 1951, DDE Personal Papers, Box 22.

49. See Roger Daniels, *The Bonus March: an Episode of the Great Depression* (Greenwood, 1971). Eisenhower on MacArthur quoted in Wilson Hicks, ed., *This Is Ike;* "Eisenhower Diary Said to Assail MacArthur and Admiral King," New York *Times,* 19 Sept. 1979. Clay to DDE, 27 June 1951, DDE Personal Papers, Box 22.

50. Cliff Roberts to DDE, 10 May 1951, DDE Personal Papers, Box 91. DDE to Swede Hazlett, 21 June 1951; Hazlett to DDE, 1 June 1951, Box 51; George Gallup, "General Ike Tops MacArthur in Poll," New York *World-Telegram and Sun,* 14 May 1951.

51. Robinson to DDE, 19 May 1951; Roberts to DDE, 18 May and 13 May 1951, DDE Personal Papers, Box 91.

52. DDE to members of Congress, 19 June 1951; Robinson to Gruenther, 17 July 1951; Robinson to DDE, 11 July 1951, including copy of Steele's suspended news report, Box 91.

53. Clay to DDE, 24 June 1951, Box 22. For the full preconvention code of participants, see Clay's interview, Columbia Oral History Project, Columbia University.

CHAPTER IV NOTES

1. DDE Personal Diary, 21 Dec. 1951.

2. DDE to Earl Schaefer, 27 Dec. 1951; Schaefer to DDE, 15 Dec. 1951, DDE Personal Papers, Box 98.

3. Clifford Roberts to DDE, 11 Sept. 1951, with editorial "International Tightrope," New York *Herald Tribune,* 11 Sept. 1951, Box 91.

4. Philip D. Reed, "The Challenge of This Conference," an address before the First International Conference of Manufacturers, sponsored by the NAM, Hotel Pierre, 4 Dec. 1951; Reed to DDE, 7 Dec. 1951; DDE to Reed, 20 Dec. 1951, Box 90.

5. Eisenhower's first speech in West Germany, at Rhein-Main Air Base, 20 Jan. 1951, Box 67.

6. Robinson to DDE, 13 Mar. 1951, Box 91; Bermingham to DDE, 14 Apr. 1951, Bermingham Papers; DDE to Robinson, 15 Mar., DDE Personal Papers, Box 91.

7. DDE to Clay, 20 May 1952, Box 22.

8. John J. McCloy to Harriman, 17 Mar. 1952, DDE Personal Papers, Box 67. For Eisenhower's effort to persuade Schumacher to cease opposition to German participation in the European Defense Force, see Douglas MacArthur II to DDE, 18 Oct. 1951, and DDE to McCloy, ibid. (documents declassified May 1975).

9. Henry Luce, "A Personal Comment on the News," C. D. Jackson Papers, Box 57, 8 Dec. 1945.

10. Eisenhower's address, San Francisco, 8 Oct. 1952, C. D. Jackson Records, Box 1. The speech, probably drafted by Jackson, presents a lengthy and specific program of psychological warfare. See also Jackson's "The Battle for Men's Minds," a speech before the American Management Association, 2 Oct. 1950, Box 83; and the text of Jackson's CBS radio broadcast on psychological warfare, 15 Sept. 1952, Box 82. Jackson deeply influenced Eisenhower's views on this subject and served as Eisenhower's political-warfare adviser during World War II and the presidency.

11. Walter Bedell Smith to DDE, 7 Sept. 1950, DDE Personal Papers, Box 101.

12. Murphy, op. cit., p. 304. See also Berenice Carroll, "The Partition of Germany: Cold War Compromise," in Thomas Hachey, *The Problem of Partition: Peril to World Peace* (Rand McNally, 1972), pp. 81–131.

13. Jackson to Daniel Lerner, 24 Aug. 1948.

14. See a sketch of C. D. Jackson prepared by J. Walter Thompson for a press release, 19 Sept. 1951, C. D. Jackson Papers, Box 82. A Princeton graduate (1924), Jackson joined *Time* as assistant to the president in 1931. He became deeply involved with several organizations to promote world trade, notably the International Chamber of Commerce, the National Foreign Trade Council (NFTC), and the International Hudson Corporation, committed to "Practical Factors" regarding "the economic development of underdeveloped countries." Jackson deplored the fact that so few businessmen appreciated the need to promote America's international economic posture. In a letter to Jack Heinz he wrote: "One of the really distressing things about the extra-curricular activities to save the world is that you are always running into the same faces. It seems incredible that out of 150 million Americans you cannot find more than 150 businessmen willing to step up to bat. Somehow or other the base must be broadened. . . ." Jackson to Heinz, 15 Feb. 1950, C. D. Jackson Papers, Box 89. See also Jackson to George Sloan, 22 Jan. 1951, ibid.; Leon Henderson to Jackson, 20 Jan. 1949, Box 51; and Jackson's testimony before the House Ways and Means Committee, 28 Apr. 1947, favoring lower tariffs and a "Reciprocal Trade Program."

15. On the origins of SAIS see Jackson's program for an "Institute for Democratic Leadership" (1941), C. D. Jackson Papers, Box 50; Jackson to Henry Luce, 29 Jan. 1942, Box 56; Jackson to Roy Alexander, 8 Sept. 1950, Box 43; Christian Herter to Jackson, 22 Sept. 1950, Box 43; Hamilton Robinson to Jackson, 25 May 1951, Box 43.

16. C. D. Jackson, "Who Will Win the Cold War Between Free Enterprise and Statism?" 24 Oct. 1949, Jackson Papers, Box 83; also, Jackson's speech before the St. Louis Advertising Club, 9 Jan. 1950, Box 83; see "The Greatest Opportunity on Earth," *Fortune* editorial, Oct. 1949.

17. Minutes of Radio Committee meeting, 15 June 1950, C. D. Jackson Papers, Box 74. The following members of the Radio Committee were present: Frank Altschul, chairman; Edmund Chester; Jay Lovestone; Edgar Ansel Mowrer; Arthur Schlesinger, Jr.; DeWitt C. Poole, president; and Spencer Phenix, vice-president, represented NCFE. Dr. William Thorbecke, director of information of NCFE, attended. The following staff of Radio Free Europe were present: Herbert Gross, Philip Barbour, Reuben Nathan, and William Rafael.

18. Jackson to William E. Daugherty, operations research officer, 17 July 1952, C. D. Jackson Papers, Box 90.

19. NCFE and Crusade pamphlets, including "To Halt Communism and Save Freedom," are in C. D. Jackson Papers, Box 74. The NCFE in 1949 consisted of, among others: Laird Bell, A. A. Berle, Harry Bullis, Lucius Clay, William Clayton, Clark M. Clifford, Cecil B. DeMille, Frank Denton, William Donovan, Hugh A. Drum, Eisenhower, Mark Ethridge, James A. Farley, Virginia Gildersleeve, Palmer Hoyt, Arthur Bliss Lane, Herbert Lehman, Henry Luce, Spyros Skouras, Charles Spofford, Charles P. Taft, DeWitt Wallace, and Darryl F. Zanuck. The officers were Joseph C. Grew, chairman of the board; Allen Dulles, chairman of the Executive Committee; DeWitt C. Poole, president; Frederic R. Dolbeare, vice-president; Spencer Phenix, vice-president; Frank Altschul, treasurer; and Theodore C. Augustine, secretary. On the Free University in Exile, see A. A. Berle, op. cit., esp. pp. 595, 608.

20. Jackson to Gen. Walter Bedell Smith, 31 Jan. 1952; Smith to Jackson, 11 Mar. 1952, C. D. Jackson Papers, Box 78.

21. For the fullest account of RFE's early years, see Jackson's talk for CBS, 15 Sept. 1951, C. D. Jackson Papers, Box 82; see also his speech "Psychological Warfare—Orphan Annie to Superman," 18 May 1951, Box 82.

22. DDE to Clay, 24 Aug. 1951; Clay to DDE, 1 Mar. 1951; telegram, Clay to

DDE, 17 Sept. 1951, DDE Personal Papers, Box 22. Eisenhower's speech is quoted from his draft version, sent to Clay with the note: "If the following looks all right we can have a recording made here Friday. . . ."

23. Smith to DDE, via Robert Thayer, 10 Oct. 1951, Box 101 (declassified 10/1974). See Eisenhower's report to Smith on Reynaud's visit, 19 Oct. 1951 (declassified 8/10/1976, NLE-76-61 No. 1) and DDE to Smith, 20 Apr. 1951, DDE Personal Papers, Abilene.

24. Robinson to DDE, 21 Dec. 1950, DDE Personal Papers, Box 91. For an analysis of U.S. political warfare through 1953, emphasizing errors of judgment and timing, see the Lodigensky File, "Winning the Cold Peace: Soviet and U. S. Psychological Warfare," C. D. Jackson Papers, Box 56.

25. DDE to Clay, 16 Mar. 1951; Clay to DDE, 26 Mar. 1951; DDE to Clay, 30 Mar. 1951, DDE Personal Papers, Box 22.

26. Two German public-opinion surveys were taken, see C. T. Lanham to DDE, 6 Mar. 1952, Box 67. The surveys indicated: (a) The "Presence of Allied Troops in West Germany" enhanced a sense of security, but it was obtained "at a high cost," and "a considerable minority" "would like the foreign troops to 'go home.'" (b) The West Germans evaluated the "Fighting Qualities of the Allied Troops": "Poorly." (c) "The Negro soldier enjoys a good reputation as a potential fighter." But most of those who believed same emphasized "the unique racial characteristics of the Negro." (d) The "best" soldiers were, in the opinion of the West Germans, "the Russians," who took second place, "after the Germans," then the British, U.S., and French in that order. "The three Allied powers are rated very poorly, . . . with the U.S. closely pushing France for last place, while England rates just a trifle above."

A summation of "Report No. 120: 'German Evaluations of NATO,'" showed that "although no favorable public opinion toward NATO has yet developed in West Germany, there is no die-hard majority in opposition to any of the NATO proposals or activities." Regarding Eisenhower personally, the West Germans "expressed a 'fair' confidence in him, and felt that he would treat the Germans as equals." Of significance to the future level of U.S. participation was the fact that West German opinion recognized that "military participation would increase taxes" and felt "they should not be expected to contribute as great a proportion of their tax dollar to defense as do other Western nations."

27. DDE to Henry Luce, 17 Sept. 1952, C. D. Jackson Papers, Box 41; DDE to Henry Luce, 8 Jan. 1952, DDE Personal Papers, Box 65.

28. Bermingham to DDE, 13 Dec. 1951, Bermingham Papers; DDE to Milton Eisenhower, 20 Sept. 1951, M. S. Eisenhower Papers, Box 1.

29. Clay to DDE, 15 May, 22 Aug. 1951, DDE Personal Papers, Box 22; Bermingham to DDE, 9 Sept. 1951, Bermingham Papers. Throughout the spring and summer of 1951, Eisenhower was under intense pressure to declare himself. He refused. See esp. DDE to Clay, 30 May, Clay to DDE, 13 Aug. 1951; Bermingham to DDE, 28 Aug., 9 Sept. 1951; DDE to Clifford Roberts, 28 Jan. 1952, DDE Personal Papers, Box 91; Roberts to DDE, 22, 24 Jan., 26 Mar. 1952; DDE to Phil Reed, 12 Feb. 1952, Box 90; DDE to William Robinson, 21 Mar., 26 Mar. 1952, Box 91; Sid Richardson to DDE, 21 Dec. 1951, Box 90.

30. Bermingham to DDE, 4 Sept. 1951; DDE to Bermingham, 24 Sept., 18 Dec. 1951, Bermingham Papers.

31. Sid Richardson to DDE, 1 Dec. 1951, DDE Personal Papers, Box 90; Bermingham to DDE, 8 Dec. 1951, Bermingham Papers; Truman to DDE, 18 Dec. 1951, DDE Personal Diary, Box 1.

32. Eisenhower to Truman, in *Mandate for Change*, p. 19.

33. Robinson to DDE, 21 Oct. 1951; Roberts to DDE, 31 Oct. 1951, DDE Personal Papers, Box 91; DDE to Roberts, 8 Nov. 1951; Roberts to DDE, 15 Nov. 1951; DDE to Roberts, 24 Nov. 1951; Roberts to DDE, 3 Dec. 1951.

34. DDE to Roberts, 8 Dec. 1951; DDE to Robinson and Milton Eisenhower, 31 Oct. 1951, M. S. Eisenhower Papers, Box 1.

35. DDE to Bermingham, 7 Jan. 1952, Bermingham Papers; DDE to Clay, 8 Jan. 1952, DDE Personal Papers, Box 22; DDE to Milton Eisenhower, 23 Feb. 1952, M. S. Eisenhower Papers, Box 1.

36. DDE to Bermingham, 11 Feb. 1952, Bermingham Papers. Eisenhower sent a similar letter to Bermingham on 18 March as well. See also Bermingham to DDE regarding the Madison Square Garden rally as reported by Sid Richardson and Tex McCrary, 16 Feb. 1952, Bermingham Papers. William Robinson to DDE, 11 Feb. 1952, DDE Personal Papers, Box 91.

37. DDE to Phil Reed, 12 Feb. 1952; Reed to DDE, 22 Jan. 1952, Box 90.

38. DDE to "Luckus" Clay, 20 Feb. 1952, Box 22; Bermingham to DDE, 23 Feb. 1952, Bermingham Papers.

39. DDE to Clay, 10 Apr. 1952, DDE Personal Papers, Box 22; Bermingham to DDE, 13 Dec., 8 Dec. 1951, 25 Mar., 23 Apr. 1952, Bermingham Papers; Clay to DDE, 14 Apr., 28 Mar. 1952, 7 Dec. 1951, DDE Personal Papers, Box 22. DDE to Robinson, 26 Mar. 1952, DDE Personal Papers, Box 91. See also Bermingham to DDE, 28 Apr., 24 July 1952, Bermingham Papers.

40. Bermingham to DDE, 19 July 1952, Bermingham Papers; DDE to Luce, 17 Sept. 1952, C. D. Jackson Papers, Box 41.

41. Richard Nixon's "Checkers" speech has been widely reprinted. See esp., David A. Frier, *Conflict of Interest in the Eisenhower Administration* (Penguin Books, 1969), p. 31 and passim, Ch. 3, "The Poor Richard Show." See also Brownell's interview with Jean Smith, Apr. 1971, Columbia Oral History Project, pp. 9–11; Lyon, op. cit., pp. 453–62.

42. Bermingham to DDE, 13 Oct. 1952. All of Eisenhower's financial records, and materials relating to his personal finances, remain classified. One suspects that had his "unique income-tax benefit" received on his memoirs, via an unusual ruling by the IRS, regarding the $625,000 he received for *Crusade in Europe*, become public knowledge, more interest in his finances might have emerged. See Neal, *The Eisenhowers* (Doubleday, 1978), p. 242.

43. DDE to William Robinson, 12 Feb. 1952, DDE Personal Papers, Box 91; DDE to Earl Schaefer, 22 Jan. 1952, Box 98.

44. DDE to Clay, 20 Feb. 1952, Box 22; Robinson to DDE, 26 Feb. 1952, Box 91.

45. Robinson to DDE, 18 Feb. 1952, Box 91.

46. Walter Lippmann, "The Eisenhower Movement," New York *Herald Tribune*, 18 Mar. 1952, Box 91.

47. Clifford Roberts to DDE, 16 June 1952, Box 91.

48. DDE to Roberts, 19 June 1952, ibid.

CHAPTER V NOTES

1. See Clare Boothe Luce to DDE, DDE to Henry Luce, 15 Nov. 1952, Box 27; John Foster Dulles to DDE, 20 May 1952, DDE Personal Papers, Box 33; DDE to Dulles, 15 Apr. 1952; Lucius Clay to DDE, 2 Apr., with Dulles' foreign-policy paper, 31 Mar. 1952, Box 22; DDE to Clay, with criticism of Dulles' paper, 10 Apr. 1952, Box 22.

2. See Dulles on Dewey, and Sulzberger on Dulles in C. L. Sulzberger, *A Long Row of Candles* (Macmillan, 1969), pp. 748–49.

3. For Dulles' views, see particularly John Foster Dulles, *War, Peace and Change* (Garland, 1971 [1939]), with an introduction by Charles Chatfield; Townsend Hoopes, *The Devil and John Foster Dulles* (Little, Brown, 1973); and Michael A. Guhin, *A Statesman and His Times* (Columbia University Press,

1972). See also Eleanor Lansing Dulles, *John Foster Dulles: The Last Year* (Harcourt, Brace & World, 1963) and *Chances of a Lifetime: A Memoir* (Prentice-Hall, 1980).

4. DDE to Swede Hazlett, 23 Oct. 1954; 26 Feb. 1958, Whitman, Name Series, Box 18.

5. DDE to Emmet [Hughes], 10 Dec. 1953, Whitman Diary, Box 2.

6. Eisenhower's diary, 7 Feb. 1953, Box 1.

7. On Gruenther's command of European problems, see excerpts from a "confidential diary" kept by a journalist who accompanied Adlai Stevenson on his worldwide tour, in Ward Melville to DDE, 17 Sept. 1953, Whitman, Name Series, Box 32. See also, for example, Eisenhower to Gruenther, 3 Jan. 1955, Whitman, Box 17, and DDE to Gruenther, 15 Jan. 1958, Box 18; and Vernon A. Walters, *Silent Missions* (Doubleday, 1978), p. 283. Walters wrote that Gruenther "was universally admired and respected as a man of extraordinary intelligence, understanding and wit." For an overview of Eisenhower's advisers, see John S. D. Eisenhower to Milton Eisenhower, 24 Apr. 1972, M. S. Eisenhower Papers, Box 1; and Clay's oral history, Columbia.

8. C. D. Jackson, 7 Aug. 1954, Jackson Papers, Box 56.

9. There was significant opposition to the EDC and German rearmament. See, for example, Field Marshal Montgomery, who supported the EDC by 1953: Once "Western Germany is armed by us and integrated into the western fold, a united Germany will be achieved only by fighting. Many Germans believe this, and that includes Dr. Adenauer—he told me so himself," Montgomery to DDE, 2 July 1953, Whitman, Name Series, Box 22; J. F. Dulles to DDE, 11 July 1953, Box 22; see also Bedell Smith, Memo to AmEmbassy Paris, ordering "every effort [to] assist French EDC ratification" pursuant to C. D. Jackson's "non-attributable" plan, 1 Mar. 1954, C. D. Jackson Records, Box 2; John C. Hughes (U. S. Mission to NATO), Report, No. 3817, 26 June 1953, C. D. Jackson Records, Box 3; C. D. Jackson's "Memorandum on France and EDC," 8 Feb. 1954, Boxes 2, 43; C. D. Jackson to John Hughes, 6 Mar. 1954, 3 Sept. 1953, Box 3. For the French controversy, Eisenhower's anguish, and the British reaction, see Hagerty's diary, 14, 24, 26, 27, 29, 30 Dec. 1954. See also C. D. Jackson to Henry Luce, 4 Dec. 1954, C. D. Jackson Papers, Box 57; Jackson to DDE, 17 Nov. 1953, Whitman, International, Box 10; J. F. Dulles to Bonn, Brussels, The Hague, London, Luxembourg, Paris, Rome, "US Assurances to EDC," 9 Apr. 1954, Boxes 9, 10; DDE to Bedell Smith, re a "Substitute for EDC," 3 Sept. 1954, DDE Diary, NLE, 76–62 No. 101; Robert Cutler to DDE, 20 July 1954, "New Approach" to defense, NATO, and EDC, with international reactions, declassified, sanitized, portions deleted, Whitman, Administration; DDE's diary entry, German Rearmament, NATO, draft No. 3, 10 Jan. 1955, Whitman, Admin., Box 5.

10. On 1 Nov. 1952, the United States exploded its first H-bomb, in the Eniwetok Proving Grounds, in the Pacific. It was the equivalent of 3 million tons of TNT, 150 times the blast that destroyed Hiroshima. The Soviets exploded a similar device on 19 Aug. 1953. Eisenhower quoted in John S. D. Eisenhower's Geneva Notes, 18 July 1955, Whitman, International Meetings, Box 2.

11. DDE to Milton Eisenhower, 7 Oct. 1956, ME, Box 1.

12. DDE to Edgar Eisenhower, 8 Nov. 1954, DDE Diary, Box 5. See also, 1 May 1956, DDE Diary, Box 9; DDE cited President Hoover, who had told him that although there was "great danger lying ahead . . . you cannot go back." DDE was committed to stabilizing the situation, but he refused to "return to the days of 1860."

13. DDE to Gabriel Hauge, 30 Sept. 1954, DDE Diary, Box 4.

14. Conversation between DDE and Hauge, 13 Feb. 1956, transcribed by Ann Whitman, Whitman Diary, Box 8. For the lobbying scandal that marked the Fulbright-Harris gas bill, see DDE to Milton Eisenhower, 11 Mar. 1956, DDE Diary, Box 8; MemCon DDE with Governor Dan Thornton, 8 Mar. 1956, ibid.;

DDE to Sid Richardson, 20 Feb. 1956, ibid., Box 7; DDE Diary note, 11 Feb. 1956, ibid.; and DDE to Hauge, 13 Feb. 1956, ibid., Box 5.

15. Eisenhower's essay on capitalism and the contradictions of capitalism, 2 July 1953, DDE Diary, Box 5. See also his exchange with Allen Dulles on Macauley's statement "About America" (January 1857), on class warfare, violence, and chaos, A. W. Dulles to DDE, 20 June 1959, DDE to A. W. Dulles, 6 July 1959, Whitman, Box 4.

16. DDE to Milton Eisenhower, 6 Nov. 1953, M. S. Eisenhower Papers, Box 1; DDE to J. F. Dulles, 16 Nov. 1953, DDE Diary, Box 2; DDE to Emmet [J. Hughes], 10 Dec. 1953, DDE Diary. See also DDE to Albert M. Cole, Housing and Home Finance Administration, re appropriations for public housing and "slum clearance" projects, 26 Oct. 1953, ibid.

17. Telephone conversation, DDE and Oveta Culp Hobby, 13, 14 July, 27 Dec. 1954, DDE Diary, Box 4. Eisenhower created the cabinet-level Department of Health, Education and Welfare. See also Hagerty's diary, 16, 19 July 1954; and meeting with congressional leaders, 14 July, ibid.

18. Notes on pre-press-conference briefing, 3 June 1959, Whitman Diary, Box 10.

19. "Notes for Talk," DDE Diary, 3 Apr. 1954, Box 4; see also DDE to Charles Halleck, 29 Mar. 1954, and DDE to Gen. Bradford Chynoweth, 13, 20, 30 July 1954, ibid.

20. See the anonymous and extraordinary diary, Adlai Stevenson's worldwide tour, 12 Mar. to 12 July 1953, sent by Ward Melville to DDE, 17 Sept. 1953, Whitman, Name Series, Box 32; see also John Bartlow Martin's account of Stevenson's tour record, *Adlai Stevenson and the World* (Doubleday, 1977), pp. 36–75.

21. On McLeod and the civil service, see David Caute, *The Great Fear: the Anti-Communist Purge Under Truman and Eisenhower* (Simon & Schuster, 1978), esp. pp. 272, 307–24. A. A. Berle, p. 629.

22. Alexander Makinsky's international analysis, n.d., Sept. 1954, Whitman, Name Series, Box 21.

23. C. D. Jackson, log, 30 Nov. 1953, C. D. Jackson Papers, Box 56; DDE to Milton Eisenhower, 9 Oct. 1953, M. S. Eisenhower Papers, Box 1. For the President's explanation of the deleted paragraph in support of Gen. Marshall, see D. D. Eisenhower, *Mandate for Change, 1953–1956* (Doubleday 1963), p. 318.

24. Dillon to J. F. Dulles, 15 May 1953; Walter B. Smith to DDE, 20 May 1953, Whitman, International.

25. Clyde Miller to DDE, 8 June 1953, with flyer "Parents to Die on Wedding Anniversary . . ."; Brownell to Ann Whitman, 16 June 1953, Whitman, Administration, Box 35; DDE to Clyde Miller, 10 June 1953, DDE Diary, Box 2.

26. Allen Dulles, Memorandum on the Rosenberg Case, 22 Jan. 1953, Julius Rosenberg Papers, F.B.I. Headquarters Case No. HQ-65-58236-1489.

27. DDE Diary, 21 Dec. 1953, Box 2; Nelson Rockefeller to DDE, 3 Mar. 1955, DDE to Rockefeller, 5 Mar., Diary, Box 6.

28. See Brownell to DDE, 6 Oct. 1956, Whitman, Administration, Box 8; Brownell to DDE, 4 Mar. 1955, Diary, Box 6; Memo for the Record, Congressman Harley O. Staggers with DDE, 12 Jan. 1954, Diary, Box 3; Brownell to DDE, 9 Apr. 1954, Whitman, Box 8. See Caute, p. 50, pp. 170–72, 274–75. For an important analysis of the law to outlaw communism, see Mary S. McAuliffe, "Liberals and the Communist Control Act of 1954," *Journal of American History* (Sept. 1976), pp. 351–76. Introduced by Senator Hubert Humphrey, who wanted to make Communist Party membership a crime, and Senator Hugh Butler, who emphasized communist infiltration of unions, an extraordinary collection of congressional liberals sponsored the bill, including Wayne Morse, John F. Kennedy, Paul H. Douglas, Herbert Lehman, Mike Mansfield, and many others. Only Senator Estes Kefauver voted against it. Ac-

cording to McAuliffe, Attorney General Brownell and Eisenhower objected to outlawing the Communist Party; but not for civil libertarian reasons. They feared the Act would override the more sweeping subversive registration clause of the Internal Security Act. See also, Mary Sperling McAuliffe, *Crisis on the Left: Cold War Politics and American Liberals* (University of Massachusetts Press, 1978). Eisenhower's "Suggested Statement" on Democrats and Republicans, n.d., in Martin Dies folder, Whitman, Name Series, Box 7.

29. DDE to Ed Bermingham, 20 Apr. 1951, Bermingham Papers.

30. DDE to Earl Schaefer, 12 Apr. 1954, Whitman Diary, Box 4.

31. DDE to J. F. Dulles, 15 Nov. 1954, Whitman Diary, Box 5; DDE to Gen. Gruenther, 2 July 1954, Box 4.

32. DDE to Richard Nixon, 1 June 1953, Whitman, Administration, Box 31. For a similar exchange when Senators Jenner and Knowland urged the United States to pull out of the UN, see Hagerty's diary, 4 Aug. 1954.

33. DDE to Richard L. Simon, 4 Apr. 1956, Whitman Diary, Box 8.

34. DDE to Field Marshal the Viscount Montgomery of Alamein, 2 May 1956, MR 76–82, No. 33.

35. Record, conversation between Styles Bridges and DDE, 21 May 1957, Whitman Diary, Box 9.

36. Classified Top Secret until recently, a series of reports analyzed the costs, risks, and future of nuclear weapons. They include: "Draft, Statement of Policy on *Continental Defense:* Basic Considerations," NSC 5606, 5 June 1956, Gordon Gray, Box 4. This report includes "U.S. and Soviet Nuclear Capabilities and Missile Systems," a financial appendix of the estimated costs, FY 1955–60, for tactical warning systems, defense against overt and covert enemy action, civil defense, international collaboration and coordination, sea surveillance. The Killian Report, *Meeting the Threat of Surprise Attack: Technological Capabilities Panel of the Science Advisory Committee,* 14 Feb. 1955, declassified with exemptions (including the deletion of pp. 133–52), in Project Clean-Up, Box 14. The panel was chaired by Dr. James A. Killian. As recently as 15 Sept. 1977, David Burnham reported in the New York *Times* that a secret 52-page report revealed that the Environmental Protection Agency has failed "to establish radiation controls." "The Federal agency responsible for protecting the public against the hazards of radiation does not know the scope of the problem, does not have the resources to find out and for the last six years has failed to issue a single standard that is currently being enforced, the General Accounting Office has charged. About 22,000 Americans develop leukemia, other forms of cancer and serious genetic disorders each year because of exposure to various forms of radiation. . . ."

37. Killian Report, p. 74.

38. The Gaither Report, *Deterrence and Survival in the Nuclear Age,* Security Resources Panel of the Science Advisory Committee, 7 Nov. 1957, declassified, Gordon Gray, Box 75; quotations, p. 84. For commentary on the Gaither Report, see Chalmers Roberts, "NATO Votes Missile Bases. . . . Secret Report Sees U.S. in Grave Peril," Washington *Post,* 20 Dec. 1957. Members of the Gaither Committee included, in addition to Gaither, Sprague, and Foster: James Baxter, Williams College; Robert D. Calkins, Brookings Institute; John J. Corson, McKinsey & Co.; James A. Perkins, Carnegie Corp.; Robert Prim, Bell Telephone Laboratories; Hector R. Skifter, Airborne Instruments Laboratories; William Webster, New England Electric System; Dr. Jerome B. Wiesner, MIT. The advisory panel included: Adm. Robert C. Carney, Westinghouse Electric; Gen. James Doolittle, Shell Oil; Gen. John E. Hull, Manufacturing Chemists Association; Mervin Kelly and James Fisk, Bell Telephone Laboratories; James R. Killian, MIT; Ernest O. Lawrence, U. of California Radiation Laboratory; Robert Lovett, Brown Bros. & Harriman; John J. McCloy, Chase National Bank; Frank Stanton, Columbia Broadcasting System; I. I. Rabi, chairman, President's Science Advisory Committee. Assisting the panel were Paul Nitze, George Washington

U.; George A. Lincoln, U. S. Military Academy; Gen. James McCormick, president, and Albert G. Hill, vice-president, Institute for Defense Analyses. *Khrushchev Remembers, the Last Testament* (Little, Brown, 1974), Strobe Talbott, transl., ed., p. 450.

39. Dulles quoted in Eisenhower, *Waging Peace, 1956–1961* (Doubleday, 1965), p. 223; for Eisenhower's reaction to the Gaither Report, see pp. 219–23.

40. George Humphrey quoted in Richard Barnet, *The Economy of Death* (Atheneum, 1970), p. 93.

41. DDE on Kennedy's defense budget quoted in ibid. For the politics of the Republican Party convention of 1960, see William Robinson, Diary, account of visit with Eisenhower, 18–25 July 1960, Robinson Papers, Box 4. See also Eisenhower's telephone conversation with Nelson Rockefeller, 11 June 1960; DDE with Mrs. Hobby re Rockefeller and Nixon, 11 June, DDE Diary, Box 33.

42. Nelson Rockefeller was one of the leading exponents of the "fallout protection" shelter. In July 1959, he organized a White House conference on fallout protection. See *Report of the Special Committee on Civil Defense and Related Papers of the Governor's Conference*, Whitman, Administration, Box 34. The Gaither Committee had originally emerged out of Rockfeller's preoccupation with fallout shelters.

43. For an analysis of the degree to which nuclear war had become unthinkable but not impossible, see NSC 5605, Gordon Gray, Box 4; NSC 5810/1, 5 May 1958, NLE 76–51, No. 421. On 5 Aug. 1955, Eisenhower appointed Harold Stassen Deputy U. S. Representative to the Disarmament Commission of the UN. He considered Stassen essentially a "Secretary for Peace." See DDE-Stassen telephone call, 15 Mar. 1955, Diary, Box 5; DDE to Charles Wilson, 22 Mar. 1955, Box 6; see, for example, suggestions for negotiation, Memorandum of Conference, 1 Mar. 1956, DDE, Stassen, J. F. Dulles, the Joint Chiefs, MR 76–82, No. 19; ibid., Wilson, Humphrey, et al., 5 Apr. 1956, MR 76–82, No. 29. Several cabinet and NSC meetings dedicated to disarmament elicited deeply emotional support from Eisenhower's team. See, e.g., Rowland Hughes to DDE, 1 June 1954, 13 Feb. 1956, Whitman, Administration, Box 22. See also DDE to Charles Wilson, 5 Jan. 1955, Diary, Box 5; Hallock Hoffman to DDE, 28 Jan. 1955; DDE to Hoffman, 7 Feb. 1955, Whitman, Name Series, Box 21.

For a survey, based on recently declassified documents, of the efforts to negotiate a test-ban treaty, see esp. Robert A. Divine, *Blowing on the Wind: the Nuclear Test Ban Debate, 1954–1960* (Oxford University, 1978).

44. DDE-Styles Bridges conversation, note 35.

45. DDE Personal Diary, n.d., Jan. 1953.

46. *The Memoirs of Chief Justice Earl Warren* (Doubleday, 1977), p. 291.

47. See Eisenhower's chapter on "Civil Rights," *Waging Peace*, pp. 148–76. See Maxwell Rabb to DDE, 16 Aug. 1954, Whitman Diary, Box 3; Rabb to DDE, 29 Apr. 1959, Box 5; and Rabb's Oral History, Eisenhower Project, Columbia University; on the issue of Red Cross blood plasma, see record of conversation, DDE and Gen. Gruenther, 23 Nov. 1958, Whitman Diary, Box 10. Eisenhower's staff routinely monitored Soviet criticism. See, e.g., Special Staff Note, 15 Oct. 1959: "Moscow shows signs of reviving its routine derogatory portrayal of life in the U.S.—strikes and unemployment, racial prejudice, and cultural poverty . . . ," DDE Diary Series, Box 29.

48. Warren, op. cit., p. 291.

49. DDE to Herbert Brownell, telephone, 19 Aug. 1956, Whitman Diary, Box 8. For an example of Eisenhower's recognition of the international complexities of racism, see DDE to Henry Wallace, 1 Dec. 1956, DDE Diary, Box 12; see also record of telephone call with L. B. Johnson, 15 June 1957; record of conference with Adam Clayton Powell, 11 May 1955, Box 14. Powell, just returned from the first international conference of Asian and African nations, at Bandung, suggested to Eisenhower that to appoint black Foreign Service officers as military

and cultural attachés in Africa and Asia would be worth the equivalent of "millions in economic aid." See also DDE to Swede Hazlett, 22 July 1957, DDE Diary, Box 14.

50. Staff Note No. 506, "Moscow on Integration," 28 Feb. 1959, MR 78–168 No. 2; DDE to Milton Eisenhower, 11 Mar. 1957, DDE Diary, Box 13.

51. DDE to Nelson Rockefeller, 15 Dec. 1954, DDE Diary, Box 5.

52. On 24 Jan. 1953, one of Eisenhower's first acts in office was to appoint the Committee on International Information Activities, William H. Jackson, chair; Robert Cutler, administrative assistant to the President; C. D. Jackson, representing the Secretary of State; Sigurd Larmon, representing the director for mutual security; Gordon Gray, Barklie McKee Henry, John C. Hughes, and Abbott Washburn, executive secretary of Committee, DDE to James S. Lay, exec. sec. to NSC, 24 Jan. 1953, Whitman, Administration, Box 30. On the recommendation of the Jackson Committee, the entire structure of the NSC was overhauled. To date, only the administrative record of the effort to coordinate the activities of the NSC has been fully declassified. Minutes of NSC meetings and planning assessments for actual overt and covert national security activities remain largely closed. The recently declassified reports include: William Jackson to DDE, 1 Oct. 1954, a reexamination of the International Information Activities Committee report of 30 June 1953, Whitman, Box 24; report on NSC 59/1 and NSC 127/1, 21 July 1954, Gordon Gray, Box 23; memo for the NSC, "The Foreign Information Program and Psychological Warfare Planning," 15 Mar. 1955 (re NSC 59/1, 127/1 and NSC Actions 1197, 1198), Gordon Gray, Box 23; Robert Cutler's report to the President, 16 Mar. 1953, and subsequent reports "to the President on Operations of the NSC," Whitman, Administration, Box 30; memo for the NSC, "The Structure and Functions of the NSC," 3 July 1957, Box 11; NSC 5440, 14 Dec. 1954, "Basic National Security Policy," portions deleted, Gordon Gray, Box 1; the Rockefeller report "Proposals for Strengthening National Security—Foreign Affairs Organization," 14 Dec. 1956, draft, M. S. Eisenhower Papers, Box 6: Rockefeller's committee included Milton Eisenhower and Arthur Fleming. See also "Foreign Affairs Organization at the Departmental Level," memo for DDE from Rockefeller, Milton Eisenhower's Committee on OCB reorganization, M. S. Eisenhower Papers, Box 6. See James S. Lay and Robert H. Johnson, Organizational History of the NSC, prepared for a Senate subcommittee, 30 June 1960, Whitman, Administration, Box 30. The OCB established the office of special assistant to the President for Cold War planning. That post was held by C. D. Jackson (to Mar. 1954), Nelson Rockefeller (to Dec. 1955), William H. Jackson (to Dec. 1956), Fred Dearborn and Karl Harr (during the second administration).

The special assistants for national security affairs were Robert Cutler, Dillon Anderson, Cutler for a second shift, William Jackson, and Gordon Gray.

In addition to the White House NSC establishment, the Center for International Studies (CENIS), organized in 1951, continued to serve as a CIA-OCB think tank. Administered by MIT, it fully employed "the academic knowledge and intellectual talents available in the Cambridge community." CENIS was directed by Max Millikan, with Walt Whitman Rostow and Clyde Kluckhohn. See Millikan to Robert Cutler, 2 Mar. 1953, C. D. Jackson Papers, Box 75. After the Geneva conference of 1955, Nelson Rockefeller called a meeting of the men associated with CENIS "to consider the psychological aspects of U.S. strategy" in the post-Geneva era. They met at Quantico and submitted a report, "Psychological Aspects of U. S. Strategy," that had a long-term influence on U.S. foreign policy. According to C. D. Jackson, "Nelson Rockefeller's Quantico skull session" contained "an alarmingly large number of PhDs" but reached "a dynamic consensus." The panelists were C. D. Jackson; Ellis A. Johnson, director, Operations Research Office, The Johns Hopkins University; Henry A. Kissinger, Harvard; Col. George A. Lincoln, U. S. Military Academy; Paul M. A. Linebarger, School of Advanced International Studies, Johns Hopkins; Stacy May, consulting economist; Max F. Millikan, director, CENIS, MIT; Philip Mosely, director of studies, Council on Foreign Relations; George Pettee, assistant director, Operations Research Office, Johns Hopkins; Stefan T. Possony, air intelligence specialist; William Webster, New England Electric System; Frederick L. Anderson, major general, USAF (Ret.). See C. D. Jackson to DDE, 13 June 1955, Whitman, Box 24; Papers of the Quantico meeting, C. D. Jackson Papers, Box 73.

On 7 May 1956, C. D. Jackson, William Jackson, W. W. Rostow, Max Millikan, Irwin Canham, Sigurd Larmon, Philip Reed, and Nelson Rockefeller met at the Century Club to discuss restaffing and greater momentum for the OCB. They believed Eisenhower's Cold War was grinding to a halt. See C. D. Jackson's log, Box 56. In 1957, "a committee of outsiders" was considered to serve "as a kind of Greek chorus to the NSC." The members were to be Robert Lovett, John J. McCloy, John Foster Dulles, George Humphrey, C. D. Jackson, and Walt Rostow. See Rostow to C. D. Jackson, 20 Nov. 1957, C. D. Jackson Papers, Box 75.

53. Robert Cutler to DDE, 27 Dec. 1952, Whitman, Box 11.

54. Jackson Committee, press release, 8 July 1953, C. D. Jackson Papers, Box 52.

55. C. D. Jackson to Richard Hollander, 12 Jan. 1953, Box 49.

56. See Abbott Washburn to Gen. Eisenhower, "Development of an Integrated U. S. Psychological Warfare Program," C. D. Jackson Papers, Box 69. Jackson, Arthur Page, Washburn, and Gen. Clay had called the meeting at Princeton, 10–11 May 1952. The participants were Adm. H. B. Miller, George Morgan, DeWitt C. Poole, Walt W. Rostow, Levering Tyson, Alan Valentine, Jerome Wiesner, Frank Altschul, Lloyd Berkner, A. A. Berle, Cyril Black, Charles Bohlen, Tom Braden, Howard Chapin, John Devine, John P. Dickson, Frederic Dolbeare, Allen Dulles, Lewis Galantiere, Joseph Grew, William Griffith, John C. Hughes, Robert Joyce, R. E. Lang, John Leich. See Rostow to C. D. Jackson, 12 May 1953, App. 1, Box 85. At a second Princeton conference, the idea for the Jackson Committee emerged. See C. D. Jackson to DDE, 26 Nov. 1952, 21 Nov. 1952, Box 52. William Jackson was appointed chair at the suggestion of Walter Bedell Smith. As originally conceived the committee was to consist of W. H. Jackson, Washburn, C. D. Jackson, Sigurd Larmon, Roger Kyes, Arthur Godfrey, Frank Nash, John Hughes, Cutler, Barklie McKee Henry, and Gordon Gray; George Kennan, Adolf A. Berle, and Adm. Sidney Sauers were to have been consultants. Wayne Jackson, Pat Johnson, and Frank Lindsay were to represent CIA; Fitz Nolting and Robert Tufts were to represent State; Alan Gerhard, Charles Noyes (or Townsend Hoopes), and John McGruder were to represent Defense; and Jack Only was to represent MSA.

57. Jackson's definition was presented at a Princeton Alumni Day Panel, with Allen Dulles, Edward W. Barrett, and others, on "Why Are We in Danger of Losing the Ideological War with World Communism?" See excerpts, transcript of discussion, *Princeton Alumni Weekly,* 9 Mar. 1951.

58. C. D. Jackson to W. W. Rostow, 31 Dec. 1952, C. D. Jackson Papers, Box 75.

59. "The Soviet Vulnerability Project," of CENIS, was headed by Millikan and Rostow. They submitted their report to the still-operating Psychological Strategy Board. See Harold Stassen (then director of mutual security) to PSB, 10 Mar. 1953, C. D. Jackson Records, Box 5. The "Soviet Vulnerability Project" suggested, among other things, the exacerbation of Sino-Soviet tensions at the time of Stalin's death. For other examples of early strategy toward increased Sino-Soviet tensions, see: "Post-Berlin Thoughts on the Current Soviet Psyche," 22 Feb. 1954; Memorandum, C. D. Jackson to DDE, 24 Feb. 1954, C. D. Jackson Papers, Box 41; Rostow to C. D. Jackson, 1 July 1955, Box 75.

60. CIA, SE-39, "Probable Consequences of the Death of Stalin . . . ," 10 Mar. 1953, C. D. Jackson Papers, Box 5.

61. Emmet J. Hughes to DDE, 27 Mar. 1953, Whitman, Administration.

62. Art Minnich to Marie McCrumb, 5 June 1953; C. D. Jackson to George Morgan, acting director, PSB, 11 Apr. 1953, C. D. Jackson Papers, Box 85.

63. Basic National Security Policy, NSC 5440, 14 Dec. 1954, declassified with portions deleted, Gordon Gray, Box 1.

64. NSC 5412, 15 Mar. 1954, "On Covert Operations," Gordon Gray, Box 7.

65. DDE to George Humphrey, 27 Mar. 1957, DDE Diary, Box 13; see also John Cowles to DDE, 3 Dec. 1955, and DDE to Cowles, 7 Dec., Box 6.

66. DDE to Winston Churchill, as reported in Hagerty's diary, 22 July 1954. The United States' ambiguous attitude toward colonialism is represented by C. D. Jackson's problems as U.S. delegate to the UN's Trusteeship Committee. See "Background Conference for U. S. NGOs," 13 Oct. 1954, C. D. Jackson Papers, Box 87; log—General Comments on 9th General Assembly, UN, 20 Sept. to 18 Dec. 1954; and Jackson to Clare Boothe Luce, 4 Oct. 1954: "I don't think I am a pigmental snob, but I must say that the Western world has somewhat more experience with the operations of war, peace, and parliamentary procedures than the swirling mess of emotionally super-charged Africans and Asiatics and Arabs that outnumber us. . . . This may be a much-needed world forum, and a great safety valve, but it was also a sure way of putting white prestige on the skids, at the precise moment in history when the colonial powers were . . . trying to de-colonialize in a semi-orderly fashion," Box 56. See also Jackson to Henry Luce: It might be "inadvisable or impossible to outlaw the CP in England or France or Italy." But it seemed to Jackson "not only possible but highly desirable" to wipe out communism "in any of these Central African areas" and to take "forcefully repressive measures," 23 July 1954, Box 56. On the other hand, Jackson wrote an essay, "Anti-Colonialism": "Colonialism is today a moribund duck. The Dutch have had it; the French know it; the British will admit it; and the Belgians and the Portuguese are quietly going about their business making as much money as possible. . . ." 11 Aug. 1954, Box 56. See also Henry Cabot Lodge to DDE, "New Anti-Colonial Statement by You," 26 June 1956, declassification number NLE 76-51, No. 458. Lodge wrote that the United States was criticized from "France to Japan" for supporting the outgoing colonial powers. "The youth of the world," Lodge wrote, could "be made to like the U.S. without its costing us a nickel—merely by a different line of talk."

67. Vernon Walters, Silent Missions (Doubleday, 1978), pp. 241–63. On 7 Nov. 1952, Ed Bermingham wrote to Eisenhower that Britain's agent for Anglo-Iranian was in the United States to complain that Mossadegh intended "to drive a wedge between England and the U.S." Churchill was concerned about it. Bermingham was told that "characters in our State Department are fostering" the situation. Bermingham considered the matter urgent and potentially "disastrous." He spoke to Luther Cleveland, who agreed. But "Pete Jones being persona non grata with the British cannot be helpful at this stage." Bermingham to DDE, 7 Nov. 1952, Bermingham Papers.

68. See Joe Stork, Middle East Oil and the Energy Crisis (Monthly Review Press, 1975), pp. 49–55.

69. Kermit Roosevelt, Counter Coup: the Struggle for the Control of Iran (McGraw-Hill, 1979), p. 71. This book was withdrawn by the publisher at the request of British Petroleum. See David Ignatius, "The Coup Snafu: a Spy Book, the CIA, and an Angry Oil Firm," Washington Post, 7 Nov. 1979.

70. Eisenhower, Mandate for Change, pp. 162–66. For Eisenhower on the Shah, see draft "Toward Peace with Justice," declassified, with portions deleted.

For Iran's recent history in political and economic perspective, see "The U.S. and Iran's Revolution," essays by Richard Cottam, David Schoenbaum, Shahram Chubin, Theodore Moran, Richard Falk, in Foreign Policy, No. 34, Spring 1979; "The Iranian Revolution," guest ed. Eqbal Ahmad, with essays by Nikki Keddie,

Mansour Farhang, Richard Falk, William Dorman, Stuart Schaar, and Fred Halliday, in *Race & Class: the Journal of the Institute of Race Relations and the Transnational Institute,* Vol. XXI, Summer 1979; *The Review of Iranian Political Economy and History, RIPEH,* P. O. Box 961, Georgetown University, Washington, DC 20057. For background, see esp. Ervand Abrahamian, "The Crowd in Iranian Politics," *Past and Present* (Dec. 1968); "The Social Bases of Iranian Politics, the Tudeh Party, 1941–1953," Ph.D. dissertation, Columbia University, 1969; and "Iran in Revolution: the Opposition Forces," *MERIP Reports,* No. 75–76 (Middle East Research and Information Project, P. O. Box 3122, Washington, DC 20010).

71. Carl Solberg, *The Rise and Imminent Fall of an American Empire* (Mason/Charter, 1976), pp. 186–87; see also Robert Engler, *The Politics of Oil* (U. of Chicago, 1967), pp. 203–8.

72. Winston Churchill to DDE, 16 Apr. 1956, DDE Diary, Box 8.

73. See "Defense of the Middle East," n.d. July 1955, International Meetings, Box 2, Geneva (3), declassified with portions deleted. The Baghdad Pact was to "keep those key countries western oriented and politically stable." The United States thought it unwise "to adhere or formally associate itself with the Pact," because it would "adversely affect our influence in bringing about a reduction in Arab-Israeli tensions."

74. The Shah's toast quoted in Hagerty's diary, 15 Dec. 1954. Gen. Robert McClure's descriptions of Iran to C. D. Jackson, 14 Sept. 1953, 8 June 1954, C. D. Jackson Papers, Box 60.

75. Jackson to Gen. McClure, 30 Sept. 1953, Box 60; see also DDE to Sec. of the Army Robert Stevens, 2 Apr. 1954, urging the Army to upgrade McClure: "You know all the money and effort we have spent in that region in support of the Shah . . . ," DDE Diary, Box 4.

76. Miles Copeland, *The Game of Nations* (Simon and Schuster, 1969).

77. Robert Murphy, op. cit., pp. 375–93. See Lyon, op. cit., pp. 689–725. For a discussion of Dulles' decision to cancel U.S. support for the Aswan Dam, see C. D. Jackson to Klaus Dohrn, 9 Apr. 1957, C. D. Jackson Papers, Box 39. For an angry account of Dulles' policy, see Herman Finer, *Dulles over Suez: the Theory and Practice of His Diplomacy* (Quadrangle Books, 1964).

78. Conversation, DDE and Strauss, 14 Nov. 1956, Whitman Diary, Box 8.

79. N. C. Debevoise to Dr. Horace Craig, "Israel's Fundamental Problems," OCB, SS-5-1, MR 78-176, No. 6, 29 Oct. 1953. DDE, talk with Undersecretary of State Hoover, 23 Sept. 1955, Diary, Box 6.

80. Luce-Dulles-DDE, telephone, 5 Sept. 1953, DDE Diary, Box 3.

81. Clare Boothe Luce to C. D. Jackson, 19 June 1953, C. D. Jackson Papers, Box 57.

82. Luce to C. D. Jackson, 30 June 1953, 29 Sept. 1954, Jackson Papers, Box 57; Luce's Report on the Italian elections, 19 June 1953, Whitman, Administration, NLE 76-51, No. 408.

83. For Luce's proposals to rectify the Italian political situation, see "Estimate as of November 1," Clare Boothe Luce to DDE, 3 Nov. 1953, Whitman, Administration, NLE 76-52, No. 469, portions deleted. Stephen Shaddegg, *Clare Boothe Luce* (Simon and Schuster, 1970), pp. 223–32. Shaddegg points out that in 1948 Luce and Joseph Kennedy collected and contributed $2 million to aid the Christian Democrats.

84. See "Relazione sulla riunione presso S.E. l'ambasciatore Luce effettuatasi in Roma presso l'ambasciata Usa giovedí, 4 febbraio 1954," excerpts of documents published by Gian Giacomo Migone, *"Stati Uniti, Fiat e repressione antioperaia negli anni cinquanta,"* in *Rivista di storia contemporanea,* No. 2, Aprile, 1974; reprinted in Emilio Puguo and Sergio Garavin, *Gli Anni Duri Alla Fiat* (Einaudi, Turin, 1974). I am grateful to Carl Marzani for the documents from *The US, Fiat and Anti-Worker Repression During the Fifties.* They will soon be published

in their entirety in a volume by Gian Giacomo Migone, to be issued by Feltrinelli.

See also C. D. Jackson, "Components of U. S. Foreign Policy," Jackson to Henry Luce, 21 Dec. 1955, C. D. Jackson Papers, log, Box 56.

In addition, a clandestine public-relations operation, "Operation Enterprise," emerged in Italy during this period. See correspondence between Allen Dulles, Jackson, et al., 6 July 1954 to Jan. 1955, and "Operation Enterprise Reports," 1–18, C. D. Jackson Papers, Box 51. See Shaddegg, op. cit., pp. 253–55.

85. See Robert Murphy on Yugoslavia, op. cit., pp. 422–27; and Shaddegg, op. cit., pp. 247–53. For background, see Lorraine M. Lees, "The American Decision to Assist Tito, 1948–1949," *Diplomatic History* (Autumn 1978), pp. 407–22.

86. See DDE to Marshal Josip Broz Tito, 10 Sept. 1954, DDE Diary, Box 4; DDE to J. F. Dulles, 30 Sept. 1953, Box 2; Rowland Hughes to Harold Stassen, re: 450,000 tons of wheat for Yugoslavia, 22 Nov. 1954, NLE 76-51, No. 356; Eisenhower's press release on the Trieste accord, 9 Oct. 1954, Whitman, International; and Eisenhower on Tito as asset, pre-press-conference notes, 6 June 1956, Whitman Diary, Box 8. On 18 Dec. 1976, Italy's parliament "approved a treaty allowing a free-trade area in Trieste, formally ending more than 30 years of territorial squabbling between Italy and Yugoslavia," New York *Times,* 19 Dec. 1976, p. 5.

87. DDE to Clare Boothe Luce, 7 Nov. 1953, Whitman, Administration, Box 27, declassified with portions deleted; see also DDE to Bedell Smith regarding his "unnecessarily long letter to Mrs. Luce," 7 Nov. 1953, DDE Diary, Box 2.

88. "Notes to discuss with JF Dulles," 10 July 1954, declassified with portions deleted, MR 78-69, No. 3.

89. Hagerty's diary, 10 Aug. 1954.

90. Clare Boothe Luce, *Russian Atomic Power and the Lost American Revolution,* 21 Aug. 1954, in C. D. Jackson Papers, Box 57.

91. Eisenhower, *Waging Peace,* pp. 88–89.

92. Alexander Werth, *Russia at War, 1941–1945* (E. P. Dutton, 1964), p. 1019.

93. For conditions in Poland and Hungary during World War II, and an analysis of postwar politics, see Werth, op. cit.; C. A. Macartney, *A History of Modern Hungary,* 2 vols. (Praeger, 1957); F. L. Carsten, *The Rise of Fascism* (U. of California, 1969); István Deák, "Hungary," in Hans Rogger and Eugen Weber, eds., *The European Right* (U. of California, 1965); *Khrushchev Remembers: the Last Testament,* pp. 177–83, for events in Poland. RFE's analysis coincided with Khrushchev's statements, but was more complete. According to RFE, the "Natolin Group" backed Gomułka originally. "It was anti-liberal, and pro-Soviet." Its opponents favored liberalization, and there were "many Poles of Jewish origin, and many intellectuals," in their ranks. Therefore, the Natolin Group "started an anti-Semitic campaign and also an attack on intellectuals, and in particular against journalists." In September, Gomułka turned against the Natolin Group and turned toward the liberal wing. Then Moscow began to turn against Gomułka. But it was too late. Gomułka's popularity throughout Poland was "immense." "Never before was a communist leader so popular. This popularity might also extend to the party." RFE, Munich, to C. D. Jackson, 5 Feb. 1957, C. D. Jackson Papers, Box 44. See also Klaus Dohrn's analysis of the Polish situation, 11 Nov. 1954, Box 39; also note 101 herein.

According to David Wise and Thomas Ross, Allen Dulles' agents combed the world for a copy of Khrushchev's speech. For an undisclosed price, the CIA received a copy. It was published in every major U.S. and allied newspaper and widely distributed as a pamphlet. Thousands were dropped by balloon over Central Europe. Allen Dulles considered its publication "one of the main coups" of his career. See Wise & Ross, *The Invisible Government* (Bantam Books, 1964), pp. 128–30; Khrushchev's speech of 25 Feb. exacerbated tensions in East Europe, was questioned by the French Communist Party, was denounced by Togliatti and Nenni in Italy, and was mildly criticized by the British and U. S. Communist parties. It was also criticized by Winston Churchill, who wrote to Eisenhower: "We have only forty or fifty thousand professional communists in this country. . . . They have made an extraordinary volte-face about Stalin. I am sure it is a great blunder which will markedly hamper the Communist Movement. It would have been easy to 'play him down' gradually without causing so great a shock to the faithful. Stalin always kept his word with me. I remember particularly saying to him . . . 'You keep Rumania and Bulgaria in your sphere of influence, but let me have Greece.' To this bargain he scrupulously adhered during months of fighting with the Greek Communists. . . ." Churchill to DDE, 16 Apr. 1956, DDE Diary, Box 8.

The CIA has recently declassified its 1956 analysis of the impact of Khrushchev's speech: *The Present Communist Controversy: Its Ramifications and Possible Repercussions* (NLE 76–51, No. 251). The CIA concluded that Moscow's new flexibility, whether called Titoism, polycentrism, or decentralization, did not in fact threaten Soviet control. Although there "are risks for the Communists" in their new liberalism, and Communism "might even be infected by evolutionary socialism," the CIA thought this unlikely, unless the West acted "vigorously to exploit prevailing Communist confusion." In sum, the CIA concluded "that the present crisis, if in fact it is one, is not a grave danger for world communism. . . . We believe that the U.S.S.R.'s main concern will be the exploitation of Communism in Asia and Africa. . . ."

See also W. W. Rostow's memo on Khrushchev's speech and the challenge of the Twentieth Party Congress, Rostow to Allen Dulles, 24, 27 Feb. 1956; and Rostow to William Jackson, 29 Mar. 1956, C. D. Jackson Papers, Box 75.

For analysis of Khrushchev's speech and new Soviet policies, see Paul Marantz, "Prelude to Détente: Doctrinal Change Under Khrushchev," *International Studies Quarterly* (Dec. 1975), pp. 501–28.

95. A. A. Berle, pp. 597–600, 622, 631. See also Rostow's less-defined plan in "proposals for a project on future U.S. problems in the Satellite States," n.d. [1953], C. D. Jackson Records, Box 5. On the magnitude of the balloon and broadcasting effort, see copies of *The Crusader: News of the Crusade for Freedom*, in Clarence Francis' Papers, Box 14.

96. William Griffith complained to Jackson that U. S. Foreign Service officers "did their best to sabotage Operation Focus in every way," Griffith to C. D. Jackson, 20 Oct. 1954, 11 Mar. 1955, C. D. Jackson Papers, Box 47. Over time, the conflict between RFE and the State Department intensified. See William Griffith to C. D. Jackson, 11 Mar. 1955, Box 47; Jackson to Allen Dulles, 24 Nov. 1954, Box 40.

97. Jackson sent a full report of his conversation with John Foster Dulles to Henry Luce, 16 Apr. 1956, portions deleted, Box 59.

98. C. D. Jackson to William Jackson, 9 May 1956, Box 52. When C. D. Jackson resigned, in 1955, he was first replaced by Nelson Rockefeller. But Rockefeller never achieved the same results or maintained the same excitement about political warfare. Robert Cutler wrote to C. D. Jackson that the entire OCB operation declined after he left: "NR was entirely not able to supply what you supplied. He talked *about* the subject, but not executively *at* the subject. He is an attractive man and I like him. But the post, without your talent, proved to bring irritation and confusion, without successful guidance." Cutler to C. D. Jackson, 12 Jan. 1956, Box 37.

Rockefeller was then succeeded by William Jackson, who described the post's declining influence: He wrote that when he replaced Rockefeller as special assistant to the President for Cold War planning, he "received a letter of authority from the President which stressed the mission of assuring proper coordination and timing of the execution of foreign policies involving more than one Department or Agency. Except for the word 'timing,' there was no reference whatever to any responsibility for the psychological aspects of operations in the field of foreign affairs. . . . In no longer assigning any duties of a psychological nature to an Assistant to the President there is grave danger. If consideration of effect on public opinion is everybody's business then perhaps it is nobody's business. . . ." See W. H. Jackson, "The Fourth Area of the National Effort in Foreign Affairs," Whitman, Administration, Box 25. Eisenhower wrote to W. H. Jackson that he "thoroughly enjoyed" his paper and found it "both interesting and, I thought, correct." DDE to W. H. Jackson, 23 Nov. 1956, Box 25.

C. D. Jackson to Henry Luce, 3 Feb. 1956, C. D. Jackson Papers, Box 58.

99. Reactions to the Soviet note, Hagerty's diary, 24, 25 Jan. 1956; reference to the Soviet protest, 18 May 1965, Whitman Diary, Box 8; see also C. D. Jackson's defense of balloons to Allen Dulles, 14 Feb. 1956, C. D. Jackson Papers, Box 40. For Grew's defense of the air accident, see Whitney Shepardson, memorandum to the directors: Arthur Page, A. A. Berle, David K. E. Bruce, Frederic Dolbeare, Julius Fleischmann, John C. Hughes, Harold B. Miller, Irving Olds, George N. Shuster, Charles M. Spofford, H. Gregory Thomas, John C. Traphagen, 20 Mar. 1956, Box 45.

100. See Samuel S. Walker (one of RFE's chief strategists) to C. D. Jackson, 15 Oct. 1956, Box 44.

101. A. A. Berle, pp. 672–73; see Klaus Dohrn to C. D. Jackson, 6 Oct. 1956, C. D. Jackson Papers, Box 39; RFE's analysis, 5 Feb. 1957 (see note 94 herein). See also an important analysis of the Polish revolution that highlights the role Chinese Communist ideology played in the impetus for decentralization: William E. Griffith, "Poland After the 9th Plenum, the Victory of Gomułka and the Intrusion of China," 24 June 1957, C. D. Jackson Papers, Box 44. For Khrushchev's growing differences with China and his reaction to Mao's "Let All Flowers Bloom in the Garden and Diverse Opinions Contend," see *Khrushchev Remembers*, pp. 235–92. For contemporary documentation of the Polish revolt that includes examples of the activities of provocateurs and RFE, see Paul E. Zinner, ed., *National Communism and Popular Revolt in Eastern Europe, a Selection of Documents on Events in Poland and Hungary, February–November 1956* (Columbia University Press, 1956). On 16 July 1956, for example, *Pravda* editorialized: "The American press did not even consider it necessary to conceal the existence of a direct link between the Poznan events and the overseas centers which direct the 'cold war.' . . . The New York *Journal-American* stated on June 30 with cynical frankness that the 'Senate has decided to allocate within the framework of aid to foreign states the sum of $25,000,000 for financing secret activity behind the iron curtain like that which led to the riots in Poznan.'" Today, over twenty-five years later, it remains the case that one of the great and ongoing ironies of international politics has been that such transmitters of the Cold War as RFE have served to distort the reality of national dissension.

102. Klaus Dohrn on Cardinal Mindszenty in "Additional Notes on Church in Hungary and Poland," 12 Dec. 1956, C. D. Jackson Papers, Box 39. For a celebration of Cardinal Mindszenty, see George N. Shuster, *In Silence I Speak: the Story of Cardinal Mindszenty Today and of Hungary's "New Order"* (Farrar, Straus & Cudahy, 1956). Although Dr. Shuster worked closely with and was a director of RFE, there is no mention of that organization in this book. There is, however, an extraordinary description of Rákosi, "the Toad," and an analysis of Hungary's anti-Semitism that ignores the country's history altogether.

103. On 10 Sept. 1957, Henry Cabot Lodge addressed the General Assembly "On the Hungarian Question" and detailed the outrages committed from Nov. 1956 to the early months of the Kádár regime. See John Foster Dulles to DDE, 19 Sept. 1957, with speech, Whitman, Box 27.

For a provocative essay on the Hungarian revolution by participant Marxists who describe themselves as "proto-Eurocommunists," see Ferenc Feher and Agnes Heller, "Hungary, 1956: the Anatomy of a Political Revolution," *Radical America* (Jan.–Feb., 1980), pp. 51–65. Feher and Heller argue that the situation in Hungary was a "pure political revolution because the ruling stratum *totally* lost its legitimacy," and the "only considerations . . . related to the structure of the social order and not to external factors." For more complex analyses, see Ursula McLean, "Hungary 1956," *Socialist Europe*, No. 4, London; and Paul E. Zinner, *Revolution in Hungary* (Columbia University Press, 1962). Based primarily on extensive interviews, Zinner's book was part of Columbia University's Research Project on Hungary. It features a full and balanced bibliography, although there is no reference to the role played by RFE.

104. The United States accepted over forty thousand Hungarian refugees and agreed to pay for the resettlement of others elsewhere. The costs for "the care and resettlement of Hungarian refugees" exceeded $80 million in 1956. See State Department memo, Henry P. Leverich to William Macomber, 4 Nov. 1958, attached to DDE to C. D. Jackson, 6 Nov. 1958, Whitman, Administration, Box 24. See also C. D. Jackson to Frank Wisner for pre-1956 CIA-RFE problems involving defectors and refugees, 13 May 1954, C. D. Jackson Papers, Box 91. In 1956, private foundations helped. The international Congress of Cultural Freedom, long supported by the CIA, received "a sizable grant from the Ford Foundation to help Hungarian intellectuals"; and the Rockefeller Foundation granted a significant sum to help create the "Free Hungarian Symphony Orchestra." See Nicolas Nabokov to Jackson, 22 Feb. 1957, Box 64.

But the 1956 refugee situation was not free of problems. See Jackson to Tracy Voorhees, 29 Nov. 1956, Box 56: "When I heard on the radio that Secretary Brucker, on hand for the arrival of the first planeload, had ordered these poor people to salute and applaud the American flag, and go through what must have been to them incomprehensible military mumbo-jumbo, I was appalled. . . ." See also C. D. Jackson Papers, log, telephone call from Tracy Voorhees, 7 Dec. 1956, Box 56; State Department estimate regarding over one hundred defecting Hungarian athletes; Eisenhower agreed to "use his special fund," Whitney Tower to Sid James, "Asylum for Hungarian Olympic Athletes," 15 Nov. 1956, Box 85; notes on meeting with Vice-President, Loy Henderson, Tracy Voorhees, et al. on Hungarian refugee problems internationally and in the United States, 26 Dec. 1956, Whitman Diary, Box 8.

105. DDE to Jackson, 19 Nov. 1956, C. D. Jackson Papers, Box 41. See also Ann Whitman's diary entry, 15 Nov. 1956: "Curiously enough, I mentioned during morning the Hungarian situation to the President. . . . He shrugged his shoulders and said, or really implied, that there was nothing he could do about the Hungarian situation, that it was the Mid East that was worrying him." Whitman Diary, Box 8.

106. Jackson to Henry Luce, 26 Nov. 1956, C. D. Jackson Papers, Box 41. For Jackson's suggestions for action short of war, see Jackson to DDE, 23 Nov. 1956, log, Box 56; draft for *Life* editorial "Grasping the Nettle," 15 Nov. 1956, Box 56; a demand that Eisenhower confirm the policy of "liberation" during his second administration and "stand toe to toe with the Soviet Union" in order "to increase the area of freedom." See also C. D. Jackson's correspondence with William Jackson, 5, 8, 17 Nov. 1956, and Robert Sarrazac-Soulage to C. D. Jackson, Box 56.

Much acrimony existed between Eisenhower's staff and C. D. Jackson as a result of the United States' policy toward Hungary. See Henry Cabot Lodge's angry letter in response to *Life*'s criticism that Lodge at the United Nations "was not prepared to do anything." Lodge to Henry Luce, 4 Mar. 1957, C. D. Jackson Papers, Box 56. In June 1958, Imre Nagy and Pál Maleter were executed in the Soviet Union for "treason" (Pál Maleter, Nagy's Minister of Defense, had, during the first days of the uprising, joined the demonstrators. He and his tank unit helped bring the Army over to Nagy's side). Jackson and others demanded that the UN refuse to seat Kádár's government and in general protest the executions. Eisenhower and Dulles both rejected Jackson's arguments, as did Henry Cabot Lodge. C. D. Jackson to DDE, 30 Oct. 1958, with attachments; DDE to Jackson, 6 Nov. 1958, Whitman, Box 24. See also Jackson to Allen Dulles, 2 July 1958, C. D. Jackson Papers, Box 57. For a description of Jackson's confrontation with Lodge at the opera, see Jackson's log, 9 Dec. 1958, Box 57.

For Jackson's efforts to keep "rollback" alive, see esp. "The Kremlin's Achilles' Heel: the Eastern European Satellites," Jackson to J. F. Dulles, 29 Aug. 1958, Whitman, Box 28. On 6 Dec. 1958, Eisenhower wrote to Jackson: "I have lived quite constantly with this Kadar problem ever since you reminded me of its existence. Frankly, my *own* position is not completely in accord with yours . . . ," C. D. Jackson Papers, Box 41. On 9 Dec., Jackson wrote to Allen Dulles: "This is probably the most painful letter I have written in the past ten years. . . . I have just written John Hughes tendering my resignation as a member of the Board of the Free Europe Committee, which as you know I have considered the international cause to which I could most totally devote my mind and heart during these last many years . . . ," Box 44. On learning of his intention to resign, John Foster Dulles wrote that he, too, understood and shared Jackson's "disappointment." But, he wrote, "the fact is that there is nothing wrong with the [Kadar government's] credentials. . . . The Communists believe in using any means to achieve a desired end. We believe that means should be lawful. . . ." (J. F. Dulles to Jackson, 18 Jan. 1959, Box 40.) Not so hypocritical as astounding. Jackson was appalled. He wrote asking who was in fact trying to kid whom? It was the end of an era. See Jackson to Dulles, 9 Feb. 1959, Box 40.

107. On 7 Jan. 1957, Ann Whitman noted in her diary, "President apparently has expressed fear that some of RFE statements . . . could be considered incitements to war," Staff Note No. 57, 26 Dec. 1956, Whitman Diary, Box 8. In a press conference, Chancellor Adenauer acknowledged that RFE's broadcasts were subject to "misinterpretations," Department of State Staff Summary Supplement, 28 Jan. 1957, NLE 77–34, No. 17; "Radio Free Europe and the Hungarian Uprising," a twenty-seven-page report compiled by the Free Europe Committee to demonstrate that policy decisions during the crisis did not call for violent revolt and did not promise U.S. military support, n.d. Nov. 1956, C. D. Jackson Papers, Box 44; Jackson to Clare Boothe Luce, 28 Dec. 1956, requesting her participation on an independent outside panel to investigate RFE's role, Box 58. See also Hugh Seton-Watson, "Report on Free Europe Press Operations," 3 Oct. 1956, Box 44; Free Europe Committee's history and statement of purpose prepared for "Proposed European Advisory Committee," 1 Nov. 1958, Box 44. On 31 Dec. 1958, Jackson wrote that "if the State Department had its way, under pressure from some Ambassadors," RFE and FEC "would cease to be altogether." The U.S. ambassador to Warsaw, Jake Beame, "was urgently pleading that RFE Polish broadcasts be limited to music and news," Jackson to Arthur Page, Box 67; again, on 4 May 1960, Jackson wrote Archibald Alexander, of the FEC: "having listened to the overt, concerted attacks by the State Department and USIA on RFE," he feared that the operation may have "had it." "Pre-control" of all scripts was reintroduced. Jackson had originally abolished such "censorship." The angry reaction to prebroadcasting overview resulted in William Griffith's departure from RFE. See Griffith to C. D. Jackson, 21 Jan. 1958, Box 47: "Perhaps we will all finally conclude, as to RFE, that our reach did exceed our grasp." Griffith's departure was a blow to RFE. He was considered the political "key" with "the best concentrated knowledge of the whole, vast, sprawling, complicated thing we call the satellite system." Part of the reason he left was that he doubted "that East Europe in the near future will see startling or very interesting developments." See James Shepley to Jackson, 7 Feb. 1957; Jackson to Gen. Willis Crittenberger, 9

Feb. 1957, Box 44; William Griffith to Jackson, 30 Dec. 1957, 8 Feb. 1958, Box 47; Willis Crittenberger to A. A. Berle, Grew, Jackson, George Shuster, Whitney Shepardson, et al., "Opposition to European Advisory Group," 21 Apr. 1958, Box 44.

Radio Free Europe and Radio Liberty continued to be supported by the CIA until 30 June 1971. The funding for RFE through donations from the Crusade for Freedom had amounted to $49 million between 1951 and 1971, or less than 18 percent of RFE's operating expenses. In August 1972, President Nixon appointed Milton Eisenhower to chair a Presidential Study Commission on International Broadcasting to decide the future of RFE and Radio Liberty. John P. Roche, Brandeis University; Edmund Gullian, dean, Fletcher School of Law and Diplomacy, Tufts University; Edward Ware Barrett, director, Communications Institute; and John A. Gronowski, dean, Lyndon Baines Johnson School of Public Affairs, University of Texas, served on the commission. It unanimously concluded that "RFE and RL, by providing a flow of free and uncensored information to peoples deprived of it, actually contribute to a climate of détente." The commission urged an annual budget of $50 million for the continuation of the operation. In FY 1973, U.S. taxpayers paid over $138 million for international broadcasting activities. At the time of the congressional hearings to approve the Eisenhower Commission report, Gen. Lucius Clay and Robert Murphy were on RFE's board of directors, and RFE employed 1,541 people; RL employed 877.

On 2 Oct. 1973, by a vote of 313 to 90, the House voted to establish a Board for International Broadcasting and to continue RFE and RL. For the commission's report and the congressional debate, see Milton Eisenhower, Box 13; the *Congressional Record*, 2 Oct. 1953, H 8474 ff.; Milton Eisenhower to William Fulbright, 15 May 1973.

When I visited RFE headquarters, situated in the beautiful English Gardens in Munich, in 1974, I was told that the new public congressional funding arrangement was excellent. The amount appropriated was known in advance and there was, therefore, more fiscal security. The C. D. Jackson Room, RFE's "war room," dedicated to its first "balloonatic" and chief advocate, has been reduced in size and painted a bilious green. But the bronze plaque ("In Memoriam, C. D. Jackson, 1902–1964") was dusted and prominent, and all the transcripts around the long conference table were ready for analysis. Jackson would probably have been pleased.

108. Kennan, "Impressions of Poland, July 1958," Allen Dulles to Gen. Goodpaster, 3 Aug. 1958, DDE Diary, Staff Notes, Box 22.

109. W. W. Rostow, "Reflections on Poland and All That," 25 Oct. 1956, C. D. Jackson Papers, Box 75.

110. DDE to Jackson, 28 Jan. 1958, Box 41.

111. Jackson to Henry Luce, 22 June 1960, Box 41. For Jackson's final effort to boost political warfare in Eisenhower's administration, see the exchange of letters and documents between Eisenhower and the White House staff regarding a "stag dinner," held at Jackson's request, on political warfare. Jackson to DDE, 10 July 1959, Box 41; DDE to Jackson, 13 July 1959, Whitman, Box 24; Eisenhower prepared for the dinner by circulating David Lawrence's "A Strategy for Peace," 20 July 1959. It was much criticized. The general White House attitude toward political warfare had become exactly what Jackson feared it was: profoundly hostile. See especially George V. Allen, 20 Aug. 1959, Whitman, Box 26; and Karl Harr, 1 Sept. 1959, Box 26; see also Allen Dulles to Wilton B. Persons, 27 Aug. 1959, declassified with portions deleted, NLE 76–51, No. 431. Jackson thought the dinner "valuable." But "Jim Hagerty thought it a complete waste of time," 10 Sept. 1959, Whitman Diary, Box 11. For Jackson, the dinner was, in the long run, significant. He had gained a new respect for Vice-President Nixon. Evidently Nixon alone had agreed with Jackson's position. Jackson became more

sanguine about the future and wrote Nixon: "It was wonderful to see you again, and appreciate how much international experience and wisdom you have stored up as a result of your travels. . . . It is no exaggeration to say that with the possible exception of Allen Dulles, you have a more experienced 'feel' for these matters than anyone in the Government . . . ," Jackson to R. M. Nixon, 11 Sept. 1959, C. D. Jackson Papers, log, Box 57.

112. See *The Pentagon Papers: the Defense Department History of U. S. Decisionmaking on Vietnam* (the Senator Gravel Edition, Beacon Press, 1971), Vol. 1, pp. 211, 235–51ff. On 23 Oct. 1954, Eisenhower wrote to Swede Hazlett: "You are somewhat wrong in your statement, 'I know at one time you contemplated some really drastic action in Indo-China.' What I really attempted to do was to get established . . . the conditions under which I felt the U.S. could properly intervene to protect its own interests. A proper political foundation for any military action was essential. Since we could not bring it about (though we prodded and argued for almost two years), I gave not even a tentative approval to any plan for massive intervention." Whitman, Name Series, Box 18. See also DDE to Hazlett, 4 June 1955, ibid.; DDE to John F. Dulles, 23 Apr. 1954, DDE Diaries, Box 4, declassified, portions deleted, MR 76–50 No. 9; and Dulles to DDE on Operation Vulture, a "massive B-29 bombing" event declared "out of the question," MR 76–50, No. 6.

113. For the details of the curious Lebanon operation, see Miles Copeland, op. cit.; Robert Murphy, *Diplomat Among Warriors,* pp. 394–418.

"In answer to Lebanon's request for assistance, U. S. Marines were landed in Beirut commencing 15 July." By 26 July, there were five thousand marines, ninety-six hundred army troops, and a medium tank battalion of ninety-five tanks in Lebanon. Eisenhower explained: "American armed forces were landed in the Lebanon to insure to the people of that country the freedom to conduct their own affairs. . . . Our purpose in the Lebanon was and is in support of self-determination. We hold it to be the right of all peoples to choose their own government and to exercise their civic rights without outside interference. The government of the Lebanon . . . was threatened from outside its borders by agitation and by infiltration. It requested help."

See "U. S. Troops in Lebanon" and "Status of Forces in Lebanon," 5 Aug. 1958; and draft, presidential statement, 28 July 1958, Office of Staff Secretary, Box 43. See also, 14 July 1958, Whitman Diary, Box 10.

114. DDE to Paul Hoffman, 18 Jan. 1958, Whitman, Box 21.

115. Prime Minister Macmillan presented Britain's case at a White House "stag dinner" that included Dulles, C. D. Jackson, Bedell Smith, Robert Lovett, John J. McCloy, and others. It was a reunion of the old "Algerian hands," see C. D. Jackson Papers, log, 10 June 1958.

116. DDE to Swede Hazlett, [28] Feb. 1958, Name Series, Box 18; DDE to his staff, 11 Feb. 1958, Whitman Diary, Box 9.

117. DDE to J. F. Dulles, telephone, 27 Nov. 1958, DDE Diary, Box 23; see Christian Herter's draft, "Reply to the Soviet Government on Berlin," 22 Dec. 1958, Whitman, Administration, NLE 76–51, No. 371.

118. W. W. Rostow to C. D. Jackson, 5 Mar. 1959, C. D. Jackson Papers, Box 75. Jackson also had suggestions for activity, including reconsideration of a 1953 "Volunteer Freedom Corps" plan, which would comprise freedom fighters and refugees, trained and equipped by the Department of Defense, and reconsideration of "liberation." With "3000 refugees a month" fleeing East Germany via Berlin, he argued, "how about organizing . . . a series of slowdown strikes in East Germany." See Jackson to Allen Dulles, 24 Feb. 1959; Allen Dulles to Jackson, 7, 16 Feb., 31 Mar. 1959; Jackson to John F. and Allen Dulles, 9, 12 Feb. 1959, Box 40. See also Jackson to Allen Dulles, 16, 25, 30 Mar. 1959; 12 May 1959, ibid.

119. Memorandum for the Record, DDE to congressional leaders, 26 Mar.

1959, DDE Diary, Box 25, portions deleted, MR 76–50 No. 139; also cabinet minutes, 13 Mar. 1959.

120. Eisenhower quoted in Hagerty's diary, 13 Dec. 1959.

121. John S. D. Eisenhower, Memo of Conference with the President, 3 Mar. 1959, DDE Diary, Box 25.

122. L. A. Minnich, minutes, legislative meeting, 10 Mar. 1959, ibid.

123. Whitman Diary, 5 Mar. 1959.

124. Gen. Goodpaster, memo of conference with President, 14 Sept. 1959; Ann Whitman's note, 9 Jan. 1961, Name Series, Box 32.

125. Ibid. and memos of conference, 26, 28 Sept. 1959, DDE Diary, Box 28.

126. On the morning that Eisenhower heard that the U-2 was intact, having been shot down inside Russia, the President and his closest advisers were undergoing a secret air-raid ritual at High Point, the United States' emergency relocation site for the President and his party. See Ann Whitman Diary, 5 May 1960, Box 11.

See also William Robinson to DDE, 23 May 1960, Robinson Papers, Box 4; Ed McCabe memo for Ann Whitman, breakfast with Republican leaders, 11 May 1960, DDE Diary, Box 32; pre-press-conference notes, 11 May 1960, ibid. For the U-2 in its CIA-covert-operations context, see: Richard Bissell's Oral History interview, Eisenhower Project, Columbia University (Bissell was directly in charge of the U-2 operation from December 1954. He was director of research and development and deputy director of plans for the CIA); David Wise and Thomas B. Ross, *The U-2 Affair* (Random House, 1962); Victor Marchetti and John D. Marks, *The CIA and the Cult of Intelligence* (Alfred A. Knopf, 1974); Col. L. Fletcher Prouty, *The Secret Team: the CIA and Its Allies in Control of the U.S. and the World* (Prentice-Hall, 1973); and George B. Kistiakowsky, *A Scientist at the White House: the Private Diary of President Eisenhower's Special Assistant for Science and Technology* (Harvard University Press, 1976).

127. The description of Eisenhower at Geneva as reported in *Le Monde* via Genêt (Janet Flanner) in *The New Yorker*, Aug. 1955, is in Whitman, Box 1.

128. *Khrushchev Remembers*, pp. 410–13.

CHAPTER VI NOTES

1. Milton S. Eisenhower, *The Wine Is Bitter* (Doubleday, 1963), p. 48.

2. After several years of inquiry regarding the absence of any record of the overthrow of Arbenz's government in the Eisenhower Library, two considerable files on Guatemala were made available. Although only scattered CIA and NSC reports have so far been declassified, the State Department records relating to Guatemalan activities from 1951 through August 1954—hereinafter cited as State —were declassified after appeals through the Freedom of Information Act. Also, the Library of Congress' ninety-six-box collection of Guatemalan Government records is critical to an understanding of the Arbenz period. Largely untranslated and filed so as to emphasize the influence of "Soviet Communism in Guatemala," the researcher should read all English-language headnotes and file descriptions with care. Evidently the Library of Congress stored this collection in a vault in Virginia as originally deposited. The documents themselves were removed from Guatemala in July 1954 by the "Guatemalan National Committee for Defense Against Communism," a committee "entrusted with wide powers." Part of the cleanup for the CIA-State Department operation, the committee "seized the files of all Communist-infiltrated organizations and leading figures of the Arbenz regime." Fifty thousand of the documents were microfilmed and brought to the United States, processed, analyzed, and used to form the basis of a book, *Communism in Guatemala, 1944–1954,* by Ronald M. Schneider—published in the

Frederick A. Praeger series in Russian History and World Communism (1958), subsequently revealed to be a CIA-sponsored project. Schneider's work was done under the auspices of the Foreign Policy Research Institute of the University of Pennsylvania, which donated the documents to the Library of Congress. References to this collection are hereinafter cited as LC.

3. "Guatemala: Plot Within a Plot," *Time*, 8 Feb. 1954, p. 36; Milton Eisenhower interview with author; Eisenhower at Quantico quoted in Hagerty's diary, 19 June 1954; Minutes, meeting of Guatemalan Group, 18 June 1954, State.

4. Manuel Galich, "Ten Years of Springtime (1944–1954) in the Land of Eternal Tyranny," *Tricontinental* (Sept.–Oct. 1974), p. 19. For an analysis of Guatemala's economic history, see also "The Legacy of Underdevelopment" and "Extracting the Surplus," in *Guatemala,* ed. Susanne Jonas and David Tobis (North American Congress on Latin America, 1974), hereinafter cited as Jonas.

5. Thomas McCann, *An American Company: the Tragedy of United Fruit* (Crown Publishers, 1976), pp. 13, 56; see also Galich, op. cit., pp. 4–49.

6. A. A. Berle, op. cit., p. 470.

7. Galich, op. cit., pp. 23–25; I am grateful to Margaret Randall and Consuela Pereira, for their taped interview, 9 Mar. 1979, on the role of the teachers union and the Alianza Femenina Guatemalteca in the popular aspects of the revolution, including the literacy campaign and the buildup of unionism in the countryside. These activities are documented in the Papers of the Alianza Femenina Guatemalteca, LC, Box 6.

8. On Spruille Braden, see McCann, op. cit., p. 55. Thomas Mann quoted in Susanne Jonas, "Anatomy of an Intervention," *Guatemala,* p. 68. For the extraordinary accusation that Spruille Braden leaned left and supported Communists in Latin America, see William D. Pawley's testimony before the U. S. Senate Judiciary Committee, *Hearings, Communist Threat to the U. S. Through the Caribbean,* 86th Cong., 2nd Sess., Part 10, Pawley, 2, 8 Sept. 1960, pp. 712–22. Pawley, better known for his anti-Communist activities in China and as the creator and owner of the Flying Tigers, also testified about Communist attitudes in the State Department regarding China and Korea (pp. 722–36.) Pawley testified that he organized the Flying Tigers, although Claire Chennault, whom he "employed at the Chinese request, got the credit for it." Pawley did not protest, since "I did not do that for credit, . . . and I owned the company. . . . I was the only stockholder and president of the company and Mr. Roosevelt thought that media was a good one to use because the employment of pilots and mechanics had to be done under cover, and I provided that cover" (p. 722).

9. See, for example, *Manifesto* del Sindicato Central de Trabajadores en la Industria del Cuero, 1 May 1950, Box 27 ("Peace Organizations"), LC. Also, on 30 Mar. 1951, the Washington *Post* reported that Manuel Galich, Guatemala's Foreign Minister, had announced that no troops would be sent to Korea, because Guatemala was preoccupied with its own economic rehabilitation. He explained that the country was in no economic or military position to maintain armed forces beyond its frontiers, and the citizens of Guatemala "would not tolerate participation." See "Guatemala ante América 1951, La Verdad Sobre la Cuarta Reunión de Consulta de Cancilleres Americanos," Box 93 ("Government Publications"), LC. In addition, a committee of solidarity with the Korean people was sponsored by Guatemala's leading labor union; see the materials in the General Confederation of Guatemalan Workers' (CGTG's) file, Box 26 ("Propaganda Committee of Korean Solidarity").

10. Arbenz's inaugural objectives quoted in Galich, op. cit., p. 27.

11. For information relating to the administration of the land-reform law, see Colonel Jacobo Arbenz Guzmán's Information Bulletin, *Noticias de Guatemala,* No. 43, 2 Mar. 1954, Box 3, LC; Andrea Brown, "Land of the Few: Rural Land Ownership in Guatemala," in *Guatemala,* esp. pp. 19–20; McCann, op. cit., p. 49; DDE, *Mandate for Change,* p. 421. It is interesting that United States authorities

disagree as to the number of acres expropriated from UFCO: Eisenhower's figure is 225,000; NACLA's is 387,000; and McCann's is 178,000 acres. See also, Luis Cardozo y Aragón, "Land for the Many," *The Nation*, 14 Mar. 1953.

12. McCann, op. cit., pp. 45, 47.

13. For Guatemala's account of the plan, see Francisco Hernández Álvarez to Carlos Pellecer, 19 June 1952, Box 1, LC. The 1952 plan was recalled by Col. Anastasio Somoza, chief of staff, Nicaraguan National Guard (and younger son of President Somoza), in a conversation with Rolland Welch: Memo of conversation, "The previously proposed plan to promote revolt in Guatemala," 9 Mar. 1953; Welch to John Ohmans, 11 Mar. 1953, State.

14. A. A. Berle, op. cit., 17 Oct. 1952, pp. 610–11, 613.

15. Ibid., pp. 614–15.

16. E. Howard Hunt, *Under-Cover: Memoirs of an American Secret Agent* (Berkley Publishing, 1974), pp. 96–97.

17. DDE, *Mandate for Change*, pp. 421–22.

18. McCann, op. cit., pp. 29, 55–56, 50.

19. Virginia Bravo Letelier to the Ministry of Education, Aug. 1949, Box 26 ("Communist Control of Education"), LC. See also, "Education," Box 1; Virginia Bravo Letelier to María Villanova de Arbenz, 4 Apr. 1954, regarding Pablo Neruda's speech that "we are ready to drain our veins to defend you." The English-language headnote reads: ". . . The Communist poet of Chile, Pablo Neruda, is the intellectual wheel horse used quite effectively by the Communists. . . . This illustrates both how the Communists 'build up' their intellectuals and use them" (D 90153, LC); Mrs. Arbenz's receipts and bills, with commentary, are in Boxes 3 and 4, LC.

20. Memo of conversation between Guatemala's ambassador, Dr. Don Guillermo Toriello Garrido, Dean Acheson, Rudolf Schoenfeld (U.S. ambassador to Guatemala), 1 Dec. 1952; and Schoenfeld to Ed Clark, 19 Dec. 1952, amending the memorandum of conversation, State.

21. Memo of conversation, Dr. Toriello, Clark, and Raymond Leddy to Thomas Mann et al., 27 Jan. 1953, State.

22. A. A. Berle, op. cit., pp. 617–20.

23. Memo of conversation, Ambassador Toriello and John Moors Cabot, "Communism in Guatemala," 6 Mar. 1953; Toriello, Rubottom, and Fisher, 11 Mar.; Toriello, Cabot, and Fisher, 25 Mar. 1953, State.

24. William Krieg to John Foster Dulles, 30, 31 Mar. 1953, State.

25. Rudolf Schoenfeld to State Department, 15 Apr. 1953, "Aftermath of Baja Verapaz uprising," State.

26. Whelan to Dulles, 4 Mar. 1953, State.

27. Schoenfeld to State Department, 13 May 1953, re: "Alleged Confessions of Salamá Uprising"; Andrew Wardlaw to State Department, 27 May 1953. For other coup competitors see: The record of conversation between Col. Roberto Barrios Peña, allegedly Trujillo's candidate for Guatemala's presidency, with Leddy and Fisher, 28 Apr. 1953. Peña was also associated with El Salvador's President Osorio, and Cuba's dictator Batista. In addition to the international competition for Guatemala's future leadership, an overzealous U.S. customs officer threatened to leak the entire affair. Evidently, an agent of Samuel Zemurray, one of UFCO's founders and longtime president, was caught by a Customs Bureau informer attempting to purchase rifles, grenades, light machine guns, and "some homemade bazookas." See memo, Fisher and Leddy to Thomas Mann, 19 May 1953, "Investigation of Alleged Arms Acquisition by Zemurray for Overthrow of Guatemalan Government"; also Fisher to Mann, "Alleged Implication of Mr. Samuel Zemurray in Illicit Arms Traffic," 22 May 1953, State.

28. Office memorandum, "Relations with Guatemala," Leddy to Cabot, 21 May 1953, State.

29. In 1949, after two years of desultory negotiations with U.S. oil companies eager to begin oil explorations in Guatemala, relations were suspended. On 25 October, Murray Schutz issued an independent report on oil to the National Institute of Petroleum (*Un Estudio y Discusión del Decreto 649, la Nueva Ley de Petróleo de la República de Guatemala*), urging Guatemala "to be reasonable" with the U.S. companies, whose capital was, he argued, needed for investment and development. Schutz's report explained that such companies as Standard Oil of Ohio and Atlantic Refining transferred their interest to North America because, for example, Standard Oil received 3 million acres to explore in Alberta and Saskatchewan, and new oil fields had opened in the United States: in Montana, Wyoming, and Colorado. (Schutz's Report, Box 4, LC.) But the government refused Schutz's 1949 advice, and in 1952 Roberto Fanjul García, the Minister of the Economy and Labor, submitted an eight-page assessment of the petroleum situation to Arbenz more in keeping with the government's preferences: "The belief that it is not possible for a small country . . . to carry out oil exploration is propaganda skillfully exploited by the large international companies." Fanjul García insisted that all activity in this field be financed by Guatemalan capital. Although he recognized the need for loans from international banks, he concluded "under no circumstances will foreign capital be permitted to enter the country." See Fanjul García's report, Box 4, LC; and "The Problem of Petroleum in Guatemala," 19 Nov. 1948, Box 1, LC.
30. "Relations with Guatemala," 21 May 1953, State.
31. Ibid., and Schoenfeld to State Department, 21 Apr. 1953.
32. Hunt, op. cit., p. 99; Miguel Ydígoras Fuentes, *My War with Communism* (Prentice-Hall, 1963), pp. 49–50. Ydígoras Fuentes and his supporters protested in Washington UFCO's support for Castillo Armas. But the State Department considered Ydígoras' associates "irresponsible." See Burrows to Holland, "General Miguel Ydígoras Fuentes, Exile Leader," 1 June 1954. Also memo of conversation, César Lanuza, Woodward, and Fisher, "Guatemalan Anti-Communist Movement," 17 May 1954. Lanuza said that a purported CIA official, "Vanderbilt Spader," gave two thousand dollars to Ydígoras in April but discontinued support after "pressure from the UFCO."
33. Division of Research for Latin America, Special Paper No. 21, "Effect upon Guatemala of Arms Procurement by El Salvador, Honduras and Nicaragua," 12 June 1953; W. Park Armstrong to Cabot, 16 June 1953, State.
34. Memorandum of conversation, Guillermo Toriello, Thomas Mann, et al., 26 June 1953, State.
35. Memo of conversation, Toriello, Leddy, et al., 21 July 1953, State.
36. John Calvin Hill, "Administration Parties and Anti-Communists Prepare for November Municipal Elections," 29 Oct. 1953, State.
37. Harold E. Urist to USIA, 9 Nov. 1953, "Recent Developments in University of San Carlos," with list of students active in the Association of University Students; and William Krieg to State Department, "Guatemalan Opportunist Politicians Sense Further Leftward Trend of Government," 4 Nov. 1953, State.
38. DDE, *Mandate for Change*, p. 422; Peurifoy to Cabot, 19 Nov. 1953, State.
39. Peurifoy's preliminary call on Foreign Minister Osegueda, 2 Nov. 1953, State.
40. Leddy to Peurifoy, 6 Nov. 1953, State.
41. Peurifoy to Dept. of State, 18 Dec. 1953 re conversation between Peurifoy and Jacobo Arbenz Guzmán.
42. *Time*, and see William Krieg to Dept. of State, 18 Nov. 1953.
43. For Castillo Armas' reflections on his rivals, see "Comments of Col. Carlos Castillo Armas Relative to Guatemalan Political Exiles," 5 Nov. 1953, State; On Arenas' visit to Washington, see Raymond Leddy to William Krieg, 5 Jan. 1954; see also Krieg to John W. Fisher, 24 Nov. 1953; and memo of conversation, José Luis Arenas et al., 18 Nov. 1953, State.

44. Krieg to Leddy, 10 Nov. 1953; memorandum, "Trujillo Drops Interest in Subsidizing Guatemalan Insurrectionist Group," 3 Nov. 1953; memo of conversation, Aurelio Montenegro, Peurifoy, and Krieg, "Efforts to Overthrow Guatemalan Government," 6 Nov. 1953, State.

45. Castillo quoted by John D. Erwin in "Comments of Col. Carlos Castillo Armas Relative to Guatemalan Political Exiles," 5 Nov. 1953, State.

46. Telegram, Peurifoy to Dulles, 23 Dec. 1953, State.

47. Krieg to USIA, 26 Jan. 1954. Subsequent information revealed to the State Department that UNTL was of "relatively little importance." One trusted "source" reported that the labor union's "membership of about 3,000 Guatemalans consisted almost exclusively of unemployed workers; that it had no real following; and that its leaders were not sufficient to the task of doing serious damage to the CGTG." See Stanley Grand to DC/R, "Guatemalan Political Developments," memorandum for the files, being "a summary of conversation with a person who has excellent contacts in the Guatemalan Government and newspaper circles . . . ," 11 Mar. 1954, State.

48. Walter Bedell Smith to AmEmbassy Guatemala, 27 Jan. 1954, State.

49. Rodolfo López D., "Report on the Organization of Publicity and Propaganda," 22 Jan. 1954, Box 3, LC. See *Guatemala en Pie, y con Ella Todos los Amantes de la Libertad y la Democracia en America y en el Mundo Entero*, Boletín del Comité de Lucha Contra la Intervención Extranjera, 23 Jan. 1954. See also William A. Krauss, USIS, Guatemala; USIA, Washington, "Government Radio Station Increases Anti-U.S. Propaganda," 30 Sept. 1953, State.

50. The documents photocopied by the Arbenz government were printed in *La Democracia Amenazada, El Caso Guatemala, Febrero de 1954. Publicación de la Secretaria de Propaganda y Divulgación de la Presidencia de la República*, a ninety-eight-page bulletin containing "irrefutable proof of the vast international conspiracy. . . ." For the information about the munitions offered by H. F. Cordes, see pp. 62, 81, Government Publications, Box 94, LC. See also Krieg to Dulles, 29 Jan. 1954, State. For Trujillo's role, see Jonas, pp. 68–69.

51. Bedell Smith, press release, 30 Jan. 1954, State; see also New York *Times* "Guatemala Says Neighbors and U.S. Plot an Invasion," 30 Jan. 1954.

52. Smith to AmEmbassies, Managua et al., 1 Feb. 1954. General Somoza and his son Col. "Tachito" Somoza both denied the allegations. According to the U.S. embassy: Public opinion in Nicaragua was persuaded that a plot existed only in the mendacious tales told by Guatemalan Communists. See Rolland Welch to State Dept., 12 Feb. 1954; Welch believed that the Nicaraguan "public in general views Guatemala with disgust," Welch to Dulles, 3 Feb. 1954. See also Welch to Dept. of State, 9 Feb. 1954: "Nicaraguan Official Says Guatemalan Charges Were True": "Guillermo (Chato) Lang is a Nicaraguan of German extraction who was on the proclaimed list during the war. Because of this, and his present shady business reputation (usually in handling German goods), he is forever currying favor with Embassy officers. He is now a member of Congress, 'purchasing agent' for the President's elder son, Luis Somoza, and he is generally regarded as the presidential 'hatchet man.'" He told Welch: "Of course we were trying to help Guatemalan revolutionary leaders. Not long ago we landed arms on the east coast in boxes marked 'printing machinery' and addressed to the President's Managua newspaper, *Novedades*."

53. White to Secretary of State, 2 Feb. 1954; Krieg to Secretary of State, 2 Feb. 1954; Krieg to Dept. of State: "Guatemalan Congress Declares Castillo Armas and Ydígoras Fuentes Traitors," 3 Feb. 1954. At this session of congress, Guatemala also denounced the U. S. Senate's "aggressive campaign" led by Senator Alexander Wiley; called on the American republics for "solidarity" at this moment "when the national sovereignty of Guatemala is threatened," and thanked the congress of Chile for its motion of support. In addition, Luis Alberto Monge, the secretary general of the parent-body of UNTL—the Inter-American

Regional Organization of Workers, ORIT—refused to consent to a statement on Guatemala requested by Serafino Romualdi. Monge explained that ORIT's leadership had "nationalistic tendencies," and any statement "no matter how carefully drafted" might benefit Guatemala "rather than the free world." See Alex A. Cohen to Department of State, 9 Feb. 1954. For an analysis of the U.S.-based anti-Communist operations in the "Free labor movement" of Latin America, spearheaded by the AFL-CIO and led by Romualdi, among others, see Ronald Radosh, *American Labor and United States Foreign Policy* (Random House, 1969).

54. Krauss to USIA, 3 Feb. 1954; see also Krieg to Dulles, 2 Feb. No specific charges were made against Bannell beyond the claim that he had "printed so many lies." But Gruson was charged with having "systematically defamed and slandered this republic and its Government." He was expelled, therefore, in "the name of national decorum." The Minister of Foreign Affairs explained: "We can understand differences of opinion because this is a democracy. But when a foreigner casts scorn on the dignity of the President that is intolerable." Quoted in New York *Times* "Guatemala Ousts Two U. S. Newsmen," 3 Feb. 1954.

55. Eisenhower on Toriello, quoted in Hagerty's diary, 26 Apr. 1954.

56. Peurifoy to Dulles, 23 Feb. 1954, State.

57. Bedell Smith to DDE, memo re visit of Guatemalan Ambassador Toriello, 15 Jan. 1954, DDE, declassified, MR 76–86 No. 11 (10/1976).

58. Dulles to Peurifoy, 20 Feb. 1954, State.

59. New York *Times*, editorial, "Inter-American Conference," 1 Mar. 1954. See also "Unity Plea Opens Caracas Meeting," New York *Times*, 2 Mar. 1954.

60. Editorial, *The Nation*, 13 Mar. 1954.

61. "The Problem of Guatemala," *Time*, 11 Jan. 1954; and also "Guatemala: Plot Within a Plot," *Time*, 8 Feb. 1954, wherein *Time* editorialized that Arbenz's white paper was "completely fanciful" and that H. F. Cordes had "sold arms to Guatemala—but to Arbenz's government rather than to any rebels." *Time* also repeated the State Department's charge that the white paper was published to coincide with Caracas and was "a communist effort to disrupt" the conference. *Time* concluded, therefore, that the "real plot was . . . a sort of Reichstag fire in reverse, masterminded in Moscow and designed to divert the attention . . . from Guatemala as the Western Hemisphere's Red problem child." See also New York *Times*, 14 Feb. 1954, "U. S. Role Delicate at Latin Meeting." On 24 Feb., Paul Kennedy, in "U. S. Aims to Avoid Guatemala Test," reported in the New York *Times* that the United States would not name Guatemala, and that the United States' resolution would be "broad and general" so that Guatemala would not be able to charge "intervention." Latin American experts agreed "that a majority of the Latin American states are not as far advanced in their thinking on the dangers of Communist infiltration as is the U.S."

62. Flora Lewis, "The Peril Is Not Red in Central America," *The Nation*, 13 Feb. 1954, pp. 127ff.; F. Lewis, "Communism in Guatemala: a Case History," New York *Times Magazine*, 21 Feb. 1954, pp. 11ff.

63. For specific economic details of U.S.-Latin American relations relating to Caracas, see Stephen V. Mitchell, "Invisible Delegate: the Peon at Caracas," *The Nation*, 27 Feb. 1954, pp. 172ff.

64. Dr. Eisenhower quoted in ibid., and in "Inter-American Affairs," New York *Times* editorial, 15 Feb. 1954.

65. Milton Eisenhower's Report on Latin America, to DDE, 18 Nov. 1953, Whitman, Name Series, Box 13, DDE, quotes from pp. 4–5, 10–12, 47.

66. See George Humphrey memorandum for the President, 15 Jan. 1954, and attached responses by the Secretaries of Commerce and Agriculture and the director of the USIA, on Milton Eisenhower's Report on Latin America, ibid. For the United States' historical refusal to support Latin America economically on a par with its European or Asian commitments, see William D. Pawley's testimony,

Hearings, Communist Threat to the U. S. Through the Caribbean, Part 10, U. S. Senate, Committee on the Judiciary, 86th Cong., 2nd Sess., 2, 8 Sept. 1960, p. 723. Pawley, assigned to the economic conference at Bogota in 1948, was afraid that the United States had nothing "to offer the Latinos at Bogota, and we would go there and come out in very bad shape. . . . We did not have any money for lending in the Export-Import Bank. Jack McCloy, who was President of the World Bank, was completely unsympathetic to Latin America, had never been to Latin America in his life, and had made no loans in Latin America although the World Bank as of that date had made loans in excess of a billion dollars to other parts of the world." See also, Walter La Feber, *America, Russia, and the Cold War, 1945–1966* (Wiley, 1967), pp. 180–81.

67. See "The Americas: What They Want," *Time,* 1 Mar. 1954; "Inter-American Affairs," New York *Times* editorial, 15 Feb. 1954; and "Conference Climate," *Time,* 8 Mar. 1954.

68. For the State Department's strategy preceding Caracas, see "Draft Memorandum on Handling of Guatemala at Caracas," 10 Feb. 1954; "Guatemala and the Discussion of Communism at the 10th Inter-American Conference"; Peurifoy to Dulles, 12 Feb. 1954, urging Dulles to withhold public announcement of military aid to Salvador, Nicaragua, and Honduras until after Caracas, so it could not be used as evidence of preparation for "armed intervention," State.

69. Dulles quoted in "Success at Caracas," *Time,* 22 March 1954.

70. The delegates' day of "breast-beating" described in "The Americas: Keeping Communists Out," *Time,* 15 Mar. 1954; see also "The Americas: a Voice for Aid," *Time,* 29 Mar. 1954.

71. Arbenz quoted in ibid., 15 Mar. 1954. His entire speech was published in *Noticias de Guatemala,* No. 43, 2 Mar. 1954, quotes from p. 5ff., Box 3 ("Propaganda Arbenz Regime"), LC; see also Milton Bracker, "Arbenz Attacks Foreign Critics," New York *Times,* 2 Mar. 1954.

72. For Guatemala's preparations for Caracas, see Krieg to Department of State, "Guatemala Prints Documents on Alleged Plot for Use at Caracas Conference," 26 Feb. 1954; Krieg to State, "Guatemalan Political Leaders and Administration Call for Guatemala to Denounce 'International Conspiracy' . . . at Caracas," 23 Feb. 1954, State; see also "Guatemalan Asks U. S. Aide to Talks," New York *Times,* 23 Feb. 1954.

73. "Guatemala Joins Americas Talks, Will Send Eight to Caracas," New York *Times,* 13 Feb. 1954; U. S. Role Delicate at Latin Meeting, New York *Times,* 14 Feb. 1954; and *Time,* 29 Mar. 1954.

74. On Toriello's speech, see "The Shape of Things: No Concord at Caracas," editorial, *The Nation,* 13 Mar. 1954; "The Americas: Keeping the Communists Out," *Time,* 15 Mar. 1954; Sidney Gruson, "Latin Lands Urge Top Trade Council . . . for Over-All Planning," New York *Times,* 3 Mar. 1954.

CHAPTER VII NOTES

1. National Intelligence Estimate, from MID-John W. Fisher to Henry Holland, 19 Apr. 1954, State.

2. Eisenhower quoted in Hagerty's diary, 26 Apr. 1954; Memorandum on Guatemalan Situation for Legislative Meeting, 26 Apr. 1954, declassified MR 76–49 No. 1, DDE Papers.

3. C. D. Jackson to Bedell Smith, cc Elmer Staats, Paul Comstock, DDE, 15 Mar. 1954, C. D. Jackson Records, Box 4. The relevant OCB and CIA documents are still unavailable. See the State Department's widely distributed "Chronology of 1953 Events in Guatemala," Krieg to AmEmbassy Guatemala, 15 Mar. 1954, State.

4. Holland et al., "Memorandum on Guatemalan Situation," to Sherman Adams "for use of the President in preparing for his meeting with congressional leaders," 24 Apr. 1954; Jack Neal to Holland, "Proposed Congressional Investigations and Speeches Concerning Communism in Guatemala," 5 May 1954, State.

5. Stanley I. Grand to DC/R memorandum for files: "Guatemalan Political Development," 11 Mar. 1954—a summary of conversations between Leddy et al., of MID, and "a person who has excellent contacts in the Guatemalan Government and newspaper circles," State.

6. Report of meeting, "OAS Action Against Communism in Guatemala," 13 May 1954, State. According to documents declassified to date, a series of meetings of the Guatemalan planning group generally involved Henry Holland, John Peurifoy, Frank Wisner, Robert Murphy, Raymond Leddy, John Fisher, John C. Hill, and later, Richard Bissell, who succeeded Wisner as the CIA's chief of clandestine services. E. Howard Hunt and Tracey Barnes evidently handled the on-site activities, and relevant documents that might detail their activities have yet to appear. Their names do not appear in the State Department file.

7. E. Howard Hunt, op. cit., pp. 99–100. According to State Department memoranda of two conversations held on 26 and 31 Dec. 1953, Col. Anselmo Getella revealed his "impatience" with Arbenz, his "hatred" for communism, and his susceptibility to flattery. The documents regarding Getella's defection were allegedly prepared by "George Phihal, a British subject of Czech origin. . . ." See John Peurifoy to Raymond G. Leddy, 5 Jan. 1954, State.

8. Hagerty diary, 20 May 1954; Frank Wisner to Chief, Western Hemisphere Division, 4 Apr. 1953, C. D. Jackson Records, Box 2. (This is a "sanitized" document, with "portions exempted," NLE 76–111, No. 1; 6 Jan. 1977.)

9. D. D. Eisenhower, *Mandate for Change*, p. 424; Eisenhower quoted in Hagerty's diary, 24 May 1954; see also Hagerty's diary, 19 May. According to Peurifoy, Guatemala's press "unanimously supported Guatemala's right to purchase arms where it pleases, thereby breaking the U.S.' embargo," Peurifoy to Secretary of State, 20 May 1954, State.

10. Memo of conversation, Holland and Ambassador Guillermo Sevilla-Sacasa, of Nicaragua, to Dulles, Murphy, et al., 21 May 1954, "Nicaraguan and Costa Rican Differences Regarding Guatemala," State.

11. Murphy to Dulles, 25 May 1954; see also Dulles' expression of concern during staff meeting, 25 May 1954, W. K. Scott to Holland and Merchant, State. Hagerty also thought "the State Department made a very bad mistake, particularly with the British, in attempting to search ships going to Guatemala. . . . Somebody in the State Department (maybe Dulles) forgot that the right of search of neutral vessels on the high seas is one which we ourselves oppose. As a matter of fact, we were at war with the British in 1812 over the same principle. I don't see how with our traditional opposition to such search and seizure we could possibly have proposed it, and I don't blame the British for one minute for getting pretty rough in their answers. . . ." Hagerty's diary, 19 June 1954.

12. English to Holland, 20 May 1954, "Interference with Shipping to Guatemala"; Holland to Ambassadors Donnelly and Pawley, 27 May 1954, State.

13. D. D. Eisenhower, *Mandate for Change*, p. 425; Memo of conversation between Dulles and Sir Roger Makins, 25 May 1954, State. Britain was specifically rocked when one of its vessels, the *Springfjord*, chartered by the Grace Line, suffered a "total loss" when bombed. It was already "three quarters loaded with cargo from Salvador and Guatemala," including "cotton, coffee, lumber, and glycerine." Peurifoy to Dulles, 28 June 1954, State. According to Hunt, it was years before reparations negotiations between the CIA and Britain's MI-16 ended. Finally, Britain was "fully reimbursed" for its loss, Hunt, op. cit., p. 100. Other allied nations were equally outraged. The Netherlands, for example, billed the United States for ten thousand dollars for the detention of its ship *Wulfsbrook*, see Guatemalan Group, Minutes of Meeting, 4 June 1954, State.

14. John Hill to Peurifoy, 30 May 1954. For Guatemala's reaction to the threat of economic sanctions, see Peurifoy to Dulles, 10, 11 June 1954, State.

15. Latin America's lack of interest regarding an "invocation of Caracas" is abundantly documented. See: memo of conversation, Dulles, João Carlos Muniz, Holland, 11 May 1954; memo of conversation, Dr. Alberto Lleras Camargo, Secretary-General OAS, and Holland, 12 May 1954; Joe Martin, Speaker of the House, Muniz, and Holland, 13 May 1954; meeting, 10 May 1954, "OAS Action Against Communism in Guatemala," Holland, Cale, R. G. Leddy, et al.; Whiting Willauer to Secretary of State, 21 May 1954, memo of conversation with Dulles, Holland, and Ambassador João Carlos Muniz, of Brazil; memo of conversation, "Consultation Regarding Guatemala," Holland with El Salvador's Ambassador Héctor David Castro, 30 May 1954. Héctor Castro asserted that the United States would have to "initiate the movement against Guatemala." Any other nation doing so would only be regarded as the United States' "Trojan horse." See also memo of conversation with Don Roberto Heurtematte, ambassador of Panama, and Sowash, MID, 21 May 1954, State.

In the LC file, there is evidence that Guatemala was convinced that the United States would not achieve the necessary two-thirds vote required to call the consultative conference. See esp. Memorandum 20–21 May 1954, Minister of Foreign Relations, regarding opinion in Mexico; cables to the ambassador in La Paz, Bolivia, 20 May; memo to Zalada Martínez to the ambassador in La Habana, 21 May; cables re the "interventionist effort," Nos. 1892 and 91, Foreign Relations, Box 1, LC. Two declassified National Security Council reports indicate that the United States was prepared to mobilize overt military activities in "the event of Guatemalan aggression in Latin America." Encoded and out of context (without related CIA and NSC documents), one may conclude that had Guatemala resisted with any success, or for any length of time, the NSC had decided to use international "force" of another dimension to topple Arbenz. See, e.g., recommendation No. 3, NSC, 5419/1, 28 May 1954; also NSC 5419, 24 May 1954, DDE Library, declassified MR 78-112 No. 1, No. 2, 15 Apr. 1980. See also Memo of conversation, "Proposed Consultative Meeting," Holland with Víctor Andrade, ambassador of Bolivia, 3 June 1954, State.

16. Unsigned and undated, "Soviet Communism in Guatemala" is filed with conversations with Latin American ambassadors, May 1954, State.

17. Memo of conversation, Holland and João Carlos Muniz, to Dulles and Robert Murphy, 15 May 1954. See also Ambassador José A. Mora, who told Holland that it was "an election year" in Uruguay, 30 May 1954, and a "number of minority groups" would "seize" an OAS meeting to argue that the United States pursued a "policy of imperialism and of control over the destinies of other American countries." Similarly, Mexico's Foreign Minister Padilla Nervo was "strongly opposed to armed intervention." Memo of conversation, U. S. Ambassador to Mexico Francis White and Holland, 1 June 1954, State.

18. Hill to Henry Holland, 7 June 1954, State.

19. See minutes of the meetings of the Guatemalan Group, 2, 4, 7 June 1954, and "Assignment List for Guatemalan Group," 8 June 1954, State. Among others, the "Guatemalan Group" included Holland, Pearson, Leddy, Fisher, Hill, Burrows, Dreier, Woodward, Donnelly, Wieland, Frank Holcomb, and Dr. Eisenhower.

20. See telegrams, Peurifoy to Secretary of State, 2 June, 12:04 A.M., 5:58 P.M., 10:18 P.M. See minutes of Guatemalan Group, 4 June 1954, p. 4.

21. Leddy to Peurifoy, 5 June 1954, State.

22. Peurifoy to Secretary of State, 3 June 1954, State.

23. Peurifoy to Secretary of State, 8 June 1954; William Krieg to Department of State, 15 June 1954, "Attempt to Link U.S. with Plot Against Government," State.

24. Dulles to AmEmbassies, Tegucigalpa, San Salvador, Managua, San José, Panama, 9 June 1954.

25. D. D. Eisenhower, *Mandate for Change*, p. 425.

26. Arbenz quoted from "El Gobierno de Guatemala Declara," a broadside taken from "The Presidency Folder," Box 4, n.d. June 1954, LC. See also Peurifoy to Dulles, 1 June 1954, indicating that the Army's morale was enhanced by the *Alfhem* shipment; ibid., 9 June, that the Army had apparently agreed to arm civilians, State. For an example of truncated negotiations, see the correspondence with an Italian supply firm in Genoa that had offered Guatemala two DC-6 aircraft, three DC-4s, fourteen hundred submachine guns, ninety-two thousand Swedish carbine rifles, and other matériel, 28 May 1954, Box 4, LC.

27. Doc. No. 89, 25 May 1954, Box 72, LC; José Luis Morales to Víctor Cordillo T., and Memorandum Copy from Arbenz, Box 1 "Foreign Affairs," and Box 2, "From U.S." folders; Guatemala's ambassador in Honduras to Guillermo Toriello, 9 June, Box 1, "Foreign Affairs" folder, LC. See also Francisco Paredes Moreira to Raúl Osegueda, 9 Oct. 1953, 7 Jan. 1954; and Paredes to Toriello, 29 Jan. 1954, Box 72, LC.

28. Ministry of Foreign Relations to Guatemala's embassies in Latin America, n.d., June 1954, Box 1, LC.

29. Minutes, meeting of Guatemalan Group, 4 June 1954, p. 3, State.

30. *Llamiento de la CGTG y de la CNCG*, June 1954, Box 5, "Rallying to Defense of Regime" folder, LC. See also *Boletín del Comité de Lucha Contra la Intervención Extranjera del STIGGS*, Box 5, "Exploitation of Intervention Issue" folder, LC; and the folder of three-by-five cards from all areas of Guatemala and from all levels of society, signed by individuals who pledged their support and requested instructions to defend the country; also the urgent bulletins from "Amigos de Guatemala" from the countryside, esp. those of 2, 8, 18, 19 June 1954, Box 5, "Defense of Regime/Top Priority" folder, LC.

31. Consejo Superior de la Defensa Nacional, 19 May 1954, Box 4, LC. See also Francisco Gonzales to CNCG, 27 June 1954, Box 1—a plan to bolster local militias in cooperation with the CNCG, LC.

32. Hagerty's diary, 14 June 1954; see the summary of actions taken by Arbenz: Invasion, 14 Junio—Sumario de Expedientes, Box 1, LC.

33. Agenda for staff meeting on "Press Conference Day," 16 June 1954, Hagerty's diary.

34. Ibid.; On 15 June, Hagerty noted in his diary: Holland feared that Allen Dulles' statement would complicate the situation at the proposed Foreign Ministers meeting. The State Department, therefore, recommended that Eisenhower say nothing specific and refer simply to the threat to the Americas caused by Guatemala's arms shipment, "a threat which was being carefully studied." See also Hagerty, 18 June; and Peurifoy to Dulles, 18 June 1954: "Uprisings have started in Quezaltenango and Zacapa. Unconfirmed reports that Barrios also under attack. Looks like this is it," State.

35. Robert Murphy to AmEmbassies, 19 June 1954, re joint USIA-State Department circular; Streibert to all diplomatic missions, 19 June 1954, State.

36. Dulles to all American diplomatic posts, except Guatemala, 22 June 1954, State. On 23 June, a public-opinion survey of eleven nations for 18–22 June 1954 was circulated. According to the State Department, there were anti-U.S. demonstrations throughout Latin America. From left to right, the Latin American press headlined "misleading" accounts of "pro-Guatemalan Communist demonstrations" and called them "peaceful and spontaneous." "Nine out of ten Chileans" held the United States "responsible." Vivid liberal-conservative differences were manifested over this issue in Brazil, Colombia, Honduras, Panama, El Salvador, Ecuador, Haiti, Venezuela. In Cuba, "hundreds of young men" applied at the Guatemalan embassy in Havana "to enlist in the Guatemalan army." In Mexico, there was "strong, but by no means unanimous, support for the Guatemalan Government in

right-wing circles." In Uruguay, the Chamber of Deputies "passed a Socialist-sponsored resolution of solidarity with Guatemala." Finally, the State Department noted, the press in the Dominican Republic "is strictly government-controlled and hence echoes official opinion which on this issue was favorable to the U.S. position." The press in Peru and Nicaragua also favored the U.S. position. "Unofficial Reactions in Latin America . . . ," 23 June 1954, State. This survey did not correspond with Eisenhower's contention that "the rest of Latin America was not in the least displeased." D. D. Eisenhower, *Mandate for Change*, p. 426.

The anti-Communist labor organization, affiliated with the AF of L, ORIT, headed by Serafino Romualdi, was also "threatened by resentment among Latin American liberals" who opposed U.S. intervention. ORIT members feared that Castillo Armas would be "another Trujillo or Somoza with no comprehension of, or sympathy for, people's desire for social reform." ORIT, therefore, declined to take an immediate public position. White to Dulles, 26 June 1954; Dulles to AmEmbassy, Mexico, 26 June, State.

37. Guillermo Toriello's petition to the UN sent to the Secretary of State, 19 June 1954, including message from the Foreign Minister to the President of the Security Council of the United Nations, 20 June 1954; Peurifoy to Dulles, 18, 19 June, State.

38. Ambassador Bohlen to Secretary of State, 20, 22 June 1954, State. For the Churchill-Eden visit to Washington, see Hagerty's diary, 24, 25, 26, 28 June 1954; Henry Cabot Lodge to Secretary of State, 24 June, 11:46 A.M., 7:47 P.M., State; see also Minutes of the Guatemalan Group, 23 June 1954; and Dulles to all diplomatic posts, 22 June 1954, State.

39. "The Situation in Guatemala as of 20 June 1954," a CIA summary for the President, Allen Dulles, Whitman, Administration File, NLE 76–51 No. 258, declassified with "portions exempted" (September 30, 1976). For Guatemalan resistance, see June 1954, Boxes 71 and 72, LC.

40. Ambassador McDermott to Dulles, 25 June 1954; Ambassador Whelan to Dulles, 23 June 1954, State.

41. Peurifoy to Dulles, 23 June 1954, State.

42. D. D. Eisenhower, *Mandate for Change*, pp. 425–26.

43. For the psychological nature of the operation, see the CIA's 20 June summary; E. Howard Hunt, op. cit., p. 100; Richard Bissell's interview, DDE Oral History Project, Columbia University.

44. Toriello to Secretary of State, 25 June 1954; Toriello quoted in Peurifoy to Dulles, 27 June 1954, State.

45. Peurifoy, report of meeting with Díaz to Secretary of State, 28 June 1954; memo of telephone conversation, Holland to Dulles, Bedell Smith, Robert Murphy, 28 June, State.

46. Peurifoy quoted in Jonas, p. 72.

47. Memo of telephone conversation, Peurifoy to Holland, 29 June 1954. Dulles urged Peurifoy to keep a low profile during the conference between Monzon and Castillo Armas so as not to "be subject to serious misinterpretation," since the Americas were awash in demonstrations "against the U.S. for alleged complicity." Dulles warned Peurifoy: "Present anti-U.S. feeling serious . . . and further damage to U.S. position could only be justified on basis [of] sheer necessity." Dulles to Peurifoy, 29 June, State. For an account of the protests throughout Latin America, see Jonas, "Protest in Latin America," p. 73. Castillo Armas' entrance into Guatemala City described by Galich, op. cit., p. 33.

48. D. D. Eisenhower, *Mandate for Change*, pp. 426–27; Dulles quoted in ibid., and Hagerty's diary, 28, 30 June 1954. Hunt, op. cit., p. 101.

49. Dulles to AmEmbassies, London, New Delhi, Karachi, Rangoon, Managua, Tegucigalpa, 29 June 1954, State.

50. Dulles to Peurifoy, 12 July 1954; "Plan of Action in Event Arbenz Government Overthrown," Fisher to Woodward, 28 June; see also Andrew Wardlaw

to Department of State, 13 July 1954, regarding "financial aid" of "$5,000 per month" from United States labor organizations anticipated by Rubén Villatora's Free Workers Union, State.

51. Peurifoy to Secretary of State, 9, 19 July 1954; Dulles to AmEmbassy Guatemala, 2 July; see also Dulles to Peurifoy, 13, 17 July—on efforts to secure Grace and UFCO's accommodations. Grace, for example, was willing to nationalize "wharf Champerico" since the company "has not found this operation profitable." The State Department was, moreover, mindful of the political significance of land reform. It was well understood that some "genuine agrarian reform" was desirable and that the United States should offer to help draw up a plan to prove its "sympathy with genuine land reform." See Hill to Woodward, 27 June 1954; and Ohmans to Woodward, 29 June 1954, State. For Guatemala's new Petroleum Code, see Galich, op. cit., p. 34. According to Jonas, "several dozen US oil companies rushed in to take advantage of this giveaway measure. . . . But the oil boom died as suddenly as it began, when no large oil deposits were discovered." "Showcase for Counterrevolution," op. cit., p. 79.

52. McCann, op. cit., pp. 59–60. See also Jonas, op. cit., pp. 74–81; and the congressional hearings dominated by testimony from Castillo Armas and John Peurifoy, including photographs, with an emphasis on the number of "left" books in the Arbenz library either purchased or received as gifts and inscribed by notorious Communists; and including Mrs. Arbenz's bank accounts: *Communist Aggression in Latin America, Ninth Interim Report of Hearings, Subcommittee on Latin America, Select Committee on Communist Aggression*, HR, 83rd Cong., 2nd Sess., HR 346, 438, *Guatemala*, 27, 28, 29 September, 8, 14, 15 October 1954.

53. For Castillo Armas' literature, see "Ultimatum" and "Manifesto," Comité Cívico de Liberación, Julio de 1954, Box 4, Box 26, "Anti-Communist" files, LC.

54. For Castillo's activities, see Peurifoy to Dulles, 6, 7, 13 July and 3 Sept. 1954; the State Department's monthly report for July, Bowdler to Pearson, 4 Aug. 1954, on the disenfranchisement of Guatemala's voters. On Army's hostility to Castillo and U.S. fear of a prerevolutionary situation, see Krieg to Dulles, 28 Aug. 1954; Memo for Raymond G. Leddy, "Situation in Guatemala," 30 Aug.; Dulles to AmEmbassy Guatemala, 31 Aug.; Peurifoy to Dulles, 1, 2 Sept. 1954. For the wave of "horrible killings" of organized workers, campesinos, and supporters of Arbenz, see Alex A. Cohen's report to the Secretary of State, "Organizations and Individuals Who Publicly Identified Themselves Recently with Arbenz's Administration," 13 July 1954, and translation of the General Confederation of Costa Rican Workers, "Manifesto of Solidarity," State. See also Galich, op. cit., p. 34; and "Memo for Record: Situation in Guatemala," 24 Aug. 1954: "The political situation is tending to worsen because Col. Carlos Castillo Armas shows little political sense," State.

55. See Che Guevara's speech "On Revolutionary Medicine," 19 Aug. 1960, reprinted in John Gerassi, ed., *Venceremos! the Speeches and Writings of Ernesto Che Guevara* (Macmillan, 1968), pp. 112–19.

56. On the issue of asylum, see Dulles to AmEmbassies, 28, 29 June, 9, 17, 27 July 1954; Dulles to Peurifoy, 27 July 1954; Peurifoy to Dulles, 28 July 1954; William L. Krieg to Dulles, 10 Aug. 1954; Peurifoy to Dulles, 17 Aug.; Peurifoy to Holland, memo of telephone conversation, 27 Aug. 1954, State. I am grateful to William O. Walker III for his unpublished paper "Asylum."

57. Nixon quoted in Hagerty's diary, 11 Mar. 1955.

58. Major John S. D. Eisenhower, "Report to the President on Guatemala Trip, 29–30 July 1957, declassified with "portions exempted" (NLE 77-34II).

59. United States investment figures quoted from Jonas, op. cit., p. 81.

60. For contemporary texts regarding the rival revolutionary forces that emerged in 1960, see John Gerassi, "Guatemala": Arnoldo Cardona Fratti (César Montes?), "Dogma and Revolution," published originally in *Tricontinental*, No. 8 (Sept.–Oct. 1968); and Marco Antonio Yon Sosa, Turcios Lima, et al., "First

Declaration of Sierra de las Minas," 12 Dec. 1964, all reprinted in Gerassi, ed., *The Coming of the New International* (The World Publishing Co., 1971), pp. 467–99. See also Louisa Frank, "Resistance and Revolution: the Development of Armed Struggle in Guatemala," in Jonas, pp. 176–92; Andrea Brown, "The Vietnamization of Guatemala: U. S. Counterinsurgency Programs," ibid., pp. 193–207; Adolfo Gilly, "The Guerrilla Movement in Guatemala, Part I," *Monthly Review* (May 1965), and Part II, ibid., (June 1965); and John and Barbara Ehrenreich, "A Favorable View of the FAR," *Monthly Review* (February 1967).

For the United States' reaction to Castro's government in Cuba, see *Hearings, Subcommittee to Investigate Administration of the Internal Security Act . . . , Committee of the Judiciary, U. S. Senate,* 86th Cong., 1st Sess., to 92nd Cong., 1st Sess. (July 1959 to Oct. 1971), in twenty-five parts, *Communist Threat to the U. S. Through the Caribbean*. Guatemala's participation in the effort to overthrow Castro, long denied by the United States, was unexpectedly confirmed by Ydígoras Fuentes in his New Year's address, 1 Jan. 1962, when he announced "that in return the U.S. had agreed to lend its good offices to mediate Guatemala's ancient claim against Great Britain for the territory of Belize." On 9 Jan. 1962, the New York *Times* charged that President Ydígoras Fuentes had made a "fantastic and outrageous claim." "No American official with authority and in his right mind could have made such a promise." But Mario Rosenthal, a long-time supporter of Ydígoras and a vigorous anti-Communist, devotes a chapter of a book to "Guatemala, the U.S., Great Britain and Belize." He details the agreement made to train "armed Cuban contingents, of solid anti-Castro persuasion," and acknowledges the "secret camp" at Retalhuleu "which was not started until President Ydígoras Fuentes had Washington's solemn promise of a well-defined stand against British colonialism." He quotes Ydígoras: "Of course, such a big favor . . . [necessitated] a just price on the contribution. My government did not hesitate; it had already thought of it beforehand: to solicit good offices to convince Great Britain to give us back Belize. . . ." Rosenthal concludes his book, so full of animus against Arévalo and Arbenz, with a denunciation of subsequent United States policy and the conjecture "that the best way to be favored by the U.S. is to oppose her" might be a "cruel reality." Rosenthal's hope for the future lay in the promise of a real alliance for progress. Envisioned by Milton Eisenhower and repeated in December 1961 by Chester Bowles representing the Kennedy administration, Rosenthal dared to hope that the United States might "begin to export democracy." See Mario Rosenthal, *Guatemala: the Story of an Emergent Latin-American Democracy* (Twayne, 1962), pp. 288–307.

But Guatemala's future would over the next twenty years reflect instead the attitudes of such State Department spokesmen as Robert C. Hill. A career diplomat, ambassador to Mexico, Costa Rica, and El Salvador, and vice-president of W. R. Grace Co., Hill told the Senate that democracy could not be exported easily. It "should not be handed out to those who do not want it, or to the undeserving." Therefore, the United States frequently had no choice except between dictatorships of the Right and of the Left. This should not disturb the United States; each nation should be permitted free choice. "I mean, sir, who rules Guatemala and who rules Peru and who rules any country . . . is the business of the country itself and its people." To encourage democracy in many areas of Latin America would be "direct intervention." Hill, one of the earliest proponents of a blockade and direct activity against Castro's Cuba, concluded that the United States should abstain from such activity "unless Communism enters the picture." See *Hearings, Communist Threat to the U. S. Through the Caribbean,* Part 12, testimony of Robert C. Hill, 12 June 1961, pp. 817–18, 826.

61. For post-1954 events in Guatemala, see: Eduardo Galeano, *Guatemala: Occupied Country* (Monthly Review Press, 1970, transl. Cedric Belfrage); Marjorie and Thomas Melville, *Guatemala: the Politics of Land Ownership* (Free Press,

1971); Richard Adams, *Crucifixion by Power: Essays on Guatemalan Social Structure, 1944–1966* (University of Texas Press, 1970); Susanne Bodenheimer, "Inside a State of Siege," *Ramparts* (June 1971); Victor Perera, "Guatemala: Always La Violencia," New York *Times Magazine* (13 June 1971); Donald T. Fox, *Human Rights in Guatemala* (International Commission of Jurists, 777 United Nations Plaza, New York, NY 10017, 1979); Elberto Torres-Rivas, "Guatemala: Crisis and Political Violence," *NACLA Report on the Americas* (Jan.–Feb. 1980), pp. 16–27; Cidamo, "The Workers Movement in Guatemala," ibid., pp. 28–35; Alan Riding, "Violence Shakes Guatemala Again," New York *Times*, 22 June 1976; Cynthia Brown, "Guatemala—the Next Nicaragua," *The Nation* (25 Aug. 1979); Stephen Kinzer, "Central American Dominoes," ibid., (10 Nov. 1979); "30 Said to Die in Guatemala Protest," New York *Times*, 1 Feb. 1980; Alan Riding, "Revolutionary Wars Put U.S. in the Middle," New York *Times*, 10 Feb. 1980; and Alan Riding, "Guatemala: State of Siege," New York *Times Magazine*, 24 Aug. 1980, which concludes on a note of "irony," by quoting an unnamed U.S. official who "recently conceded: 'What we'd give to have an Arbenz now.'"

See also the publications of the Committee of Solidarity with the People of Guatemala, P. O. Box 13006, Washington, DC 20009; Guatemala News and Information Bureau, GNIB, P. O. Box 4126, Berkeley, CA, 94704; and Noam Chomsky and Edward S. Herman, *The Washington Connection and Third World Fascism* (South End Press, 1979), which places Guatemala's political-economic environment in a global context.

CHAPTER VIII NOTES

1. For the historical roots of U.S. business expansionism, see, for example, William Appleman Williams, *The Contours of American History* (Quadrangle, 1966); *The Roots of the Modern American Empire* (Random House, 1969); and *Empire as a Way of Life* (Oxford University Press, 1980); Gerald E. Markowitz, "The Progressives in American Foreign Policy, 1898–1917," Ph.D. dissertation, University of Wisconsin, 1971; Joan Hoff Wilson, *American Business and Foreign Policy, 1920–33* (Beacon Press, 1971); Lloyd C. Gardner, *Architects of Illusion: Men and Ideas in American Foreign Policy, 1941–1949* (Quadrangle, 1970); Mira Wilkins, *The Emergence of Multinational Enterprise: American Business Abroad from the Colonial Era to 1914* (Harvard University Press, 1970); and *The Maturing of Multinational Enterprise: American Business Abroad from 1914 to 1970* (Harvard, 1974). For an important example of business diplomacy during World War II, see John A. De Novo, "The [William S.] Culbertson Economic Mission and Anglo-American Tensions in the Middle East, 1944–45," *Journal of American History* (Mar. 1973), pp. 913–36. See also Gabriel Kolko, "American Business and Germany, 1930–1941," *Western Political Quarterly* (Dec. 1962); Deborah Wing Ray, "Takordi Route: Roosevelt's Pre-War Venture Beyond the Western Hemisphere," *Journal of American History* (Sept. 1975), pp. 340–58. The essays in David Horowitz, ed., *Corporations and the Cold War,* are particularly relevant (Monthly Review Press, 1970).

2. "The International Chamber of Commerce is the business man's international body. It is his spokesman on world affairs." Based in Paris, established in 1919, the ICC had fifty-four members in 1949. See Transcript and Minutes of the Reorganization Committee Meetings, U. S. Associates of the ICC, 7, 17, 29 Jan. 1949. Present were H. J. Heinz II, chairman; Philip Cortney (president, Coty); Stanley C. Allyn (National Cash Register); Gardner Cowles (president, *Look* magazine); Alexander Fraser (president, Shell Union Oil); Rudolf S. Hecht (Mississippi Shipping); Sigurd S. Larmon (president, Young & Rubicam); C. D.

Jackson (vice-president, Time, Inc.); Philip D. Reed (General Electric); Wilbert Ward; Lowell P. Weicker (president, E. R. Squibb & Sons); and Alvin E. Dodd and Kay Smallzried, staff. C. D. Jackson Papers, Box 89.

3. Harry S Truman to Nelson Rockefeller, 24 Nov. 1950, Box 75.

4. Rockefeller quoted in John Gerassi, *The Real Rockefeller: the Story of the Rise, Decline and Resurgence of the Presidential Aspirations of Nelson Rockefeller* (Atheneum, 1964), pp. 127–30. For analyses of the postwar business-government alliance, see the articles in David Horowitz, *Corporations and the Cold War*, esp.: David Eakins, "Business Planners and America's Postwar Expansion"; Lloyd C. Gardner, "The New Deal, New Frontiers, and the Cold War: a Re-examination of American Expansion, 1933–1945"; William A. Williams, "The Large Corporation and American Foreign Policy"; and G. William Domhoff, "Who Made American Foreign Policy, 1945–1963?" See also Domhoff's *The Higher Circles* (Vintage Books, 1970).

5. See the literature of the U.S.-ICC, Committee on Business Participation in Foreign Economic Development. Quotations from "Intelligent International Investment," 6 Apr. 1949, C. D. Jackson Papers, Box 89. Members of the Committee on Business Participation included: Warren Lee Pierson (Trans World Airlines), H. W. Balgooyen (American & Foreign Power Co.), Walter J. Braunschweiger (Bank of America), Joseph O. Hanson (Swift International), George Nebolsine (Cahill, Gordon, Zachry, Reindel), Milo Perkins (director, Board of Economic Warfare during World War II, president, Federal Surplus Commodities Corporation), Edgar W. Smith (General Motors Overseas Operations), William R. Strelow (Guaranty Trust), Francis Adams Truslow (New York Curb Exchange), Leo D. Welch (Standard Oil of New Jersey), August Maffry (Irving Trust). The literature of the International Hudson Corporation is also pertinent. Organized as a business corporation "to facilitate transactions in the field of international commerce and economics" and to provide advice and assistance to American and foreign business enterprises and governments, International Hudson coordinated connections between markets, investors, suppliers, and governments, among other services. It relied for its services on "a panel of men of experience in international affairs": James F. Brownlee (director, American Express,); Ross Cissell (vice-president, International Hudson); William H. Davis (Davis, Hoxie & Faithfull, formerly chairman National War Labor Board); Herbert Feis (formerly adviser International Economic Affairs to Department of State); Thomas K. Finletter (on leave of absence, ECA, Coudert Brothers); Leon Henderson (president, International Hudson, chief economist, Research Institute of America); C. D. Jackson; Isador Lubin (president, Confidential Reports, Inc.,); Donald M. Nelson (formerly president, Society of Independent Motion Picture Producers); Philip Reed; Harry J. Rudick (vice-president, International Hudson; Lord, Day & Lord); Beardsley Ruml (chairman, Board of Directors, R. H. Macy); H. Chr. Sonne (president, Amsinck, Sonne & Co., chairman, National Planning Association); Constantine De Stackelberg (vice-president, International Hudson); Adlai E. Stevenson (Sidney, Austin, Burgess & Harper); Wayne Chatfield Taylor (on leave, ECA, chairman of the Board of Directors, International Hudson).

Initially organized to complement the International Bank for Reconstruction and Development (World Bank), the International Monetary Fund, and other public agencies, International Hudson was to facilitate private economic transactions with "strategic bearing on international relations." See, particularly, Minutes, 12–13 Feb. 1949, Meeting on "Practical Factors in the Economic Development of Underdeveloped Countries." International Hudson Papers are in C. D. Jackson Papers, Box 51.

6. Weicker's statement was used as part of U.S.-ICC's brochure to attract new members, Philip Reed to Norman Taber, 9 Jan. 1950, Box 89.

7. "Intelligent International Investment," fn. 5, p. 10. On 27 Jan. 1949, The

U.S.-ICC agreed on a "Statement of the Over-All Problem": "Business must be ready to step in in 1952 when the European Recovery Act, and other temporary measures, go out of the picture. Private business throughout the world has about three and a half years to inform itself. . . . It is either now that business seeks to give its best capacities to the building of an economically strong world—or it is never."

8. C. D. Jackson to the Export Managers Club of New York, "1947—Year of Decision," 1 Apr. 1947; see also Jackson to the St. Lawrence Advertising Club, 9 Jan. 1950; testimony before the House Ways and Means Committee, 28 Apr. 1947; and "Total Business Diplomacy," 3 Apr. 1950, Box 83.

9. Interview, confidential source; DDE to Swede Hazlett, 12 Sept. 1950, DDE Personal Papers, Box 51.

10. See Fred J. Cook's still timely book *The Warfare State* (Macmillan, Collier, 1962, 1964), pp. 18–21; 23–33. For examples of Eisenhower's fiscal moderation, see chart of military programs cut, and savings, Thomas Gates file, n.d., FY 1962, Whitman, Admin., Box 16. See also the Republican National Committee's impressive convention propaganda *Battle Line*, 25 Oct. 1960, which reported, for example, that, according to the Commerce Department, the 1939 American dollar has declined fifty-three cents between 1940 and 1960; under Roosevelt the decline was twenty-three cents; under Truman it was twenty-five cents; but under Eisenhower it declined only five cents, DDE Diary, Personal Papers, Box 34.

11. Hoffman to DDE, 31 Dec. 1952, Whitman, Admin., Box 21.

12. DDE to Charles Percy, 19 May 1954, Diary, Box 4. See Burton I. Kaufman, "The U. S. Response to the Soviet Economic Offensive of the 1950s," *Diplomatic History* (Spring, 1978), pp. 153–65; and Kaufman, "Mideast Multinational Oil, U. S. Foreign Policy and Antitrust: the 1950s," *Journal of American History* (Mar. 1977), pp. 937–59. For an update of the impact of this oil cartel, see Clyde H. Farnsworth, "Tax Loophole for Multinationals," New York *Times*, 21 Aug. 1977. The United Fruit Company case was quoted in Joseph Rand, Memorandum to Antitrust Task Force Members, CFEP 524, 17 Jan. 1956, a fifty-six-page report on *Effects of Existing Anti-trust Laws on US Foreign Activities*. The report concluded that relaxation of the Sherman Antitrust Act provides "entry for American business into otherwise inaccessible markets" and is "warranted as long as the present pattern of mass bargaining power continues abroad."

See also Joseph Rand to Clarence Randall, 29 July 1959, 10 May 1960, 6 Apr. 1960, 5 July 1960, Rand, Box 1, Personal Papers, Abilene. Eisenhower assigned Attorney General Brownell to study "whether operations of U.S. companies abroad are subject to anti-trust laws" and to keep the study "confidential," DDE Diary, 7 Aug. 1954, Box 4. For the effort to stimulate private capital investment abroad by relaxing antitrust regulations, see "Antitrust Limitations on U. S. Foreign Economic Activities," Henry Chalmers, Department of Commerce, to Edward A. Foote, Department of Justice, 24 June 1955, Rand, Box 12. For historical background, see "Advance Clearance of Business Agreements in International Trade," Cartel Memo 98, 18 Nov. 1944, Rand, Box 12. See also discussion of Webb-Pomerance Law, 17–20 May 1955, "to evaluate the effect of foreign cartels and combinations on . . . export trade of the U.S. . . . ," idem. See McCann, for the United Fruit Co. case, pp. 62–66, 79, 188–189. For the related tariff debates, see esp. DDE's Diary essay on the briar pipe case, 9 Feb. 1953, Personal Diary; and Hagerty's diary, 27 July 1954, regarding the Swiss watch tariff controversy.

13. Council of Economic Advisers, "The Administration Program for Economic Expansion," 17 May 1954, White House Central Files, 558; see also Milton Eisenhower to Gabriel Hauge, 2 Mar. 1954, with a special report "from the Advertising Fraternity on America's Economic Future," Oct. 1953, ibid.

14. The foreign trade missions were the responsibility of: John H. Davis, Assistant Secretary of Agriculture for Marketing and Foreign Agriculture; Fred J. Rossiter, Assistant Administrator, Foreign Service and Trade Programs, Agriculture; W. Arthur Minor, Foreign Management, Agriculture; L. N. Hoopes, Agriculture; Marshall M. Smith, Commerce; James C. Foster, International Resources, Bureau of Foreign Commerce; A. N. Overby, Treasury; George H. Willis, Office of International Finance, Treasury; Thorsten Kalijarvi, Economic Affairs, State; William Turnage, Economic Affairs, State; Dr. D. A. FitzGerald, Director for Operations, FOA; Clarence Francis, chairman, foreign trade missions. See Clarence Francis, Box 7, Abilene, esp. minutes of meeting, 10 Mar. 1954.

15. Eisenhower, address to the Congress on "The Foreign Economic Policy of the United States," 30 Mar. 1954, White House Central Files, Box 558. See Eisenhower's early efforts to facilitate this program: DDE to Cabinet, 12 July 1954, and to Rowland Hughes and Nelson Rockefeller, 30 July; and William Finan to Hauge, 30 July 1954, "Study of Organization for the Formation and Execution of Foreign Economic Policy," ibid.

16. DDE to C. D. Jackson, 14 Apr. 1954, Whitman, Admin., Box 19.

17. Jackson to John Foster Dulles, with draft memo of Plan, 9 Apr. 1954, C. D. Jackson Papers, Box 68; Jackson to DDE, 29 Apr. 1954, Whitman, Box 19.

18. "Five Key Reports to the Government: a Summary": (1) Report to the President on Foreign Economic Policies, by Gordon Gray and Edward S. Mason (131 pp., GPO, Nov. 1950); (2) A Report to the President by the International Development Advisory Board, The Rockefeller Report (120 pp., GPO, Mar. 1951); (3) *Resources for Freedom:* a Report to the President by the President's Materials Policy Commission, 5 Vols. (GPO, June 1952); (4) A Trade and Tariff Policy in the National Interest, a Report to the President by the Public Advisory Board for Mutual Security, the Bell Report (78 pp., GPO, 1953); (5) Report of the Commission of Foreign Economic Policy, The Randall Report (94 pp., GPO, Jan. 1954), in C. D. Jackson Papers, Box 68. Hauge to DDE, 3 May 1956, NLE 76–51, No. 368.

19. Dulles quoted in Walter La Feber, *America, Russia, and the Cold War, 1945–1966* (Wiley, 1967), p. 180. See the 284-page transcript, "Proceedings of the Off-the-Record Conference Held Under the Auspices of Time, Inc., 15–16 May 1954, at Princeton," C. D. Jackson Papers, Box 68; Interim Report, Max Millikan and W. W. Rostow, "Notes on Foreign Economic Policy," 21 May 1954, idem. The Princeton Conference attendees were Samuel Anderson, Commerce; George B. Baldwin, CENIS; Lloyd Berkner, president, Associated Universities Inc.; Richard Bissell, CIA; Robert Bowie, State; Arthur Burns, chairman, Council of Economic Advisers; Gen. Robert Cutler, White House special assistant for National Security Affairs; Allen W. Dulles; Arthur Flemming, director, Office of Defense Mobilization; Robert Garner, The International Bank; Gabriel Hauge; C. D. Jackson; John K. Jessup, Time, Inc.; Edward S. Mason, Harvard University; David J. McDonald, president, United Steel Workers of America; Thomas McKittrick, Chase National Bank; Max Millikan, president, CENIS; H. Chapman Rose, Treasury; Walt W. Rostow, CENIS; Harold E. Stassen, director, Foreign Operations Administration; Charles L. Stillman, Time, Inc.; Abbott Washburn, USIA; John MacKenzie, Atomic Energy Commission; and Jerome Wiesner, Harvard.

After the Geneva Conference, Nelson Rockefeller convened Quantico II, in November 1955, to discuss "The Psychological Aspects of U. S. Strategy" in the post-Geneva environment. Although the meeting was to deal with political warfare, economic considerations were emphasized. The meeting engendered papers and discussions that were, like the Princeton session, influential for decades to follow. See esp. Max Millikan, "Economic Policy as an Institute of Political and Psychological Policy"; Stefan Possony, "General Guidelines for an American Long Range Psychological Plan"; George A. Lincoln, "The Middle East and Africa—a Working Paper"; Paul M. A. Linebarger, "Policy and Opinion in South and Southeast Asia"; Stacy May, "Latin America—as a Demonstration Area of U. S. Foreign Policy in Action"; Ellis A. Johnson, "The National Costs and Policies Required to Maintain a Modern Weapons System"; Henry A. Kissinger, "Psychological and Pressure Aspects of Negotiations with the U.S.S.R."; Stefan Possony, "Investigation of NATO"; and Possony, "The Atoms for Peace Program." The other panelists were Frederick L. Anderson, C. D. Jackson; Philip E. Mosely, director of studies, Council on Foreign Relations; George Pettee, Operations Research Office, The Johns Hopkins University; William Webster, New England Electric System. The Quantico II Papers are in C. D. Jackson Papers, Box 73.

C. D. Jackson to Nelson Rockefeller, 10 Nov. 1955, Box 56; Jackson to Rockefeller, 29 July 1955, including a legislative and committee history of foreign economic policy, 1945–55, ibid; and the Rockefeller brothers' "America at Mid-Century" series, notably Panel Report III, *Foreign Economic Policy for the Twentieth Century*, 15 June 1958, White House Central Files, Box 561. The Rockefeller Brothers Fund reports were subsequently published, see esp. *Prospect for America* (Doubleday, 1958).

20. Jackson, "Proposal for a New U. S. Foreign Economic Policy," 20 July 1954, C. D. Jackson Papers, Box 26.

21. Gen. Paul T. Carroll to DDE, n.d. [August 1954], Whitman, Administration, NLE 76-51 No. 413; Carroll to DDE, 27 Aug. 1954, ibid., No. 412. For the Food for Peace Program, the use of surplus agriculture as an economic-warfare measure, see the papers of Ezra Taft Benson and the voluminous files of PL-480. See also C. D. Jackson Papers, 2, 22 July 1953, Box 56.

22. Carroll to DDE, idem.; and Jackson to DDE, 16 Aug. 1954, Whitman, Admin., Box 24; Jackson to Herbert Hoover, Jr., 4 Nov. 1954, C. D. Jackson Papers, Box 56.

23. Eisenhower quoted in Hagerty's diary, 13 Dec. 1954; see also Hagerty's diary, 2 Dec. 1954; and Millikan Memo to Jackson, 12 Nov. 1954, C. D. Jackson Papers, Box 64.

24. Hauge to Humphrey, 25 Mar. 1953, Gabriel Hauge, Box 1, Abilene.

25. Milton Eisenhower, telephone call, 28 Oct. 1954, Whitman Diary, Box 3; DDE to Milton Eisenhower, 25 Oct. 1954, Whitman, Name, Box 12; DDE to Milton Eisenhower, 23 Nov., 1 Dec. 1954, ibid.

26. Hagerty's diary, 25 Dec. 1954.

27. See Whitman Diary, 8 June 1955, Box 5. Gabriel Hauge also opposed a $1.00 minimum wage, see Hauge, memo, 22 June 1955, Whitman Diary, Box 19.

28. Dulles quoted in Hagerty's diary, 13, 14 Dec. 1954.

29. Clarence B. Randall, "Our Foreign Economic Policy," stenographic transcript of address to the 59th Annual Congress of American Industry, 3 Dec. 1954, White House Central File, Box 558.

30. John H. Stambaugh to Gabriel Hauge, "Foreign Economic Battle Plan," 6 Jan. 1955, White House Central File, 558; Hauge, "The Economics of Eisenhower Conservatism," address before The Commonwealth Club of California, 14 Oct. 1955, White House Central File, 559; C. D. Jackson to Bernard Baines, 15 Mar. 1956, C. D. Jackson Papers, Box 33.

31. Jackson to Klaus Dohrn, 12 Jan. 1955, Box 39.

32. Shepley to Jackson, telephone call, log, 7 June 1956, Box 56.

33. Joseph Rand to Clarence Randall, 8 Jan. 1958, Rand, Box 1.

34. Hoffman to DDE, 17 Dec. 1956, Whitman, Admin., Box 21; Hauge to DDE, 8 Aug. 1956, with clipping, Box 19.

35. Humphrey to DDE, 15 Apr. 1955, Box 20.

36. Jackson to Humphrey, 6 Dec. 1955, C. D. Jackson Papers, Box 56.

37. Humphrey to DDE, 7 Sept. 1956, Whitman, Admin., Box 23. See also

Humphrey to DDE, 28 June 1955, with an article by Sylvia Porter, "one of the smartest commentators on our financial and economic affairs," according to Humphrey. Porter's article "We Have Made It," New York *Post*, 24 June 1955, was written on the tenth anniversary of the UN; it celebrated the "giant and unprecedented" contribution to "real peace": The George Humphrey-D. D. Eisenhower defense cuts. "War is no longer bolstering any boom for us. . . . Our annual rate of spending for defense" was $11–13 billion below the Korean peak. Yet, wrote Porter, U.S. business "was expanding on its own . . . to fill the demands of us as civilians." America's nonmilitary economic strength would enable the country to remain "a bulwark of the free world." Humphrey wanted Eisenhower to take heed. See also Humphrey to DDE, 6 Dec. 1956, Whitman, Admin., Box 23: "The most effective thing we can do today is protect the soundness of the dollar," stabilize the cost of living, and reduce government expenditures.

38. Henry Cabot Lodge, Note to Correspondents, Press Release No. 2401, 30 Apr. 1956, Whitman, Admin., Box 21. See John Foster Dulles to DDE, 10 Jan. 1957, ibid. Dulles told Eisenhower that Humphrey was, "of course, ardently opposed to this type of scheme. He feels that our international exchange position is such that we must seek ways of reducing our contributions abroad with their consequent drain of the dollar." Paul Hoffman to George Humphrey, 22 Mar. 1957, with reprint of Hoffman's article "Blueprint for Foreign Aid," New York *Times Magazine*, 17 Feb. 1957, C. D. Jackson Papers, Box 49.

39. Lodge, "Economic Aid for Underdeveloped Countries," Memo for DDE, 15 Mar. 1956, NLE 76-52, No. 459; ibid., 5 Mar., 3 Mar. 1956, No. 464, No. 463; Lodge, Memo, "Proposed U. S. Reaction to New Soviet Tactics to Penetrate Africa by Technical, Economic and Political Means," 5 Mar. 1956, NLE 76-52, No. 465, Paul Hoffman to DDE, 17 Dec. 1956, Whitman, Admin., Box 21. See also Herbert Hoover, Jr., to DDE, 15 Mar., NLE 76-51, No. 342, A State Department Assessment of Henry Cabot Lodge's Views and Lodge's Statement to the Fairless Committee in support of multilateral aid for mutual security, including SUNFED, 30 Nov. 1956, MR 76-51, No. 402. Paul Hoffman, a statement before the House Foreign Affairs Committee, 9 Oct. 1956, in C. D. Jackson Papers, Box 49. See Memo of Conference with President to Promote the Foreign Aid Program, with Adm. Radford, Gen. Goodpaster, 6 June 1956, DDE Diaries, Box 9; and Legislative Leadership Meeting on Foreign Economic Policy, 6 Mar. 1956, Supplementary Notes.

40. Humphrey to Paul Hoffman, 26 Mar. 1957; and Humphrey to DDE, Whitman, Admin., Box 23.

41. See "Staff Paper on Tax Amortization," DMB Meeting No. 76, 13 July 1955, Rand, Box 9; Rand to Hauge, Tax Amortization of Foreign Facilities, 13 July 1956, ibid. The tax amortization section (168) of the Internal Revenue Code authorized "a five year depreciation deduction against income taxes for facilities certified as necessary" to the national defense. See Rand to Hauge, ibid., a list of the companies granted tax write-offs at an estimated cost of $350 million. The companies were primarily iron ore and bauxite mining facilities in Mexico, Venezuela, Canada, the Dominican Republic, the British West Indies, and Jamaica.

See "Summary of Progress on 14 Point Tax Proposal," n.d., 1957, Rand Box 9, Abilene: "Despite high level urging . . . that the 'Government should move promptly to increase the incentives for private investment abroad,' and specific appeals for tax incentives by the Vice President, Secretary [of Commerce Sinclair] Weeks, Under Secretary Dillon, the Business Advisory Council, and others important in Government and industry, the Treasury position that we could not afford the tax revenue losses has continued to prevail."

42. Humphrey to DDE, 7 May 1956, Whitman, Admin., Box 23.

43. The following charts were part of the "Summary of Progress on 14 Point Tax Proposal":

DIRECT U. S. PRIVATE FOREIGN INVESTMENTS

	1950	1957	Increase	Petroleum as a Percentage of Total	
	(Millions of Dollars)		(%)	1950	1957
Africa[a]	107	319	198	48	42
Un. of S. Africa	140	305			
Middle East[b]	731	1,284	76	95	92
Far East[c]	320	716	124	38	43
Latin America	4,445	8,308	87	28	35

[a] Excludes Union of South Africa and estimated value of ships registered in Liberia.
[b] Includes Egypt and Afghanistan; excludes Greece and Turkey
[c] Excludes Australia, New Zealand, and Japan.

U. S. PRIVATE DIRECT FOREIGN INVESTMENTS*
(Millions of dollars and approximate percentage of increase over previous period)

	1950	1953	% Increase	1955	% Increase	1957	% Increase
World Total	11,788	16,286	(38)	19,313	(18)	25,252	(31)
Latin America	4,735	6,034	(27)	6,608	(10)	8,805	(31)
Australia	201	326	(63)	498	(53)	601	(21)
New Zealand	25	34		42		51	
India	38	68	(79)	95	(40)	110	(16)
Indonesia	58	88	(52)	86	–	150	(75)
Philippines	149	188	(26)	229	(22)	307	(34)
Japan	19	92	(380)	128	(39)	181	(41)
Liberia	82	186	(113)	277	(49)	380	(41)
Union of S. Africa	140	212	(51)	259	(22)	305	(18)

* Based on statistics contained in the "Survey of Current Business" of September 1958, U. S. Department of Commerce.

See Charles Silberman and Lawrence Mayer, "The Migration of U. S. Capital," *Fortune*, Jan. 1958, pp. 125–28. By 1958, the net value of all U.S. investment abroad was an estimated $37.5 billion, double what it was in 1950. "The value of private investment abroad is actually growing several times faster than the value of U.S. domestic investment."

See also "Administration's Views on Legislation to Promote U. S. Private Investment Abroad," statements by Undersecretary of State Douglas Dillon and Assistant to the Secretary of the Treasury David Lindsay, *Department of State*

Bulletin, 27 July 1959, pp. 128–35, testimony on behalf of HR 5, Foreign Investment Incentive Tax Act of 1959, introduced by Hale Boggs.

44. C. D. Jackson, "Report on Meeting Organized by Clarence Randall for me to present WEP," 6 Feb. 1957; to Henry Luce, 7 Feb. 1957, C. D. Jackson Papers, Box 57.

45. DDE to George Humphrey, 27 Mar. 1958, Whitman, Admin., Box 23; see Humphrey to DDE, 26 Mar., ibid.; and DDE to Paul Hoffman, 8 Mar. 1957, for DDE's analysis of Humphrey's position and his own theoretical opposition to "the kind of government spending in which we are now indulging," DDE Diary, Box 13; Paul Hoffman to DDE, 22 Mar. 1957, Whitman, Box 21. See also Humphrey to DDE, 16 Jan. 1957, including article "The Way to Cut Defence," *The Economist,* 15 Jan. 1957, Whitman, Admin., Box 23.

46. DDE to Percival Brundage, 30 Aug. 1957, Whitman, Admin., Box 9.

47. See "Humphrey Expected to Quit Soon . . . ," New York *Herald Tribune,* 27 Apr. 1957; Sylvia Porter, "Humphrey's Farewell," New York *Post,* 1 May 1957. See also, D. D. Eisenhower, *Waging Peace, 1956–1961* (Doubleday, 1965), pp. 127–47, "A Family of Controversy." By implication, Eisenhower designated the beginning of the process of Humphrey's resignation with Humphrey's comment at a news conference, 15 Jan. 1957: "I would deplore the day" that expenditures could not be reduced. "If we don't, over a long period of time, I will predict that you will have a depression that will curl your hair."
See Humphrey to DDE, 21 Nov. 1957; and DDE to Humphrey, 23 Nov. 1957, Whitman, Admin., Box 23, for further discussion on Humphrey's continued demand for budget cuts.

48. C. D. Jackson to Herbert Agar, 11 Feb. 1958, C. D. Jackson Papers, Box 57. John Foster Dulles to DDE, 13 Sept. 1958, C. D. Jackson, Box 41. The Colombo Plan, for the countries "of the arc of Asia," where three quarters of a billion people lived and earned an average estimated income of fifty dollars a year per capita, was a pilot project for regional development. Colombo members included Australia, Burma, Cambodia, Canada, Ceylon, India, Indonesia, Japan, Laos, Malaya, Nepal, New Zealand, Pakistan, Philippines, Singapore, Thailand, U.K. with Borneo and Sarawak, U.S.A., and Vietnam. See Clarence Francis to Members of the ICASD, 1, 7 Sept. 1955, on the Colombo Plan, Clarence Francis, Box 9, Abilene.

49. Adlai Stevenson, address to the National Conference of Organizations on International Trade Policy, 27 Mar. 1958, in Rand, Box 10, Abilene.

50. Colonel Kintner in Slater to Dodge, 4 Feb. 1959, Joseph Dodge, Box 1; see Allen Dulles, address to The Edison Electric Institute, "The Challenge of Soviet Power," 8 Apr. 1959, Box 5.

51. Dulles, idem; and "Sino-Soviet Economic Offensive and Its Effect on U. S. Foreign Policy," Task Group 4, 24 Mar. 1959, Box 3. See esp. Tab A, Bibliography; see also David Whitnack, Division of Functional Intelligence, to Carl Robert Slover, President's Committee to Study U. S. Military Assistance, 5 Feb. 1959, Tab F, ibid. "Grant Aid Extended by the Sino-Soviet Bloc to Free World Less Developed Countries," an estimated total of $2.4 billion in economic and military aid was expended by the Sino-Soviet Bloc between 1954 and 1958. See also Biweekly Report: Sino-Soviet Bloc Economic Activities in Underdeveloped Areas, No. 2, 5 Mar. 1956, declassified with portions deleted, NLE 76-51, No. 197; Joseph Dodge to DDE, Report to the President on External Economic Activities by the Soviet Bloc, 28 Feb., 13, 17 Mar. 1956, ibid., Nos. 198, 195, 194; and China's offer to supply India with fifty thousand tons of steel, Paul Cullen to Gen. Goodpaster, 9 Mar. 1956, ibid., No. 196. Office of Intelligence Research and Analysis, Department of State, Intelligence Report No. 7681, 142-page report with tables, "The Sino-Soviet Economic Offensive in the Less Developed Countries of the Free World," 12 Mar. 1958, Rand, Box 8.

52. C. D. Jackson to DDE, 6 Mar. 1958, C. D. Jackson Papers, Box 57.

53. The Fairless Committee, the President's Citizen Advisers on the Mutual Security Program, was commissioned on 27 Sept. 1956. Chaired by Benjamin Fairless, the committee initiated a series of panel discussions between private citizens and government officials, and consulted many specialists. See the Committee's Report to the President, 1 Mar. 1957, Whitman, Administration, Box 29. Members of the committee included Colgate Darden, Richard Deupree, John L. Lewis, Whitelaw Reid, Walter Bedell Smith, and Jesse W. Tapp.

54. The Draper Committee, the President's Committee to Study the U. S. Military Assistance Program, compiled voluminous analyses and reports. Quotations from pp. 15–16, Paul Nitze, "The Purposes of U. S. Military and Economic Assistance," in Joseph Dodge, Box 1. Chaired by William H. Draper, the committee comprised nine retired generals and three former members of the Department of Defense.

See Douglas Dillon to William Draper, 20 Feb. 1959, IDA Log No. D-S 597/25, Dodge, Box 3, with enclosures, "Objectives of Long-Term U. S. Foreign Economic Assistance, Economic Growth of the Free World," talking paper by General W. B. Smith. For the organization of IDA, see Edward Galbraith to Randall, 30 Sept. 1960, Rand, Box 2.

See also the correspondence and enclosures between Joseph Slater and Joseph Dodge, 27 Dec. 1958, 22 Jan. 1959, Dodge, Boxes 1, 2.

See also National Advisory Council on International Monetary and Financial Problems, 30 Nov. 1959, Don Paarlberg, Box 7, particularly "Financing Foreign Trade—a Comparison of Methods; and Committee for International Economic Growth, Fact Sheet No. 6 [n.d. December 1958], "New Proposals for Economic Development of the Free World," with a focus on Asia, the Middle East, Africa, and Latin America, Dodge, Box 2.

55. OCB, Special Report on Military Training in the U.S. of Foreign Nationals from Selected Countries, declassified with portions deleted, including all of pp. 23–30; also, names of countries deleted; 18 Mar. 1959, Gordon Gray and Karl Harr, NSC, EO 116525 (B) (3); see also DOD, MAP Training, Follow-Up Activities, to OCB discussion, 12 Dec. 1958, Gordon Gray, NSC. See also Gen. James A. Van Fleet's "Observations During Trip to Korea, Japan, Formosa—May, June 1956," an angry demand for a thorough reevaluation of the entire program: "In short, most of what we are doing overseas is WRONG." Van Fleet particularly deplored the waste, the "spectacular" fancy-drill teams, rest-and-recreation trips to Japan, private cars, a variety of expenditures that "hurt morale and [would] eventually lead to hate," in C. D. Jackson Papers, Box 89.

56. Green, Fulbright, et al. to DDE, 25 Aug. 1958, Dodge, Box 2.

57. Christian Herter to William Draper, 17 Feb. 1959, Dodge, Box 3, including an assessment of "Regional Aspects of the MAP" and the "Militaristic Image." The United States' contribution to NATO represented 35 percent of the MAP; 23 percent went to the Near East, "where two-thirds of the world's proven oil reserves are located, and where we have other vital foreign policy interests"; 27 percent went to the Far East to protect that area against "Chinese ambitions." There the United States created defense forces in the "new" countries of Laos, Cambodia, and Vietnam; and underwrote large military programs in Korea and Taiwan. Thailand and Burma also received military aid. Latin America received less than 2 percent and Africa less than 1 percent.

58. Robert Amory to William Draper, 30 Jan. 1959, Dodge, Box 3, CIA Report, "Certain Problems Created by the U. S. Military Assistance Program." See also Evaluation of the "Military Assistance Program for the President's Committee . . ." [n.d., 1959], declassified, Dodge, Box 4; an evaluation of achievement to date and anticipated activities to 1963. By 1958 grant-military assistance was made to two hundred divisions in thirty-four countries, a 50 percent increase in the number of nations involved over 1950. Eleven Latin American nations were

added. Between 1950 and 1958, $11.751 billion in military assistance matériel was delivered. Military Assistance Advisory Groups (MAAGs) trained and reorganized the Greek Army; rebuilt the "shattered South Korean army," developing eighteen active army divisions and a marine division; revitalized the Taiwanese forces; and strengthened the Turkish Army. The report concluded that the entire program was thrifty, since in FY 1959 the cost of a U.S. soldier was estimated at $3,713; while the same average cost for soldiers of twenty-five Allied nations was estimated at $800 annually.

59. Spyros Skouras to DDE, 10 July 1959, DDE Diary, Box 27.

60. Quotations from Waldemar A. Nielse, "Why We Are Losing the Ruble War," *Harper's Magazine,* Sept. 1958. Joseph Slater, of the President's Committee to Study the U. S. MAP, considered this article "one of the best," with recommendations "of direct interest to the working of this committee," Slater to Dodge, 27 Dec. 1958, Dodge, Box 1; "Briefing Session," 17 June 1958, Program No. 13, transcript, The Educational TV and Radio Center of the National Broadcasting Company, Erwin Canham, host, Robert Strausz-Hupé, Merrill Mueller, J. Sterling Livingston, Robert Sprague, and Jerome Wiesner, White House Office of the Special Assistant for Science and Technology, Box 4.

61. DDE to C. D. Jackson, 30 Apr. 1957, Whitman, Box 24, C. D. Jackson Papers, Box 41.

62. Willard Garvey, text of statement "Everyman a Capitalist—Everyman a Homeowner," 14 Dec. 1960, Rand, Box 5. See "A Chronology of Low Cost Private Housing as a Builders, Inc., Concept" [1959], ibid. Willard Garvey was a partner in C-G-F Grain Co., "the largest grain storage company in the world," and board chairman of Petroleum, Inc., a drilling and producing oil company in Kansas. In October 1960, for example, the United States approved a $2.5 million Development Loan Fund loan to Panama's National Savings Bank to initiate a five-hundred-unit private home ownership program. See CFEP 587/2, "Encouraging Private Home Ownership in the Developing Countries," 18 Sept. 1959, Rand, Box 4.

63. Quotations from CFEP 587/2, ibid.

64. John Maynard Keynes, quoted in Louis Turner, *Multinational Companies and the Third World* (Hill & Wang, 1973), p. 3.

65. John Knox Jessup, "U. S. Council Comments on the UN Experts Report on National and International Measures for Full Employment," 9 Nov. 1950, C. D. Jackson Papers, Box 88. See also Abbott Washburn, draft, "Information Paper on the American Economy," 1 Dec. 1955, White House Central File, 559—a USIA paper to counter Communist propaganda through the People's Capitalism campaign: "The economy of the U.S is modern capitalism. It is capitalism in the service of the people. . . ." The U.S. system "guarantees each individual the freedom to (1) Choose his own job, to work where and when he wishes. (2) To keep the rewards of his labor—to spend, to save, and to invest as he wishes. This is the basic right to private property: to own his own land, his own home, and other possessions. (3) To start a new business, to compete in a free market. (4) To form unions, to strike, and to join other groups." The United States' *"modern people's* capitalism . . . serves the people in a way that no other system has ever approached. It produces *the most for the many."*

The USIA's "People's Capitalism" campaign was for global consumption and fully enhanced by the energies of the Advertising Council, under the presidency of Theodore Repplier. See Sherman Adams to H. Christian Sonne, chairman of the National Planning Association, 14 June 1956, White House Central Files, 560. See also Walter Reuther to DDE, 3 Feb. 1958; and DDE to Reuther, 12 Feb. 1958, idem—an exchange on full employment.

For the origins of the People's Capitalism crusade, see Theodore Streibert to DDE, 22 Sept. 1955, C. D. Jackson Papers, Box 90: "Recently, G. Keith Funston, President of the N. Y. Stock Exchange, said we ought to call the American economy a 'People's Capitalism.' Ted Repplier and Harold Stassen are also using this term. Paul Hoffman speaks of 'Mutual Capitalism,' and some are calling it 'New Capitalism.'" The concern was U.S. identification "with the old form of capitalism. . . . Communist propaganda fosters this identification, tieing it up with colonialism and imperialism. If we can succeed in clarifying the true nature and benefits of our system, we will destroy one of the main propaganda weapons against us." See also C. D. Jackson to Abbott Washburn, 30 Jan. 1956, ibid.; George C. Lodge, assistant secretary of labor for international affairs. "The Economic System of the United States," 6 Jan. 1960, Rand, Box 7; Theodore S. Repplier, "People's Capitalism," address to the Advertising Council, 27 Oct. 1955, C. D. Jackson Papers, Box 90; the correspondence of James Lambie on People's Capitalism, Box 43; and Theodore Streibert to DDE, 13 Sept. 1956, Whitman, Admin., Box 41, with Henry Hazlett's "People's Capitalism," *Newsweek*, 17 Sept. 1956, enclosed.

See also "International Trade to Provide a More Uniform Standard of Living Throughout the World," Reuben G. Gustavson, president, Resources for the Future, Rand, Box 9; "Jobs and Our Foreign Trade Policy," Committee for a National Trade Policy, 25 Apr. 1958, Box 10. For an update on the concept of full employment, see esp. Robert Lekachman, "The Specter of Full Employment," *Harper's Magazine*, Feb. 1977, which analyses the demise of the [Hubert] Humphrey-Hawkins Full Employment Bill, which was a revived version of the 1945 bill.

66. George Humphrey to Neil McElroy, 21 Nov. 1958; Humphrey to DDE, 25 Nov. 1958, Whitman, Admin., Box 23.

67. Joseph Alsop, "Matter of Fact: the Protocol of Humphrey," Washington *Post*, 13 Mar. 1959; Humphrey to Alsop, 25 Mar. 1959; Humphrey to DDE, ibid.

68. For the politics of the congressional cuts in the Mutual Security Program, see Douglas Dillon to DDE, 15 June 1959, Whitman, Admin., Box 12; and "Salient Points Regarding Congressional Reductions in Military Assistance and Defense Support," FY 1958, Whitman, Administration, Box 29; DDE's crayoned notes, Mutual Security Folder [1958], ibid.

69. DDE to C. D. Jackson, 14 May 1960, C. D. Jackson Papers, Box 41, with text of DDE's 2 May 1960 address.

70. Eisenhower's statement before the NSC quoted in Benson to DDE, 18 June 1959, Whitman, Admin., Box 7. See also Milton Eisenhower to Gabriel Hauge, 26 Oct. 1956, White House Central Files, 559, including Milo Perkins' report, on foreign economic policy, recommending an updated Paley Report.

71. Eisenhower's "Directive Concerning Steps to Be Taken with Respect to the U. S. Balance of Payments," 16 Nov. 1960, Rand, Box 2; see Press Release, 17 Nov. 1960, White House Central Files, 562. This directive noted that the "once war-devastated nations" of Europe and Japan "have now become fully competitive with the U.S. in the markets of the free world."

72. Philip A. Ray, Staff Notes, "Special Budget Message Proposal to Tax Unrepatriated Income of Foreign U. S. Business Operations," 12 Jan. 1961, DDE Diary, Box 36.

73. Staff Notes, No. 607, 8 Aug. 1959, DDE Diary, Box 28.

74. Rand to Randall, 19 Aug. 1960, Rand, Box 5.

75. Originated and dominated by European statesmen and business leaders, the Bilderbergers during the Eisenhower years were concerned primarily with McCarthyism (which they abhorred), East-West trade (which they sought), international crises (as they emerged), Atoms for Peace and nuclear development (which they approved), European integration (about which there was ambivalence), and global economic growth. Economic competition and tension between U.S. and European interests were vigorously explored. See especially: Emilio G.

Collado, "The Effects of the Change in Relative Economic Strength Between the United States and Western Europe on the Atlantic Alliance," 21 Apr. 1961; James S. Duncan, "The Impact of Communist Economic Penetration in the Western World," Apr. 1961; George W. Ball, "The Struggle with the Communists for the Uncommitted Peoples—Suggestions for an American View of Its Ideological and Political Aspects," Mar. 1955; Raymond Aron, "The Actual Causes of Tension Between Europe and the United States," a criticism of U.S. diplomacy during Suez, and especially U.S. anticolonialism, Feb. 1957; Lincoln Gordon, "Political and Economic Institutions of the Western Community," Feb. 1957; Denis Healey, "The Diplomacy of Liberation" and "Nationalism and Neutralism in the Western Community," Feb. 1957; and Rudolf Mueller, "The Weakness of Western Society," Jan. 1958.

The papers presented at Bilderberg meetings, transcripts of many of the sessions, as well as summary and preliminary reports and steering-committee meetings, 1954–64, are in C. D. Jackson Papers, Box 29. For examples of the Bilderbergers' relationship with the Eisenhower administration, see: C. D. Jackson Log, 4 Aug. 1953, Box 56; Jackson to Prince Bernhard, 2 Oct. 1953, Whitman, International, Box 37; Walter Bedell Smith to DDE, 11 Mar. 1955, ibid.; Prince Bernhard to DDE, 27 Apr., 30 Oct., 16 Nov., 23 Nov. 1954, ibid.; DDE to Prince Bernhard, 7 May 1954, DDE Diaries, NLE 76-62, No. 63; Gabriel Hauge to DDE, 23 May 1956, Whitman, Admin., Box 19; DDE to Hauge, 30 Mar. 1955, ibid. See also Report by Heinz Committee for Bilderberg Group, "Economic Aspects of Competitive Coexistence as They Relate to Underdeveloped Areas," 11 Mar. 1955, C. D. Jackson Papers, Box 29.

For a historical review of the origins of the Bilderberg group, see Joseph Rettinger, "The Bilderberg Group," Sept. 1955, idem. For Prince Bernhard's implication in the Lockheed scandal and its effect on the Bilderbergers, see: Clyde Farnsworth, "Bernhard, a Prince of Dutch Commerce and a Master of Public Relations," New York *Times*, 18 Feb. 1976; "Prince Re-Emerging on the Dutch Scene," New York *Times*, 29 Aug. 1977. Although little of substance has been written about the Bilderbergers, see esp. Eugene Pasymowski and Carl Gilbert, "Bilderberg: the Cold War Internationale," *Congressional Record*, extensions of remarks, 15 Sept. 1971, E9616–9624.

76. Recent works on the multinationals have become an international publishing industry. See esp.: *Multinational Corporations in World Development*, Department of Economic and Social Affairs, ST/ECA/190, United Nations, 1973; Mira Wilkins, *The Maturing of Multinational Enterprise* (Harvard University, 1974); Richard J. Barnet and Ronald Müller, *Global Reach: the Power of the Multinational Corporations* (Simon and Schuster, 1974); Louis Turner, *Multinational Companies and the Third World* (Hill & Wang, 1973); James D. Cockcroft, André Gunder Frank, and Dale L. Johnson, *Dependence and Underdevelopment* (Doubleday, Anchor, 1972); Raymond Vernon, *Storm over the Multinationals: the Real Issues* (Harvard University, 1972).

See also: Clarence Randall, *The Communist Challenge to American Business* (Little, Brown, 1959); Harry Magdoff, *The Age of Imperialism: the Economics of U. S. Foreign Policy* (Modern Reader, 1969); Michael Hudson, *Super Imperialism: the Economic Strategy of American Empire* (Holt, Rinehart & Winston, 1968); Charles Levinson, *Capital, Inflation and the Multi-nationals* (Macmillan, 1971); Joyce Kolko, *America and the Crisis of World Capitalism* (Beacon Press, 1974). Notable collections include: *Les Multinationales*, a special issue of *Les Cahiers Français*, No. 190, 3–4/1979, ed. Bernadette Madeuf (Paris: La Documentation Française, 1979); Ralph Andreano, ed., *Superconcentration/Supercorporation: a Collage of Opinion on the Concentration of Economic Power*, (Warner Modular Publications, Book 1, 1973); *Peace and Change* devoted two issues to the papers presented at the Fourth Biennial conference of the Conference on Peace Research in History, "Toward a Historical Understanding of the Multinational Corporation" (1974), Spring 1976 and Fall 1976 issues. See also the issues of *The Multinational Monitor,* a monthly published by the Corporate Accountability Research Group, P. O. Box 19312, Washington, DC 20036.

77. Milton Eisenhower to DDE, 2 June 1961, M. S. Eisenhower Papers, Box 1.

78. DDE to Charles E. Wilson, 20 Oct. 1951, quoted by Wilson in "A Sound Economy Essential to Freedom." See Wilson to DDE, 23 Feb. 1959, White House Central Files, 561.

79. D. D. Eisenhower, *Waging Peace,* pp. 615–16. For an analysis of Eisenhower's "other warning," "Yet in holding scientific research and discovery in respect, as we should, we must also be alert to the equal and opposite danger that public policy could itself become the captive of a scientific-technological elite," see Herbert F. York, *Race to Oblivion: a Participant's View of the Arms Race* (Simon and Schuster, 1971).

INDEX